THE DOCTRINE OF THE BUDDHA

THE DOCTRINE OF THE BUDDHA

THE RELIGION OF REASON

BY
GEORGE GRIMM

"Among beings there are some whose eyes are not quite covered with dust: they will perceive the truth."

GYAN

Published by

Gyan Publishing House
5, Ansari Road
Daryaganj, New Delhi-110002
Phone: 011-47034999, 9811692060
E-mail: books@gyanbooks.com

Distribution Network
gyanbooks.com
India, USA, Canada, UK, Australia, France

ISBN : 978-81-212-2897-8 (PB)
First Published, 1926

2nd Impression 2021

Printed at: Gyan Press, Delhi.

The Doctrine of the Buddha
Author: George Grimm

THE DOCTRINE OF THE BUDDHA

THE RELIGION OF REASON

BY

GEORGE GRIMM

"Among beings there are some whose eyes are not quite covered with dust: they will perceive the truth."

PUBLISHED BY THE
OFFIZIN W. DRUGULIN, LEIPZIG
MCMXXVI

CONTENTS

PAGE

PREFACE vi

THEME AND BASIS OF THE DOCTRINE OF THE BUDDHA 1

THE FOUR MOST EXCELLENT TRUTHS

I. THE MOST EXCELLENT TRUTH OF SUFFERING

1. THE CRITERION OF SUFFERING 37
2. PERSONALITY 47
3. THE WORLD OF SUFFERING 82
4. THE SUBJECT OF SUFFERING 116

II. THE MOST EXCELLENT TRUTH OF THE ARISING OF SUFFERING

1. GENERAL INTRODUCTION 201
2. OLD AGE AND DEATH—BIRTH AS IMMEDIATE CONDITIONS OF SUFFERING 210
3. THE CONDITIONS OF REBIRTH 213
4. THE PROCESS OF REBIRTH—THE LAW OF KARMA . . 227
5. THE CONDITIONING OF THIRST 264
6. THE SAṄKHĀRĀ 272
7. IGNORANCE — SUMMARY OF THE CHAIN OF SUFFERING 285

III. THE MOST EXCELLENT TRUTH OF THE ANNIHILATION OF SUFFERING 297

PAGE

IV. THE MOST EXCELLENT TRUTH OF THE PATH LEADING TO THE ANNIHILATION OF SUFFERING

A. THE EXCELLENT EIGHTFOLD PATH IN GENERAL . . . 365
B. THE SEVERAL STEPS OF THE PATH
1. THE GOING INTO HOMELESSNESS 397
2. MORAL DISCIPLINE 416
3. THE PART OF CONCENTRATION IN THE NARROWER SENSE 423
4. THE ABSORPTIONS — THE HIGHER KNOWLEDGE 444
C. THE MEANS OF CONCENTRATION 457
D. THE FOUR HOLY STATES 468

APPENDIX

1. THE DOCTRINE OF THE BUDDHA AS THE FLOWER OF INDIAN THOUGHT 485
2. THE METAPHYSICS OF THE BUDDHA 503
3. RIGHT COGNITION 521

KEY TO THE QUOTATIONS 533

The progressive numbers in the text refer to the Key to the Quotations at the end of the volume.

PREFACE

I

No seeing man possessed of even half an eye, will be disposed to dispute that our present age is a thoroughly irreligious one. Even the religion which men still profess to follow, almost everywhere has degenerated into a mere affair of external observances. Above all, this irreligiousness has laid hold of the lower classes of the population whose idol to a very large extent has become Lenin, the deceased leader of the Russian Communists who declared all religion to be opium from which the people, but most of all, the youth, to-day as well as to-morrow, must be delivered. For the irreligious man, however, there exists only his *present* form of existence, which precisely therefore becomes for him the summation of all possible possessions. From this mental attitude there springs an unbridled impulsion towards making the very most of this present fleeting form of existence. Hence the vast majority of men abandon themselves to the grossest sensual enjoyments. They have no feeling save only for the pleasures of a well-filled stomach, the delights of lust, the satisfaction of personal vanity in all its varied manifestation, and the titillations of a sensuous art in common or refined forms. Even science has turned entirely in this direction in its endeavour, as the so-called "applied sciences," to produce the means required for the satisfaction of this craving of the senses.

In the satisfaction of this craving men do not shrink from the exploitation, nay, the spoliation, of the economically weaker. Hence those weaker are little by little filled with deeper ill-will against their exploiters. To remove their weakness they "organise" themselves. Against them the masters also organise themselves; and thus the combat of individual against individual has become a war of the different classes of mankind against one another. The war of species in the animal kingdom finds its resurrection among men in the shape of the class war.

At the present day, this social war rages throughout entire civilised humanity. What in the normal course of things will be the final issue, cannot be a matter of much doubt. The proletariat is not only superior in numbers, but in the compulsory military service which the possessing classes themselves forced upon them, they have been given the *physical* weapon, in manhood suffrage the *political* weapon, and in compulsory education the *mental* weapon. And thus the whole of civilised humanity is driving on towards the red revolution, is going the way of Russia, in whose present condition some States, of course, will land earlier, and some later. *This red world revolution* will constitute the great danger of the future. The terrible spectre of the social question will tower giant-high into the heavens, and with its awesome shadow outdarken all others. To avert the final catastrophe there exists only *one* resource, as surely as there is only *one* effective means of releasing the tension of that spring which impels to the social warfare found in the unbounded craving for ever more refined forms of sensual enjoyment. This sole means resides in giving back again to mankind *religion*, and to the upper strata of humanity no less than to the lower. For religion opens out to man the prospect of survival after death, and thereby requires of him that he no longer direct his efforts toward the utmost possible unrestrained satisfaction of his sense cravings, but also take into account the consequences that in a future life may follow upon such brutal egoism. The religious consciousness declares unmistakably and unanimously that self-seeking—and the greater it is, all the more so—in the period after death leads to an abyss; and further proclaims with one voice that besides the happiness of the satisfaction of sensual craving there is another and purer happiness which stands throned beyond sense enjoyments, which springs out of inward quietude, inward peace, which descends upon a man in all the greater majesty the more he renounces all sensual enjoyment and all outward possessions,—a happiness that not even death can disturb. Whoso once has understood this, withdraws from the social warfare; he is a man subdued. And so the social question disappears, without remainder over, in the solution of the religious question. In very truth the social question is also a religious question; nay it is *the* religious question. Therefore like a Sphinx big with threats of doom, again and again it can loom up and grin at men only when the religion of a people is lost to them. *A religious people knows no social question.* Whoever therefore really desires to help present-day humanity, can *only* help it by again restoring to it its sense of religion.

It might be thought that all this goes without saying, is so clear that at least every man of the better class of mind, at the very least, the *leaders* of mankind, would see it quite well, and therefore would feel bound to direct all their energies towards making a home for religion among the nations. But the terrible thing is precisely this, that of men of this better class of mind hardly any more are now at all to be found, and that, particularly for the leaders of mankind the religious factor no longer has any existence at all, so that they are veritably like captains who with their own hands steer the already wrecked ships of state into the maelstrom that roars in wait for it at the end of the long voyage of the social problem. Or does even the mere *word* religion ever come to the lips of these statesmen? For the rest, one need only cast one's eye over our journals and magazines, over the huge bulk of our collective literature. Where and when does one find even the very slightest reference to religion and the *religious* happiness? When by way of exception, such a thing once in a while is ventured upon, is it not made precisely an occasion for blame of its author? *This* fact only needs to be thoroughly reflected upon in order to recognise the full, the terrible completeness of the religious degeneration of present-day humanity. One may justly doubt if at any period in the known history of mankind such a degree of general religious, and therewith, of moral, degeneracy has ever been reached. The ancient peoples, as a rule, held fast by their gods to the end, or until they had taken to a higher religion. In *this* light no prophecy as to the impending fate of the civilised peoples of to-day can be black enough not to fall short of actuality.

But this is not yet the whole truth. Even if there dawned on us the insight, "We need a religion!" we no longer have with us a religion with the help of which the religious revival might be initiated and carried out. For Christianity which alone could come into the reckoning, for every unbiassed mind has quite obviously exhausted its mandate, has for ever lost its influence over the great masses of the working population, as in the broadest circles of the intellectual.

So then our doom is inescapable? Perhaps. Perhaps we are face to face with the signs of a frightful downward movement of humanity initiated by the most barbaric of all wars, since in the course of the world's history such downward movements repeat themselves with the same regularity as the upward movements, a confirmation of which is to be found in the 26th Discourse of the Dīgha Nikāya.

Perhaps, however, once again as so often before in history, in times of greatest danger a way of escape is opening up. Perhaps slowly and very gradually, in spite of everything, the religious renovation of humanity is setting in, as the only remedy.

But where is the religion that might accomplish this miracle? To-day, assuredly, in many quarters we find the position taken up that the era of institutional religion is absolutely over. We are told that to-day there can only be individual religion, or, strictly speaking, individual religions, each man having to be himself the founder of his religion. But this very position itself is a direct symptom of decadence. It fails to recognise the fundamental fact that in the sphere of knowledge it is always only the single super-eminent minds that have pointed out to mankind the road, so that, where such *geniuses* as leaders are lacking, the consequences are, not only mental shallowness with all its aberrations, but also the most revolting perversities in practical life, as well among individuals as among nations. The normal intellect, even if it does happen to have passed through all the schools of science, is scarcely capable of finding its way in the involved paths of every-day life, to say nothing of the deeps of actuality. This latter is successfully accomplished only by the genuine geniuses who are so rare that, as Schopenhauer says, they reach hands to one another across the centuries.

This holds good, above all, of the *ultimate* explanation of actuality, and with that, in particular, of our place within this actuality as living beings. That is to say: it holds good, above all, of the domains of religion and philosophy. In this sphere to receive only partially reliable, nay, even only plausible, explanations, from all time has seemed to mankind something so surpassingly difficult, and therefore so great, that those who here were able to convince and inspire, were forthwith regarded as divine beings, and venerated as such.

And now to-day, in this domain, Mr. Smith and Mr. Brown and Mr. Jones and Mr. Robinson will each be sufficient to himself with the fruits of his own individual mind! The upshot, however, is simply this: mankind threatens to go under in the morass of so-called civilisation. Only a giant mind with a giant understanding might yet save it. A giant mind with a giant *understanding!* Modern science has not only, with perfect right, banished from its domain all mere *faith*; it has also so completely driven out of the masses belief in every authority, more especially, religious authorities, that even these masses are only impressed by what they themselves are able to comprehend, and what with the hammer of steelhard logic can be pounded into their heads. This, too, is precisely the reason why not only the so-called scientists, but also the general masses have shaken off all religion, since up to now religion has been offered to them only in the garb of dogmatic articles of faith. And exactly because of this it can only compel into its service a religion which appeals not to faith but to *reason*, thus, a *philosophical* religion, or, if one prefers it, a *religious* philosophy, which in its obvious rightness, with goodwill may be grasped by any average mind. Where, however, is this religion to be found? Where is the giant who promulgates the religious Idea in its highest completeness, and at the same time in entire nakedness, stripped of every vestige of ecclesiasticism, free from sacerdotalism, from prayer and sacrament, free from sacrifices, in particular, free from every sacrifice of the intellect, so free, indeed, from every trace of such a thing, that on the contrary, the religious Idea is grasped all the more surely and completely in all its conquering irresistibility, the keener the intellect that measures itself against it? Let our mental eye roam over all the religious and philosophical systems of the present and the past; and where shall we find one which claims to be able, solely of itself, to point out the supreme actuality, and along with that, also, and before all else, the place which man occupies within this *genuine* actuality, and therewith is able to show each man his ultimate destiny in an intelligible manner, that is, with compelling logic; and whose founder in his own person had realised this ultimate goal of mankind? We shall find no such system. There has never been any *religion* which has appealed, not to faith solely but to reason: and no *philosopher* yet has claimed for himself that in his own person he has realised the supreme summit. Thereby, however, without further argument it is established beyond dispute that the entire Occident, from the very earliest beginnings of its history, has not produced any such system. For this at least, before all else, its discoverer would have had to *know* and *experience* within himself.

So then, the religious hero of our time has still to arise? Not a few believe so. But if this were really so, then it would stand ill with us. For until he came, if he came at all, everything might long since have slipped back into the abyss of barbarism. But by good fortune the giant of mental giants with his giant truth, in his Teaching, already for the last two thousand years has been living among mankind, and for an appreciable period of time has been dwelling also among us Occidentals, where we need him most:

> "The Truth has long ago been found,
> And noble minds together bound.
> That ancient Truth, lay hold of it!"

Of course, against such a contention modern sentiment will rear itself up in proud revolt. Just imagine! The solution on the basis of knowledge of the religio-philosophical problem, and therewith, of the basic problem of all, has not been reserved for modern scientists! And not only that! *We*, the glorious sons of the twentieth century after Christ, who have not merely climbed to the crowning peak of civilisation in the invention of instruments of wholesale murder hitherto held to be absolutely impossible, but also to the summit of knowledge in general, up to this day do not even know anything of that solution of the foundation problem of all already arrived at twenty-five hundred years ago! Is not that a tremendous assertion? To be sure it is a tremendous assertion. But is it bound on that account to be a false assertion? May it not be that present-day humanity, precisely because of its high *civilisation*, that is, of its *materialisation*, among its most scientific minds, yea, among these most of all, has sunk so far below the *religious* level of that giant mind, that this Beyond of their horizon remains like some far-distant star that still shines serenely on, even though for weak eyes it has become invisible?

To every age is given its own definite strivings and achievements; as, on the other hand, it has its own defects and weaknesses, peculiar to itself. Our age, in its boundless greed for sensual enjoyment has climbed the ladder of civilisation apparently right up to the topmost rung, so that this ladder already begins to shake and totter; and correspondent with this achievement, it also, positively, no longer possesses any religious feeling. The very opposite pole to this sort of development is represented by *Ancient India*. There for centuries men devoted themselves to the solution of the religious problem on the basis of knowledge, to the also total neglect of *material* development. Why should they not have achieved the final solution of this problem, even as our investigators have attained to the solution of the problems of physical science? Is the axiom that unceasing effort, in particular, unwearied, *concentrated* mental effort, in time must surely attain that which is attainable at all, valid only for us moderns? What conceit! And so the next step will be that at least the more thoughtful and quietly reflective minds of our day, were it only for the purpose of completing their entirely one-sided modern education, will turn full of expectation towards the conclusions which that ancient India has to present to them,—has to present to them through its greatest scion, the King's son, and later the beggar-monk, Siddhattha Gotama. Yea, they will wait upon his message all the more eagerly in that he not only claimed of himself that he had penetrated the supreme actuality—he called himself the *Buddha, the awakened to actuality* out of the dream of life—but that, as the *only* one among mankind so far as our vision extends, himself in his own person fully and completely realised his Teaching with all the tremendous demands which it makes upon him who would follow it out to its consummation, and during all the rest of his life never for a single moment was unfaithful to it.

Alone of itself this *compels* for him the high esteem, nay, the veneration of every man who is not yet wholly depraved, as already, indeed, during his lifetime it led hearts to him in flocks. Already in those days the Brahmin woman Dhanañjāni spoke for many thousands when in answer to one of her own caste who had scolded her thus: "Perverted is this Brahmin woman, Dhanañjāni, depraved is this Brahmin woman, Dhanañjāni, who, there where are Brahmins, knowers of the three Vedas, can praise this shaveling ascetic," replied: "Thou knowest nothing, good friend, of the virtue and wisdom of the Exalted One. If, good friend, thou didst know of the virtue and wisdom of the Exalted One, thou wouldst not even think of reviling him, the Exalted One."

II

The Buddha lived in India in the sixth century before Christ. The period of his teaching activity extended over a space of about fifty years. His sayings and discourses were at first circulated only by word of mouth. Immediately after the death of the Buddha, according to tradition, his monks assembled together at the Council of Rājagaha in order to fix the various Discourses and sayings that had been handed down. Thus was laid the ground-plan of the Pāli Canon which contains the collected discourses and sayings of the Buddha, including those of his leading disciples. Later on the Canon was further completed, particularly at the second Council of Vesāli which was held about a hundred years after the First Council, and in its main features was brought to a formal close at the Third Council under King Asoka (264—227. B. C.). Still later, the material was sorted out into different collections, altogether, into three collections called the Pitakas, Baskets, namely, the Sutta Pitaka, the Basket of Instructive Discourses, the Vinaya Pitaka, the Basket of the Regulations concerning monkish discipline, and the Abhidhamma Pitaka, consisting for the most part of expositions of a scholastic nature, of the two first Pitakas, which expositions were only conceived a considerable time after the death of the Buddha. The total varied content of these three Baskets was then called the Ti-pitaka, the Three Baskets.

But in this form also the sayings and discourses of the Buddha were handed down to posterity only orally, in accordance with the ancient, venerated usage upon which was based the transmission of the Vedas. The fixing of the Tipitaka in writing followed only a few decades before the beginning of our era under King Vaṭṭagāmini in Ceylon, to which Island the Canon had been brought by Mahinda the son of King Asoka. This definitive fixing of the Pāli Canon, accordingly, only took place about four hundred years after the Buddha's death.

With this, it cannot at all be determined whether the Pāli in which the Canon has come down to us was also the actual speech of the Buddha himself, or whether his words were only translated from his native language into the Pāli idiom. From all which it is evident without further words that one cannot speak in any positive manner of a verbal authenticity of the Pāli Canon in the sense that all contained within it can be guaranteed to come from the Buddha and from his immediate chief disciples. One part of the Canon, and indeed a very extensive part, has not merely been collected only at a considerable time after the death of the Buddha, but in general only *conceived* by third parties, on the basis of the original texts which they themselves knew only at second-hand; this is especially true of the greater part of the Abhidhamma.

These portions of the Canon, precisely on this account, and indeed quite self-evidently, must be left entirely out of the reckoning in the attempt to determine the original contents of the Buddha's teaching. For thus far one can, at most, only reasonably establish from them how the later editors of these portions of the Canon on their part understood the original texts which had merely been handed down to them by others. To draw upon their expositions in the determining of the Buddha's teaching would be exactly the same as if one should seek to determine authentically the views of Jesus from the writings of the *Patres Ecclesiae*, the Church Fathers who lived in the first centuries after him. Every one who has only taken even the merest glance into their writings knows to what results such an undertaking perforce would lead. At most these writings can only serve to show how the teachings of Jesus, with the lapse of time, were deformed and transformed. Even the Apostolic Fathers, who were so called, because, rightly or wrongly, they passed for having been immediate disciples of the twelve apostles, can no longer be held as authorities. For the Law of Epigony is borne out precisely, and more than anywhere else, in the domain of the ideas of the giants of the mind, inasmuch as their ideas, so soon as their promulgation and interpretation are no longer under their own control, in an incredibly short time, become vulgarised, when they are not actually mutilated and defaced, or, indeed, twisted into their direct opposite. One need only imagine, for example, what would be the result if some one sought authentically to establish what was the philosophy of Spinoza or Berkeley, instead of from the original works themselves, from expositions by third parties, thus, after their passage through the heads of these third parties; and sought to lend, as it were thereby, a special character to this determining of their philosophy, by assuring us that these third parties had lived not so very long after Spinoza or Berkeley!

At bottom, all such expositions are only *attempts at interpretation*, thus mere *commentaries*. And so, all the later conceptions also of the Pāli Canon, precisely the same as the post-canonical Miliṅdapañha and the actual commentarial literature, are only similar commentaries on the Buddha's teaching. More especially are Indian commentators quite particularly dangerous for the determining of the system commented upon, as Deussen points out in the following passage:—

"It consists with that complete lack of historical sense which is characteristic of the Indian, that the Indian expositor does not so much place himself at the standpoint of his texts in order with loving devotion to make these clear, as rather only utilise the words of the author to be explained in order in them to develop and make good his own progressed standpoint. Every philosophical commentary is to be looked upon as the expression *of a particular, further developed standpoint*, which, as such, demands, and also often merits, special treatment. Much confusion has arisen in European expositions of Indian philosophy through the scraping together of everything that could possibly be got at for the building of a system; and thereby there has often been given a confused, incoherent picture of the teaching concerned which, philosophically, has been simply unthinkable." Of these sins, however, it is not European scholars alone who have made themselves guilty. Much greater sinners in this direction as regards the determining of the *original* Buddha-doctrine have been, for many centuries, nay, actually for two milenniums, the Buddhist monks of Asia; and sinners in this direction particularly, they still are to-day. Among them the Abhidhamma, indeed, the Milindapañha, and the yet later actual Commentaries are worshipped as the acme of the highest wisdom, with such a reverence, nay, with such an inexhaustible enthusiasm, that, in the end, one might easily quite forget that in addition to the authors of this *exegetical* literature there also once lived a *Buddha*. And so, in this inversion of the proper relationship, in accordance with which latter the surrogate must always yield place when one can get at the original itself, there also resides, at bottom, a serious crime against the majesty of the Buddha. For at the very least, by such an attitude it is imputed to the Buddha that he did not in his discourses express himself clearly enough, or at any rate, not so clearly as the gentlemen of the Abhidhamma, and the rest of the exegetical gentlemen would have known how to do!

What an enormity such an accusation is, will be clear without further words if one reflects that a perfect Buddha knows how to cast the highest truth in such a form that even a robber chief along with his band, even a leper, "a poor, wretched, unfortunate man," even a cow-herd, yea, even a seven-year-old boy—Bhadda in the Theragātha, v. 479—can comprehend its meaning without anything more added, and also immediately realise it. Why then do you need an Abhidhamma? Why a Buddhaghosa? Why all the other commentators when you could have the Buddha-word in the *original?* Does not the Buddha suffice you? Would you have it otherwise, or would you have more? Do you not see that of you also these words of the Master hold good: "And the Exalted One, perceiving in mind the thoughts of that monk, turned to the monks and said: 'It may well be, monks, that some vain man, out of ignorance, plunged in ignorance, overpowered in mind with thirst, *thinks himself bound to go beyond the message of the Master*'"? Were it not more fitting that at least towards these products of late epigones of the Buddha, also in so far as they have been incorporated into the Canon, that you should take up the position already adopted by Purāna towards the reports of a third party concerning the discourses of the Master himself, as told of in the Cullavagga, II, I, II? Purāna comes to Rājagaha where, after the death of the Buddha, his disciples have gathered together. He is called upon to take part in the Council, but courteously declines the invitation since he prefers to hold fast to what he himself has learned from the lips of the Master.

And finally, to come to the test of facts: When did the great Saints of Buddhism live? *After* the rise of Abhidhamma, or already before its rise? What, thus, has produced them,—the Abhidhamma, with its, for most people, impenetrable desert of learnedness, or the Master's Discourses in their genial simplicity? Has the Abhidhamma yet begotten any saints at all? Yea, truly, it was only during a brief and splendid noontide that the Buddha-dharma shone out in full splendour, visible to all. Incredibly, nay, uncannily soon broke in upon it the long, pale night of mere scholastic learnedness, and added to that, a learnedness no longer on a level in any wise with the Dharma.

To-day, Southern Budhism has fallen so low that it expressly forbids its monks to try to lay hold of the teaching of the Buddha by the exercise of their own powers of understanding. The "collective opinion" of the Three Councils, the so-called Theravāda-interpretation, as it is preserved in the Island of *Laṅkā* (Ceylon), is the sole standard of truth. Here, thus, we have exactly the standpoint of the Catholic Church which likewise forbidding all individual explanations of the Bible, for a thousand years has held valid *only* the explanation of this Bible given through the Councils. Of a truth Deussen is right when he says: "The Buddhism of to-day is a magnifying mirror of the mistakes of Catholicism." To be sure, one thing only is lacking, namely, that the Southern Buddhist *Church* should entirely forbid to its *faithful* the reading of the Buddha-word in the original, and refer them exclusively to the so-anxiously guarded Theravāda-interpretation, as, in fact, the Catholic Church forbids to its laity the reading of the Bible alone. Is not that mental emasculation? Is it not a travesty of the Buddha who has set forth Sammādiṭṭhi, the winning of Right Understanding, as the first and most fundamental member of his select Eightfold Path; and who ever and again declares that we must *only* adopt that which *we ourselves* have recognised to be right? "Then, monks, what you have just said is only what *you yourselves* have recognised, what *you yourselves* have comprehended, what *you yourselves* have understood; is it not so?" "It is even so, Lord."*

III

So then the prophecy of the Buddha that his teaching would decline five hundred years after his death has actually been fulfilled. What for the last two thousand years has

* Majjhima Nikāya, 38th Discourse.—The word "Diṭṭhipaṭinissagga," Renunciation of Cognition, upon which the Southern Church relies, has a *radically* different meaning. It is precisely *through* the acquisition of right cognition that we must overcome also every thirst for cognition and thereby every activity of the mind, in exactly the same way that willing is overcome by willing:—"Chanden' eva chandaṁ pajahati." (*Cf*, below, p. 356; further, the 117th Discourse of the Majjhima Nikāya!)

been presented in Asia as Buddhism is as little the old Buddha-teaching as that any one of the present-day Christian sects represents the Christianity of Christ. As well the Northern as the Southern Buddhism of Asia are, in the sense of the above-quoted words of Deussen, *independent developments* of the original teaching of the Buddha which already had set in not very long after his death.

In contrast thereto the present work sets forth the *original*, genuine teaching of the Buddha. This, to be sure, is a very bold claim. But the author has an infallible criterion for it, furnished by the Buddha himself. The Buddha, in fact, calls his teaching the *dhamma anitiha*, the truth *that carries its confirmation within itself*, stands in no need of external authorization. Elsewhere the Buddha-doctrine is called, "The cognised in itself, *the doctrine of actuality to be seen with one's own eyes*." According to this, the genuine Buddha-doctrine is a securely self-contained, *incontestable* system of iron logic, in which latter precisely is mirrored the internal evidence of the structure of the teaching.* Just such an incontestable system, self-evident in itself, does the present work set forth. In doing so, it builds exclusively upon the sayings of the Buddha himself, and his leading disciples who lived contemporaneously with him. So, then, it presents itself as the original teaching of the Buddha as surely as that there cannot be a duplicate truth.

Looked out upon from this watch-tower, the reader obtains also immediate certainty as to whether the passages from the Canon relied upon by the author are really the genuine words of the Master and of his disciples. For the criterion of their genuineness here lies in their known objective truth, certainly the most elevated criterion one can have, compared with which all philologico-historical formal criticism,

* Therefore the doctrine of the Buddha bears also the epithet "vibhajjavāda," which Childers and Rhys Davids render, "Religion of Logic or Reason."

altogether apart from its general barrenness, becomes quite superfluous.

A simile may serve to illustrate how the author, out of the Buddhist Canon has reconstructed the old Buddha-doctrine.

Men have been digging in the ruins of an ancient city. According to tradition there stood in the middle a great temple, the ground-plan of which is still recognisable. The investigators now apply themselves to the identification of the huge blocks of stone lying around, as forming part of the temple. Concerning almost every single stone a learned contention is spun out as to whether or not it belongs to the temple, so that no end to the disputing seems in sight. An architect for a long time listens in silence. Then he comes to a bold resolve: he will build up the temple again with the original stones. So he has workmen come; points out stone after stone; has each fitted into its proper place, until at last the whole temple without a gap anywhere, is reconstructed in all its splendour and in a pleasing harmony of all its parts, wherein every block exactly fits in with every other. Is not the whole contention as to the genuineness of each separate stone thereby decided in the simplest and surest manner?

Perhaps the reader will recognise even as immediately, in the passages quoted in "The Doctrine of the Buddha" under his hands, the original blocks of the words of the Master, and in the whole system, the *dhamma anitiha*. Assuredly he has recognised it if in the reading of the book he has also experienced in himself the truth of those other words, that the teaching of the Buddha is like the paw of the lion: "What it strikes, be it lofty or low, that it strikes soundly."

And so, may the Teaching of "the greatest among gods and men," anew in undiminished strength shed abroad its glowing radiance and still bestow blessing on all that are of good will, even as gold loses nothing of its lustre though it has lain buried in the ground for thousands of years.

The printing of the present work has been made possible by the generosity of Mr. Basile Giurkowsky. To him therefore in this place is expressed the heartiest thanks.

George Grimm.

THEME AND BASIS
OF THE DOCTRINE OF THE BUDDHA

Schopenhauer has pointed out to us the great truth that the nature of all that exists consists in willing. Every creature, from the first moment of its existence to its last breath, wills, and all its powers, mental as well as physical, are exclusively for the service of this will; yea, they are nothing but will itself made visible. If man no longer wills, if he has become entirely without will, each of himself, feels that he has become impossible as a human being; we feel that because of the annihilation of his will, and thereby of his real nature, he must vanish from the world. And if mankind were not to will anything, if every being were to be entirely without will, then the whole world within a very short time would simply disappear, because every kind of existence is based solely upon will.

Because all existence is will, everything that is in harmony with this will is happiness, and everything hindering it is suffering,—suffering meaning impeded will. Thus happiness and suffering, in the last analysis, only reveal the extent to which the will of the individual is able to maintain and effectuate itself.

Obvious as all this is to everybody who has once grasped it, there is equally as little doubt that every act of will at every moment is impeded on all hands. Even where will seems to get fulfilled, its consequences at length turn round against itself, and at last in inevitable death, it suffers complete shipwreck.

Thus is it to-day, thus has it been through all the past, and thus will it continue to be as long as there are men, or even living creatures at all. For everybody feels—and the reasoning man perceives it—that those circumstances which are in opposition to a real and permanent gratification of our will are dictated by the law of nature, representing an iron necessity, connected as inseparably with every act of will as heat is connected with fire. For where life is—and where will is, there is life, will being nothing else but the will to live—there, even when every possibility of development is taken into account, at last must be death, and therewith, an inevitable, ever repeated ultimate collapse of life and thus of will.

Clear as all this is, there can hardly be a man who at least once in his life has not put to himself the timid question, if there is really no way out of this terrible self-dissension of our nature which always wants what must be impossible according to the very nature of this will; whether there is not at least a possibility of escaping *death*. Is this not strange? Is not the simple putting of this question more inexplicable than the problem of death itself? For if suffering, if above all, death, is conditioned by the very law of nature, how should it be possible to evade them? How can man in face of the unequivocal language of nature, demonstrating to him on every corpse the inevitableness of death, entertain the thought that it might be possible to conquer death?

And still this question is not only the question of every single human being, but has been the great question of mankind from its first beginnings, and will remain so as long as there are men. It is the chief, properly speaking, the only theme, as well as the strong point, of all religions, and is the source of every philosophy. Free mankind from evil, first of all from death, and religion and philosophy will not only be counted superfluous, but truly have become superfluous. Not even a god does man need, if rid of suffering and become immortal; from which it is clear that the concept of god is ultimately nothing but an expedient for solving the problem of suffering and death. On the other hand, men are content with the most absurd dogmatical forms of belief, if only they make claim to vanquish suffering and death.

"If our life," says Schopenhauer, "were endless and free from pain, perhaps it would never enter any one's head to ask why the world is here, and constructed just as it is. Accordingly we find that the interest awakened by philosophical or religious systems has its strongest point in the dogma of some kind of existence after death; and though the latter systems make the existence of their gods the chief point and seem to defend this with most zeal, this is ultimately only because they have bound their doctrine of immortality to it and think both inseparable; really they only care for this. For if it could be secured otherwise, their lively zeal for their gods would very soon cool down; and it would give place to almost complete indifference, if, on the other hand, the utter impossibility of immortality could be proved to them." In entire agreement with this, it is just that doctrine, materialism, which, holding to the ocular evidence of nature itself, teaches the annihilation of man by death, that, as Schopenhauer goes on to say, has never been able to obtain a permanent influence over mankind. This proves that the solution of the problem given by materialism goes against the inner nature of man, and therefore cannot possibly be true. For viewed simply from the standpoint of materialism, man is merely a part of nature, her mere product and nothing more. But if this is so, then his nature must be in harmony with it; and thus in his feelings, it would be impossible for him to be in conflict with her dictates.

Accordingly the situation is such, that in the innermost

depths of human nature the conviction is firmly established that in spite of all seeming impossibility, there must be a way and a bridge leading beyond suffering and death.

But has mankind succeeded in finding out such a way? Here, without more ado, this much is clear, that an answer is only to be expected from the religions. For philosophy that alone might come into question here, certainly in its greatest representatives has looked astonishingly deep into the mystery of death; but of the philosophers, none even claims to have discovered a practicable way that leads beyond death. But all religions are built upon faith, so much so that according to our current notions, this trait is the direct and formal nature of every religion. A system abhorring faith can *eo ipso* on no account be taken as a religion. But not every man is able to believe. "There is," as Schopenhauer says, "a boiling point on the scale of civilization, where all faith vanishes, and man longs for better insight."

As soon as he has come thus far, he is irrecoverably lost for faith, and therewith for religion. "For faith,"—again according to Schopenhauer—"is like love; it cannot be enforced; it will only thrive on the soil of ignorance." But apart from that, mere faith is always a precarious matter, particularly if, as in our case, the various religions and creeds teach different things about the way in which man may vanquish death, and if, at the same time each one claims the direction shown by itself to be the right one, and that faith is to be given only to itself, not to the others. Upon which shall we rely? There is no other way than to examine the different religions with regard to their compatibility with reason. To reason indeed, they all themselves appeal, in their eager efforts to snatch away one another's adherents. But precisely in this do they all sign their own death-warrant. For with this they, in the last resort, allow the reason of man to judge as to what is true and what is not true. But on the other hand, they themselves with their doctrines always come into the most violent contradiction with the demands of this same reason; a fact which has found its classical expression in the saying "Credo quia absurdum est."

This is becoming evident precisely in our time, when the conviction of the inadequacy of religions slowly begins to become a phenomenon of the multitude, and just in the direction here in question, the "shall-believe" is more and more opposed by the "want-to-know." But who is able to satisfy this craving, since all our philosophy too, here fails completely? Indeed, we seem to have come to the standpoint of many, that here all knowledge is impossible and, mere faith having become untenable, complete resignation remains the only possible thing. Yet here, just in time, in consequence of those secret conjunctions in the course of the world's events, thanks to which, help or compensation comes for every state that has grown untenable, salvation arises, as so often before, out of the East: *ex oriente lux!*

Let us once more call the situation to mind: "The age of science no longer wants to believe, but to know." More than that, it is no longer satisfied with that feebler kind of knowledge, namely, the purely abstract, gained by mere concepts or even consisting in mere concepts, as is particularly made evident by the rejection of every philosophy founded upon pure concepts, such as was in vogue during earlier days. Our age demands immediate insight; it also wants to base metaphysical concepts upon self-experience, accessible to everybody. For self-experience alone gives real certainty. Fully to understand this we must recall the incomparable elucidation of the relation between direct knowledge and abstract knowledge given by Schopenhauer, that diamond of his philosophy, which relation may be briefly explained thus:

Abstract knowledge receives its entire content only from

direct, sense-perceived knowledge; it borrows its materials entirely from the latter. Therefore it is not able to give really new knowledge, but only serves to condense our direct knowledge, once gained, into settled concepts, and thus to fix it and transmit it to others. Accordingly truth, that is, the adequate apprehension of something existing in the intellect of man, may ultimately be gained only through our own immediate perception. As Schopenhauer says: "Perception is not only the source of all knowledge, it is itself very knowledge. As out of the immediately radiated splendour of the sun we enter into the borrowed and reflected light of the moon, so do we pass from the sense-perceived, immediate representation bearing its own evidence and warrant in itself, to the abstract and discursive notions of reason which receive all their content only from this direct sense-perceived knowledge, and in relation to the same. As long as we remain simply percipient, everything is clear, fixed and certain. There are neither questions, nor doubts, nor errors. One neither wants, nor is able, to go further; peace is found in immediate perception; contentment in the present. But with abstract knowledge, with reason, in the theoretical there arises doubt and error, and in the practical, sorrow and regret."

Thus, only direct sense-perceived knowledge gives complete satisfaction. Whoever possesses *it*, has no more need of faith, every form of faith melting before it like liquid wax; for him who possesses it, all merely abstract knowledge also, with all its sources of error, has become superfluous: he who has become certain of the existence of a thing through himself perceiving it, as little needs to believe in this existence, as to have it proved to him.

Only this highest degree of truth can permanently satisfy man with regard to the primal problem also, as to whether it is possible to overcome suffering and, above all, death.

This highest degree of truth our age demands, also in this connection.

And now, hearken! Thousands of years ago, there lived in India a man, who, as no other has done, succeeded in crystallizing out this great, primary problem of mankind in all its purity, free from all accessories of any kind, more especially, purified from other obscure, refuse by-products of the longing for metaphysical knowledge. He claimed for himself to have solved the problem in such a manner, that every one by his own direct perception, by his own immediate insight might convince himself of the correctness of the solution, and even at any time, if only he wishes to do so, may test it upon himself. Thus he does not, as do our religions, merely draw a bill of exchange payable after death in an uncertain future. And it happens that the doctrine of this man whom many call the greatest of the Aryans and therefore the greatest of men, precisely at this moment is making its way among us Europeans who look longingly for a teaching that on one hand may present to us the kernel of all religions and all metaphysics, pure and unmixed, and on the other that guarantees its solution in accordance with the methods of exact science, by self-experimentation. This is the doctrine of Gotama the Buddha, the Awakened One, the culminating point of Indian wisdom. Is it any wonder that all those who cannot pass with indifference over the great question of suffering culminating in death, or as children of an era that craves for knowledge, are no longer able to believe, but want to know, begin more and more to swarm round this doctrine which begins for them to take possession of the throne of religions that satisfy them no longer? Give me the name of another mortal who has set forth with equal clearness the great problem of mankind, how to escape suffering and death, and made it the exclusive theme of his doctrine and his life, as the Buddha has done!

The solution of this problem of suffering, from the very beginning was the great task he set himself. For its sake he who had the claim to the crown of his father, an Indian petty king, renounced this crown as well as riches, wife and child and "just entering on his princedom, in first manhood, in the bloom of youth, dark-haired, against the wish of his parents weeping and lamenting, with shorn hair and beard, clad in garb of yellow, he left home behind and retired from the household life to the homeless life," to find out if it were not possible to put an end to this whole chain of suffering. Though the story about the motives of his flight from the world in its details is nothing but a legend, still this legend is so beautiful and is so much in line with the spirit of his doctrine, marking out and defining its contents from the beginning so distinctly and faithfully, that it may be rendered here.

Already when Prince Siddhattha—this was the Buddha's original name—was born, the Brahmins living as priests and astrologers at the court of his father, King Suddhodana, predicted the future destiny of the child. They prophesied: "If Prince Siddhattha mounts the throne, he will become a king of kings, a ruler of the world; but if he renounces the throne and chooses the life of an ascetic, then he will become an overcomer of the world, a perfect Buddha." And the ascetic Kaladevala came from the wilderness of the Himālaya and threw himself down before the child, speaking thus: "Truly, this child will some day become a most perfect Buddha and show men the way to liberation." And he wept, for he knew that at his advanced age, he could not live to see that day. But the king, by every means at his disposal sought to hinder the fulfiment of this prediction, as he wished Prince Siddhattha to become a monarch dominating the world. As the Brahmins had told him that the sight of human suffering and of earthly transitoriness would cause the prince to fly from the world, he kept away from his son everything that might have given him knowledge of human misery and death. He furnished him with every kind of pleasure and all royal splendour, to chain him to worldly life as closely as possible. As he grew up a youth, his father had three palaces built for him, suited to the three seasons of the Indian climate, the hot, the cold, and the rainy. They were all furnished with magnificent splendour. Wide gardens and groves extended all around, with clear ponds girdled with lotus flowers, cool grottoes, murmuring cascades, and garden beds full of beautiful flowers. Within these gardens and groves the prince spent his youth, but he was not allowed to leave them; and to every poor, sick or old man, entrance to them was strictly prohibited. The sons of the country's most noble families were his companions. In his sixteenth year his father had him married to the Princess Yasodhara, and besides that, he provided him with a whole harem of beautiful girls skilled in all manner of dances and songs, and in all kinds of musical instruments in use among Indian princes. Then one day, in driving through the park, he suddenly noticed an infirm old man, his back bent down under the burden of many years, who with the aid of a staff crawled painfully along. Full of astonishment Siddhattha asked his driver Channa, what this curious creature might be, and Channa replied that it was an old man. "Was he born in this state?" the prince went on asking. "No, my Lord, once he was young and in full bloom like you." "Are there more of such old men?" the prince inquired, growing more and more astonished. "Very many, my Lord." "And how could he fall into this miserable state?" "Such is nature's course, that all men must become old and feeble, if they do not die young." "And I too, Channa?" "Yes, my Lord, you too." This accident put the young prince in such a pensive mood, that he gave the order to turn home, as he had lost all delight in his beautiful surroundings. Some time afterwards in driving out again, he caught sight of a leper, and when Channa answered his questions about this apparition, he was so deeply impressed in mind that from then on, he shunned all pleasures and began to think about human misery. After a longer time had elapsed, the prince encountered a third apparition. He saw a decayed corpse lying at the wayside. Greatly perturbed he turned home at once and cried out: "Woe to men! Of what use to me is all royal splendour, all this pomp and all these pleasures, if they are not able to save me from old age, from sickness and death? How unhappy is mankind! Are there no means to put an end to suffering and death ever renewing themselves with every new birth?" Henceforth, this question incessantly occupied him. Riding out at a later time, he found an answer. An ascetic appeared to him, wearing a garb of yellow as do the Buddhist brethren, his awe-inspiring features clearly reflecting the deep peace of his mind.

This apparition indicated to him the way in which he had to seek the solution of his great problem. His resolution to quit the world like that reverend ascetic and to go out into the wilderness, slowly ripened. And then, all at once he put this resolution into effect, in the unshakeable conviction that it would be given him to discover the end of every form of suffering.

To this problem, for him the greatest, the six following years of most horrible self-mortifications were devoted; as the custom of India of that day held this to be the way leading soonest to the perception of truth. As he said himself: "Whatever feelings painful, burning and bitter, ascetics and brahmins ever have undergone in the past, undergo in the present, or shall undergo in the future: this is the utmost; further they cannot go."[1] To this one goal was devoted that time of quiet inward contemplation, in which he next immersed himself when he had convinced himself of the uselessness of all painful asceticism, and which at last brought him the solution of his great problem. In triumph he first communicated it to the five monks who had surrounded him during the time of his self-martyrdom, but who had left him when he had recognized this way as erroneous. "An Exalted One, O monks, is the Accomplished One; a Supremely Awakened One is He! Give ear, O monks, the deathless has been attained. I will instruct you, I will impart to you the doctrine. Following my instructions, ye shall know and realize that utmost noble goal of the holy life for yourselves even in this present lifetime."[2] And in fact, like the Master, they also soon attained to "the incomparable security, the birthless, the free from growth and decay and disease, the deathless, the sorrowless, the stainless."[3] They attained the end of suffering.

This gospel of the ending of suffering henceforth constituted the only theme of the Buddha, the Awakened One, as thenceforward he called himself. To its propagation the following forty-five years of his life were devoted. Every day, yea, every hour he could say of himself: "As before so also now, I preach only Suffering and the Cessation of Suffering."[4] "As the great ocean, ye disciples, is penetrated by only one taste, the taste of salt, even so, disciples, this Doctrine and this Order are penetrated by only one taste, the taste of salvation."[5] This, the sole content of his teaching, he made externally knowable by condensing it into the Four Most Excellent Truths of Suffering, within which everything good is contained: "Just as all living creatures that go upon feet find passage-way in the footsteps of the elephant, the footprint of the elephant being by them held in the highest esteem by reason of its great size, even so, all things whatsoever that are good and salutary are contained and comprehended in the Four Most Excellent Truths, namely in these: the Most Excellent Truth of Suffering, the Most Excellent Truth of the Arising of Suffering, the Most Excellent Truth of the Ceasing of Suffering and the Most Excellent Truth of the Path that leads to the Ceasing of Suffering."[6]

Certainly his knowledge was not restricted to these four excellent truths; his mind had penetrated the abysses of existence in other directions also, more deeply than any other mortal; but with deliberate intention he communicated nothing of it to mankind, but exclusively limited himself to the four excellent truths: "Once upon a time, the Venerable One was staying at Kosambi in a Sinsapa-forest. And the Venerable One took up a few *sinsapa* leaves in his hand and said to his disciples: "What do you think, my disciples, which is more, these few *sinsapa* leaves I hold in my hand, or the other leaves in the *sinsapa* wood above?"—"The few leaves, Lord, that the Venerable One holds in his hands, are small in number; much more are the leaves in the *sinsapa* forest above."—"Even so, disciples, what I have perceived and have not communicated to you is much more than what I have communicated to you. And why, O disciples, have I not revealed this to you? Because, O disciples, it would not be of advantage to you, because it does not promote the higher life in all its purity, because it does not lead to disgust with the world, to annihilation of all lust, to the ceasing of the transitory, to peace, to the higher knowledge, to awakening, to Nirvāna. Therefore I have not communicated it to you. And what, disciples, have I communicated to you? What Suffering is, disciples, I have communicated to you; what the Arising of Suffering is, disciples, I have communicated to you; what the Ceasing of Suffering is, disciples, I have communicated to you; and what is the Path that leads to the Ceasing of Suffering, disciples, I have communicated to you."[7]

The Buddha even goes so far as to reject every setting up of problems that go beyond this exclusively practical purpose, all theoretical questions and all speculative enquiries, particularly those about the essence of the world or of ourselves, as a mere overflow of our tendency towards polymathy and terminating only in "a blind alley of views, a cave, a gorge of views" and thus only involving the inexperienced mortal still deeper in suffering.[8] Accordingly, the Buddha especially does not teach any system of philosophy; not only no kind of metaphysics, but also no ontology nor dianoiology. Concerning the world in itself, its origin, its duration, its laws, he is indifferent, since any such predictions and statements are ultimately without any practical purpose for mankind. All this has interest for him only in so far as it is of practical value for the annihilation of suffering. Therefore in his teaching those philosophers who, corrupted by the thirst for knowledge for its own sake, wish to have every enigma of existence solved, will lose their labour, since, if the saying holds good of any one, it holds good of the Buddha: "Non meum est docere doctores." It is not my task to teach scholars. Apart from this, the enigma of the world belongs to those enigmas "with which to dabble only leads to perplexity;"[9] while those dabbling with it resemble men born blind, who have been led to touch an elephant. The first of them touches the head, the other the trunk, the third one the foot, the fourth one the tail, and now each of them cries out: "The elephant looks like this; no, he looks like that," until the combat of opinions turns into a combat of fists.[10] Such investigators entirely mistake the situation wherein they find themselves. This is like that of explorers who have ventured into a lonely desert and on every side are beset by wild animals. Instead of thinking about defending themselves against these animals and saving their lives, they enter upon zoological studies of them, which end in themselves being devoured by the beasts, together with the results of their studies. The Buddha himself sums up their standpoint as follows.

"It is as if, Mālunkyāputta, a man had been wounded by an arrow thickly smeared with poison, and his friends and companions, his relatives and kinsfolk, were to procure for him a physician or surgeon; and the sick man were to say, 'I will not have this arrow taken out until I have learnt whether the man who wounded me belonged to the warrior caste, or to the Brahmin caste, or to the agricultural caste, or to the menial caste!' "Or again he were to say, 'I will not have this arrow taken out until I have learnt the name of the man who wounded me and to what clan he belongs.'

"Or again he were to say, 'I will not have this arrow taken out until I have learnt whether the man who wounded me was tall, or short, or of middle height.'

"Or again he were to say, 'I will not have this arrow taken out until I have learnt whether the bow which wounded me was a *cāpa*, or a *kodanda*.'

"Or again he were to say, 'I will not have this arrow taken out until I have learnt whether the bow-string which wounded me was made from smaller-wort, or bamboo, or sinew, or *maruva*, or from milkweed.'

"Or again he were to say. 'I will not have this arrow taken out until I have learnt whether the shaft which wounded me was feathered from the wings of a vulture, or of a heron, or of a falcon, or of a peacock.'

"Or again he were to say, 'I will not have this arrow taken out until I have learnt whether the shaft which wounded me was wound round with the sinews of an ox, or of a buffalo, or of a monkey.' That man would die, Mālunkyāputta, without ever having learnt this.

"In exactly the same way, Mālunkyāputta, any one who should say, 'I will not lead the religious life under the Blessed

One until the Blessed One shall elucidate to me, either that the world is eternal, or that the world is not eternal . . . or that the saint exists or does not exist after death,'—that person would die, Mālunkyāputta, before the Accomplished One had ever elucidated this to him.

"The religious life, Mālunkyāputta, does not depend on the dogma that the world is eternal, nor does the religious life depend on the dogma that the world is not eternal. Whether the dogma obtains, that the world is eternal, or that the world is not eternal, there still remain birth, old age, death, sorrow, lamentation, misery, grief and despair, for the extinction of which in the present life I am prescribing."[11]

Thus again it is nothing but a sign of the surpassing wisdom of the Buddha, that of the ocean of wisdom wherein he had plunged, he only has communicated just as much as is necessary to save us from our desperate situation; anything more would only distract our mind from the great goal of concentrating all our forces upon this salvation.

But of course the four excellent truths do not exhaust all truths, as the Buddha acknowledges. Naturally he admits all verities the human mind has ever found and may still find. Some of them he even incorporates into his teaching, e. g. the doctrine of reincarnation, simply because they are true! "That of which the wise declare that it does not exist in the world, that I also declare not to exist; and what the wise declare to exist in the world, that I also declare to exist."[12] But just because these verities were known to mankind apart from him, and might well have been discovered without a "Perfectly Awakened One," he does not acknowledge them as distinguishing points in his doctrine. What he has given to mankind is something entirely unique, something it might never obtain again through any other man with the exception of another Perfectly Awakened One, it is "that doctrine that is peculiar to the Awakened Ones."

Certainly mankind itself, in its greatest representatives, has gained deep insight into suffering, into its origin, annihilation, and the way leading to this annihilation. Since the fact of suffering dominates the whole cosmos as well as the life of every single being, it would be quite incomprehensible, if this were not the case. But these were only single glimpses of light, only partial insights that could lead to no decisive results. This holds good of the modern philosophy of Schopenhauer, who, like no other European, has shown the essence of all life to consist in suffering, but who has not been able to find the way and the bridge leading out of suffering. Not less does it hold good of the ancient Upanishads, which in their greatness are only surpassed by the Buddha's doctrine. But they too fall below it inasmuch as they do not make the fact of suffering their only content, do not see suffering always and everywhere, and therefore do not know a clearly visible way to its complete annihilation.

The Buddha thus brings immediately before our consciousness as does no other, the principal and cardinal problem of our life, how to escape suffering and, above all, the suffering of death. But he does more: he promises us its solution in the highest possible form of certitude, that is, by the awakening of our own direct cognition. His doctrine is, first, free from every wrapping of a mythological or allegorical character, such as is peculiar to religions. "As if there were somewhere near a village or a town a big *sal* tree, and in the changing season, there fell leaves and twigs down from it, there fell branches and bark and greenwood, so that later on it was free from leaves and twigs, free from branches and bark, consisting of kernel wood only,—even so here the exposition of Lord Gotama is free from leaves and twigs, free from branches and bark, consisting of pure kernel wood."[14]

Then, next, the Buddha rejects every kind of theorising:

"The Accomplished One is free from every theory, for he has seen," he says of himself.[15] Not even with logical conclusions which in one way or another forsake immediate perception does the Buddha concern himself. The sole criterion of truth for him is, and always remains, one's own, immediate, intuitive apprehension of truth. It is only the self-evident consequence of this standpoint, that he does not claim any belief in his own purely descriptive exposition of the things he says he knows by his direct perception; and that he even admonishes his disciples to accept nothing, even from himself, simply on good faith, but to accept only as fact what they themselves have beheld. "Now, ye monks, thus knowing, thus perceiving, will ye speak thus: 'We hold the Teacher in reverence and what we say is only said out of reverence for the Teacher?'"—"Nay, verily, Lord."—"Then, monks, what you say is only what you yourselves have recognised, what you yourselves have comprehended, what you yourselves have understood, is it not so?"—"It is even so, Lord."—"Well said, monks! Given are ye, my monks, to this Teaching, the clearly visible, the timeless, the all-inviting, which is to be understood by every reasonable man."[16] And further on: "Do not believe, O Bhaddiya, in hearsay, nor in traditions, nor in rumours, nor in the word handed down, nor in purely logical conclusions, nor in external semblance, nor because of agreement of anything with the views you cherish and approve of, nor because of your own thinking of anything that it is true. Neither shall you think: 'The ascetic, the Buddha himself, is my teacher,' but if you, Bhaddiya, yourself, gain the insight: Such things are evil, such things lead to misfortune and suffering: then you may reject them."[17] Especially does he often warn against holding any transmitted dogmas of belief; because "one may remember well or may remember badly."[18] In the same manner he compares believers to "a row of blind men chained together, of whom not one, of the first, nor of the middle, nor of the last, sees anything."[19] Particular warning he also gives against trusting to the speculations of any speculating philosopher, for such an one "may philosophize well or philosophize badly."[20] Only our own immediate insight is of value; and the Buddha's doctrine itself also has value only in so far as it makes this our own insight possible. "And the Teacher expounds the Teaching, more and more deeply, more and more highly, in all its divisions obscure and clear. According as the Teacher proceeds to expound the Teaching to the monk, more and more deeply, more and more highly, in all its divisions obscure and clear, so, penetrating ever further into the Teaching, he arrives at certitude as respects point after point in the Teaching. Wheresoever, disciples, for such reasons, upon such grounds, through such tokens, faith is fixed on the Accomplished One, has struck root, is settled fast, such, disciples, is called *reasonable* faith, faith *grounded in sight*, firm, not to be shaken by any ascetic or recluse or god or devil or by any one whatsoever in all the world. In this wise, disciples, is the Teaching tried in respect of the Accomplished One. In this wise also is the Accomplished One well tried in respect of the Teaching."[21] "Not directly at the beginning, ye disciples, may certainty be attained; but gradually striving, gradually struggling, striding on pace by pace, certainty is attained. But how, gradually striving, gradually struggling, striding on pace by pace, is certainty attained? There, ye monks, a man full of trust comes near. Having come near, he associates. Associating, he listens. With open ears he hears the Teaching. Having heard the Teaching, he retains it. Having retained the sentences, he contemplates their content. Contemplating their content, the sentences give him insight. As the sentences give insight to him, he approves them. Approving them, he weighs them. Having weighed them, he works, and because he works earnestly, he in his own person realizes the supreme truth, and, wisely penetrating, beholds it face to face."[22]

According to this, the Buddha only asks one thing from his disciples, namely, the treading of the way shown by himself, upon which one may oneself win the intuitive apprehension of truth. This minimum of trust, to try, at least once, the way shown by him to the discovery of truth, even he cannot omit, but as *anima candida*, as a man who obviously has no selfish purpose in view, he may certainly demand it. But this minimum of trust, entirely indispensably in the world, once given to him, and the way shown be him and described by him with the accuracy of an ordnance map, once entered upon, all the rest follows of itself. Very soon the foretold glimpses of light and undivined results will appear, one after the other, like the stations a traveller on a road reaches one after the other; thus the faith first given will change into unshakeable certainty as to the correctness of that part of the way not yet accomplished. "Whoever, ye monks, is a worldly master who deals with worldly things, even such an one is not treated like a merchant or a dealer, by people saying of him: 'Thus we want it, then we will try; if we cannot get it thus, we do not want to try.' How much more, O disciples, the Accomplished One, who is entirely free from worldly matters! To the trusting follower, to the follower training himself in the Master's Order with earnest zeal, the confidence dawns: Master is the Accomplished One, his disciple am I; the Accomplished One knows, I do not know. To the trusting disciple, to the disciple who trains himself in the Master's Order with earnest zeal, the Master's Order imparts itself, refreshing and precious; in him the confidence dawns: Let skin and tendons and bones shrivel up within my body, let flesh and blood dry up: whatever may be accomplished by manly virtue, manly strength and manly valour, not till it is accomplished, shall my strength lessen.'"[23] Thus then, the Buddha does not want more faith than must be given to a *guide*, but certainly not less than a guide must claim: "This, oh Brahmin, I can do in regard to this: A guide is the Accomplished One."[24]

According to the standpoint thus taken up by him, all purely abstract notions are wanting in his Discourses, and only such occur as may be immediately drawn from perception and are therefore without more ado, evident in themselves, just as in a guide-book difficult technical terms of physics, geology and other branches of science are out of place.

If the Buddha thus wishes to bring about the individual's own direct perception of truth, the question arises as to what may be the nature of this perception that can lead to such extraordinary results as he promises. Its peculiarity cannot lie in the object, since the Buddha also has to do only with the world about us. Therefore it cannot be anything else but a peculiar mode of looking at things that he wishes to teach us. And indeed its secret consists in an extraordinary deepening of the normal manner of looking at things. Here the Buddha is in perfect harmony with Schopenhauer. Like this philosopher he first proceeds from the fact that there are various degrees of this cognition through the medium of the senses, from the dull gaze with which the beast looks at the world, to the look of the genius, penetrating into all depths. It is precisely the realization of this mode of viewing things, called by Schopenhauer the *genius-like* one, in the form of pure contemplation, which is the goal the Buddha sets before every one. He not only gives in detail the several steps leading upwards to it, but he also teaches the ever greater perfecting of this pure contemplation itself, right up to the culminating point where "it draws aside the veil of the world."[25]

As regards the antecedent conditions under which this pure contemplation comes about, the Buddha also agrees with Schopenhauer. Just as for Schopenhauer it sets in through the cognizing part of consciousness becoming entirely separated from the willing part, just as according to him it is conditioned by such a deep silence of will, on one hand, and such an energy of the perceptive function, on the other, that even individuality vanishes from the consciousness and man is left alone as the pure subject of cognition; even so also, according to the Buddha, by eliminating all and every motion of will, such a complete tranquillity of the mind—*samatha*—must be produced, that "thoughts about Me and Mine no more arise", and on the other hand the utmost energy in perception must be produced, if the "eye of knowledge" is to open; in particular, the "hindrances" of mental sloth and of dubiety must be abandoned. And as, according to Schopenhauer, in order to obtain thoughts of genius one must be so completely alienated from the world that the commonest events seem to be quite new and unknown, so also, according to the Buddha, the "penetrating insight" presupposes "loosening" and is in itself conditioned by "alienation," "far from lusts, far from unwholesome states of mind." Indeed, we find the adequate expression for the "pure subject of cognition," again in the words wherein the disciples often characterize their Master, calling him, "the One who has become eye, who has become knowledge."

But in two points the Buddha here deviates from Schopenhauer, or rather, surpasses him: First, in regard to the object of contemplation. For he teaches, laying, for the rest, great stress upon the contemplation of the world alone accessible to us as the normal and sufficing one, that in the highest stage of "alienation," of "loosening," when in complete equanimity everything has been abandoned and thereby the sight can be directed exclusively inwards, in inner enlightenment a higher form of perception will appear like a chicken from an egg, reaching far beyond the limits of birth and death and thus make possible for us complete clearness concerning our situation. Schopenhauer has certainly pointed to this region, styled by him "illuminism," as to something really existing, and given it its place, but he did not enter it, well knowing that he could not, because he did not know the necessary antecedent conditions. But according to the Buddha, contrary to Schopenhauer's view, —who on this point, since all experience was here wanting to him, was unable to give a competent judgment— also this higher kind of perception may very well be conferred on others, and he imparts this knowledge to us in the clearest possible manner. To be sure, also according to him, it is accessible only to a few, *but it is not at all necessary for the annihilation of suffering.* As for the rest—and with this we come to an essential difference between the Buddha and Schopenhauer, connected, as we shall see later on, with the different answer given by the Buddha to the fundamental question of Schopenhauer's system—man may very well develop in himself the faculty for the apprehension of the world peculiar to the genius. He even may come thus far, that he is able to bring it about every time he wants to, "just as he wishes, in its fulness and width" contrary to the view of Schopenhauer, according to whom the cognition of the genius is not perhaps difficult, but does not at all lie within our power, and is only a state of mind exceptionally occurring in a "festival hour," a "lucid interval" of the genius, who must himself be born as such. To make accessible this genius-like mode of looking at things is precisely, as said above, the direct aim of the doctrine of the Buddha.

To teach this art, he only needs to have a "reasonable man" before him, "not a hypocrite nor a dissembler, but a straightforward man."[26] Him he offers to lead by a quite definite mode of training, up the mountain of pure cognition, from which, as Schopenhauer promises, in the individual, not only the general, the Ideas, may be seen, but something quite different, something unparalleled, namely, the ocean of suffering heaving deep below his feet, while he himself is throned upon an inaccessible height, whither not even the smallest drop of this ocean sprays up, and where therefore purest happiness reigns. "It is, as if near a village or a town there were a high rock, and two friends were approaching it. Having reached it, one of them remains standing at the base of the rock, while the other one climbs to the top of the rock. And the friend below, at the foot of the rock, cries up to the friend who has climbed up to the top of the rock: 'What now, friend, are you seeing from the rock?' But that other replies: 'I see, dearest one, from the rock a serene garden, a magnificent forest, a landscape all in bloom, a bright pool of water.' But the other says: 'This is impossible, dearest one, this cannot be, that from the top of that rock you can see a serene garden, a magnificent wood, a landscape all in bloom, a bright pool of water.' Then the friend comes down from the summit, and takes his friend by the arm and leads him up the rock, and, having given him a little time to rest, asks him: 'What now, friend, are you seeing from the top of the rock?' And the other one says: 'Now, friend, I see from the rock a serene garden, a magnificent wood, a landscape all in bloom, a bright pool of water.' But the other one says: 'Just now, dearest one, we heard you speaking thus: 'It is impossible, it cannot be, that from the top of that rock you can see a serene garden, a magnificent forest, a landscape all in bloom, a bright pool of water.' And now again, we have heard you speaking thus: 'I see there from the top of the rock a serene garden, a magnificent forest, a landscape all in bloom, a bright pool of water.'

And thereupon the first one replies: 'So long, dearest one, as this high rock was obstructing me, of course I could not see what was to be seen.'"[27]

Certainly, also according to Schopenhauer, when we have become the pure subject of cognition, we reach a state free from pain, the greatest and purest happiness of life. But this happiness is perishable. For it consists only in a temporary quieting of the ceaseless torment of willing, in a passing silence of will, in the fetters of which we remain chained, after as before, since ultimately, we ourselves are will. But according to the Buddha, following the way of pure contemplation, we are also able to attain *permanent*, total annihilation of willing, and therewith may see the fetters wherewith willing had bound us, lying for ever broken at our feet.

That these two, Schopenhauer and the Buddha, did not see quite the same from the mountain of knowledge, is explained, first by the fact that Schopenhauer, so to say, had only climbed the first slopes of the mountain, while the Buddha *from the summit* "looked down into this world of pain."[28] Schopenhauer, the man of will, convinced as he was of the impossibility of influencing his will, was incapable of making any attempt to develop within himself the genius' mode of contemplation, but had to wait in patience till a lucky hour of itself should bring a cognition more or less free from willing, the depth and duration of which he was unable in any way to determine. The Buddha, on the other hand, who by the extreme purity of his entire mode of life, in advance had cleansed his cognition from all the perturbations of willing, had thus acquired the power of transporting himself, at will and for as long as he liked, into the deepest contemplation, to remain in a state of pure cognition, wherein the whole truth of the world then revealed itself to him.

A further reason why, to both of these great men the same view did not offer itself from the mountain of cognition, is this, that each of them had fixed his gaze upon quite a different field of sight. Schopenhauer wanted to explain "the primary phenomena in the individual and in the whole as the world," and therefore he only saw the "Ideas" the *form* of these primary phenomena, and as their *content* the immeasurable ocean of will, so immense that it swallowed up the philosopher himself, and he thought himself to consist of it, thus, without any hope of escaping it, unless this ocean should some time or other dry up of its own accord. The Buddha, renouncing every explanation of all other phenomena, wanted nothing but simply to find the end of suffering. Therefore, at last, behind the ocean of will he found another realm, the realm of freedom from suffering, the narrow entrance to this realm at the same time disclosing itself to him.

Precisely this exclusive limitation of all his striving to this one point, how to escape suffering, led him at last to his goal. And so he made this point the foundation of his unique way of salvation, which may be briefly characterized as a direct envisagement growing more and more deep, an ever purer contemplation, of suffering, regarded according to its compassing bounds, its causes, and its relation to ourselves. This contemplation constitutes the goal of all insight, and the source of all wisdom. All virtue, ultimately, serves only it, by creating in a pure heart wherein the storms of willing are laid to rest, the indispensably necessary antecedent condition for it. He only who by the practice of ceaseless mindfulness of such sort that he performs everything he thinks, says and does with full consciousness, little by little has trained his mind so that it is able to dwell incessantly and exclusively in the contemplation of suffering,—only he, "wisely penetrating" will struggle through to that point where, at first far away, like the holy grail, but in time becoming more and more distinct, rises "the island, the only one" where there is no more suffering, and especially, no more death. Such an one alone is at all competent to pass an authoritative judgment upon the truth or untruth of the Buddha's teaching. Else he resembles the friend who refuses to climb the rock from which the most enchanting view offers itself, but who nevertheless denies that this view may be seen from above. He resembles the man born blind, for whom things visible do not exist because he does not see them: "As if, O Brahmin, there were a man born blind, not seeing things black or white or blue or yellow or red or green, nor seeing what is equal and what unequal, nor stars nor sun nor moon. And as if he thus should speak: 'There is neither black nor white; there is none who might see black or white; there is neither blue nor yellow; there is no one who might see blue or yellow; there is neither red nor green, there is no one who might see red or green; there is neither equal nor unequal; there is no one who might see equal or unequal; there are no stars, there is no one who might see the stars; there is neither sun nor moon, there is no one who might see sun or moon. I myself do not know anything about them, I do not see them, *therefore* they do not exist.' Just so, O Brahmin, is the Brahmin Pokkharasāti, the Opamañña from Subhagavana, blind and without eyesight. That he should perceive the utmost reality, the highest truth, is impossible."[29]

From this, to be sure, there results a certain exclusiveness in the doctrine of the Buddha; it presumes men who not only have become clearly conscious of suffering as the primary problem of their existence, but who have come so far as to expect salvation, if such a thing is to be hoped for, no longer from without, but only through their own strength. For such, as is said in the Samyutta-Nikāya, to seek to win peace through others, as priests or sacrificers, is the same as if, a stone were thrown into deep water, and now people, praying and imploring. and folding their hands, came and knelt down all round saying: 'Rise, O dear stone! Come to the surface, O dear stone! Spring up on to the shore, O dear stone!' But the stone remains at the bottom.[30] Of such men at any time there never have been too many. Most men find it convenient to take no notice at all of suffering in any form, to say nothing of occupying themselves minutely with it. For them, there is of course no help, therefore they are not taken into account by the Buddha. He calls them "uninstructed men, unperceiving the Noble Doctrine, unacquainted with the Noble Doctrine."[31] They are those, who, according to Schopenhauer, represent the factory wares of nature, to whom one may also belong even if one is a scholar; they are the great mass to which, as says Thilo, commonly belongs one more person than each individual thinks! "With them Lord Gotama has nothing in common."[32] But with those also he has nothing in common who, though they do not blindly pass over the fact of suffering, do not wish to be enlightened about the fact that liberation from suffering cannot be realized through any kind of grace, especially not by the help of some personal god, but exclusively by our own strength and by personal action.

Thus the doctrine of the Buddha, having for its organ, the most exact of all methods, that of natural science, in experimentally realizing truth, requires true men, "no hypocrites, nor dissemblers, unassuming, resolute, stout-hearted, possessing insight, clear-headed, steadfast, of collected and unified mind, wise and intelligent,"[33] who alone are capable of applying the experimental method. With them, "the noble ones, knowing the doctrine of the noble ones, inclined towards the doctrine of the noble ones,"[34] he has communication, as with the true aristocrats of mankind, "to whom this world is too mean,"[35] who therefore wish to grow out of it. To them as prize he offers a solution of the great problem of the world's suffering, which, being based upon one's own immediate perception, provides unshakeable certainty: "Whoso has not properly understood the four excellent truths", says the Samyutta Nikâya, "he goes from one teacher to another and looks searchingly into his face thinking: 'Does this one really know something, see something?' It is as if a feather or a flock of cotton, light, at the mercy of the wind, blown about a plain, were carried now here, now there, now by this wind, now by that, by reason of its very lightness. But whoso has truly understood the four excellent truths, he no longer goes from one teacher to another and searchingly looks into his face to see if this one may really know something, see something. It is as if a brazen columm, or a post of a gate, stood there, deeply founded, well dug into the ground, without tottering or shaking. If now from this or that quarter, wind and weather come mightily storming on, it cannot tremble, shake and totter, and why not? Because of the depth of the foundation, because the column is well dug in."[36]

And this system, warranting to the noblest of men such a goal by the application of the surest, and thereby most modern method, is said to be no longer suited to our times! *For such a contention we must seek the reasons*, for such must exist. And here in the end we find, when such statements are not based on pure unreason, always the same reason given, either directly, or with some variations, namely, that it does not suit the modern criticizers of the Buddha's doctrine of salvation,—he himself calls them men "who only learn the doctrine so as to be able to give discourses and express opinions about it"[37] instead of practically testing its truth,—that according to him, salvation from suffering is identical with salvation from the world itself, and that the Buddha asks of his disciples that they try this method of salvation in earnest. This is said to be no longer up to date. Now it may be admitted that precisely in our time, notwithstanding its high civilization, or perhaps just because of it,* mankind is devoted in quite a terrifying degree to a materialistic conception of the world, even where theoretically this is held in abhorrence, and just on this account, all consciousness of the unsuitability of their continued stay in this world, and thereby of the necessity of salvation, is wanting in men. Of course, we will not deny either that the utmost our modern thinkers are able to fulfil in this direction consists generally in writing books full of learning about salvation, and about those who have lived and taught *practical* salvation; or, sitting at a well-spread table, to expatiate movingly upon the grandeur of renunciation of the world. But this does not exclude the fact that there are also in our time some few who do not feel at all satisfied with this world, and therefore try to grow out of it; for whom, therefore, the gospel of salvation through one's own strength during this *present lifetime* and, in such wise that its occurrence is *directly perceived, experienced within oneself,* is the most tremendous event that can happen in the world. For such the doctrine of the Buddha is modern, quite as modern as any branch of natural science whose methods it shares. To those few, the doctrine of the Buddha, who himself for this very reason called it "the timeless," will be for all time modern, in the same way that the definitive solution of a problem remains valid for all time. You may lose the interest in the problem,—whether that, in our case, is an advantage, each may judge for himself; you may even try to find a still simpler solution than the

* Civilization alone, without culture, that means, without improvement of the heart, is nothing but refinement of every form of pleasure-seeking, and therefore ultimately producing, an enhancement of egoism, and thereby of the struggle of everybody against everybody.

one here given. But so long as you have not succeeded in doing this,—and try to name another who has solved the problem of salvation, attainable for every reasonable man, with the same immediate security giving directly perceived certainty as the Buddha has done—so long is it simply folly to try to discredit the solution given because it was already reached two thousand years ago.* So long also is it folly—let each consider within himself, if this expression is too strong!—to belittle the solution of this problem given by the Buddha as unmodern, merely because it can be fully realized, as we shall see later, only by going away into homelessness (Pabbajjâ), that means, by becoming a monk. Who wants the goal, must also want the only known means thereto. Further on we shall speak more in detail about this going into homelessness, and especially about the collision of duties possibly occurring thereby. Here, where we only have to touch upon the suitability of the step to our age, we should only like to point out what, after all, is only self-evident, that whoever desires in this present life to obtain *entire* deliverance from the world, in this very life must wholly forsake it, must leave it entirely behind him. Here also the old saying holds good: "You can't wash a hide without making it wet." The Buddha would not have been the great genius he was, if he had not recognized that to reach this perfect salvation in this present lifetime only a very very few are fit and ready. Therefore it is again nothing but foolishness to fear that our enlightened Europe might become overrun by actual living Buddhist monks. For this reason the Buddha does not expect anyone to take this way, if on any grounds he does not think himself fit to do

---

* From the outset it is probable that the solution of the problem of salvation, if at all possible to the human mind, has been attained in ancient India, where as in no other country, this problem had drawn men into its circle, in an unexampled manner, as far as the speculative, as well as the practical side of the problem is concerned.

so. On the contrary, to all those who are already alive to the consciousness of their eternal destiny lying beyond the world, but who prefer to make their way towards this goal within the world, he points out the nearest way for them, so that they need not return after death into this our world, but may realise the great goal in one of the highest worlds of light. Yea, because he knows the path leading out of the world, he also knows the paths leading within the world to a fortunate rebirth, and shows these also with indisputable certainty. His doctrine, therefore, is modern in this sense also, that it assures to each man who does not belong to the great multitude in the sense given above, that is, to the man of the world who is concerned about his future after death, the measure of freedom from suffering and of wellbeing procurable for him. "If this doctrine should be attainable only for Lord Gotama and the monks and nuns, but not for his male and female adherents, *living the household life,* clad in white, *abstaining in chastity,* and not for the male and female adherents, *living the household life, and satisfying their desires,* then this holy life would be incomplete, just because of this. But because this doctrine may be attained by the Lord Gotama and the monks and nuns, as well as by the male and female adherents, *living the household life,* clad in white, *abstaining in chastity,* and by the male and female adherents *satisfying their desires,* therefore this holy life is perfect, just because of this."[38]

After all, for the expert, even to-day, it still holds good what the Brahmin Moggallâna, a contemporary of the Buddha, exalts in his teaching: "Just as among the odours of roots the black rose-garlic is thought the most excellent of its kind; and among the odours of kernel wood the red sandal wood is thought the most excellent of its kind; and among the odours of flowers the white jasmine is thought the most excellent of its kind; even so also, is the doctrine of Lord Gotama the best in our times to-day."[39]*

* The question put so often as to whether the spreading of Buddhist ideas among ourselves is desirable, considering the peculiar character of our civilization which lays the chief stress upon the living out of our personality as it is euphemistically called—for in truth this is nothing but a living out of our desires — is, first, wrongly put, and, second, without purpose. Rightly put, it ought to run: Is the solution of the enigma of man given by the Buddha, correct, or is it not? If it is correct, then all the other solutions dissenting in theory *or practice* from the Buddha, are wrong, without further words. The opponents of Buddhism, therefore, in so far as they are playing an honest game, will have to refute his teachings; which ought not to be difficult if they are erroneous since they are not founded on any revelation, but only on perception. On the other hand, the question is purposeless. Everyone who takes the trouble to make himself acquainted with the doctrine of the Buddha has himself personally to come to terms with it. What attitude others may adopt cannot concern him in any way, since he alone will reap the fruits of his doing. For this reason the Buddhist naturally concedes the same right to every other system. Buddhism is the religion of unlimited tolerance.

THE MOST EXCELLENT TRUTH OF SUFFERING

THE CRITERION OF SUFFERING

Suffering is impeded volition. This sentence, coined by Schopenhauer, is so clear and so true that it needs no further proof. Everything running contrary to my volition and to my wishes is suffering, and everything occurring in harmony with my wishes, but finding resistance, is, as far as this goes, also suffering. Therefore the Buddha also proceeds from this self-evident definition of suffering, when, in the first of the four excellent truths, defining suffering as follows: "Birth is Suffering, old age is Suffering, disease is Suffering, death is Suffering, to be united to the disliked is Suffering, to be separated from the liked is Suffering, not to get what one desires is Suffering. This, friends, is what is called Suffering."[40] So far every man will be in perfect accordance with the Buddha. But herein lies the peculiarity of his doctrine, that according to him there is nothing at all but suffering in the world. For immediately after the words as given above, the Buddha proceeds: "In short, the five groups of grasping are Suffering." Later on, we shall return to these five groups of grasping. At present it will suffice to define them briefly as representing all objects of will at all possible; thus the words say: All activities of will are suffering, or, since we already know the nature of everything existing to consist in volition: Everything is full of suffering, just because of its nature. "Suffering only arises where something arises, Suffering only vanishes where something vanishes."[41] Against this part of the first of the four excellent truths the average man revolts; this he thinks he ought to reject as a perversion, sprung from world-sundered and world-estranged brooding, a perversion recognizable as such, through its taking only a fleeting glance at life. For what an immense quantity of pleasure, of lust, of the purer joys of family life, in nature and in art, life offers! How dare one overlook all this? How can one shut his eyes against it? No, not everything in life is suffering; it is not even true, that suffering predominates therein; but in spite of suffering, existent without doubt, the world is beautiful and worthy of being enjoyed.

If nevertheless the Buddha should be right, then without further argument it is clear that the average man must have made a terrible mistake in his judgment of the content of life according to its actual value. This, of course, is not impossible. For the question of life's value cannot be answered off-hand simply from clear and pure perception, in which everything is fixed and certain. But this answer represents a *judgment*, that is, a bringing together of the materials, offered by perception, into a relationship of concepts by means of the activity of reason. Now the part that error plays in the action of reason is often immense, especially if the subsuming of countless isolated accidents of manifold kind, reaching into the past and the future, under one or under a few fixed concepts, is involved. Free from error such can only be when done with the utmost care, looking out over the past and the future; and this is given only to very few. The great mass of mankind when using their reason in this manner, falls into the greatest errors, so that such an error "may dominate centuries, throw its iron yoke upon whole nations, stifle the noblest feelings of mankind; and cause even him whom it is not able to deceive, to be put in fetters by his own servants, its dupes." Such an error, then, is "the enemy, against whom the wisest minds of all times have waged unequal combat. Only what *they* have won from him, has become the property of mankind."

May it not be that here also, in this question as to the value of life, such a fundamental error of the multitude, even of mankind taken as a whole, might come into operation, an error that only an enlightened mind like a Buddha might be able to remove? Only the utmost carefulness and thoughtfulness, the primary antecedent condition of a correct judgment, can, on our part, lead to a correct answer.

In applying it, there has first to be exposed a fundamental error which is generally made when judging as to the value or worthlessness of life, making it in advance, impossible to understand the doctrine of the Buddha. It is this: that a thing which man desires with such unexampled ardour as he does life, must at all events be desirable. But this is a gigantic paralogism. Imagine a man condemned to lifelong imprisonment with the prospect before him of an endless chain of misery. Will he not, facing sudden death, nevertheless cry out: I want to live, to live? Or go to the death-bed of a man who has been sick for years and is at last tormented by the most torturing pain. Will not he too, for all that, only too often exclaim in his pains: I want to live, to live! Will not they both want to live even when you tell them that death means for them redemption from severe and incurable suffering, that further life for them means nothing but further suffering? Will they not answer again and again: I want to live, to live at any price, even at this price, that my whole life be nothing but suffering? From this it is evidently clear, that man in general will take upon him a life full of suffering, even a life consisting of nothing but suffering, if only he can, and is allowed to live. But from this it follows as evidently, that this boundless clinging to life cannot be founded upon an understanding that life is not identical with suffering but is something fundamentally different and really worth striving for; the reason for this clinging to life, as we shall see later on, being something entirely different. Therefore it is not legitimate to take this human impulsion towards life into account in deciding the question as to whether in life suffering preponderates, or whether perhaps indeed, life and suffering in the last analysis are identical concepts. On the contrary, the question really is if at the bar of purified cognition this impulsion will not prove to be entirely mistaken. With this, the principal weapon with which the average man comes forth against this part of the doctrine of the Buddha, in advance falls to the ground. For it is just this clinging to life as such, which is the chief argument by which he is guided in examining the question as to whether life is really worth living. The argument: "Certainly life is worth living, else I should not crave for it thus irresistibly," will either lead him to the negation of the doctrine of the Buddha without any more ado; or if he nevertheless occupies himself with the arguments adduced by the Buddha, it forms, for all that, the basis of his reasoning, generally remaining hidden from the reasoner himself, but in advance, influencing his investigation in a decisive manner, and determining its results from the beginning. Thus he shows a lack of heedfulness, whereby he blocks up his own way to the understanding of the first of the four excellent truths. Whoso wishes to understand this, before all else must be able entirely to put aside his unparalleled attachment to life in his examination of the question as to how far suffering dominates in life. Even if he thinks this attachment to be something unassailable, he must not allow it to influence him in any way. In other words, he must be able to face the question in an entirely objective manner, like one looking down upon life from some high watch-tower, as if removed from it, and therefore in no way influenced either by desire or dislike. Only then will he be able quietly to compare the pros and cons, and thus only gain the balance needed for judging as to the *justification* of this his craving for life itself. A lustful man is not the proper authority for judging as to a woman's beauty or ugliness; and a man possessed by the desire for life is not the right person to decide as to the worth or worthlessness of life. But how very few of those who self-complacently criticize the "pessimism" of the Buddha, fulfil this fundamental antecedent condition of an objective judgment!

Not less important in judging life is another circumstance reckoned with by only very few: Happiness is satisfaction of the will, suffering is obstruction of the will. Now everything occurring in the world is not a single accident consisting by itself, but, just as it is itself the effect of a cause, on its own side, it will become again the cause of new effects. Accordingly, with every event there is bound up a countless number of motions of will, partly pleasant, partly unpleasant. The question therefore arises: In what way can judgment be given as to whether an event may be called a happy or an unhappy one? To answer this question, we shall do best to come down to immediate experience. Somebody has won the first prize in a lottery. This, beyond doubt is a satisfaction of the will in a very high degree, and, in addition, an immense piece of good fortune. Now this man who until then, has led a life free from sorrow, in consequence of this event goes wrong, turns an idler and a spendthrift, squanders all his gains and, at last, despised by all, finds himself in deepest misery, ruined and without the energy to work himself again out of his misery. What now will be his judgment, and that of others, in regard to the prize he lately won?

Unquestionably, that this seeming good fortune in reality was the greatest misfortune of his life. Or take another case: A certain person thinks good eating and drinking the chief good in his existence. Therein he takes pride and comfort, and does not hesitate at times to set forth this happiness of his life in the right light before others. But by and by, in consequence of this life, there supervenes a grave malady, say, cancer. Will he now, writhing in torments, still think the time of good eating, recognizing it as the cause of his present suffering, a happy one, and remember it with pleasure, thinking, "still it was nice"? Or will he not rather curse it as the source of his present suffering? Or, suppose a man tormented by thirst, sees a cool drink. Full of greed he drinks of it, and feels a momentary pleasant sensation running through his body. Afterwards he feels pains and thus sees that he has drunk poison. Will he still have the courage to call this cool drink a good? Or will he not rather, recognizing this "good" as the cause of his keen pains, now look back upon it as a misfortune, and therewith register it under the heading of suffering? From this it is evidentially clear that a momentary sensation agreeing with our will, does not give us the right to enter it in our book of life as a good. Even innumerable pleasant motions of will, released by some event, lose afterwards all their value, yes, may even become accurst, if one single moment in the long chain is miserable, and this single decisive moment happens to be the last one in the chain of effects produced by the so-called happy event. This single last moment alone gives to the whole chain of perhaps years-long impulses of will, its definitive character. When itself is full of misery, it sucks up the happiness of years, as a sponge the water surrounding it. It may even erase it utterly from the account of life as if it had never been there. But equally well it may erase the misery of years like a corrosive acid. A person may have been the unhappiest of men during his whole life. But if now, in this moment, he becomes really happy, if he really feels himself quite well, if his feeling of happiness is not darkened by any prospect of the future, then the whole past full of suffering will be utterly forgotten. He will feel as if liberated from a heavy oppressive nightmare that now has vanished in the abyss of the past, and therefore counts no more.

Certainly it cannot be otherwise. It is always only the present that is real; hence it is always only the satisfaction of will and thereby happiness, or, on the other hand, the obstruction of will and thereby unhappiness which I feel *now* that is real. Happiness or unhappiness belonging to the past, are, like everything gone by, nothing but a shadow without reality. Especially is bygone happiness, brought into relation to my present woe, apt only to intensify the latter, according to the law that a fall is accompanied by more painful results, the greater the height from which it takes place.

Accordingly only the last moment of life counts in the evaluating of a life as a happy or an unhappy one, and ultimately, the last moment of consciousness before death. For only *this* present will then be real. If I, in *this* moment, feel well and thereby happy, a whole life full of greatest misery will count nothing against this; and if I feel unhappy, this feeling is not modified by even the happiest past, but rather increased to unbearableness by the frightful contrast with the latter.

In regard to this, above everything else entire clearness must be reached through deep reflection, before one is competent to pass judgment as to how far life is to be put on record as happiness or as suffering. From this fundamental fact therefore the Buddha too sets out in developing the first of his four excellent truths, the truth of Suffering. It forms the clue to their understanding.

According to the arguments just advanced, the following chain of thought forms the foundation of all the expositions of the Buddha on suffering. I may be made as happy as possible by a satisfaction of my will: but in that moment where, by the taking away of the object conferring this satisfaction of will, it has changed into suffering,—into suffering that will be the greater, the greater the luck has been that granted the possession of the object—only the fact of suffering will be real, and thereby will furnish exclusively the standard for evaluating the object as one happy or painful for me. The object was such that at last there has remained to me only one thing: suffering. If I am honest, therefore, I can only post it up in the book of my life with this as final result, i. e. as a negative entry. As there depends very much, strictly speaking almost everything, on this cognition, we will come down once more to immediate experience. A person may find the complete and exclusive satisfaction of his will in possessing or cherishing some object, in his wife or his children, or in the realization of some idea grown dear to him. And now this object upon which his interests are entirely concentrated, is snatched away from him, further occupation with it becomes impossible to him; thereupon life itself will become worthless to him, and he will break out into the lamentation: Life has no more value for me.

After this, however, according to the Buddha, the decision of the question, as to how far life must be looked upon as suffering, depends upon this other, as to whether there are objects of the will which cannot be taken away from man, and thereby satisfactions of the will which do not become suffering. Only such with inner justification might be registered as wellbeing, as happiness; every other satisfaction purified cognition cannot honestly register otherwise than under the heading of suffering. But an object of will that cannot be taken away, necessarily presupposes that it is not perishable. For in the moment when it perishes, when it dissolves, it is irrecoverably lost for will, even if will clings to it ever so much. The question, therefore, amounts to this: Are there imperishable objects of will? Or, to put it otherwise: The real, ultimate criterion of suffering is *transitoriness*: "Whatever is transitory, is painful."[42]

Indeed this dictum forms the basis of granite upon which the whole doctrine of the Buddha about suffering is built: "That there are three kinds of sensations, I have taught: Pleasure, pain, and that which is neither pleasure nor pain.... And again I have taught: Whatever is felt, belongs to suffering. Thus alone in regard to the impermanence of things I have said that whatever is felt belongs to suffering, having regard to the fact that things are subject to annihilation, to destruction; that pleasure in them ceases, that they are subject to cessation, to changeableness."[43]

As we see, these words not only give transitoriness as the infallible criterion for what may be looked upon as suffering, but they also contain the statement that everything follows this law of transitoriness: all things are impermanent, are subject to annihilation, to destruction.

Really to recognize this, and to its whole extent, is the point on which everything depends. Certainly, the mediate objects of our willing, the objects of the external world, everybody without further ado will concede to be transitory without exception, because here the continual change, the incessant dissolution is evident. But the matter becomes quite different, when the *immediate* manifestation of our willing in that which we call our personality, comes into question. This personality is said to be the only thing in the world which lies outside the realm of transitoriness, either entirely and to its whole extent, so that man, neck and crop, as it were, would be immortal, or partially so, if at least its kernel should be permanent and thus imperishable. This kernel some think to find in the soul: others, as Schopenhauer and his disciples, in will manifesting itself in the personality.

That even the powerful genius of Schopenhauer thought himself forced to recognize in the personality, if only in its last substratum and with manifold reservations, the only insurmountable barrier to the law of transitoriness comprising everything else, shows clearly how deeply rooted in man is the illusion that personality includes the imperishable, the eternal. Even thus from of old, within that part of the personality that was thought to be removed from the realm of transitoriness, there was found the island in the ocean of worldly misery, to which one only needed to flee, perhaps as pure spirit, to escape from suffering. And precisely for this reason, mankind never has been able to penetrate to the first of the four excellent truths that everything, everything without exception in the world, is suffering.

Here within the personality lies the great obstacle to the acknowledgment of the first of the four excellent truths. Everything else, as said above, is obviously perishable and therefore, according to our exposition above, painful. To eliminate this obstacle had to be the main task of the Buddha in the direction here in question; and this, in fact, it was. For he always limited himself to this; but he also takes every imaginable trouble to make clear that everything connected with personality, and therewith personality itself, is without exception subject to the iron law of transitoriness, and thereby, of dissolution and decay, therefore painful throughout its whole extent. This he does by dissolving personality into its parts: corporeal form, sensation, perception, mentations and consciousness, and by showing the characteristic of transitoriness present in each of them.

It is clear, however, that here we are only able to follow the Buddha further, if we have first convinced ourselves that the dissolution of personality into the five components just enumerated, as given by him, is really correct and exhaustive, that it is to say, if the essence of personality shall have become quite clear to us. Therefore we shall first have to deal with this question.

PERSONALITY

"Personality, personality, is said, Venerable One; but what is personality, does the Blessed One say?" Thus the adherent Visākha asked the sage nun Dhammadinnā, his former wife. "The five groups of grasping are personality: that is the Grasping-group of the corporeal form, the Grasping-group of sensation, the Grasping-group of perception, the Grasping-group of the activities of the mind, the Grasping-group of consciousness. These five groups of grasping, friend Visākha, constitute the personality, so the Blessed One has said."[44] After this, according to the Buddha, personality consists of five groups: the body, the sensations, the perceptions, the activities of the mind, and the consciousness. But these groups are not simply groups, but more closely defined as groups *of grasping*. Therefore to understand the definition given by the Buddha, insight must be gained into two things. First, that personality is really exhausted by these five groups, that it is summed up in them; secondly, why the Buddha calls them just groups *of grasping*.

The answer to this last question is the fundamental antecedent condition for understanding the essence of personality. Therefore it properly ought to be given first. For in order to comprehend something as the sum of a number of definite groups, before all, the general character of these groups itself must be known, consisting in our case precisely in this, that it is groups of *grasping* which constitute the personality. But as far as we have got at present, a thorough treatment of this question is for systematical reasons not yet possible. Therefore we cannot do otherwise than anticipate the result of our later expositions and assume it until then as established. This result is, briefly, as follows. According to the Buddha, our essence is not exhausted by our personality; we only grasp it, we only cling to it, though so tightly that we imagine ourselves to consist in it, "as if a man with hands besmeared with resin caught hold of a twig."[45] Therefore it is nothing but an expression of this fact, when the Buddha calls the five groups forming our personality, groups of grasping, Upādānakkhandhā.*

We must always bear in mind this character of the five groups, when under the guidance of the Buddha we now try to comprehend them as the sole and complete components of our personality, and this in accordance with the principle of the Buddha *intuitively*, in such a manner that we look through their machinery in form of the personality precisely as through the composition and the working together of the parts of an ingeniously constructed machine we have fully understood.

The basis of the personality is formed by the material body. It originates in the moment of generation by father and mother from the several chemical materials the Buddha

---

*) The word we translate here by personality is Sakkāya. It is composed from sat-kāya: kāya meaning, as the definition given at the beginning of this chapter indicates, the summary of the five groups: corporeal form, sensation, perception, mentations, consciousness; *sat* meaning *"being"*. By Sakkāya therefore the summary of the five groups is defined as the real being—that is, of ourselves,—expressing thus that we entirely consist in these five groups.

Just this same content our conception of personality possesses. For it is thought of as a being existing for itself, that exhausts itself in the marks—just these five groups—wherein it appears. Sakkāya and personality are thus indeed equivalent terms.

sums up under the four chief-elements, the earthy, watery, fiery and airy one. These materials constitute the female egg as well as the male spermatic cell, and, further, they furnish the matter for building up the body, which is drawn from the blood of the mother, and worked up into the form of the new body. This upbuilding being finished, the body is born and further sustained in similar fashion, in that, by taking nonrishment to replace the particles incessantly streaming away, new substitutes are brought in from the four chief-elements: "This my formed body is composed of the four elements, generated by father and mother, built up from rice, porridge and sour gruel."[46]

This body, constituted thus, shows itself endowed with organs of sense equally consisting of the four chief-elements. By this, that is, by the "body endowed with the six organs of sense," we have what is generally, and also by the Buddha himself, designated as the body or, more exactly, as the corporeal form, *rūpa:* "Just as the enclosed space which we call a house comes to be through the conjunction of timbers and bindweed and grass and mud, in the selfsame way, through the conjunction of bone and sinew and flesh and skin, there comes to be this enclosed space which we call a body."[47]

The corporeal form thus consists exclusively of the four chief-elements. The materials from which it is built up, are throughout identical with the inorganic substances of the external world, they are directly taken from it, and afterwards they return to union with it. Only when incorporated into the body they are brought into the form peculiar to this, just as the materials from which a house is built up have also be worked into a form belonging to this kind of structure.

Evident as this fact is, and unconditioned as it is generally conceded to be from the purely rational point of view*, nevertheless it is known with perfectly clear consciousness only by very few; which is a clear proof, how very shallow the "normal" perception is. But this fact *must* be penetrated by longer reflection in its full significance, if we wish fully to understand the essence of personality! The basis of this personality, the body together with the organs of sense, is nothing but a mere collection and transformation of dead matter from external nature; nay, in the main, it consists simply of worked-up dung.

One would imagine that, with this state of things really penetrated, even now it ought to a matter for some astonishment that men should cling to a structure with such a basis, namely, to this same personality, as to the highest they know. But just from this it will probably also become clear why the Buddha lays such stress upon the penetration of this basis of our personality as of a mere conjunction of the substances comprised in the four chief-elements:

"What now, brethren, is the earthy element? The earthy element may be either internal or external; whereof the internal division is as follows. Whatsoever is found in the subject proper to the person, of a hard or solid nature, such as the hair of the head or of the body, nails, teeth, skin, flesh, sinews, bones, marrow, kidneys, heart, liver, pleura, spleen, lungs, intestines, mesentery, stomach, excrement and whatever else of hard or solid nature exists in the subject proper to the person,—this is called the internal earthy element. Whatsoever exists of the earthy element, whether belonging to the subject or foreign to the subject, all is designated as the earthy element. And what is the watery element? The watery element may be either internal or external; whereof the internal division is as follows. Whatsoever is found in the subject proper to the person, of a

* "Think, o Man, that you are dust and shall return to dust," the Catholic church also calls to her adherents before every corpse.

fluid or watery nature, such as bile, phlegm, pus, blood, perspiration, fat, tears, sperm, spittle, nasal mucus, oil of the joints, urine and whatever else of a fluid or watery nature exists in the subject proper to the person—this is called the internal watery element. Whatsoever exists of the watery element, whether belonging to the subject or foreign to the subject, all is designated as the watery element. And what is the fiery element? The fiery element may be either internal or external; whereof the internal division is as follows: Whatsoever is found in the subject proper to the person, of the nature of heat or fire, such as that wherethrough warmth is present, whereby digestion takes place, whereby the physical frame becomes heated, whereby what is eaten and drunken, tasted and swallowed undergoes complete transformation, and whatever else of a hot or fiery nature exists in the subject proper to the person—this is called the internal fiery element. Whatsoever exists of the fiery element, whether belonging to the subject or foreign to the subject—all is designated as the fiery element. And what is the airy element? The airy element may be either internal or external; whereof the internal division is as follows. Whatsoever is found in the subject proper to the person, of the nature of air or wind, such as the up-coming airs and the down-going airs, the wind seated in stomach and intestines, the airs that traverse the limbs, the incoming and outgoing breaths—this and whatever else of an airy or windy nature exists in the subject proper to the person is called the internal airy element. Whatsoever exists of the airy element, whether belonging to the subject or foreign to the subject—all is designated as the fiery element."[48] Thus the Buddha entirely equilibrates the materials building up our body with those of the external world; he even identifies them with the latter.

But the body composed thus, together with the organs of sense, is, as said above, nothing but *the basis* of the personality, not personality itself. To produce this, the four other groups, sensation, perception, mentations and consciousness, must be developed. This is done by the six organs of sense beginning their peculiar activity, consisting in catching each a certain side of the external world, the eye the forms, the ear the sounds, the nose the odours, the tongue the savours, the body the touchable, the organ of thought, the brain, having as a collective basin the data of the five other senses for its objects. "Five senses there are, friend,—the sense of sight, the sense of hearing, the sense of smell, the sense of taste and the sense of touch, each having a different sphere, a different field of action; none sharing in the sphere or field of action of any other. As regards these five senses that have different spheres or fields of actions, each distinct and apart from all the others, what is their mainstay; what is that which does share in the sphere and field of action of each?"—"As regards these five senses, friend, Thinking is their mainstay, Thinking is that which participates in the sphere and field of action of each."[49]

But that this process of the senses may begin, that the external "bodies may bring the organs of sense each to the kind of activity peculiar to them," first the organs of sense themselves must be able to fulfil their functions, or, as the Buddha puts it, the organs of seeing, hearing, smelling, tasting, feeling must be "intact." Then the objects corresponding to the several organs of sense must come within their reach, and at last the action of seeing, or of hearing, and so on, must be stirred and incited through the influence of the outer object, or, as the Buddha puts it, there must be a corresponding interlocking of the organs of sense and of the forms, sounds, odours, savours, objects of touch and ideas coming within their reach. If all this is the case, then by the interlocking of the organ and of the object of sense, *consciousness arises:*

"If, friends, the organ of vision exists intact, but external forms do not come within its range and hence the proper interlocking is lacking, then the corresponding parcel of consciousness does not arise. And if the organ of vision is not defective and outward forms do come within its reach, but the appropriate interlocking fails to take place, then again the corresponding parcel of consciousness does not arise.* If, however, the organ of vision is uninjured and outward forms come within its reach and the proper interlocking takes place, then the corresponding parcel of consciousness arises.

As with the organ of vision, so with the organ of hearing, the organ of smell, the organ of taste, the organ of touch, the organ of thought.** If each is whole and intact, but the corresponding external object does not come within its range and hence the appropriate interlocking is lacking, then the corresponding parcel of consciousness does not arise. And if the internal organ is whole and intact and the corresponding external object does come within its range, but the proper interlocking fails to take place, then again the corresponding parcel of consciousness does not arise. If, however, the internal organ is whole and intact, and the corresponding external object comes within its range, and the appropriate

---

* If, for example, I am absent-mindedly looking out of my window upon the street, then, though various forms may come within reach of my sight, nevertheless there is no "corresponding interlocking" of eye and form, and therefore no consciousness of these things arises within me.

** Also to the organ of thinking an object must correspond. As said above, these objects to the organ of thinking are the objects of the other five senses, that is, all possible appearances of the world, either directly as concrete and immediate perceptions, or indirectly as formations of the imaginative faculty raised by means of association of ideas out of our memory, or as abstract notions formed earlier and again become objects of the activity of the organ of thinking. In harmony with this, the Buddha calls the objects of the sense of thought, *dhammā*, that means realities in the most extensive sense. Accordingly, we shall continue to translate Dhammā, as meaning the objects of the organ of thought, by "realities"—but alternately, for sake of greater clearness, by "ideas."

interlocking takes place, then the corresponding parcel of consciousness arises."[50]

In another passage[51] the Buddha describes this process as follows: "Through the eye and forms consciousness arises: 'visual consciousness' accordingly is the term applied. Through the ear and sounds consciousness arises: 'auditory consciousness' accordingly is the term applied. Through the nose and smells consciousness arises: 'olfactory consciousness' accordingly is the term applied. Through the tongue and flavours consciousness arises: 'gustatory consciousness' accordingly is the term applied. Through the body and objects of taction consciousness arises: 'tactile consciousness' accordingly is the term applied. Through the organ of thought and ideas consciousness arises: 'mental consciousness' accordingly is the term applied. Just as with fire, o monks, when by means of one or another conditioning cause a fire burns up, exactly according to that is the name applied. Thus, if a fire burns up by means of logs, then 'log-fire' is the name applied. If a fire burns up by means of faggots, then 'faggot-fire' is the name applied. If a fire burns up by means of grass, then 'grass-fire' is the name applied. If a fire burns up by means of cow-dung, then 'cow-dung-fire' is the name applied. If a fire burns up by means of chaff, then 'chaff-fire' is the name applied. And if a fire burns up by means of rubbish, then 'rubbish-fire' is the name applied. In the selfsame way, O monks, when, on account of any conditioning cause whatsoever, any consciousness whatsoever springs up, exactly in accordance therewith is the name applied."

If this exposition is closely thought over, it yields a surprising result. Consciousness is nothing substantial whatever. It is nothing but the effect of a fixed conditioning cause, namely, of the interlocking of one of the activities of the six senses and its objects. It is only present, if and for as long as this cause exists, and vanishes again into nothing as soon as this cause disappears. It flames up in the moment when an organ of sense is excited through an external object corresponding to it, as fire flames up if a match is rubbed on its rubbing-surface. Again it disappears, if the organs of sense are put out of action, just as the fire is extinguished, if the wood through which it had flamed up is withdrawn from it. If I do not see, that means, if I do not put my eye, directing it towards an object, into action, then there does not burn—we may directly say, 'burn'—any visual-consciousness within me, if I do not hear, no auditory-consciousness, and if all activities of the senses, thinking included, have ceased, then there no consciousness at all is burning: it is *extinguished*. "From whatever reason, ye monks, consciousness arises, just through this one, and through this one only is it effected." "Apart from conditioning cause there is no coming to pass of consciousness,"[52] in short, consciousness is something causally conditioned.

If through the starting of an activity of sense the corresponding consciousness, as visual consciousness, auditory consciousness, and so forth, flames up, then only am I *touched* through the external object. "In dependence upon the eye and forms there arises visual consciousness; the conjunction of these three constitutes contact. In dependence upon the ear and sounds there arises auditory consciousness; the conjunction of these three constitutes contact. In dependence upon the nose and smells there arises olfactory consciousness; the conjunction of these three constitutes contact. In dependence upon the tongue and flavours there arises gustatory consciousness; the conjunction of these three constitutes contact. In dependence upon the body and objects of contaction there arises tactile consciousness; the conjunction of these three constitutes contact. In dependence upon the organ of thought and ideas there arises mental consciousness;

the conjunction of these three constitutes contact."[53] Before this contact, that is, before consciousness flames up in which I am first touched by the object becoming apparent in it, this external object, inciting the functioning of the senses, even my own body, is, for me, entirely non-existent. Only in consequence of the up-flaming of consciousness am I touched by the external object so that I am first struck by *a sensation*, and this sensation then arouses *the perception* of an external object. Now I perceive the object of the sensation as form, sound, smell, flavour, as pressure or, by means of thinking, as a concrete or abstract idea: the object of sensation as such becomes *apparent* to me. The several stages of this process may be clearly observed in the lowest kind of sense, the tactile sense. If, lightly slumbering, in the darkness I hit a thing with my arm, then in consequence of this interlocking of the organ of touch and its object consciousness flames up, the contact between me and the thing occurring first in this. But if my sleep is so deep that no interlocking of the organ of touch and of the external object takes place, and thereby no consciousness is aroused, then I am not touched by this. But if I am touched, then within me, first, a mere sensation arises, without the object arousing this sensation being directly perceived as such. This is only effected by and by through continuous touching.

The thing perceived thus arouses in me the will to recognize it more clearly in its relations to its surroundings and, first of all, to myself. This means that it becomes an object for my central organ of perception or for my organ of thought, this organ having for its task the penetrating of those relations of the objects perceived. As soon as I perceive something, my activity of thinking begins: *I consider* the object perceived.

Precisely through this is the latter distinguished from the other appearances which, besides this, I have to confront.

Where, in seeing appearances no *will* arises to make them the objects of thinking, there they are not seen as *individual* things, they are not distinguished from each other. Whoever without having his organ of thought in any way incited thereat, wanders through a place, will certainly not be able to say in the end which *individual* things he has seen; he will only be able to speak of the place as a whole. This will be still more the case, if he has been entirely absorbed in looking at a magnificent landscape, without *thinking* about it in any way. For it is peculiar to aesthetic contemplation never to behold the *individual* parts but always only the harmonious whole. Thus it is only in consequence of the activity of thinking setting in with regard to an appearance that we become conscious of this appearance as an individual one, that we distinguish it from the countless other appearances. These latter I do not consider, and just for this reason they flow together into an undefined totality. Thus only through this distinguishing activity of thinking is the totality of appearances presenting themselves to me through the senses, broken up in respect of time and space into a world of distinct things, *the Papañca:*

"Out of contact springs sensation. What one senses, that he perceives. What one perceives, that he thinks. What one thinks, that he distinguishes. What one distinguishes, that, in consequence of this, presents itself to him as a totality of single perceptions, namely as past, future and present forms, entering consciousness by the eye, as past, future and present sounds, entering consciousness by the ear, as past, future and present odours, entering consciousness by the nose, as past, future and present flavours, entering consciousness by the tongue, as past, future and present objects of contaction, entering consciousness by the body, as past, future and present ideas, entering consciousness by the organ of thought."[54]

Therewith the whole mechanism of the personality is given. To put it otherwise: all the five groups are now clearly defined, for "every corporeal form* peculiar to what is formed thus** ranks as component of the group of form. Every sensation peculiar to what is formed thus ranks as component of the group of sensation. Every perception peculiar to what is formed thus ranks as component of the group of perception. Every mentation peculiar to what is formed thus ranks as component of the group of activities of the mind.*** Every consciousness peculiar to what is formed thus ranks as component of the group of consciousness. Now we understand: 'Thus is the grouping, the collecting, the placing together of these five groups of grasping.'"[55] Now, we may add, the origin of personality is understood as the origin of what man generally looks at as representing his essence.

Reviewing this whole history of the origin of personality, it becomes clear without further ado that the five groups into which the Buddha has analyzed it, really exhaust it

---

* This means our body, that "comes to be through the conjunction of bone and sinew and flesh and skin." See above!

** This means, the personality.

*** The fourth one of the groups (khandhā) constituting the personality, is the group of the *saṅkhārā, saṅkhārākkhandha.* To understand the word *saṅkhāra* is of fundamental importance for the understanding of the whole doctrine of the Buddha. Therefore we will come back to its meaning later on. Here we only wish to lay down the following: *Saṅkhārākkhandha* contains within itself all inner emotions arising in us in consequence of the sensation and perception of a sense-perceptible object, that is, first, the said considering or *thinking,* further on, the willing originating from this thinking, in all its possible varieties, as desire, joy, enthusiasm, antipathy, wrath, anger, sadness, fear etc., in short, the whole complex of mentation and volition setting in, in dependence upon feeling and perceiving a certain object of sense. We comprehend this whole complex of mentation and willing as the totality of the motions *of the mind* roused by a concrete sensation and perception. Therefore the expression "group of activities of the mind" is entirely adequate to *saṅkhārākkhandha.* Strictly speaking, also the mentations are expressions of willing, namely, the immediate realisation of willing in thinking. This is also adequately expressed by the term "mind," wherein the relation to willing widely prevails.

completely. We shall find nothing in it that may not be classified among one of these groups. But going further, it becomes clear that the four groups of sensation, perception, activities of the mind, and consciousness, are always found together. If through the collision of an organ of sense with an object corresponding to it, consciousness flames up, then at once sensation and perception of the object as well as the functions of the mind appear as inevitable consequences in consciousness: "Whatever there, in dependence upon eye-contact, in dependence on ear-contact, in dependence on nose-contact, in dependence on tongue-contact, in dependence on body-contact, in dependence on mind-contact arises of sensation, arises of perception, arises of activities of mind, arises of consciousness," it is said in the 147th Dialogue of the Majjhima Nikāya which passage is given in more detail in the "*Milindapañha*," as follows:

"The king said: May it be possible, reverend Nāgasena, to separate these phenomena bound together in a unity, from each other, and to show their diversity, so that one might be able to say: 'This is contact, this is sensation, this is will, this is consciousness, this is idea, this is discursive thinking'?" "No, O king, that is impossible."—"Give me an explanation."—"Suppose, O king, that the cook of a prince was preparing a soup or a gravy and adding some sour milk, salt, ginger, cummin, pepper and other spices. If the prince now should speak to him thus: 'Extract singly the juice of the sour milk, as well as that of the salt, of the ginger, the pepper, the cummin and the other spices you added!'—might this cook, O king, be able to separate the juices of those spices mixed thus completely, and to extract them and to say: 'This here is the sour, and that the salt, this is the bitter, this is the biting, this is the acrid and that the sweet'?"—"Certainly not, sir. That is impossible. But nevertheless all the spices together with their characteristic qualities are contained therein."—"Just so, O king, it is impossible really to separate those phenomena bound together into a unity and to show their diversity and to say: 'This is contact, this is sensation, this is perception, this is will, this is consciousness, this is idea, this is discursive thinking'."

Consciousness, sensation, perception and activities of the mind thus have their sufficient cause in the interlocking between the organ of sense and its corresponding object. They are the respective product of the activities of the senses, always occurring joined together, and always generated anew by these with the exactness of a piece of mechanism. Indeed, if we sift the matter to the bottom, the corporeal form together with the organs of sense, that we have called the *basis* of personality, is nothing but the mechanical contrivance of the six senses, *the six-senses-machine,* having for its purpose to bring us into contact with the external world by generating consciousness and thereby sensation and perception of it. The five different organs of sense of this machine are just so many different tools for effecting the interlocking of the five different groups of components of the external world; the sixth organ, the brain, being, as said above, only the focal and collective point of the remaining activities of sense, their "mainstay." Whatever namely the world may be, at all events it is composed of those "marks," those "characteristics,"[56] entering consciousness as forms, sounds, odours, flavours, objects of touch in form of perception, and furnishing furthermore the materials for the products of the sense of thought. In these elements the world is summed up: "Everything will I show you, my monks. What is everything? The eye and forms, the ear and sounds, the nose and odours, the tongue and flavours, the body and the objects of touch, the organ of thinking and ideas. This, ye monks, is called everything."[57]

The internal evidence of this sentence will afterwards become clearer to us. Here it may suffice to prove that according to the Buddha, the world is nothing but a world of forms, of sounds, of odours, of flavours, of objects of touch and of ideas, for the comprehension of which, including their working up by means of the sixth sense in the form of the activities of the mind, the machine of the six senses is designed and put together.

To be sure, this may not yet be entirely intelligible from the foregoing expositions. How can a formation consisting exclusively of the four chief-elements, that means, of dead matter—and our body, as far as we have yet learnt to know it, is nothing else—how can it bring forth, if put into activity, consciousness and thereby sensation, perception and thought, in short, the summation of all those phenomena we call spiritual ones? If a body composed of dead matter is set into motion, always none but purely mechanical movements are brought forth, but never the so-called spiritual phenomena, even if this body possesses the form of a human body, as for instance a human corpse, which is certainly a very clear proof that in the material body, as such, and alone, the sufficient cause of those spiritual phenomena cannot be contained. But on the other hand we have seen in the foregoing, that the spiritual phenomena are bound to the material body, inclusive of its organs, and conditioned by them. It follows from this that the material body, inclusive of its organs built up in the same manner from the matter of external nature, must be endowed with *special qualities* to be able to arouse consciousness and to produce their peculiar effects of seeing, hearing, smelling, tasting, touching and thinking. This may be made clear by an analogy.

If I give a piece of common iron to somebody and ask him with it to attract and keep fast other particles of iron without immediately touching them, he will rightly declare this to be an impossibility, since the qualities necessary for this are wanting to iron as such. But if he understands something of physics, he will add that he could easily fulfil the task proposed, if a piece of magnetic iron were be handed to him. For some pieces of oxide of iron or loadstone possess the quality of attracting and holding fast, particles of iron. This quality is called magnetism; and a piece of iron possessing it, is called a natural magnet. This kind of iron thus possesses a quality not possessed by common iron, it develops something analogous to life by causing motion from within; and it develops this quality because it is magnetized. But what is this magnetism? Surely something added to the iron. This is already proved by the fact that by touching or stroking with a natural loadstone, magnetism may be transferred temporarily to iron and permanently to steel, both thereby becoming artificial magnets. But, for the rest, this something is entirely unknown to us. Perhaps it is something infinitely subtle, infinitely ethereal, not perceivable as such, first of all, not weighable; perhaps it only consists in a change of a certain kind, produced in the molecules of the iron themselves. However this may be, at all events magnetizing, that is, the procedure by which unmagnetical iron becomes magnetical, gives to the iron a mysterious capacity, otherwise totally alien to it. This capacity itself is only able to exist in dependence on iron, thus, it vanishes, if not earlier, then at latest, along with the destruction of the piece of iron itself. Precisely the same relation, as that between unmagnetical and magnetical iron, exists between inorganic and organic matter. Inorganic matter can never, in no case, support the processes of consciousness consisting in sensation, perception and thinking. To become capable of this it must become *especially qualified*. As iron must be made *magnetic*, it must be made *organic;* as iron must become *magnetized,* it must become *organized.* This precisely is done by building it up in the maternal womb into a corporeal form of a certain kind. As many a piece of oxide of iron is already magnetized by nature, so here, in the maternal womb from the very beginning, the material body, including its purely material organs of sense, are *organized,* that is, they are made capable of serving as organs of sense. Certainly we can just as little tell how this organization here is effected, and wherein it consists. We do not know if perhaps the material body is loaded with a kind of ethereal fluid, neither weighable nor perceivable as such; or if there happens only a change of the state of the molecules of matter. But here too we know at least this much, that organization is something added to inorganic matter, giving to the organs of sense formed by it a mysterious capacity entirely foreign to their essence. This is the capacity of causing consciousness to flame up as soon as they are put into activity, and of thereby engendering sensation and perception. This transmutation of inorganic matter into organic, is equivalent to that of dead matter into living matter, for the latter expression denotes just the capacity of arousing sensation. Thus vitality and the organization of a corporeal form, mean the same thing.* This vitality is completely bound up with the material body, just as magnetism is only able to exist in dependence on iron, and disappears, at the latest, with the decomposition of the same. In the same manner, vitality can only exist in dependence on the material body, and must at last totally disappear upon the disintegration of such a body.

Thus the machine of the six senses now becomes quite intelligible. It consists of the body endowed with vitality,

* "To live and to be organic are reciprocal concepts." (Schopenhauer.)

or, if you prefer to say so, loaded with vitality, or, in short, enabled to live. Only organs of sense already capable of living, and only such as still possess the faculty of life, are able to perform their functions. This, too, is the meaning of the words, of the twenty-eighth Dialogue of the Majjhima Nikāya, that the organs of vision, of hearing, of smell, of taste, of touch and of thought must be intact, if the sensing process is to set in.

But there is reason for showing in still more detail that our expositions really correspond to the doctrine of the Buddha, which alone is to be reproduced here.

The monk Mahākoṭṭhita wanted to know how our bodily organs of sense come into possession of their peculiar faculty of arousing consciousness, and thereby sensation and perception, as he expresses himself in questioning Sāriputta: "Five senses there are, brother: sight, hearing, smell, taste and touch. By reason of what do they continue their existence?" From Sāriputta he gets the following answer: "The five senses, O brother, exist by reason of vitality."[58]* Thereby Sāriputta expressly declares the functions of the senses to be nothing but manifestations of vitality having their sufficient reason therein. The Buddha himself expresses the same thought by using the term *nāma-rūpa* for the six-senses-machine or the corporeal organism. For by *rūpa* he means the body consisting of inorganic matter, and by *nāma* the faculty of sensation, of perception, of thought, of contact, of attention and so on: "And what, ye monks, is *nāma-rūpa?* Sensation, perception, thinking, contact, attention—these, friends, are called *nāma*. The four chief-elements and the corporeal form that comes to be by reason of the

* The sixth sense, the sense of thought, is not mentioned here, obviously because Sāriputta has explained just before that it is nothing but the centre of the other senses, their "mainstay", and therefore must exist under the same fundamental antecedent condition as the other ones.

four chief elements—this, friends, is called *rūpa.* Thus that is *nāma,* and this, *rūpa.* This, ye monks, is called *nāma-rūpa.*[59] As the *faculties* comprised under *nāma** form the kernel of what is called life,** the meaning of *nāma-rūpa* again, is that of a body capable of life.*** Moreover, *nāma-rūpa* may also be translated by mind-body, since *we* call the faculties comprised under *nāma* the mental ones and, by a collective term, the "mind."† That especially the relation of *nāma* to *rūpa* is the same as the relation of magnetism to iron, is clear from the following.

Nāma-rūpa is the six-sense-machine which alone makes possible contact between us and the objects of the outer world, and thereby, sensation and mentation. The Buddha states this elsewhere as follows: "If, Ānanda, you were asked: 'Is contact due to a particular cause?' you should say: 'It is.'

---

* That the Buddha means by *nāma* only the *faculties* of sensation, of perception, of thought, of contact etc., is clearly evident from the chain of causality (Paṭicca-samuppāda) that will be treated of later on, Nāma-rūpa being adduced there as an antecedent condition of concrete contact, sensation, perception etc. In the Dialogues a word will often be found to mean a certain quality, as well as the *capacity* to develop it.

** As a rule, only the faculty of *sensation* is given as the characteristic quality of life. This is certainly correct. For perception, thought, and attention etc., are only the necessary consequences of sensation in the higher grades of life.

*** The faculty of life, appears in two directions, once as the capacity of the vegetative functions of the body, and then as the capacity of the sensitive functions—sensation, perception and thinking—of the organs of the six senses, including the brain as their centre, or, as we would say, of the central nervous system. *Nāma* comprises especially this second side of vitality, the capacity of sensuous functioning. But as this capacity, being the higher degree of vitality, presupposes the lower one, that is, the capacity of vegetative life, and therefore includes it as self-evident, the Buddha in defining *nāma* as above, might conveniently leave this latter and lower side of vitality unmentioned. We are doing precisely the same in defining life simply as the capacity of sensation.

† The expression *nāma-rūpa* is taken from the Veda, where it designates what possesses name and form, that is, the single individual. "The world here then was not developed, it developed itself in names and forms, so that it was said: 'The individual called thus and thus by his name—*nāma*—possesses this or that form—*rūpa.*' This same world is developing still to-day into names and forms, so that it is said: 'The individual called so and so has this or that form.'" (Bṛihadaraṇyaka Upanishad 1, 4, 7). "Name and form are the reality." (Ibid. 1, 6, 3.) The same reality of the individual the Buddha, of course, also means by *nāma-rūpa.*

And to the question: 'From what cause is contact?' you should say: 'Name and form is the cause of contact.'"[60] Thereby he explains *nāma-rūpa* as follows:

He distinguishes between *nāmakāya* and *rūpakāya*, these terms designating the mental and the material body. Proceeding from this he explains that, if the mental body were not there, then the material body would not be attainable by us,* hence, could not exist. And if, on the other hand, the material body were not existent, then "those modes, features, characters, expressions," in which the mental body manifests itself, that is, sensation, perception and mentation, would not be possible for us, so that really only by the conjunction of these two "bodies" is the possibility of contact and thereby of sensation and mentation given: "Therefore, just this is the ground, the basis, the genesis, the cause of contact, to wit, *nāma-rūpa*."[61]

Hence, the six-sense-machine—*nāma-rūpa*—according to the Buddha, actually consists of two co-ordinate components which only in their conjunction yield the capacity of engendering consciousness and thereby sensation and perception. These two are the material and the mental body. We see these two components related to each other in very much the same way that we relate magnetism to steel, which acquire the power of attracting and repelling other iron particles only in their union. To make this agreement outwardly recognisable also, we only need to say, correspondent to the expression *nāma-rūpa*, instead, "magnet" "magnet-iron," and then to define this concept, in connection with *nāmakāya* and *rūpakāya*, the mental and the material body, as the combination of the "magnetic body" and the "iron body."

To be sure, how the relation between this spiritual and this material body is more exactly constituted, we do not

* Here we must especially bear in mind that, in respect of our real essence, we are behind our personality.

know, as little as up till now we have succeeded in explaining fully the relationship of magnetism to steel, its vehicle. The Buddha also does not tell us; but just as we are able to describe magnetism only from the effects through which it becomes visible, he too contents himself with defining the mental body according to "those modes, features, characters, expressions, in which it manifests itself."[62] At all events we must be careful not to take the rendering of the expression *nāmakāya* by "mental body," here chosen by us, in the sense wherein it is generally understood among ourselves, as signifying a substance indestructible and immaterial which might inhabit the material body. By "mental body" as we have already said, nothing is designated but that unknown factor which transfers the coarse material body into that condition where it is able to produce sensations and perceptions for us. In the doctrine of the Buddha the contrast of mind and matter, as understood by Christian theologians, does not exist. Mind and matter are for him nothing completely distinct, but hold place in one and the same scale, matter being at the same time something coarsely mental, mind and soul at the same time something subtly material. In other words: The mental body is something material in exactly the same sense that the magnet in relation to coarsely material iron may be called something mental. This conception of the Buddha is in perfect harmony with our modern physiology, for which it is also certain that the so-called mental or spiritual processes must ultimately be nothing but material processes, though of the subtlest kind, such as perhaps we may imagine the oscillations of the ether to be. Positively speaking, we shall doubtless come nearest to the truth by defining the relation of the mental or spiritual body to the material one thus, that the spiritual body represents a more intimate determinant, that is to say, a quality, of the material body, in the same way that magnetism constitutes a quality of iron. There also results from this, that vitality (which, as explained before, is, according to the Buddha, fundamentally identical with the faculties comprised within the idea of the mental body) and the animal heat of the material body, mutually condition each other. For after Sāriputta has explained the senses as being conditioned through vitality, the dialogue between him and the monk Mahākoṭṭhita runs on thus: "And by reason of what, does vitality exist?"—"Vitality exists by reason of heat."—"And by reason of what does heat exist?"—"Heat exists by reason of vitality."—"Then we understand the venerable Sāriputta to say that heat exists by reason of vitality, and we also understand the venerable Sāriputta to say that vitality exists by reason of heat. But what, friend, are we to take as the meaning of such words?"—"Well, I will give you an illustration, friend, for by means of an illustration many an intelligent man comes to an understanding of the word spoken.* Just as in an oil lamp that is lit, by reason of the flame light appears, and by reason of the light the flame,—in the selfsame way, friend, vitality exists by reason of heat, and heat exists by reason of vitality."[63] Vitality thus stands to animal heat, filling and penetrating the material body, in the same relation as the light stands to the flame, and thereby, like animal heat, it is itself a quality of the material body. Here, again, we have an analogy with magnetism, this, as Schopenhauer says, being no primary force of nature, but reduceable to electricity, the latter itself again, standing in interchangeable relations to heat (thermo-electricity).

Lastly the perfect correctness of the analogy between the relation of the material and the mental body and that of iron and magnetism may be inferred from the further fact that, as magnetism can be transferred from a magnet to

* For the same reason the comparison with magnetism is here carried through.

other pieces of iron, so the mental or spiritual body, by a saint in the state of highest concentration, may in a certain sense be *exteriorized*.

"With his mind thus concentrated, made completely pure, utterly clear, devoid of depravity, free from dirty spots, ready to act, firm, and imperturbable, he applies and directs it to the calling up of the mental body. He calls up from this body another body, having form, made of thought-stuff, having all limbs and parts, not deprived of any organ. Just, O king, as if a man were to pull out a reed from its sheath. He would know: 'This is the reed, this is the sheath. The reed is one thing, the sheath another. It is from the sheath that the reed has been drawn forth'—just so, O king, the monk calls up from this body another body, having form, made of thought-stuff, having all limbs and parts, not deprived of any organ."[64]

According to this, the similarity between mineral magnetism and what until now, following the Buddha, we have defined as vitality or spiritual body, is indeed so great that we can quite understand, why these latter days have coined the expression "*animal* magnetism" for the latter quality.

Summing up what we have been saying, the result is that the six-sense-machine—*nāma-rūpa*—consists of two components, one of which,—*rūpa*, the body built up from the dead materials of the outer world, is the supporter of the other component, namely, vitality, called also *nāma* or *nāma-kāya*, mental body, in such a way that the latter constitutes a closer definition, that means, a *quality* of the material body, in the same manner as magnetism constitutes a quality of iron. As magnetism makes iron magnetic, vitality makes the material body organic, that is to say, it changes inorganic matter into organic matter, the latter only in the form of a corporeal organism being *capable* of arousing consciousness and thereby of bringing about contact with the outer world.*

That is, only this *faculty* of the six-sense-machine, namely, "the body endowed with the six senses, as condition of life"[65] is thereby explained. To generate real life, that is, consciousness, and thereby sensation and thought, it is further necessary that the machine of the senses, or the body made capable of life, is also set in activity.** Only if this setting in activity has taken place, that means, only if the six senses begin to work, does consciousness flame up in the manner already described. Thereby we for the first time come into contact with the world, to which, of course, the six-sense-machine also belongs. This contact, in consequence of the peculiar construction of the organs of the senses, assumes the forms of sensation and of perception, as well as, later on, those of the activities of the mind.***

---

* It will be noticed that, in using this term, "corporeal" corresponds to *rūpa* and "organism" to *nāma*. —

It is in perfect harmony with these expositions, if *nāma-rūpa* is, in the Milindapañha, defined as follows:

"The king said: 'Master Nagasena, you were talking about *nāma-rūpa*. What means *nāma* and what means *rūpa*?'

'What there is of coarse matter about a creature, that is *rūpa*, and what there is subtle, spiritual, mental about it, that is *nāma*,'

'How is it, Mastet Nagasena, that not *nāma* alone is reborn, or *rūpa* alone?'

'Because, O king, both are inextricably connected; only as a unity may they come into existence.'

'Give me an illustration!'

'Just as, O king, a hen cannot lay the yolk and the egg-shell separately, because the yolk and the egg-shell are thus mutually dependent that they may only originate as an unity: in the same manner, O king, there would be no *rūpa*, if there were no *nāma*. For *nāma* and *rūpa* are thus mutually dependent that they may only originate together. Thus it happens from time immemorial.'"

** This actuating of the body made capable of life is effected by *thirst* animating and stimulating us to come by means of the six senses-machine into contact with the world, and by the adhering to *nāma-rūpa* caused by that thirst, these factors also effecting the building up of the machine itself. Later on, we will speak more at length about this.

*** From these expositions results also the insight that eye-consciousness, ear-consciousness etc. does not arise in the brain,—as to-day is inferred from the fact that,

Hereby the bodily organism, *nāma-rūpa* as the six-sense-machine and thereby the one substratum of the personality, is fully comprehended. But the personality has still another substratum, to wit, *consciousness*. For the possibility of coming into contact with the world depends, as has been made fully clear in the foregoing exposition, not only on the existence of the bodily organism, but also on this organism arousing consciousness in its sixfold sensual activity. If in consequence of the activity of the organism no consciousness should flame up, then in spite of this activity of the senses we should not be touched by the world, or to express it otherwise, we should not feel nor hear anything. Therefore personality is only the homogeneous result of the bodily organism and of the element of consciousness. This second substratum also must be inspected somewhat more narrowly.

Next, the possible objection that consciousness cannot be regarded as a separate basis of personality, because it is itself only produced by means of the corporeal organism, must be rejected. To recognize this objection as untenable, the mere hint suffices that a burning match also consists of two wholly different elements, wood and fire, though the latter is only produced by contact of the former with the rubbing-surface of the match-box. In the same manner consciousness only flames up through the interlocking of an individual organ of sense with an object of the outer world corresponding to it. With the element of fire consciousness also shares another quality, that of having to be kindled always anew.

But for the rest, the relations between the corporeal organism and consciousness are much more intimate then those between fire and match. For the relation of the two

---

if a nerve leading from an organ of sense to the brain is severed, nothing more is seen or heard etc.,—but they arise immediately in the eye, the ear etc., the severing of the respective nerve only interrupting the contact with the source of the current, so that the nerve, so to say, is no longer charged with vitality.

latter objects is simply conditioned, that is, it is nothing but a connection between cause and effect. But the corporeal organism and consciousness are *mutually* conditioned.

Next, we know already that consciousness is conditioned through the corporeal organism, being a product of it. But on the other hand, the existence of the corporeal organism itself is also conditioned through consciousness. For if the corporeal organism did not generate consciousness, then there would not be any sensation. But a body without sensation, though *capable* of living, would be destined to destruction, as is clear without further argument, only from its being unable to take nourishment. Even the embryo within the maternal womb could not develop to maturity, if it did not develop in its later stages some activity of the senses, in consequence of which consciousness is aroused in it. For we know that it shows life of its own from the sixth month of pregnancy, manifesting itself through its own movements. Now we know vitality to be identical with the faculty of sensation, and real life with real sensation. Thus the embryo possesses sensation even in this stage of development; and, because we know sensation without consciousness to be impossible, it also must have consciousness. Certainly this is only the lowest kind of sensation, nothing but sensation of *touch*, that is aroused through the organ of touch being spread over the whole body, to wit, the respective parts of the nervous system. Such sensations may also be felt by a worm, and therefore consciousness resulting thereby is only such as corresponds to this lowest degree of sensation, without perception attached to it.* All the other senses are still inactive, therefore do not generate consciousness; first of all, the brain does not yet produce consciousness of thought and therefore, of course, no self-consciousness. But nevertheless, the embryo also must in time develop at

* *This* kind of consciousness is therefore exhausted by concrete sensation.

least this touch-consciousness, if it is to come to maturity. So here also, consciousness is the antecedent condition for the further development and evolution of *nāma-rūpa* or of the corporeal organism. Consciousness must even descend into the impregnated ovum in the moment of conception, if this is to be enabled to develop into an embryo. Certainly at this period consciousness is still so weak, that it only arouses vegetative irritations, because it is produced by organic matter not yet differentiated, to wit, not yet differentiated to organs of sense. Therefore in the first instance it is only a kind of consciousness, and only arouses sensations or analogies of such, as are possessed by the germ of a plant in development. Only by and by, as the evolution of the embryo goes on, this plant-like consciousness is raised to animal touch-consciousness. Therewith the mutual conditionality of both factors, the corporeal organism and consciousness, is established.

"Just as, O friend, two bundles of reed are standing there, leaning against each other, in the selfsame way, O friend, consciousness arises in dependence on corporeal organism *(nāma-rūpa)* and the corporeal organism in dependence on consciousness."

"Ānanda, if it be asked: 'Does the corporeal organism depend on anything?' the reply should be: 'It does.' And if it be asked: 'On what does the corporeal organism depend?' the reply should be: 'The corporeal organism depends on consciousness.'"[66]

"Ānanda, if it be asked: 'Does consciousness depend on anything?' the reply should be: 'It does.' And if it be asked: 'On what does consciousness depend?' the reply should be: 'Consciousness depends on the corporeal organism.'"[67]

"This truth, Ānanda, that on consciousness depends the corporeal organism, is to be understood in this way: Suppose, Ānanda, consciousness were not to descend into the maternal womb, pray, would the corporeal organism consolidate in the maternal womb?"

"Nay, verily, Reverend Sir."

"Suppose, Ānanda, consciousness, after having descended into the maternal womb, were then to go away again, pray, would the corporeal organism be born to life in the world?"

"Nay, verily, Reverend Sir."

"Suppose, Ānanda, consciousness were to be severed from a child, either boy or girl, pray, would the corporeal organism attain to growth, increase and development?"

"Nay, verily, Reverend Sir."

"Accordingly, Ānanda, here we have in consciousness the cause, the occasion, the origin and the dependence of the corporeal organism."

"I have said that on the corporeal organism depends consciousness. This truth, Ānanda, that on the corporeal organism depends consciousness, is to be understood in this way: Suppose, Ānanda, that consciousness were to gain no foothold in the corporeal organism, pray, would there in the future be birth, old age and death and the coming into existence of misery's host?"

"Nay, verily, Reverend Sir."

"Accordingly, Ānanda, here we have in the corporeal organism the cause, the occasion, the origin, and the dependence of consciousness."*[68]

But what is this consciousness, *viññāṇa*, in reality? The Buddha defines it as an element *(dhātu)* "invisible, boundless, all-penetrating."[69] The objects enter this element at the same time, the interlocking of the sensual activities and of their corresponding objects having aroused it. Only by their entering the element of consciousness are the objects of the senses able to touch us, and only thereby sensation

---

* The corporeal organism—Nāma-rūpa—is the reason, the corporeal organism is the cause that the group of consciousness is able to appear. (Majjh.-Nik. III, p. 17.)

and perception of them becomes possible for us. The whole world, therefore, is for us existent only as far as it is irradiated by this element, and it vanishes again for us as soon as this element is temporarily or for ever extinguished. "Everything has its stand in consciousness" and "When consciousness ceases, this here also ceases," the Buddha therefore teaches further on.*[70] Because this element thus forms the indispensable antecedent condition, or the medium through which we become conscious of the objects of the world—this becoming conscious consisting in contact, sensation and perception—*therefore* it is called the element of consciousness.** Also in this way the relation of consciousness to the corporeal organism is the same as that of the fire to the match. Things must, in the same manner, first enter the fire to be perceived in the darkness: "This is my body, built up of the four chief elements, sprung from father and mother, and that is my consciousness, bound to it, on that does it depend," it

* It is well known that the modern empirical theory of the sensual perceptions, built upon the sensualism of Locke, suffers from a great defect. According to this theory sensations and perceptions arise only through the external object irritating the organ of sense. But here it remains entirely unintelligible how the irritating objects are felt and perceived as being *outside* of the organs of sense, the whole process occurring only *in* or *about* the organ of sense and therefore not being able to reach out of the realm of the same (the problem of the excentricity of sensation and perception). Now compare with this the doctrine of the Buddha as expounded above: Just where the defect of the modern empirical theory becomes visible, the factor discovered by the Buddha is introduced, and thereby completely remedies this defect. For through contact of the organ of sense and the immediate object of sense, for instance of the molecular current of the ether striking the surface of the eye, an invisible element called consciousness is aroused. In a moment, with the speed of thought, it spreads along the molecular stream to the object, emanating that stream comparable to an electric current running in the same manner with the speed of lightning through the whole conducting wire, be this as long as it may. Only thus sensation and perception of the external objects are made possible for us, who stand likewise as something inscrutable behind the whole process. This element, like space more subtle than the subtlest radiant matter, is boundless as is space. This boundlessness reveals itself especially by the help of space, consciousness illuminating the latter in its entire endlessness as soon as the organ of thought is directed upon it.

** Instead of being or becoming conscious, we may also say *cognitive*. "For consciousness consists in recognizing" (Schopenhauer).

is said in the Dīghanikāya II, 84, just as we may say: "This is the match, built up of wood and of chemical stuffs, sprung from the chemist; and that is the fire, bound to it, on that does it depend."

Now we not only understand the five groups as representing the only and complete components of personality, but we also, as promised, see through their mechanism, just as we may see through the plan and the working together of the parts of a machine we have thoroughly understood. Personality itself is such a machine at work, but with its products included.

The machine is represented by the corporeal organism we have just on this account called the six-sense-machine. It possesses the peculiarity of being only able to exist and to work after the accession of another element wholly different from it. This heterogeneous element is consciousness, possessing on its part the peculiar quality of being generated always anew as soon as the six-sense-machine begins to work. As soon as it flames up in this manner, it produces, according to its being aroused by the respective organ of sight, of hearing, of smell, of taste, of touch or of thought, the *sensation* of seeing, of hearing, of smelling, of tasting, of touching, of thinking, and the respective *perception* of the object felt in this way. Out of this sensation and perception, later on, the activities of the mind arise.*

* That sensation, and thereby perception and the activities of the mind, themselves conditioned by sensation, are especially conditioned by the corporeal organism, is particularily emphasised in the following passages: "Within a monk who thus gives heed to himself and dominates his recognizing, who persists without relaxing in wholesome striving and in working upon himself, there arises a pleasant sensation or arises an unpleasant sensation, or arises a sensation which is neither pleasant nor unpleasant. Then he recognizes the following: 'Within myself this sensation has arisen. It has arisen in dependence on a cause, not without a cause. In dependence on which cause? In dependence on this body." (Sam. Nik. IV, 211.)—"A monk, the mind of whom is released, knows: When the body dissolves, all sensations will be extinguished. It is, O monks, as if a shadow might originate, conditioned by a tree. Suppose that a man, provided with an axe and a basket, should go and fell that tree at the root. Having felled it at the root, suppose he should dig out the root and pull it out together with

Accordingly, the corporeal organism and consciousness are the two chief groups uniting themselves again to produce the three other groups of sensation, of perception, and of the activities of the mind as their common result.*

They are, in their mutual conditionality, the real substrata of the personality and produce the "body endowed with consciousness," as it is always said in the Dialogues.

"In so far only, Ānanda, as one can be born, or grow old, or die, or dissolve, or reappear, in so far only is there any process of verbal expression, in so far only is there any process of explanation, in so far only is there any process of manifestation, in so far only is there any sphere of knowledge, in so far only do we go round the wheel of life up to our appearance amid the conditions of this world,—*in as far as*

---

the tender fibres. Thereupon he should saw the trunk into pieces and split these and so reduce them to chips. The chips he should let become dry by wind and sun, then he should burn them and change them to ashes, and the ashes he should give to the winds or let them be carried away by the streaming floods of a river. Thus the shadow conditioned by the tree would be radically destroyed, like a palm-tree disrooted from the soil, it would be annihilated and not be able to arise again. In exactly the same (radical) manner all sensations will be extinguished when the body dissolves." (Angutta Nik. II, p. 198.)

* The first one of the five groups, the group of corporeal form, or of corporeality, *rūpakkhandha*, therefore is meant as being the same we already know as *nāma-rūpa*. This is beyond doubt. For on one side, *rūpakkhandha* comprises within itself the body *able to live*: "If corporeality,—that is, *rūpa*, the object of the first group—was the self, ye monks, then it could not be *exposed to malady*." (Mahavagga I, 6.) On the other hand, as we have seen, *nāma-rūpa* is just this body able to live.—That the first group nevertheless is only designated as *rūpakkhandha*, without mentioning *nāma*, has its reason only therein that, in speaking of *rūpa*, vitality is considered to be included as self-evident, as we too, when we mean a living body, simply speak of a body. *Rūpa* is only specially designated by *nāma* and thereby designated as *nāma-rūpa*, if the vitality of *rūpa* is to be rendered especially conspicuous. Such is the case in the passages of the *Paṭiccasamuppāda* cited above, wherein the proof had to be given that only a body *able to live* might be a sufficient cause for producing concrete sensation and perception. Therefore *rūpakkhandha* is, properly speaking, *nāma-rūpakkhandha*. By the way, that *nāma* must be contained in *rūpakkhandha*, follows already from *nāma* not being able to be separated from *rūpa*, but both being absolutely inseparable, so that where one of them is, the other also must be present (cf. above p. 70 note *).—If, on the other hand, also the three other *khandhā*, *vedanā*, *saññā* and *saṅkhārā* are comprised in other passages under the designation of *nāma*, the meaning is simply this: *Rūpakkhandha* or, properly

this is, to wit, the corporeal organism together with consciousness."*[71] Now we may, without further ado, fix an essential quality pertaining to all the five groups wherein personality consists. The Buddha lays decisive stress upon this quality, he even dissolves personality into the five groups only for its sake. If we survey our whole series of deductions once more, the following total view presents itself.

The material substratum of the personality is the corporeal organism, or the six-sense-machine as we say. This machine fitted out with the organs of the senses and besides that, only with the necessary contrivances for its further maintenance and continuous supplying with fuel like any other machine, in the maternal womb—we shall see later by what—is built up out of parts of the outer world, these being at the same time assimilated by the maternal organism, or changed from dead into vital matter and thus organized, and further, kept working through an unbroken supply of food. As long

---

speaking, *nāma-rūpakkhandha* comprises the body endowed with vitality, especially with the faculty of producing the so-called mental processes. But *vedanākkhandha, saññakkhandha* and *saṅkhārakkhandha* are the groups of those mental processes themselves, comprised under the term *nāmakkhandha*, because they are *based* upon *nāma* as the respective *faculty* or *quality* of the material body as of a living entity.

The group of consciousness, *viññāṇakkhandha,* does not belong even in this sense to the *nāmakkhandha,* as, following the expositions given above in the text, consciousness is a separate element accessory to *nāma.* Therefore it is also said in the passage given afterwards: "Nāma-rūpa *together with* consciousness."

* Here the following passage of the Dīgha Nik. XXIII may be brought to notice: ". . . . If there, O Kassapa, the iron ball is combined with heat, combined with air, blazing, flaming and flaring, then it is lighter, more flexible and pliable. But if the iron ball is no more combined with heat and air, but has cooled down and become extinguished, then it has become heavier, more stiff and rigid. Just so, warrior king, is this body, if combined with vitality, with warmth, with consciousness, lighter, more flexible and pliable; but if this body is no longer combined with vitality and warmth and consciousness, then it has become heavy, more stiff and rigid."

So here instead of "*Nāma-rūpa* together with consciousness" it is said: "this body combined *with vitality, with warmth,* with consciousness," from which it results again obviously that *nāma* is the same as "combined with vitality, with warmth." Besides this, the relation of vitality to the material organism is defined also in this passage in exactly the same manner as the relation of magnetism to iron, the body endowed with vitality being compared to a *heated* iron ball.

as this machine is in order and goes well, it also fulfils its purpose of making possible the element of consciousness and thereby, of sensation and perception and, later on, the activities of the mind. If it is not able to work any more, then consciousness too is at an end, and thereby also sensation and perception and naturally also new activities of mind and especially, new willing, just because they are mere products of the six-sense-machine and of consciousness. Only a new-built six-sense-machine may again bring forth these phenomena. Also sensation, perception and the activities of the mind are therefore nothing persistent, as little as the element of consciousness, but they are only the respective results of the six-sense-machine *in conjunction* with the element of consciousness and ultimately conditioned by the former. Since, as we have seen, this six-sense-machine itself, that is, the corporeal organism, is again a product of the four chief elements, the five groups constituting personality are thereby *causally conditioned:* "And thus has the Blessed One spoken: 'Whoso perceives the Arising of things through cause, the same perceives the truth. Whoso perceives the truth, the same perceives the Arising of things through cause.' In dependence upon cause, verily, have these five adherence-groups arisen."[72]

Now we also understand something further. Because our body endowed with organs of sense is the apparatus by means of which we come into connection with the world, the body, by coming into action, generating the element of consciousness and only thereby sensation and perception of the world, *the beginning as well as the end of the world is conditioned by it.* If the body is dissolved by death, the entire world vanishes for us. And if there should be, as the Buddha promises, a definitive overcoming of the world, then we may say now already that it will be possible only through this, that there exists a way to the final, extinguishing of every corporeal organism— remember here that the Buddha teaches incessant rebirth—and thereby of consciousness, thereby of personality, thereby at last of the world itself:

"Once the Blessed One was staying in the Jeta grove near Sāvatthī, in the monastery of Anāthapindika. And Rohitassa, a heavenly spirit, radiant in beauty, as night fell, lit up the whole garden, and betook himself to the Blessed One. Arriving thither, he respectfully saluted the Blessed One and stood beside him. And standing beside him, Rohitassa, the heavenly spirit, spoke thus to the Blessed One:

'May it be possible, O Lord, through going to know, to see or to reach the end of the world, where neither birth is, nor growing old nor dying, neither originating nor perishing?'

'It is impossible, O friend, thus I say, through going to know, to see or to reach the end of the world, where neither birth is, nor growing old nor dying, neither originating nor perishing.'

'Wonderful it is, O Lord, astonishing it is, O Lord, how the Blessed One tells me thus correctly: "It is impossible, O friend, thus I say, through going to know, to see or to reach the end of the world, where neither birth is, nor growing old nor dying, neither originating nor perishing." Once, in a former birth, O Lord, I was a hermit, called Rohitassa, the son of Bhoja, and by dominating magic I was able to walk through the air. Such, O Lord, was my speed, that I, during the time an archer, strong, well trained, skilled and expert, takes to shoot with a light arrow, without using his strength, across the shadow of a palm-tree, could make a stride as far as the Eastern Sea is away from the Western Sea. In possession of such speed, capable of making such strides, O Lord, the wish arose in me to reach, by going, the end of the world. And without eating and drinking, without chewing or tasting, without voiding excrement or urine, without being hindered by sleep or weariness, I spent and lived a hundred years. And having gone through a full hundred years, I died on the way, without having reached the end of the world. Wonderful it is, O Lord, astonishing it is, O Lord, how the Blessed One tells me thus correctly: 'It is impossible, O friend, thus I say, by going to know, to see or to reach the end of the world, where neither birth is, nor growing old nor dying, neither originating nor perishing.'

'Certainly it is impossible, O friend, thus I say, by going to know, to see or to reach the end of the world, where neither birth is, nor growing old nor dying, neither originating nor perishing. But neither is it possible, O friend, thus I say, to make an end of suffering without having reached the end of the world. But this I declare, O friend: *Within this body, six feet high, endowed with perception and cognition, is contained the world, the origin of the world, and the end of the world, and the path leading towards the end of the world*'."[73] Or, as we have heard above, but only now are able to understand completely: within *nāma-rūpa,* to wit, our corporeal organism, together with consciousness, everything is contained "that lies in the domain of concepts, in the domain of explanation, in the domain of manifestation, in the domain of knowledge."

If thus the corporeal organism together with consciousness offers us *the possibility* of coming into contact with the world, this world *becomes real* for us in the same measure that the six-sense-machine is set in action and thereby all the five groups appear, thus, in the measure that we develop into personality: Within and with this personality we experience what we call the world or the All. And because this living and moving and having our being in the All seems to us the highest ideal, therefore we know no higher bliss than our personality, wherein each of us sees for himself the realization of this whole process of the world.

Further, it follows from this point of view, how wise it was of the Buddha to furnish the proof of the great universal law of transitoriness and therewith of suffering, especially by means of the five groups constituting personality. For if we recognize all the five groups of personality as transient, then everything is known as transient, and full of suffering, because for us everything consists only in and through our personality.

To this proof we may therefore now return.

THE WORLD OF SUFFERING

The whole world, its beginning as well as its continuing and its end, is for us connected with our personality. The five groups constituting personality are causally conditioned in this manner that the corporeal group represents the basis of the four other groups, sensation, perception, mentation and consciousness,* and even through the activity of the organs of sense, at first of all, produces them. The body itself is a product of the substances comprised within the four chief elements; it is "built up of the four chief elements," and is therefore itself conditioned by these. Our personality, and thereby our whole world, ultimately share the fate of the four chief elements, they are *transient* like these.

These are axioms which everybody who once has understood them, perceives without more ado; they have become self-evident for him. Just this self-evidence is what the Buddha wants us to comprehend. Ultimately, he only works

* Consciousness, according to Indian custom, is put at the end as being the most important.

with self-evident ideas, what is ocularly recognized, being always self-evident.

First then, it is in question for the Buddha to illustrate the transitoriness of the four chief elements, as plainly to our sight as possible:

"A time will come, when the external watery element will rise in fury, and when that happens, the external earthy element will disappear. In that day this great external earthy element will unmistakably reveal itself as transient, will show itself subject to ruin, destruction and all vicissitude.

"A time will come when the external watery element will rise in fury and sweep away village and town and city and province and kingdom. Yea, there will come a time when the waters of the great ocean will be hundreds of miles deep, many hundreds of miles deep. And a time will come when the waters in the great ocean will stand no more then seven palm-tree's height in depth, then six, then five, four, three, two and, at last, only one palm-tree's height in depth. There will come a time when the water in the great ocean will stand only seven men's height in depth, then only six, then five, four, three, two, and finally, only one man's height in depth. And a time will be when the water in the great ocean will only come up to a man's middle, then to his loins, then to his knee, then only to his ancle. Yea, there will come a time when there will be no more water left in the great ocean than will cover one joint of the finger. In that day this great external watery element will unmistakably reveal itself as transient, will show itself subject to ruin, destruction and all vicissitude.

"A time will come when the fiery element will rage furiously and devour village and town and city and province and kingdom, and, spreading over meadows and pastures, jungle and plain and pleasure-grove, will only cease when there is naught to devour. And there will come a time when men will seek to preserve fire with a fan made out of a fowl's wing, or from scraps of hide. In that day this great external fiery element will unmistakably reveal itself as transient, will show itself subject to ruin, destruction and all vicissitude.

"A time will come when the external airy element will rage in fury and carry away village and town and city and province and kingdom, and there will also come a time when, in the last month of the hot season, not a blade of grass stirring in the water-courses, men will seek to make a little wind with a fan made from a palm-stalk. In that day this great external airy element will unmistakably reveal itself as transient, will show itself subject to ruin, destruction and all vicissitude."[74]

If thus all matter comprised under the heading of the four chief elements shows itself subject to the great law of transitoriness, the same is of course the case with all things formed by it, especially with our body. Therefore the Buddha, immediately after having described the incessant vicissitude of all material things, proceeds thus: "What, then, of this fathom-long body? Is there aught here of which may rightly be said 'I' or 'Mine' or 'Am?' Nay, verily, nothing whatsoever"—that means, also our body is "subject to ruin, destruction and all vicissitude." Accordingly then also the transitoriness of the remaining components of our personality is self-evident, being based upon the body, including its organs:

"The corporeal form, O monks, is transient, and what underlies the arising of the corporeal form, what conditions it, that too is transient. Corporeal form arisen from that which is transient, how could it be permanent?

"Sensation is transient, and what underlies the arising of sensation, what conditions it, that too is transient. Sensation arisen from that which is transient, how could it be permanent?

"Perception is transient, and what underlies the arising of perception, what conditions it, that, too, is transient. Perception arisen from that which is transient, how could it be permanent?

"The activities of the mind are transient, and what underlies the arising of the activities of the mind, what conditions them, that, too, is transient. The activities of the mind arisen from that which is transient, how could they be permanent?

"Consciousness is transient, and what underlies the arising of consciousness, what conditions it, that, too, is transient. Consciousness arisen from that which is transient, how could it be permanent?"[75]

Accordingly in regard to all the five groups of personality upon which all our volition is concentrated—the Buddha calling them therefore the five groups of *grasping*—as well as to all external objects of will, included in the five groups, the saying holds good: "Arising shows itself, passing away shows itself, during existence vicissitude shows itself."[76]

But thereby it is also established that the whole personality, thereby also the whole world made accessible to us through this, is painful. For "whatever is transient, that is painful:"

"What think ye, monks? Is body permanent or is it transient?"

"It is transient, O Lord."

"But that which is transient—is it painful or is it pleasant?"

"It is painful, Lord."

"What think, ye, monks? Is sensation, is perception, are the activities of the mind, is consciousness permanent or transient?"

"They are transient, Lord."

"But what is transient—is it painful or pleasant?"

"It is painful, Lord."[77]

This painfulness in consequence of transitoriness shows itself in the body as "decay, death," in the four other groups as "pain, sorrow, grief and despair."

Thus, at last, there remains of every satisfaction of will, nothing but suffering caused by its loss. Only with this final effect, as we have shown, can it be entered up in the book of life. The latter, therefore, at last, must show nothing but negative entries. In other words: the Buddha is right in valuing everything ultimately as suffering.

To the average man this generally only becomes clear when this book is definitively closed, when death comes near. Then, with the complete breakdown of all willing, when he sees everything torn from him, his prosperity, his dearest relations, even his own body in the pangs with which he is writhing, and together with these, the whole of the rest of the world, then also for him only an ocean of misery remains, and this ocean of suffering only will then be real. Let us only stop and consider: What, to us, to-day, is yesterday with all its pleasures? Nothing but a mere shadow. But to-morrow, to-day will be just such another shadow; and the day after to-morrow, to-morrow will be the same: and at last, face to face with death, our entire life will be all a mere shadow. All its comforts are then over, definitively over, and nothing will remain but suffering, nameless suffering. Whoso wishes fully to experience this, and thus wishes to pass a competent judgment on the first of the four excellent truths of the Buddha, let him betake himself to some death-bed and carry out his contemplation *there,* and best of all, to the death-bed of some sensualist. Does not this sensualist resemble a merchant who, after having started his business with a million, has revelled in a life of pleasure, until he has squandered all he had and finds himself face to face with nothing? Have not, as in the books of this merchant, so in the book of life of that dying sensualist all active entries vanished and only the passive ones remained?

Certainly, the will to life struggling for its right to existence and defending itself daily in innumerable brains, has still one last resource left, so as not to be obliged to modify its judgment on the value of life, namely this, that at last also to a dying man, and indeed the more he has worked during his lifetime, the happifying consciousness remains that at least *the fruits* of his labours, pains and troubles, are reaped by his relatives, and lastly by mankind as a whole, contributing thus to the general evolution. To this the Buddha, if he were still alive, would reply: You fool, you are talking of the evolution of mankind. Look a little closer at this evolution. Certainly mankind rises higher and higher, until,—why! until the whole towering edifice, the whole superior civilization you dream of, falls a victim to the law of dissolution and decay, as so often has happened during the limitless past. Thereupon the play may begin anew, and go on and on thus through endless time, only interrupted by world-catastrophes again and again occurring, in which, together with everything alive, the whole staging of life also will entirely disappear through the planets falling into the sun, until it is built up again anew. But meanwhile every single man perishes through inevitable death again and again, with the prospect that also his children and grandchildren, as well as the innumerable generations coming after them, only live to die, as he himself has to die, and that with them also the fruits of his own labour he left to them, wherein only he ultimately saw the value of his life, will crash down into the bottomless abyss of the past. In short: *There is no evolution such as you dream of.* As to life, death is just as essential as birth, old age just as essential as youth;* even so, there is no evolution of the world that is not inevitably followed by decay. Evolution and decay are nothing but the two sides of *one* process, to wit, of *becoming:* Everything appears in the first part of its *becoming* as evolution, in the second one as decay.

This impossibility of any lasting satisfaction of will, which prevails throughout the whole world, and therefore the final domination of suffering, is so evident, so obvious, that it can nowise be refuted, but only ignored. And as a matter of fact, incredible as it is, the will of man, this his foundation, is so strong, that it enables him to ignore even this fundamental truth which lights up the whole essence of the world, if he does not want to see it. By means of empty sophisms he slurs it over, or even babbles in high-sounding phrases about reaching a final state of mankind full of bliss. And this his opinion is not altered even by the consideration that this happy, final state of his, if it is to be reached at all, ought to have been reached long ago, having regard to the endless time that has flowed into the ocean of the past.**

---

* Compare with this the words of the Buddha in regard to Ānanda's wondering to himself that the Master no longer looked so imposing as once he did: "Thus it is, Ānanda, that upon youth follows age, upon health, sickness, upon life, death."[78]

** Compare Du Prel, "The Enigma of Man:" "As a whole, it may be said, that the solution of the enigma of man proposed by materialism is very comfortless...... To compensate us for this comfortlessness, materialism puts the accent on the life of *the species.* Nature is thus said not to care for the individual, but for the species only. By making continual progress, mankind is said to approach a state that may be thought to develop at last into the golden age. To work as a serving member to reach this state, is said to be the task of the individual. But, sad to say, this solace does not last long. For, apart from the fact that species also die out, it is quite an arbitrary proceeding to remain fixed at the biological standpoint in regarding the matter. As a naturalist, the materialistic observer must take the higher standpoint of astronomy. There will be a time when the earth, through the decline of the isothermal lines from the poles towards the equator, will at last become uninhabitable, and afterwards the earth will dissolve into a current of meteorites and fall into the sun. Therefore, even if mankind should reach a golden age, it yet would lack an heir. But what has finally to come to a definitive end, in any case is devoid of purpose. From the materialistic point of view, individual death makes bygone life just as purposeless as the bygone

With such men there is nothing to be done. They are, as said above, in regard to their valuation of life, under the ban of their blind cleaving to it. They cannot keep to pure observation of the problem in an objective manner, and thus they are "incapable of seeing clear," as the Buddha says. But it is impossible for the *objective* observer, after what we have just said, to come to any other judgment in regard to life than to that given by the Buddha. Only too well he will comprehend the truth of the words:

"Impermanent are all the compounds of existence!
Painful are all the compounds of existence!"[79]

But also this insight that life must ultimately in every direction necessarily change to suffering, and therefore at last become itself suffering and nothing but suffering, might still be bearable. Also with this view before us we might still withdraw to that standpoint that just therefore, because only the present time is real, it is the highest wisdom to enjoy this present and to make this the purpose of life, indifferent to any later judgment on the whole life. We might also console ourselves about the sorrowful end with the thought that this end too will come to an end, and therefore be at last overcome. But this too, according to the Buddha, would be self-deceit, and in fact, the worst of all. For our present existence is not our whole life, it is

---

history of civilization becomes purposeless through the dying out of mankind. At no point of evolution can a purpose be seen, if no purpose can be seen in the final point.—Certainly, from the astronomical point of view the play always begins anew, by solar systems dissolving into cosmic nebulae, and these developing again into solar systems. But the results of these biological and cosmological processes are always lost again. Purposelessness does not become more rational by always renewing itself. Thus, every reason for enthusiasm is lacking in the history of the species, the reality of which in addition to that does not exceed that of its individuals. An artist always destroying his own works deserves no admiration, but ought to be confined in a madhouse, all the more so, indeed, the more genius is displayed in his works. Hence it is nothing but a mere phrase, if materialism tries to fill us with enthusiasm for the grandeur of nature. According to its own premises, it ought rather to depict nature as a materialized absurdity."

only a tiny section of our life. This itself is without beginning and without end, if we do not make an end to it: "Without beginning or end, ye monks, is this round of rebirth *(saṁsāra)*. There cannot be discerned a first beginning of beings who, sunk in ignorance and bound by thirst, ceaselessly transmigrating, again and again run to a new birth."*

It is only from this standpoint that the flood of suffering, the dreadfulness and awfulness of life is to be seen in its full measure.

For the Buddha teaches the round of rebirth, within which the creatures are wandering incessantly, to consist of five fates: "Five in number, Sāriputta, are the fates that may befall after death; namely these: passage into the hell-world, the animal kingdom, the realm of shades, the world of men or the abodes of the gods. The hell-world I know, Sāriputta; and the road that leads to the hell-world, and the course of conduct that brings down to it, following which, at the break-up of the body, after death, descending upon a sorry journey downwards towards loss, a man is born in the hell-world—this also I know. The animal kingdom I know, Sāriputta; and the road, the course of conduct, following which, at the break-up of the body, after death, a man is born into the animal kingdom—this too I know. The realm of shades I know, Sāriputta; and the road, the course of conduct which, at the break-up of the body after death, bring a man to the realm of shades—this too I know. The world of men I know, Sāriputta; and the road that leads to the world of men, the course of conduct, through the following whereof, at the break-up of the body after death, a man is born into the world of men—this too I know. The gods I know, Sāriputta; and the road that leads to the abodes of the gods, the course of conduct through the following of which, a man, at the break-up of the body, after death, journeying happily, is born into the heaven-world—this also

* Saṁsāra means: a course (sar) returning (sam) to its starting point.

I know . . . And, Sāriputta, penetrating the mind and heart of a certain person, I perceive: 'This person so acts, so conducts himself, follows such a course, that at the break-up of the body after death, descending upon a sorry journey towards loss, he will come to the hell-world.' And after a time, with the pure, the superhuman, celestial Seeing, I behold that person descend upon that sorry journey towards loss, I see him in the hell-world in utter anguish, subject to pains bitter and grievous. Just as if there were a fiery pit, over the height of a man in depth, filled with red-hot embers, smokeless, glowing; and a man should approach, scorched by the noonday sun, half dead with the heat, exhausted, tottering, athirst, making straight for that pit of fire, and an observing man should see him and say: 'This good man so acts, so conducts himself, follows such a course, that he will certainly come into that fiery pit', and not long thereafter he should actually see the man fallen into the pit of fire in utter anguish, subject to bitter and grievous torment; in the selfsame way, Sāriputta, I behold a person so conduct himself that after death he comes to the hell-world, there to undergo the extremest pangs of sharp and piercing agonies.*

* In the 129th Discourse of the Majjhima Nikāya, it is said: "If man, ye monks, might say, rightly: 'Utterly unwished for, utterly unwelcome, utterly unpleasant,' he might rightly of the hell-world say: 'Utterly unwished for, utterly unwelcome, utterly unpleasant.' Not even by means of a simile might the greatness of the sufferings of the hell-world become quite clear."—As one of the monks, nevertheless, asks for a simile, the Blessed One asks, if a criminal receiving daily, morning, noon and night, three hundred strokes with a sword, would not be sad and sorrowful. The answer is: "Even if chastised with one stroke of the sword only, this man would be sad and sorrowful, how much more after three hundred strokes." Thereupon the Blessed One took up a stone of moderate size, of the size of a fist, and turning to the monks said: "What do you think, O monks, which is larger, this stone of moderate size, of the size of a fist, or Himālaya, the king of the mountains?"—"Very small, O Lord, is this stone of moderate size, of the size of a fist, that the Blessed One has there, against Himālaya, the king of the mountains; it cannot be reckoned, it cannot be counted, it cannot be compared."—"Even so, monks, what a man, chastised with three hundred strokes of a blade, experiences of sadness and sorrow, cannot be reckoned, counted or compared against the sufferings of the hell-worlds."

But again, Sāriputta, penetrating the heart and mind of a certain person, I perceive: 'This person so acts, so conducts himself, follows such a course, that after death he will come to the animal kingdom,' and in due time, with the pure, the superhuman, celestial Seeing, I behold him born into the animal kingdom', in great misery and subject to grievous and bitter sufferings. It is as if there were a cesspool over a man's height in depth filled with filth; and a man should approach, scorched by the sun, half dead with heat, worn out, reeling, parched with thirst, walking directly on towards that cesspool. And an observing man should see him and say: 'This good man, as he is now going, will surely come into that cesspool.' And in a short time he should see the man fallen into the cesspool, in great misery and subject to bitter and grievous suffering. In like manner also, Sāriputta, do I behold a man follow such a course that after death I see him born into the animal kingdom, there to undergo bitter and grievous misery and suffering.* — Again, Sāriputta, penetrating the heart and mind of a certain person, I perceive: 'This person so acts that after death he will come to the realm of shades, and later I actually see him in the spirit-world, sore afflicted and distressed. It is as if upon a piece of poor soil there were growing a tree having but

* Compare the 129th Discourse of Majjh.-Nikāya, cited above: "If I should try, O monks, to expose to you in any way the state of those which have become animals, nevertheless, monks, it would hardly be possible to explain in words, the greatness of the sufferings of animals.

"It is as if, monks, a man should throw a drum-net with only one hole into the ocean and it would be driven by the eastern wind to the west, by the western wind to the east, by the northern wind to the south, by the southern wind to the north. And there should be an one-eyed turtle coming up to the surface of the ocean once in every hundred years. What do you think, monks, would this one-eyed turtle get its neck into that one-holed drum-net?"—"Hardly ever, Lord, but if at all, then only after a very long time had elapsed."—"Rather, monks, might this one-eyed turtle get its neck into the one-holed drum-net than a fool, once sunk into this depth, come again into the world of men. And why so? Because there is, monks, no just conduct, no straightforward conduct, no wholesome acting, no charitable acting. There, monks, they are accustomed to devour each other, and to kill the weaker ones."

few branches which, scanty of foliage, yielded but little shade, and a man devoured by the fierce noonday heat, utterly exhausted with thirst and weariness, should come staggering along the road straight on towards this tree, and one observing him should say: 'This good man is making straight for that tree,' and a short time thereafter, he should actually see the man, either seated or lying down beneath the tree, sore afflicted and distessed. In similar wise, Sāriputta, do I see a man so comport himself that after death I behold him come to the realm of shades there to suffer much affliction and distress. — Again, Sāriputta, penetrating the heart and mind of a certain person, I perceive: 'This person so acts that after death he will reappear as a man,' and some time later I do indeed see him as a man, in the enjoyment of many pleasures. Somewhat as if upon a piece of good soil there were growing a tree, many branched, thick of foliage, yielding abundant shade, and one drew near, oppressed by the noonday heat, thirsty and weary, and made straight for this tree; and an observer should see him and remark: 'This good man is coming straight to that tree,' and later on he should see the man sitting or reclining in the shade of the tree, experiencing much pleasurable sensation. Similarly, Sāriputta, do I behold a man so conduct himself that after death he comes again into the world of men, there to experience much pleasurable sensation. — Again, Sāriputta, penetrating the heart and mind of a certain person, I perceive: 'This person so acts that after death, journeying happily, he will come to the heaven-worlds,' and later I behold him in the heaven-world, enjoying the height of felicity. Just as if there were a palace, having a pavilion, smooth within and without, with an enclosed, finely casemented alcove, and therein a couch at either end cushioned in purple and provided with coverlets long-fleeced and white and flower inwoven, hung also with choicest antelope skins; and a man should draw near, spent with the noontide heat, reeling with exhaustion, parched with thirst, and should move straight on towards this same palace, and an observer should see him and say: 'This good man is coming straight on towards that palace'; and later should indeed behold the man arrived at the palace and, in the pavilion sitting or reclining upon the couch, enjoying the greatest felicity. In like manner also, Sāriputta, do I see a man so act that after death I behold him arrived in the heaven-world, enjoying the greatest felicity."[80]

Among these five fates ultimately only the last one, the abode in the heaven-world, could be desirable. But according to the Buddha this one is just as much subject to the great law of transitoriness as the abode in the four other ones, objectification in the animal world and in the hells also finding always its end, though possibly only after enormous stretches of time. "Up to the highest world of the gods every existence becomes annihilated"—"The Thirty-three Gods and the Yāma Gods, the Satisfied Gods, the Gods Who Delight in Fashioning, the Gods Who Have Control of Pleasures Fashioned by Others, they all, bound with the fetters of desire, return into the power of Māra which means into the power of death."[81] Unfailingly, therefore, always again descent to the lower worlds will follow.

But moreover, this pleasant prospect of staying in a heaven, or even only in the realm of mankind, is open only to very few beings, in complete accordance with the doctrine of the Christ, according to whom, also "many are called, but few chosen":

"Just as, monks, here on the soil of this India there are only a few beautiful gardens and woods, fields and ponds, but far more mountain slopes and gorges, streams difficult to pass, wild virgin forests and heights impossible to climb; in like manner, monks, only a few creatures who have died as men are reborn as men, but far more creatures who died as men, come back to existence in a hell, among animals, or in the realm of shades."[82]

Thus every being is eternally wandering to and fro within Saṁsāra through the five realms, finding itself reborn by the incessant change of the five groups constituting its personality, now as a man, now as a spectre, now as an animal, now as a devil, now and then as a god. "In wombs we are germinating, in other worlds we are germinating, in the changing circle we are returning now and then."[83]

We must try to make directly clear to ourselves what this means. First, we must become clear about the endlessness of this our wandering through the worlds:

"Suppose, O monks, a man should cut off the grasses and herbs, twigs and leaves of this entire continent of India, should collect them and heap up one handful of them after the other, saying: 'This is my mother, this is the mother of my mother', and so on,—there would be no end of the mothers of the mother of this man. But he would reach the very last bit, the end of all the grasses and herbs of this continent of India,—and why? Without beginning or end, monks, is this round of rebirth. There cannot be discerned the first beginning of beings, who, sunk in ignorance and bound by thirst, are incessantly transmigrating, and again and again run to a new birth . . ."

"As if, monks, a man should heap up this great earth by handfuls, to form a ball of earth, saying: 'This is my father, this is my father's father,' and so on—there would be no end of the fathers of the father of this man, but this great earth would be used up, would come to an end. And why? Without beginning or end, O monks, is this round of rebirth. There cannot be discerned the first beginning of beings, who, sunk in ignorance and bound by thirst, are incessantly transmigrating, and again and again run to a new birth.

"And thus, O monks, during a long time you have experienced suffering, you have experienced pain and misery and have enlarged the burying-ground truly long enough to be disgusted with every kind of existence, long enough to turn from every kind of existence, long enough to deliver yourselves from it." * [84]

But the Buddha is not content to describe in this general manner the endlessness of the round of our rebirths. He also shows separately, of what kind our single existences have been, first, within the realm of mankind itself.

"What do you think, O monks? Which may be more, the flood of tears you have shed on this long way, running again and again to new birth and new death, united to the disliked, separated from the liked, complaining and weeping, or the water of the four great oceans? . . . .

"Through a long time, you have experienced the death of the mother, the death of the father, the death of the son, the death of the daughter, the death of brother and sister, through a long time you were oppressed by sickness. And while the death of the mother, the death of the father, the death of the son, the death of the daughter, the death of brother and sister, the loss of wealth, the pain of sickness was your lot, while you were united to the disliked, separated from the liked, running from birth to death, from death to birth, you have shed on this long way truly more tears than water is contained within the four great oceans.

---

* In the Samyutta Nikāya V, p. 258, it is said that in consequence of the countless bodies deposited only by one man in the course of his re-births, the heap of bones thereby made would be immense. To the height of a mountain the heap of bones would mount during only one world-cycle, following upon the ceaseless change of birth and death, if one, in thought, gathered together the bones of only one single creature; yea, a veritable mountain chain of chalk would be accumulated. Compare also the passage in Jātaka, No. 116, where it is said that there is no spot on earth that is not composed of the dust of beings who have died. Recall also Voltaire's saying: "*Le globe ne contient que des cadavres*," the globe contains nothing but corpses.

"What do you think, monks? Which may be more, the blood that on this long way, while you were always running to new birth and death, was flowing at your decapitation, or the water of the four great oceans? . . . .

"Through a long time, you have shed, sentenced to death as murderers, more blood in being executed than there is water contained within the four great oceans. Through a long time, you have shed, caught as robbers, more blood in being executed than water is contained within the four great oceans. Through a long time, you have shed, detected as adulterers, more blood in being executed than there is water contained within the four great oceans."[85]

But thereby the abundance of suffering lying behind us is not yet exhausted. Much worse were those sufferings that arose for us, as we were straying through *the lower abysses* of existence:

"What do you think, O monks? Which may be more, the blood that was flowing at your decapitation, while you were again and again running to new birth and death, or the water of the four great oceans? . . . .

"Through a long time, you have as cows and calves truly shed more blood in being decapitated than there is water contained within the four great oceans.

"Through a long time, you have as buffaloes and buffalo-calves truly shed more blood in being decapitated than water is contained within the four great oceans.

"Through a long time, you have as sheep and lambs truly shed more blood in being decapitated than there is water contained within the four great oceans.

"Through a long time you have as he-goats and she-goats truly shed more blood in being decapitated than there is water contained within the four great oceans.

"Through a long time, you have as deers and stags

truly shed more blood in being shot than there is water contained within the four great oceans.

"Through a long time you have as swine and pigs truly shed more blood in being slaughtered than there is water contained within the four great oceans.

"Through a long time you have as hens and doves and geese truly shed more blood in being butchered than there is water contained within the four great oceans.

"But how is this possible? Without beginning or end, O monks, is this round of rebirth. There cannot be discerned the first beginning of beings, who sunk in ignorance and bound by thirst, are incessantly transmigrating and again and again run to a new birth.

"And thus, O monks, through a long time you have experienced suffering, pain and misery, and enlarged the burying-ground; truly long enough to be disgusted with every kind of existence, long enough to turn away from every kind of existence, long enough to deliver yourselves from it."[86]

It is clear that, if all this is really so—not to speak of the stay in the hells—if this is really our past fate and will be our future one, then the saying "All life is suffering" becomes true in its most horrible sense. But not a few will declare that they are unable to follow the Buddha any further on this way, even if they agree with this judgment on the value of our *present* life. For here every possibility of our own immediate insight, which, also according to the Buddha, forms the only real criterion of all truth, seems to be wanting. To such we reply that the Buddha does not at all want them to take his sayings, cited above, without criticism and upon mere faith. The declaration that we ought only to believe what we ourselves have recognized as true holds good also in this case, and to give immediate insight into the round of our rebirths is the special theme of the second of the four excellent truths, as we shall see later on. It may even happen that on the way shown by the Buddha we may gain an immediate perception of our own existences before our birth, and of the vanishing and reappearing of the other creatures, by developing the "pure, superhuman, celestial eye."

Meanwhile, precisely this truth as to the nature of our existence before and after birth is such that it may be also found without immediate insight, in a purely indirect way, since to a purely sober judgment of things it appears as the only possible one. For this very reason it is not peculiar to the Buddha, but forms part of the original faith of mankind* and as such lies at the base of all the great religions of the earth, with the sole exception of Judaism, and of the two religions originating from it, Christianity and Mohammedanism.

This indirect path to its confirmation we also will tread first, as it were, by way of introduction. It is the path of *hypothesis*. Human reason, as long as immediate insight into any occurrence is impossible, seeks to find out truth in this form, not only in daily life but also within the domain of science. For a mere hypothesis also may come near to immediate truth. This is the case, for instance, with the theory of the origination of the world put forward by Kant and Laplace, or the theory of the ether. Here the criterion of a hypothesis in regard to its being inwardly well founded, consists in its explaining the occurrence concerned as completely as possible and in its being in perfect harmony with the whole course of nature. Thus a great obstacle to the theory of Kant and Laplace being accepted as entirely correct, is that the relation of the densities of the planets and of the sun cannot very well be brought into harmony with it.

* This is proven by the fact that the doctrine of reincarnation already forms part of the religious systems of the most primitive peoples, such as the *Arunta* and other tribes of Central Australia.

If these fundamental axioms are applied to the doctrine of the Buddha as far as the nature of our existence before and after birth is concerned, the following conclusions are reached. His doctrine embraces three statements:

1. There is an existence after death;

2. This existence is effected by rebirth, strictly speaking, *by palingenesis;*

3. It takes place within the five realms mentioned above.

The first statement has always been accepted as true by the immense majority of mankind, at every time and in every place. The agreement goes so far that it can hardly be explained otherwise than through the saying of Spinoza: "We feel by immediate consciousness that we are immortal."* Only when men try to transfer this immediate truth, founded in the depth of their essence and therefore only felt, into abstract knowledge, only when, to put it otherwise, they try to understand it in accordance with the law of sufficient reason, only then do contradictions appear. Against this truth those only fight who call themselves scientific materialists, a class of men already very well known to the Buddha:

"There, Sandaka, a teacher defends this view: 'There is no such thing as alms or sacrifice or offering. There is neither fruit nor result of good or evil deeds. There is no such thing as this world or the next. There is neither father nor mother, nor beings springing into life without them. There are in the world no recluses or Brahmins who have reached the highest point, who walk perfectly, and who having understood and realized, by themselves alone, both this world and the next, make their wisdom known to others. A human being is built up of the four elements. When he dies, the earthy in him returns and relapses to the earth, the

* If we want to see clearly how deeply rooted in man this consciousness is, we must think of the inappeasable anxiety which seizes every man immediately before death, as to what his future will be afterwards. It seizes even those who in days of health have nothing but a superior smile for every belief in a life after death.

fluid to the water, the heat to the fire, the windy to the air, and his senses pass into space. The four bearers, on the bier as a fifth, take his dead body away; till they reach the burning-ground men utter forth eulogies, but there his bones are bleached and his offerings end in ashes. It is a doctrine of fools, this talk of gifts. It is an empty lie, mere idle talk, when men say there is profit therein. Fools and wise alike, on the dissolution of the body, are cut off, annihilated, and after death they are not."[87]

But curiously, though obviousness is on its side—for with death, what we are accustomed to call man, evidently dissolves—materialism, as Schopenhauer says, and as we mentioned before, never has been able to gain a permanent influence over mankind. The reasons for this are evident. Materialism is just as much a hypothesis as any other scientific system which tries to explain the phenomenon of life. But as said above, a hypothesis cannot be correct, if it is contradictory to a fundamental fact of the course of nature. But to this course of nature surely there belongs not only man and all his activities but also the immediate consciousness of living on after death; for, as said above, it represents a common property of mankind. Accordingly it must be included in an explanation of life. Many try to explain it in this way, that from this consciousness only a longing for living on after death peculiar to man may result, but not the fact of the realization of this longing. But there is this to be said in reply, that the mere fact of such a longing being present in every man and therefore being essential to us, gives security for the realization of this longing in some way or other, in accord with the axiom, *natura nihil frustra facit,* Nature makes nothing in vain. We could not possess this longing at all if it were not to be satisfied. When a naturalist has discovered the existence of a peculiar longing in any creature, without anything more he will be so certain that this longing is capable of being satisfied that he would consider it folly to cease searching for *the object* of this longing on the ground that there could not possibly be any such object. On the contrary, he will not stop searching until he has found this object, feeling certain that Nature works on the lines of least resistence, and therefore creates no wants for which there is no satisfaction. Besides this, materialism already is wrecked on the fact of the existence of moral and therefore unselfish actions, since such are certainly to be found, and belong as much to the phenomena of life as birth and death, with which, therefore, a hypothesis claiming to explain the phenomenon of life cannot be allowed to conflict. Even the materialist will esteem and admire a man who, without hesitation, sacrifices his own person for others. But how will he reconcile this esteem and admiration with his own system, according to which it must be senseless to annihilate oneself to save the life of another person who is nothing to me; for what bond, according to the system of materialism, can bind me to another man? Am I not a fool in sacrificing my own life for another person, since in accordance with the materialist view of the world, life must be the highest thing for me, everything without a remainder being annihilated for me with the annihilation of my own life? And where would be the equivalent for the sacrifice of life for another man, felt also by a materialist to be a noble deed, if with death everything is over? For this also belongs to the phenomenon of life, and must therefore be taken into account in giving an explanation of this phenomenon, that in us there dwells an ineradicable feeling that every action must somehow have its reward. If a materialist answers: 'The equivalent of the action must be sought in the fact that it makes for the benefit of another creature'; then the further question must be answered: 'But how, if the man sacrificing his life, sacrifices it for a *lost* cause? For instance, what about those five hundred Switzers who sacrificed themselves for Louis XVI when the Tuileries were stormed by the people? Was not their death, regarded from a purely natural point of view, entirely worthless? Nevertheless, who will dare to say that it would have been the same thing for these noble men, if, instead of giving their lives for their master, they had weakly betrayed him and sided with the people? But if it is not the same, when and where can the equivalent for which human feeling impatiently longs, take place, if complete annihilation follows death? And thus is it with every good and, still more, with every heroical deed which does not bear the fruits expected.*

By such reflections also does the Buddha silence the materialistic doctrine that with death, all is over. "There, Sandaka, a reasonable man is reflecting thus: 'This dear teacher sets up such a meaning, such a doctrine: [to wit the materialistic one, as reproduced by the above words]. If it is true what he is saying, then every moral action upon the earth is purposeless. Then we both are grown exactly the same . . . . Therefore it is too much if this dear teacher goes naked, shaves his crown; crouches down on his heels, plucks out both hair and beard; and if I, living in

---

* *Du Prel* calls that trait in man by which he feels himself responsible for his actions even beyond death, *moral instinct*. "Man is the highest fact of nature, and morality is his highest function. Instinctively we place morality higher than knowledge. In a moral man, we will hardly miss knowledge, but genius without morals we feel to be repulsive. Stupidity rouses regret or a smile, but immorality rouses indignation. Consequently, the real test of philosophical systems is their aptitude for forming the basis of a moral system. But moral instinct is illogical if human individuality exists only between the cradle and the grave. If the visible part of our career alone had validity, and we went towards our annihilation with full consciousness, then we should resemble men condemned to death, only that our way to the scaffold would be a little longer, and the time uncertain when we should reach it. The law allows the condemned criminal the satisfaction of his wishes for the last days of his life, as was already the case with the ancient Greeks. But we ought to make this claim for the satisfaction of our wishes, for the whole duration of our life, neglecting all preparations for the other world, if as materialists we look upon death as annihilation."

a house full of children, using silk and sandal wood, ornaments and odoriferous ointments, finding pleasure in gold and silver, shall have in future just the same fate as this dear teacher.' And he perceives: 'This is not the path to truth, and turns away unsatisfied from such path.'"[88]

Indeed, the knowledge that materialism makes all true morality impossible, is decisive in making every moral man refuse it. For, as a moral man, he immediately feels the whole importance of moral action and rejects materialism merely from this immediate feeling, felt truth being nothing but truth immediately perceived, only not yet abstracted into notions. And only to men who already have gained this height of moral action does the Buddha address himself.

But if the fact of death not being our end is established for a man, then the second question for him is: Of what kind is his continued existence after death? Here two chief doctrines are opposed to each other, first, the doctrine of personal continuance, mainly represented by the Christian doctrine of the immortality of the individual in an eternal heaven or in an eternal hell; and secondly, the doctrine of palingenesis.

Which is truth? Here also for every one who has not yet himself recognized it, only the standpoint of the reasonable man remains, which, in the words of the Buddha himself, may be defined as follows: "There a reasonable man reflects thus: If some of those dear recluses and Brahmins teach personal continuance, I cannot see it, and if other dear recluses and Brahmins teach that there is no personal duration, neither do I perceive this. But if, without having seen or perceived it, I now should decide in favour of one of these doctrines, and say: 'This one only is true, and the other teaching is foolish', then this would not be well done. For we may easily trust to something that is hollow and empty and wrong, and we may fail to trust to something that is right and true and real. And thus who seeks for truth, if he is a reasonable man, will not draw readily the one-sided conclusion: 'Only this opinion is true, and the other opinion is foolish,' but to gain insight into these statements, it is of importance to regard their content."[89] To use our own way of thinking, this means: Here also for everybody who cannot blindly believe but wants to know, to begin with, only hypotheses come into question which must be examined for their value according to the rules applying to them. Especially must they be examined to see if they do not come into contradiction with other facts established beyond contradiction. For in this case even their simple possibility must be denied, and therefore they are to be rejected from the beginning.

Now we have seen that the body obviously perishes in death, its components then returning to the common stock of inorganic substances of external nature, and that together with the annihilation of this *basis,* the remaining components of the personality also, namely sensation, perception, mentation and consciousness, dissolve into nothing and become impossible. We may be influenced by dogmatic prejudices to ignore this obvious demonstration of nature, or even in spite of it, hold fast to the belief in personal continuance; but if one does not set up will instead of cognition as the source of truth,—and every belief is ultimately a function of will, and will, as we know, cannot be instructed,—but if we share the standpoint that all verities can only be based upon perception and must be rooted in it, then it is established beyond doubt that, if a man dies, not only his corporeal part but also everything mental in him, sensation, perception, mentation and consciousness, thereby the whole of personality, perishes. This is so clear to every unprejudiced observer that materialism just from this fact derives its chief weapon against every belief in continuance after death. Certainly, in doing so, it commits itself the unpardonable mistake of concluding from the impossibility of one alternative that the other one, the palingenesis we will afterwards speak of, is also impossible.

In particular, the Christian doctrine of personal survival after death in an eternal heaven or an eternal hell, presupposes the belief in a personal god, and, together with this dogma, leads to monstrous contradictions: How can human insight bear the thought of a god who ought to be the sum of infinite goodness, wisdom, and power, creating beings whom he knows to be condemned in an overwhelming majority to eternal damnation in a hell, since "many are called, but few are chosen." Certainly, these beings choose their gruesome fate themselves, as their will is free. But how can a most gracious god bestow such a horrible gift, when he knows beforehand, in virtue of his omniscience, how dreadfully they will misuse it! What should we think about a father who should send his child into the world or even only generate it, knowing for certain that it would later on commit "voluntarily" a crime that would be punished with life-long imprisonment, and thus remain through all its life in deepest despair! But what would such a deed be in comparison to that other one, to give existence to a being, even to the greater majority of beings, so that those beings, namely, the animals, who have no free will and are therefore without fault, live always in terror and fear* without any prospect of compensation—because, according to the Christian doctrine, animals are not immortal;—while the others, men, are to be doomed in consequence of this their

* We cannot imagine what a fear-filled life most animals are leading. Only look at some tiny little bird taking its food! It will turn its head at least *ten* times in every direction so as to spy out in time a supposed enemy, before it risks picking up *once* a grain of seed. The average man thinks this behaviour dainty and droll, but whoso looks deeper will recognize just from this, that these harmless creatures also are living in a state of constant fear and anxiety.

free will to eternal hell, foreseen by their creator to be the consequence of this free will which he gave to them! Must not the intellect first be created, that may bear such a thought? Is it not, moreover, contrary to every law of thought that the fault of a poor finite creature, which itself must therefore be limited and finite, should be revenged by an infinite punishment? And then, as Schopenhauer quite correctly remarks: Is it conceivable that the same god who orders men to overlook and to forgive every offence, acts himself in quite a different manner, inflicting eternal punishment even after death? But the most senseless thing is that this god who wants me to believe in this dogma of eternal punishment in hell, under threat in case of my unbelief, of having that dogma made good on my own person, on the other hand has endowed me with a power of insight which simply will not let me believe such a dogma because of its opposition to all reason.

It is not saying too much to assert that a hypothesis involving such consequences and contradictions cannot possibly stand the trial at the assize of intellect and must therefore be dismissed without more ado.*

Accordingly palingenesis remains as the only possible form of existence after death. For to a man for whom the fact of his living on after death is established, but who has to reject on the other hand all doctrines of personal continuation—not only the Christian one, but all others beside that teach personal continuation in the form of metempsychosis or transmigration of souls—only the possibility of continuation *involving the annihilation of personality* offers itself. This annihilation is contained in palingenesis. For palingene-

* The doctrine of personal continuance after death is nothing but a hypothesis naturally in this case too, if it is proclaimed as the revelation of a personal god, for this argument is itself nothing but a mere hypothesis, inevitably leading to irreconcilable contradictions.

sis means decomposition and renewal of the entire individual, thus that the dying creature perishes entirely, together with its consciousness, but that there remains a germ from which a new individual arises together with new consciousness, "man thus ripening like corn, and ripening always again and again." This doctrine of continuance after death is the only one which stands in no contradiction to any other fact of the course of nature. And because it is the only one, in accepting which, continuance after death can be imagined without falling into logical contradictions, already for this reason it must be accepted as true by every one for whom the fact of continuance after death as such is established.

But this hypothesis—nothing more than a hypothesis is at first in question—is not only incontrovertible in all its parts and consequences, through its being in harmony with the whole process of nature, so much so that even Hume, though "excessively empirical," as Schopenhauer calls him, says in his sceptical treatise on immortality, that this system is the only one of its kind to which philosophy can pay heed, but it is also, according to Schopenhauer, a postulate of practical reason. This is plain from the fact that everybody comes to it of himself, that at least it becomes immediately clear to everybody who hears about it for the first time, "if the brain, confused from early youth by having become imbued with false fundamental doctrines, does not with superstitious fear, flee it from afar."

Palingenesis thus has always been the conviction of the choicest and wisest of mankind.

But how palingenesis, this renewal of existence, effects itself in the moment of death, this is the great mystery: "Every new-born creature enters its new existence full of freshness and gladness, and enjoys it as a boon: but there is no boon and there cannot be a boon. Its fresh existence is paid for by the old age and the death of a worn-out creature that has perished but contained the indestructible germ from which this new existence originated: they are *one* being. To point out the bridge between the two would certainly mean the solution of a great problem," says Schopenhauer; of a problem, we may add, that from all time has been insoluble. Nobody has effected its solution, with the sole exception of one man, and this sole exception is again—the Buddha! To his insight of genius it was possible to look even into this most secret workshop of nature, and thus to find the solution of this problem, a solution as simple as only truth can be. For truth is always simple, so simple that, as Goethe once remarked, men are always angry that it is so simple. But of this we will speak later. Here we have only to establish that palingenesis is the only possible form of continuance after death, and that this only possible form of continuance is taught by the Buddha.*

What might cause offence in his doctrine, as far as the mode of rebirth taught by it is concerned, can therefore only be its third element. He teaches that palingenesis is not confined to the realm of human beings only,** but

---

* As soon as we have reached the insight that palingenesis is the real form of our living on, then, without further ado, the insight into the beginninglessness of the round of our rebirths and thereby into the immeasurable spaces of time we have already wandered through is reached too. For if the birth that has opened my present life was not my first one, then neither was the preceding one the first one, and so on without cessation, back to the beginningless infinity of the past. If we look down upon the immense spaces of time with which the Hindu is wont to reckon, with a supercilious smile, thinking our passing present life to be our life as such, then we only show the narrowness of our mental horizon. On this we smile again, having won the right standpoint by ascertaining that we are essentially outside of time, and time is therefore not able to harm us in any way, as will be seen in our next chapter. Therefore it is also self-evident that by entering it, we are able to see it pass in its entire endlessness, though becoming always other beings.—Besides this, modern astronomy too reckons with the same immense spaces of time.

** Here it must be noted that rebirth as a man need not necessarily take place upon *our* earth. Quite in harmony with modern astronomy, already ancient India had reached the insight that the universe consists of countless world-systems and therefore also of countless earths.

extends just as well to the world of animals, and to that of spectres, as to hells and heavens. To this it might be objected that, on one side, realms of spectres, heavens and hells are beyond all possible experience; and that, on the other hand, the supposition is senseless and in contradiction to every idea of evolution, that man might fall back into such depths as the realm of animals or a hell would mean.

Concerning the first objection it declares ordinary experience to be the only experience possible. To this it must be replied, following a saying of Goethe: Certainly we must give in at the boundaries of experience, but not at the boundaries of our own narrow-minded individual experience, but at the boundaries of the experience of mankind. This means: the realm of the eternally unknown begins only where even the greatest of mankind are not able to penetrate. But by these greatest ones, ultimately not the intellectually, but also *morally* eminent must be understood, those who have fought the heaviest battle, and won the greatest victory, to wit, the victory over themselves. Measured with this measure, all our so-called great men dwindle down to dwarfs. Now these morally great men, the Christ not less than the Buddha, and their saints not less than those of other religions, assert that they know these three realms inaccessible to normal perception, even though designating them by names totally different and taken from the range of ideas wherein they were living. What gives us the right to disbelieve their assertions? Perhaps that they as morally great men were incapable of uttering a conscious falsehood? Or this, that, though separated by thousands of years and of miles, they saw the same? Or perhaps that especially the Buddha and his disciples lay stress upon complete sobriety and carefulness in regard to all inner experiences, especially in regard to those occurring upon the highest stages of holiness and conferring a vision that embraces the whole round of rebirth, as the fundamental presupposition of right insight?*

Certainly we do not say too much if we assert that the reality of an occurrence of *outer* history, if testified to by such a multitude of unimpeachable witnesses as such holy men are, would be doubted by no reasonable person. If here nevertheless, especially by modern "enlightened" persons, such doubts are raised — but this is never done by people who have an eye for the *real* boundaries of the possible and for the criterions of reality — then this can only have its grounds in the *improbability* of the existence of such realms. For their existence can only be thought improbable; in no case impossible or contradictory to facts otherwise known. But are they really so improbable? On the contrary, it is improbable that the form of life existing upon our earth should be the only one that Nature, otherwise inexhaustible, has brought forth. But if the probability of the contrary presses itself upon us on the path of pure reasoning, then it is further just as probable that those forms of life we have to suspect otherwhere exhaust, with due regard to the inexhaustibility of Nature, all possibilities of a happy as well as of an unhappy existence, in as far as they may be brought into harmony with the fundamental laws of the universe, especially with the universal law of transitoriness. On a small scale we see the same thing upon our earth, where also to states of highest bliss, those of pain hardly imaginable are opposed; and to lives radiant

* Such inner illumination has even been represented as a diseased state, and the Christ as well as the Buddha, therefore, thought to have been insane! Such results are reached, if the critic's own "Pelagian common sense," as Schopenhauer calls it, is made the measure of all things. It must be a curious mental sanity which declares men to be insane who developed their mental faculties so far as to be able to triumph over all their passions, even over every kind of motion of the will in a way that seems impossible to us average mortals, and thus to acquire the highest powers of sense and mind! Is not this owning to some confusion of conceptions in regard to what is sanity and insanity?

with the most extraordinary good fortune, are opposed such as only form a chain of endless tortures, as in the animal world. Why should nature not do on a grand scale, what we see every day occurring on a small scale? Why, in short, should not extremes of existence exist, extending in the direction of happiness as well as in that of unhappiness? Of course, the extreme in the direction of untainted happiness, such as is said to be found within the heavens, we easily agree with; but in any case, this much is clear, that if there are heavens, according to the law of polarisation there must also be states of the opposite extreme, designated as hells, in whatever form we choose to picture these states. Therefore, whoso does not want to miss a heaven, must also reckon with a hell.

Therewith we come to the second objection, to wit, that the supposition that man can fall back into such depths is absurd. But there is nothing at all absurd here, at the most only something may be contrary to our will. This means that against this possibility nothing at all may be adduced from the standpoint of reason and experience, but that the only thing opposed to it is our will, thirsting for wellbeing, and, as it always does, falsifying insight in this case also. Because human will abhors a form of existence "consisting only of suffering," such as the view of a reappearance in a hell, or in animal form insinuates, therefore man simply shuts his eyes to all such eventualities, trying to persuade himself that such things cannot be. But what can be and what cannot be, is not decided by our will, but by the laws dominating the world; and it has always been fatal to truth when, faced by it, people have attempted to adopt the standpoint: *Sic volo, sic jubeo: stat pro ratione voluntas.*

This influence of will in the investigation of truth is often to be found concealed behind even the most "scientific" theories. Especially is it concealed within the theory of "evolution" with which the possibility of a relapse of man into lower realms of existence is thought to be refuted. Because man perceives in nature a progressive development in the forms of life, and because it thus pleases his will, he rashly infers an unlimited development of his own species, though nature teaches him by clear evidence that there is no such development: every evolution being, as hinted above, only the first half of a process, namely, of becoming, the second half of which must always bring about decay and, at last, the complete collapse of the thing that seemed at first to develop. This is a law that holds good for the greatest as well as for the smallest things. But when, by and by, man gains the insight that the unlimited development of a species is an illusion, then he at last transfers the realization of the thought of evolution to the single individual, rather than believe in the purposelessness of his striving and of his volition. He imagines a metaphysical goal to be set up for the individual beyond the realm of transitoriness, and thinks that the individual ripens more and more towards this goal until this is actually reached, either in death, or at least after a series of existences following each other, as a traveller on foot comes nearer to his goal with every step he takes, even if he does not notice it.* If the thought of evolution is formulated thus, then it comes near to truth in as much as man looks for the centre of gravity *within himself* and no longer in the species, in harmony with his own inner nature which is only able to regard itself as the centre of the whole world and thereby as the object of all its endeavours. But even daily experience ought to tell us that progressive evolution does not take place here either. Of course we have to bear in mind that evolution is only to be taken as a purification

* This conception is not at all a production of modern times, as the Buddha had already to refute it. Majjh. Nik. I, p. 518.

of character; that is to say, *moral* evolution is to be attained, since it is a question not of a physical, but of a metaphysical goal. But how little of such evolution is to be found! Do we not rather almost as a rule perceive just the opposite of it? Is life not serving in general to develop *selfishness,* the opposite of moral purification, in every direction? How very few men are there who at the end of their life are free from qualms of conscience, this sole measure of all moral progress, and thereby feel within themselves the immediate certainty that they really have made moral progress and may die in peace and full of trust without being in need to pacify their minds artificially by an imagined external forgiving of sins through a priest, or through the belief in a god forgiving sins! So here is no development either; nay, many men in the course of their life are sinking through their instincts and inclinations down to the level of beasts, or even reach such a degree of bestiality as even beasts do not descend to, for which reason the decent section of their fellow-countrymen do their utmost to keep them at a distance as much as possible, the state even enforcing their actual exclusion from human society. Is it absurd, if eternal justice, inexorably at work, in the moment of death, when alone a new settlement in a corresponding environment is possible, actually undertakes this settlement, sending the being there where it belongs according to its entire character, and where the dispositions peculiar to it are not regarded at all as unnatural, but as quite natural and proper, that is, sending it to the animal realm or even to a hell, to balance at the same time all the misery it has caused? Certainly not for ever, for *everything* in the world, in Saṁsāra, has an end, the stay in the animal world, or in hell, also.

This hypothesis, which besides does justice to the idea of the unity of all life, in as much as according to it, animal as well as devil have the prospect somewhere and some time of coming up again and attaining human existence, truly seems much more in accordance with reality than that evolution-idea, according to which everything happens so nicely in agreement with our will, that one cannot help suspectin gthat here once more the wish is father to the thought.

Certainly, from this point of view a truly horrible prospect opens before us in the future: we are not by a "law of evolution" born onward and upward to ever purer regions, but as through times long past, so also now, and through all future time, we wander through the gruesome abysses of existence. And in view of the endless number of the rebirths still in store for us the possibility, even the certainty exists, that we ourselves may sink down to the deepest of those abysses, to the animal-world and to the hell-worlds, thus into states of greatest misery, so that we might experience for ourselves the truth of the words of *Jacob Boehme*: "If all the mountains were books, and all the lakes ink, and all the trees pens, still they would not suffice to depict all the misery."

But is it the fault of the Buddha, of the Christ, of all the men of sanctity to whom a glimpse into these abysses has been granted, that by some incomprehensible fatality we are involved in such a world? Are they bound to be wrong, merely because we cannot believe in such a dreadful situation, like a child who cannot believe that the beautiful flowers it is gathering are growing above an abyss hidden precisely by them, and on that account finally itself must tumble into this abyss?

But if our stay in the world is of this sort, if wheresoever we may look, in the infinitudes of space and time, ultimately we only see suffering, often *only* suffering for immeasurable time, then even the most inveterate "optimist" will certainly not venture to doubt the first of the four excellent truths that all life at bottom is suffering. Rather will he be unable to do otherwise than concede the truth of these other words of the Master also: "The whole world is devoured by flames, the whole world is enshrouded in smoke, the whole world is on fire, the whole world is trembling."[90] And so, full of expectation, he will listen to the further message how he may escape this world of suffering for ever. But this problem presupposes for its solution before all else the elucidation of the relation in which we stand to our ever-changing personalities during the round of rebirth* and therewith to the world itself. Therefore we will now turn to the consideration of this relation, the more so, as it forms the bridge to immediate insight into the endless round of rebirth of which we have been treating above.

THE SUBJECT OF SUFFERING

I am: that is the most certain axiom there is. It belongs to those axioms that are evident in themselves without any proof. Indeed, it holds good before every proof; for whatever I want to prove, that "I" want to prove, and to prove for *Myself*. This axiom is more certain than all perception, which, in general, is the most reliable criterion of truth we have. For every perception is effected through *me*, and therefore already presupposes me as the perceiving subject. I may be in doubt as to *what* I am; I may even doubt if I really *"am,"* that is, I may doubt if the definition of my essence can and may be undertaken by means of the idea of being that is itself only gained through perception. I may even prove irrefutably that "I" is indeed nothing but a mere

* Personality is to be understood in the sense given above, as the totality of the five groups of grasping, be it in the form of a human, or of an animal, or of any other organism.

thought for which no substantial equivalent can be found. All this we may do. In fact, I may prove whatever I like: the reality of myself is not in the least affected thereby, and I will pass over all these proofs with a smile, even if I acknowledge their validity. For I cannot argue away my own existence even with the help of the deepest-going analysis; and if somebody should try to prove to me that I am really nothing, then I should answer, if I thought it worth while to answer at all: "But, my good friend, if I do not exist, why do you trouble yourself at all to prove to me that I don't? In all your arguments you always presuppose me as the person to whom you address them, in the same way that you presuppose yourself in setting them forth. For how could you undertake to prove that we do not exist, if you had not existed in advance to give this proof?" Indeed, it is really ridiculous to raise the question at all as to whether I am. Everybody feels at once, without further words, that such questions as "Am I?" or "Am I not?" do not in truth cast any doubt upon the actuality of my self, but only seek to express that perhaps I may not be what I think myself to be, that even the predicate "am" may not be applicable to my essence. But in this case an unprejudiced man will only give this answer: "Very well! Then I am not what up to now I thought myself to be. Perhaps I am something that neither you nor any other man is able to find out, but in spite of all, I am; in this case, I am something inscrutable."

All this is so clear that, as said above, it cannot be proved, but only made clear by words. It is so clear that the contrary, namely, that I am not, in any sense at all, may be "tongued" but cannot be "brained," it can be *said* in words, but it cannot be *thought*. Therefore the fact of his reality is self-evident for every man, self-evident for the unprejudiced normal man as well as for the greatest geniuses, self-evident especially for our great philosophers, for all great founders of religions and, of course, for the Buddha too.

For them it is the fundamental fact which they do not even discuss, and for the greatest of them the "Ego" is the first cause of things:

"What is the first cause, what is Brahman—(here a general name for "principle")—? Whence are we?

Through what do we exist, and upon what are we founded?

> Governed by whom, ye wise ones, do we move
> Within the changing states of pain and pleasure?
> Can time, nature, necessity, or chance,
> Primordial matter, mind, or a combination
> Of these be thought of as the primal cause?
> Never! For the 'Ego' there exists."

Thus says the Çvetāçvatara-Upanishad, expressing thereby the belief that all the principles enumerated here cannot be thought as existing for themselves alone, but only as determinants of the Ego—Ātman—which, therefore, when everything is taken into account, is the first cause.

If, however, proof is required for this fundamental fact, that I am, then the Buddha provides such proof, and, in accordance with the self-evident nature of the fact to be proved, it is the most striking that could possibly be given: "You are, because you suffer,"—a statement the truth of which is experienced immediately every moment we live. But why at this point is this self-evident fact, that I am, thus urged? Simply because self-evident facts are precisely those that are only too easily overlooked, and on that account, curiously enough, ourselves also. Later on, we shall have occasion to find this amply confirmed.

Because our *I* is thus the fundamental fact with which every one is confronted, the fundamental question of all philosophy is not, as is generally assumed: "What is the world?" but "What am I?"* To deal with this fundamental question the Buddha also was led. For precisely because man is a being exposed to suffering, for him who had set before himself the goal of bringing this suffering to an end, the question arose: "What am I?" If he wished to find a successful issue to his great task, he necessarily had to get clear ideas as to this question, at least in so far as he could state this with certainty: "Is the necessity of suffering grounded in our own essence, suffering thus being merely an emanation of the same? Or is it something that reaches us only as an alien element?" Only in the latter case is there a possibility of freeing ourselves from it; whilst in the former case, every effort to escape it must be in vain from the very outset. For from my own essence, which just means, from myself, I can as little flee as the hand can throw itself away. No one can jump out of his own skin: "What thinkest thou, Aggivessana: Whoso clings to suffering, gives himself to suffering, holds by suffering with the view: 'This is mine, this am I, this is myself'—can such an one comprehend suffering or keep clear of suffering?"—"How might that be? That he cannot, honoured Gotama!"[91]

Thus also the Buddha, precisely through his problem of the annihilation of suffering, found himself confronted by the great question: What is the proper essence of man? Or, what amounts to the same thing: What is his true *I*? Indeed, according to him, the importance of this question is so great that he has placed the answer to it in the very heart of his doctrine, as also is evident from the answer he gave to thirty Brahmin youths who asked him as to the whereabouts of a runaway woman: "Which is of greater

* This incorrect formulation of the cardinal problem is largely responsible for the sterility of Western philosophy, since, in defining the problem as a question of what *the world is*, it is assumed as self-evident that I myself belong to this world. But precisely thus the possibility of understanding myself as extra-mundane is shut off from the very outset.

importance, O youths, to search for this woman or to search for your *I*?"[92]

This question as to our true essence may be approached from two sides: We may try to answer it directly or indirectly, namely, by determining what I am *not*, at all events. Which way is the better, cannot be decided beforehand. Nevertheless, without further words this much is clear, that the indirect way is certainly the safer one. What I am *not*, can be determined with certainty, at all events; but a positive answer to the question as to what I am, may easily raise doubts as to whether I actually am that wherein the answer asserts my essence to consist, as is amply proved by our divers philosophical systems. Therefore it must, from the outset, inspire us with confidence in the Buddha that he prefers the safer indirect way. For the characteristic mark of his doctrine consists in pointing out to us, step by step, so that we can safely and comfortably follow him, what in any case, we are *not*, the Buddha summing up the result each time in the great formula: "This belongs not to me; This am I not; This is not myself." To this path he was already led by the manner in which he put his problem as to whether the elements of suffering form a constituent part of the essence of a human being.

Besides, this indirect method of solving the problem is also the natural one. For the contrast between *I* and not-*I* dominates the whole world and every individual being. It is merely a matter of drawing the boundary-line between *I* and not-*I* correctly, and making the cut which divides them, in the proper place. The Buddha has drawn this dividing line between *attā* and *anattā*, between *I* and not-*I*, with great exactness. He invites all to examine if he has determined the boundary in the right manner. Let us accept his invitation.

First, of course, we must discuss the criterion according

to which the Buddha distinguishes between *attā* and *anattā*. It is clear that this criterion, in correspondence with the tremendous importance of the question that by its help is to be answered, must be put beyond all doubt, so beyond all doubt that we may be able resolutely to stake our whole destiny upon the consequences resulting from it. The Buddha, of course, does not leave us in the dark as to this criterion. It may be gathered from nearly all his discourses, and is expressly formulated in the 148th Discourse of the *Majjhima Nikāya* in the following words: "'The eye is the *I*', such a statement is inadmissible. We perceive the originating and perishing of the eye. But if originating and perishing are perceived, the result would follow: My *I* is originating and perishing. Therefore it is inadmissible to assert the eye to be the *I*. Consequently the eye is not the *I*." Accordingly the Buddha makes the following formula, the criterion for determining the boundary between *I* and not-*I:* What we perceive originating and perishing, that cannot be assumed to be my Self, cannot be my *I*. This formula must become quite clear to us, in order that we may be able, despite its extraordinary simplicity, to penetrate it in all its depth and inner obviousness. Note especially that the Buddha does not say: What originates and perishes, is not my *I*, not my Self. This sentence might be disputed; as it might not be clear at once, why not even something transient might not constitute my essence. But the Buddha says: "What I *perceive* originating and perishing, that cannot be my *I*, my Ego;" and this statement will certainly not be doubted by any thinking creature. For what I *perceive* to originate and to perish must, with logical consequence, be something different from me. If a thing passes before my physical eye, then it is irrefutably certain that it cannot be identical with my eye; and if with my ear I hear a sound begin and die away, not even a fool would assert that it was his ear itself that had just died away. Just because I exist, beyond doubt exist, I cannot be that which I perceive disappear before my physical or spiritual eye, before myself as *the perceiving subject*. For if the *I* were identical with the disappearing object, along with its disappearing, I also should have ceased to exist. But there I am; I am still there after the thing is gone. Therefore it was not my *I* nor anything belonging to me which just now disappeared. On the contrary, *it is precisely its disappearance that causes me astonishment, surprise and—pain.*

For it is just through my not-myself being involved in this passing away, that pain and suffering in consequence of transitoriness alone become possible at all. For this suffering—and the Buddha does not know any other suffering, as we have amply shown—consists just in the state desired giving place to another state not desired. But this presupposes something to exist that *experiences* this passing from the state desired into the state not desired, which therefore itself does not participate in this incessant change, but on the contrary feels it as painful; and this something is nothing but my self. This something am I, with the whole reality of pain felt by me. To express it otherwise: I cannot be identical with *the cause* of my pains.* On the contrary, if I were identical with the thing I behold perish, I could not experience pain through this passing away, because whatever in its own essence is transitory—and everything I see to be transitory is transitory in consequence of its inner nature—cannot experience this transitoriness as painful, since

* This idea may also be expressed thus: In every change something perishes, and something new is formed. But the something that has perished cannot be unhappy because it does not exist any more; and the something that has newly arisen cannot be unhappy either, because it has not experienced the change but on the contrary has only just arisen out of it: to say nothing of the fact that it ought to feel *glad* about this change, just because its own existence is due to it. Therefore a third something must be present which feels the change to be painful. This third something *I* am.

it is *not contrary to its nature, but only the outcome of its innermost essence.* Just as, for example, gas that has become free does not hesitate about expanding into empty space, but on the contrary endeavours to do so with the utmost violence, since this is in accord with its nature. Therefore also the second criterion for determining the boundary between *I* and not-*I* of which the Buddha makes use, is evident in itself, to wit, *that I cannot consist in that which because of its transitoriness causes pain to me.**

Both criterions for the determining of the realm of the not-*I*, to wit, that of perceived transitoriness and that of suffering in consequence of this transitoriness, in the Discourses are always condensed into this sentence: "Is this permanent or transient?"—"It is transient, O Lord."—"But

---

* Compare with our expositions the form in which *Schopenhauer* has put the paralogism of personality given by *Kant*. As the matter is of fundamental importance, the following passage may be quoted verbatim:

"With regard to all motion, of whatever kind it may be, it can be established *a priori* that it becomes perceivable only by comparison with something at rest. From this it follows that the course of time also, together with everything within it, could not be perceived if there were not something that had no part in the same, with the motionlessness of which we contrast the motion of time. To be sure, we here judge according to the analogy of motion in space, but space and time must always serve to illustrate each other. Therefore we must also represent time under the figure of a straight line, in order to construct it intuitively *a priori*, and make it apprehensible. Next we cannot imagine, if everything within our consciousness was going on together at once in the ordinary flow of time, how this going on could nevertheless be perceived. For this to happen we must assume something to remain at rest, which time with its contents flows past. Therefore there must be something immovable within consciousness itself. This can be nothing but the perceiving subject itself gazing unmoved and unchanging at the course of time and its changing contents. Before its gaze, life runs its course like a play. How little part itself takes in this play, even we feel, if we vividly call to mind in old age the scenes of youth and of childhood ...... Taken as a whole, the truth underlying the error of rational psychology—some truth underlies, as a rule, every error—seems to have its root in this. The truth is, that even in our empirical consciousness *an eternal resting-point may be pointed out, but only one point, and that it may only just be pointed out,* but no materials for further argumentation may be taken from it. Here I refer to my own doctrine, according to which the recognizing subject is all-perceiving but cannot be perceived: nevertheless we take it as the fixed point which time passes together with all ideas, while, its course itself certainly can only be recognized in contradistinction to something at rest." (Parerga I, p. 114.)

that which is transient—is that painful or is it pleasurable?"—"It is painful, O Lord."—"But that which is transient, painful, subject to all vicissitude—is it possible thus to regard it: This is mine, this am I, this is my Self?"—"That is not possible, O Lord."

Now in what has gone before we have found nothing permanent within the world, but recognized everything as transient, as subject to incessant change, especially everything constituting our personality; on which account precisely, everything, the components of our personality included, changes finally always to suffering also. Accordingly, the question as to what is not-*I*, of which I can in no case consist, is, in effect, already decided: Everything is not-*I*, *anattā*. On one side stands *I*; on the other, the whole gigantic cosmos, the duration, origination and dissolution of which I recognize in and through my personality.

Indeed, if we are not in advance hindered by rigid contrary views, if we look down in equal-minded reflectiveness, in tranquil contemplation upon the elements of the cosmos in their combination as personality, we can almost lay our hands upon the truth when the Buddha says:[93]

"The eye* is the *I*', such a statement is inadmissible. We perceive the originating and perishing of the eye. But if originating and perishing are perceived the result would be: 'My *I* originates and perishes'.** Therefore it is inadmissible to declare the eye to be the *I*. Consequently the eye is not the *I*.—'Forms are the *I*,' such a statement is inadmissible. We perceive the originating and perishing of the forms. But if originating and perishing are perceived, the result would be: 'My *I* originates and perishes'. There-

---

* That is, seeing.

** To repeat it once more: This is impossible, because, if I myself together with the eye, were always changing and vanishing and originating, change, as such, could not be perceived, nor felt as joy and sorrow.

fore it is inadmissible to declare forms to be the *I*.—'Eye-consciousness is the *I*'—'eye-contact is the *I*'—'sensation is the *I*'—'thirst* is the *I*,' such a statement is inadmissible. We perceive the originating and perishing of thirst. But if originating and perishing are perceived, the result would be: 'My *I* originates and perishes.' Therefore it is inadmissible to assert thirst to be the *I*. Consequently the eye is not the *I*, the forms are not the *I*, eye-consciousness is not the *I*, eye-contact is not the *I*, sensation is not the *I*, thirst is not the *I*.

'The ear is the *I*'—'the nose is the *I*'—'the tongue is the *I*'—'the body is the *I*'—'the organ of thought is the *I*,' such a statement is inadmissible. We perceive the originating and perishing of thinking.** But if originating and perishing are perceived, there the result would be: 'My *I* originates and perishes.' Therefore it is inadmissible to assert the thinking to be the *I*.—'Objects of thought are the *I*,' such a statement is inadmissible. We perceive the originating and perishing of the objects of thinking. But if originating and perishing are perceived, the result would be: 'My *I* originates and perishes.' Therefore it is inadmissible to assert objects of thought to be the *I*.—'Mind-consciousness is the *I*'—'mind-contact is the *I*'—'sensation is the *I*'—'thirst is the *I*,' such a statement is inadmissible. We perceive the originating and perishing of thirst. But if originating and perishing are perceived the result would be: 'My *I* originates and perishes.' Therefore it is inadmissible to assert thirst to be the *I*. Therefore thinking is not the *I*, objects of thinking are not the *I*, mind-consciousness is not the *I*, mind-contact is noth the *I*, sensation is not the *I*, thirst is not the *I*"

---

* This means, *desire* always arising anew from sensation and from perception. Of this thirst we shall give later on a detailed description.

** Thinking, that means, in effect, the *organ* of thought.

In short: as soon as the process of the originating of my personality and thereby to me, of the whole world, is analyzed, and therein every single component of this process as well as this process itself is examined by the criterion for defining the boundary between the realm of *I* and that of not-*I*, it becomes clear that nothing of this belongs to my *I*, but that everything lies outside of the same. For I stand behind the entire process and its constituent parts; in hours of contemplative analysis I look down upon them as a cold, dispassionate spectator, as the pure subject of cognition. I observe their incessant arising and passing away, by which I myself, the observer, remain entirely untouched:

"The monk, O monks, betakes himself to the depths of the forest or to the foot of a tree, or to any solitary spot, and sits himself down with legs crossed under him; and, body held erect, earnestly practises recollectedness. He considers this body of his, encased in a skin and filled full of all manner of uncleannesses; looks it up and down from the soles of the feet to the crown of the head, and thus reflects: 'This body has a shock of hair on the upper extremity and scattered hair all over it; it has nails and teeth, skin and flesh. There are in it sinews and bones and marrow of the bones, kidneys, heart and liver, diaphragm, spleen, lungs, stomach, intestines, and mesentery; excrement, bile, phlegm, pus, blood, sweat, lymph, tears, semen, spittle, nasal mucus, oil of the joints, and urine.'

"It is as if there were a sack, tied up at both ends, filled with diverse grains—paddy, beans, pulse, sesame and rice—and a keen-sighted man were to open it and scrutinise its contents, saying: 'This is paddy, these are beans; that is pulse; this is sesame; and this is rice.' In like manner, also, does the monk consider this body, encased in its skin and filled with all manner of uncleannesses, scrutinising it up and down from the soles of the feet to the crown of the head.

Again: the monk considers the body, however situated, however occupied, in respect of its constituent elements, reflecting: 'This body is compounded of the four elements, earth, water, fire and air.'

"Again, O monks, as if the monk should see a dead body lying at the burying-place, one or two or three days dead, bloated, bluish-black in colour, a prey to corruption, he compares it with his own body and concludes: 'This my body is even as that; shall so become, inevitably, without escape.' Again: as if the monk should see a dead body lying at the place of burial, a blood-bespattered frame-work of bones hung with mere rags of flesh, held together only by the sinews; or a blood-bespattered skeleton totally stripped of flesh, held together only by sinews; or a skeleton wholly bare of flesh and blood, held together only by the sinews; or the bones detached from the sinews, and scattered hither and thither, here a bone of the hand, there a bone of the foot, here a shin-bone, there a thigh-bone, here the pelvis, here the spine, there the skull;—as if he should see all this, he compares it with his own body and concludes: 'This my body is even as that; shall so become, inevitably, without escape.' Again: as if the monk should see a dead body lying at the place of burial, the bones white and of the colour of musselshells; or gathered together into a heap after the lapse of a year; or weathered away and turned to dust;—as if he should see this, the monk compares it with his own body and concludes: 'This my body is even as that; shall so become, inevitably, without escape.'

"Thus as respects his own body, he keeps watch upon the body; as respects other bodies he keeps watch upon the body; both as respects his own and other bodies, he keeps watch upon the body."[94]

And what does he find in this keeping watch upon the body? The old fact: he observes: The body arises, the body passes away; the body arises and passes away, but I remain untouched by this. What I am seeing before me, is nothing but a formation arisen out of the four chief elements, which I perceive always to renew itself out of them, and under my eyes hurry incessantly towards definite decay, until at last it entirely dissolves and returns to union with the matter of external nature; in short: he finds out: "It is a body," "subject to dissolution and decay,"—and nothing else, especially not my *I*, not my Ego. For how could this be my ego which I perceive passing away before mine eyes? "This consideration is constantly before his mind, even because it conduces to understanding, to clear comprehension."[94] For only now do we begin to think about ourselves, are we surprised at ourselves, perceiving that we cannot really consist in what up till now we have thought ourselves to consist.*

---

* If we wish to perceive quite clearly that the body cannot be our *I*, we may think about the following: It is well known that the incessant change of matter within our body has this effect, that after ten years at most no atom within it remains the same. In the meantime, from nourishment newly taken in, an entirely new body has been built up. Now take a captive sentenced to ten years imprisonment who as a matter of course thinks his body his *I*, or at least, an essential component of the same, and set before him, at the beginning of his term of punishment, all the food he will consume within the coming ten years, in the shape of tins of preserved food, and tell him: "Here in these tins of food is contained your self as it will be after some years."—Further, collect in a barrel all his excreta during his ten years imprisonment. At the end of this time lead him to the barrel and tell him: "Here in this barrel your bygone self is lying; only look at it!" One would imagine that the monstrosity of the view that the body and its substances have anything to do with our real self must here leap to the eye. Let none object: "My essence does not consist in the material substances, but in *the form* they have assumed," for this form is nothing existing in itself, but is only substance itself endowed with form, only the temporary state of the substance. Certainly this form conditions the diversity of beings, but even on that very account with the effect that this diversity itself is only formal; materially everything is the same, nothing but—dirt! The most admirable form cannot cover up this fact. Whoever feels shocked by this truth, let him imagine a man whose form has again dissolved, that is, a putrefying corpse, and on the other hand look closely at a crushed snail, and then answer the question if both are not *materially* exactly the same. "It is significant of the value of everything existing, that its charms reside only in its form, which is as fugitive as that—substance—is consistent; every moment it is changing and can only stay as long as it clings parasitically to substance (now to this and now to that part of it), but perishes as soon as it loses this stronghold." (Schopenhauer.)

Thus, as with the body, so is it with the whole process of sensation and perception: "Again: the monk keeps watch upon the phenomena of the six subjective-objective spheres of sense.—And how does he keep watch upon the phenomena of the six subjective-objective spheres of sense? The monk, O monks, understands the eye and understands forms; and the connexion that comes to be because of these two, —that also he understands. He understands the ear and understands sounds; and the connexion that comes to be because of these two,—that also he understands. He understands the nose and understands odours; and the connexion that comes to be because of these two,—that also he understands. He understands the tongue and understands objects of taste; and the connexion that comes to be because of these two,—that also he understands. He understands the body and understands objects of touch; and the connexion that comes to be because of these two,—that also he understands. He understands the mind and understands ideas; and the connexion that comes to be because of these two, —that also he understands. He is aware when the connexion arises that has not yet arisen; is aware when the connexion that already has arisen is overcome; is aware when the connexion that has been overcome appears no more for ever.

"But how, as respects sensation, does the monk keep watch upon sensation? The monk, O monks, in experiencing a pleasant sensation, is aware, 'I experience a pleasant sensation'; in experiencing an unpleasant sensation is aware, 'I experience an unpleasant sensation'; in experiencing a sensation neither pleasant nor unpleasant is aware, 'I experience a sensation neither pleasant nor unpleasant'.

"But how does a monk keep watch over the mind? The monk, O monks, perceives as craving, the mind bound by craving: and as uncraving, the mind free from craving. He perceives as hating, the mind bound by hatred; and as unhating, the mind free from hatred. He perceives as deluded, the mind bound by delusion; and as undeluded, the mind free from delusion.

"Thus, as respects phenomena in himself, he keeps watch upon phenomena; as respects phenomena in others, he keeps watch upon phenomena; both as respects phenomena in himself and in others, he keeps watch upon phenomena.[95] And thus here also he perceives: They are mere phenomena, mere processes, restlessly fluctuating within myself: visual contacts, auditory contacts, and so forth . . . ., sensations rising and dissolving again, thoughts coming and going, and nothing else. Especially are these also not my *I*, not my Self. For here also the reasoning holds good: How could that be my *I*, my Self, my real essence, which I perceive thus fluctuating before me, vanishing and arising always anew? Thus this observation also becomes for us a new support in trying to discover our Self, our innermost essence, because "it conduces to understanding, to clear comprehension." For now we may perceive surely enough that our true essence has nothing whatever to do with one of these five groups constituting our personality, but must lie beyond them, and that the nun *Vajirā* is right in telling Māra the tempter: "Only a heap of changing processes, (Saṅkhārā) is this; there is not found a being here."[96]

Now, too, the conclusion of the Master may be fully understood:

"What thinkest thou, Aggivessana, is the body permanent or transient?"

"It is transient, honoured Gotama!"

"But that which is transient—is that painful or is it pleasurable?"

"It is painful, honoured Gotama!"

"But that which is transient, painful, subject to all vicissitude—is it possible to regard it: 'This is mine; this am I; this is my Self'?"

"This is not possible, honoured Gotama!"

"What thinkest thou, Aggivessana, sensation, perception, activities of the mind, consciousness,—are these permanent or are they transient?"

"They are transient, honoured Gotama!"

"But that which is transient—is that painful or is it pleasurable?"

"It is painful, honoured Gotama!"

"But that which is transient, painful, subject to all vicissitude—is it possible to regard it: 'This is mine; this am I; this is my Self'?"

"That is not possible, honoured Gotama!"[97]

Accordingly, the matter stands really thus as the Buddha recapitulates it in the following words:

"Wherefore monks, whatsoever there is of body, whatsoever there is of sensation, whatsoever there is of perception, whatsoever there is of mentations, whatsoever there is of consciousness, in the past, in the future and at the present moment, our own or a stranger's, gross or subtle, mean or exalted, remote or close at hand—all body as it has come to be, all sensation, all perception, all the activities of the mind, all consciousness as it has come to be, is, in the light of the highest wisdom, to be regarded thus: 'This belongs not to me; this am I not; this is not my Self.'"

Now we may also understand why we are so helpless against the five groups constituting our personality. They all follow their own laws. Those of our body, even today, we do not yet know thoroughly; sensations are coming and going against our will, thoughts and moods are vexing us without our being able to drive them away. How could all this be, if they really did belong to our essence, if we were consisting in them? What really and essentially belongs to us ought to be entirely at our own unqualified disposal, and our volition could not possibly come into conflict with our faculties, because volition and the organs of its realization, would be in the same degree essential to us. A faculty belonging really, that is essentially, to us, we should absolutely dominate, because our essence would consist in putting it into action. Only what is foreign to us, we must first bring into our power. But this is exactly the case with the five groups which constitute our personality. Most men cannot dominate them at all; nobody can dominate them entirely; and very few come near to it. And those few have only reached this through incessant exercise and effort. From this point of view also it is a contradiction to assert our essence to consist in the elements of our personality and thereby, in this personality itself. This contradiction the Buddha deals with in the thirty-fifth Dialogue of the Majjhima Nikāya:

"What thinkest thou, Aggivessana, Does a reigning warrior King, such as King Pasenadi of Kosala, or King Ajātasattu of Magadhā, *within their own domains* possess the power of pronouncing and causing to be carried out sentences of death, outlawry and banishment?"

"Reigning warrior kings, such as King Pasenadi and King Ajātasattu, indeed, possess such powers, honoured Gotama; and even this company of notables of Vajjī and of Mallā *within their own domains* exercise powers of life and death, outlawry and banishment; how much more, duly appointed Kings, like King Pasenadi of Kosala and King Ajātasattu of Magadhā. These have such powers, honoured Gotama, and are worthy of such powers."

"What thinkest thou then, Aggivessana? In as much as thou hast but now said: 'Body is my Self,' dost thou possess this power over body—'Let my body be thus, let not my body be so'?"

"That I have not, honoured Gotama."

"Pause and consider, Aggivessana, and, having well considered, then give answer, for thy last does not tally with thy first nor thy first with thy last. In as much as thou hast but now said: 'Sensation is my Self—Perception is my Self—the Activities of mind are my Self—Consciousness is my Self,' hast thou this dominion over consciousness—'Let my consciousness be thus, let not my consciousness be so'?"

"That I have not, honoured Gotama."

Further: if we consisted of the five groups, if our essence were exhausted by them, then they ought to be to us the most natural and familiar thing of the world. They would be nothing but our self, our *I*, and thereby, completely recognized and defined. But compare with this, how curiously not only the child, but also the grown-up man, during all his lifetime, regards and studies his body, wonders at it as at a riddle, a mystery, exactly as he would behave if suddenly he were to come across something entirely strange with which he had never before had anything to do. But not less does the man of a reflective mind, the man whose gaze has not become dulled by habit, himself wonder at his faculties of sense, at the sensations, moods and thoughts arising within himself; and he asks himself: "How have I come into possession of all these things? Must I really have them?" A question that would be quite impossible, if he were nothing but these processes themselves. Then he would be comprehended in these processes, more especially, in the consciousness produced by them. This consciousness would be produced with the same machine-like self-evidence as steam by the steam-engine. Consciousness and thereby man himself would be the adequate product of the conditions of their existence, would find their exhaustive and sufficient cause in them, would without remainder be comprehended in them. Whence then should come astonishment of the consciousness and of the *I* produced in it, at their own existence and at the whole process producing them?* But this astonishment exists, an dnot only mere astonishment of consciousness at itself, but the astonishment of somebody who wonders especially at this consciousness, indeed therefore, of one who must be standing behind it. It is the great wonder how I acquired "this body endowed with sensuality and consciousness," or, to express ourselves popularly, how I ever got into this world. It is that great wonder which forms the original basis of every religion and every philosophy, and overcomes perhaps every man at least once in his life, in a contemplative hour.

Take notice, how this fundamental feeling of mankind expresses itself also in language, that most immediate product of direct perception: "I enter the world," "I leave the world," "Life pleases me," "I cling to life," "I take away my life," in which it is to be noted that life is nothing but the five groups in action. How could I cling to life, how especially could I take away my life, if I myself *were* life, that is, if I consisted in the five groups? Especially, to take away my own life would, in this case, be just as impossible as, (to repeat this simile once more) it is impossible for the hand to throw itself away, or for a machine to commit self-annihilation. How could it be possible to annihilate my *real* self, that is, that wherein I ultimately consist, be this what it may, since it constitutes my *essence* to be what I am? Even the mere will to be some *other* thing than I am in reality is contrary to my essence and therefore cannot arise; how much more is the will to self-annihilation contrary to my essence! *Omnis natura conservatrix sui!* I can only throw away or annihilate something wherein I do *not* consist, and

* Astonishment arises only if no sufficient explanation in accord with the law of sufficient reason is possible.

which is therefore *alien* to me. This thought, wisely considered, alone must make it clear that I am something standing *behind* life, behind the five groups, something only *adhering,* only *clinging* to life and to the five groups constituting personality, as to something *alien* which I think desirable.

Let us just attempt the counterproof! If personality constitutes my essence, then of course every part of it must form a part of this my essence, and with the successive falling away of these parts I ought to become ever less. Now let me imagine that I have lost hair and teeth: have I thereby become less? A ridiculous question! Further: Suppose I lose a leg, both legs, an arm, both arms; have I thereby become less? In this case also I know myself to be quite whole and complete; I have become *poorer,* but not *less.* How could this be, if my essence consisted of my body? Certainly, the so-called vital organs of our organism cannot be taken away without our ceasing to live. But are they therefore our essence? Suppose that medical science were in a position—and to-day indeed it is not very far from it—to amputate these vital organs also, piece by piece, and by and by to replace them completely by new ones, in such a manner that another part is always removed when the last removed part has been completely replaced, until at last all the organs, the brain included, have been, so to say, changed in this manner. Should I then have become another man? Again: A ridiculous question! The whole procedure that had given me a new body in a visible manner—in reality Nature herself effects just such a change, as we have seen above—would not touch me in the least. But from this once more it becomes evident that I cannot consist in my body.

Even so is it with the functions of the senses. If I become deaf, that is to say, if I lose the sense of hearing, I again become poorer, but not less, and it is the same, if I lose the sense of smell, of taste and even of feeling. I would always become poorer and poorer, but in no wise less. I would feel always entirely and completely the same as I was before. It could even happen that I might be-glad about this poverty of sense faculty thus come over me. If, for instance, a man very sensitive to noise, who therefore would prefer to hear nothing at all, but for some reason is unable to repair to the stillness for which he longs, loses the power of hearing, he will certainly bear this loss very easily, perhaps he will even rejoice over it, since thereby a perennial source of pain to him is for ever closed. It may even be that a man grows weary of all his five senses, feels them as a burden from which he would like to be freed, in the immediate consciousness that he in his real essence will not be touched thereby. Certainly, there remains the sixth sense, thinking, to which this does not seem to be applicable. For, as Schopenhauet says, everyone identifies his essence with consciousness, again in harmony with the words of the Buddha: "Of the body built up from the four chief-elements also an inexperienced average man may grow weary, but what is designated as thinking or as mind or as consciousness, thereof the inexperienced average man cannot get enough, cannot break away from it. And why not? For long has the inexperienced average man clung to it, tended and cherished it (and thought): 'This belongs to me, this am I, this is my Self.'"[98] This means: Since, lacking the necessary reflectiveness, we are inclined, first of all, to regard at least the noble parts of our body as belonging to our essence, we thus ultimately cling to thinking, and therewith to consciousness resulting from it, as to our real essence. But just as, for instance, the loss of sight and of consciousness of seeing based upon it, does not fundamentally touch my self, just as little am I touched in my real essence, if

I not only stop the activities of the five outer-senses, but also cease to think, and thereby take away the basis of all consciousness. This is proved to me every night anew in sleep, where I am without consciousness, but nevertheless existing. Nobody will say that he perishes in falling asleep, and originates anew in awakening; on the contrary, he will think it not bad to be in the state of a deep, sound sleep.* To put it briefly: In looking critically at all the components of my personality, I recognize clearly that none of them belongs so essentially to me that in losing it I should become not only poorer, but less. But further, I recognize just as clearly that neither can I consist in the interaction of these components as their product. For I look down upon this interaction with its incessant changes, I observe it in all its details, as one only can look down upon something alien, as one only can observe something foreign to himself. The Buddha is therefore undoubtedly right in teaching that our real essence does not consist in the components of our personality, and therefore not in this personality itself.

But precisely on this account do I exist, apart from this personality and uninjured by its decay. Therefore a man, even if it is convincingly shown to him a hundred times over that his essence can in no case consist in what he calls his personality, will pass on with a superior air, smiling tranquilly, over any conclusion as to his non-existence that

---

* We may also say: In a sleeping man, every kind of consciousness, also consciousness of thought, has ceased to exist; and yet, he exists. Therefore consciousness of thought does not belong to his essence; it is *anattā*. But what besides, in addition to this, exists in him, to wit, his corporeal organism, we have already recognized as *anattā*, as not our Self. Therefore he exists, though he is nothing of what he seems to be *for us*. Moreover, the fact that I am also still existing in deep dreamless sleep, must be strictly differentiated from the question as to whether such an existence is desirable. Only this latter point is really doubted by man, not the former fact.—The question of the value of an existence without any activity of the senses or of the mind, will be dealt with later on.

may be drawn from that fact. As shown above, he will not even be able to understand the objection, as it is really meant, to wit, that he does not in any wise exist at all, but will answer: "Very well! If I do not consist in my personality, then I am something else." Accordingly, even at the stage we have now reached, he may consider it a debatable point as to *what* he is, but never as to *if* he is.

* * *

"Then I am something else." But what is left, if nothing constituting man's personality forms the real essence of man?

In putting this question, the problem of the *nature* of our Self, of our essence, takes a new direction. Until now, so to say, we have gone straight ahead in our search for the right answer, investigating the components of our personality lying before us and generally assumed to constitute the essence of man, to see how far the latter assumption can be justified. We always had something tangible before us, and in our enquiry, for that very reason, stood on the solid ground of reality. But now, having thus far reflected upon ourselves that it has become clear to us that our essence is in no wise identical with our personality, we are threatened with the loss of our support in perceptible reality, we are in danger of getting on to the swampy, shaky ground of empty notions, or even into the barren domain of metaphysical speculations. Double cautiousness is therefore needed.

For if we proceed to ask what this "other thing" might be, wherein I am ultimately said to exist, we shall probably get the answer: "Well, my essence consists *in my soul*." But this answer will most likely be given with some hesitation, because the person answering will almost certainly feel that the counter-question will immediately follow: "But what is this soul?" How much this counter-question is justified, will become clear, if we remember that the word "soul" only represents a special expression for the real essence of man, so that the sentence: "My essence consists in my soul" is nothing more than a piece of empty tautology. We therefore cannot help but try to define this soul a little more exactly. The answer will not long be wanting; theologians and commonplace philosophers have so long trumpeted it abroad in the world that every child knows by heart: "*The soul is an immaterial and therefore spiritual, therefore simple, therefore imperishable, substance.*" For how many thousands of believing men does this definition of their essence constitute the magic formula that banishes every doubt, the granite foundation upon which they have based their whole view of the world and therewith all their action, without—and herein lies the tragedy of the affair—even once making the attempt to investigate the solidity of this foundation. At the bottom, however, this is not in the least to be wondered at. The fact that man *is*, in some sense or another, *is*, as the fundamental and original fact of all being, stands beyond question. Therefore it only seems self-evident that he then must be *something*, *is* something; and if it is not comprised within the perceptible components of his personality, it must naturally lie *behind* them as pure spirit, which is only another word for the so-called spiritual substance.

And yet the belief in this immaterial and simple substance, this "spirit" dwelling within us, is just as untenable as the belief that our essence consists in our personality. It is even much more untenable, a mere creation of the brain, the outcome of confused and careless thinking. To understand this is not difficult. With a little reflection, the baselessness of this assumption might be gathered at once from what has been said in our previous pages. But as it is just this notion of the purely spiritual or of a spiritual substance or of pure spirit, that is so often misused, and with us, so to say, constitutes a big bag into which theologians and commonplace philosophers put everything they cannot prove and explain, it will be better to submit these notions to special analysis in thoughtful reflectiveness, a course, recommended by the Buddha as a sure remedy against all errors, and thus to reduce them to their real content. Let us therefore without fear look somewhat nearer at this "spirit"!

Spiritual substance or pure spirit are mere abstract notions. To value them adequately we must remember the invaluable expositions of Schopenhauer concerning the essence of notions. According to him, notions are the product of reflection on the world as given by perception. They arise through the forming of one notion out of a number of perceived separate things. In this one notion everything individual and special about the separate, single things is omitted, and only what is common to the whole class of things thought of under the homogeneous notion is preserved. Thus, man has formed the notion "oak" to signify all the innumerable but similar single trees given him in perception, which are comprised under this notion. Notions are therefore nothing originally real, but an artificial product of reason distilled from the world given in perception. They take their substance and their content exclusively from the perceptible world, and therefore possess reality only in so far as they lead back to something given by perception. From this it follows self-evidently, first, that a notion having no perceptible substratum is an empty creation of the brain, a "mere word inside the head;" and secondly, that also a notion correctly arrived at, that is, one really derived from perception, can, and may, be only "for immanent, but never for transcendent use." This means that it may never be applied beyond the realm of experience from which alone it has been abstracted, and within which therefore it alone is valid.

Let us apply this insight to the notions of spiritual substance or pure spirit. How were they formed? Or, what is the same thing: From which elements of perception did they originate?

We saw that personality is nothing but a "heap of processes" (Saṅkhārā). These processes are of three kinds: —the purely corporeal, that is, the activities of the several bodily organs, the circulation of the blood, inhalation and exhalation,—the Buddha always mentions inhalation and exhalation as fundamental activities conditioning all other corporeal processes,—further, the functions of the senses, upon which sensation and perception are based; and, finally, the action of reason, consisting in deliberation and consideration.* The two last-named kinds of activities, that is, the purely sensual ones,—to wit, seeing, hearing, smelling, tasting, touching, and the perceiving action of the mind—on one side, and the action of reason, to wit, abstract thinking, on the other side, together with their respective product of consciousness, we call mental processes, in contradistinction to the corporeal ones. Since now these mental or spiritual processes presuppose, of course, a substratum on which they effect themselves, but the body together with its organs of sense, the brain included, is thought not to constitute a sufficient substratum for these so-called mental or spiritual processes, a special substratum is simply postulated for these "spiritual" functions; and so we get the "spirit," the spiritual substance, which is said to be hidden as a peculiar something, and as their substratum, behind these spiritual functions. Fundamentally, that is, for him who recognizes, by the help of the Buddha's not less startlingly simple than genius-like elucidation, that all the so-called spiritual functions, the functions of the senses in the proper sense, as well as those of mind and of reason, are nothing but mere functions of

* See below, the chapter on the Saṅkhārā.

the organs of sense, including the brain, effecting the arising of consciousness, the assumption of a spiritual substance or of an actual "spirit" means nothing more than a hypostasis of those so-called spiritual functions themselves. It is the same tendency of the human mind towards personification, which makes a native of the South Sea Islands, who for the first time sees a steam-engine at work, suppose that within the machine an imprisoned "spirit" is working, and run away from it in terror. It is the same tendency which always causes man, if he does not understand a process in its inner connection, to substitute for the purely natural connection not yet accessible to him, an independent force supposed to exist solely for this special purpose.*

Between the natural man and the scholar, there is in such a case only this difference, that the scholar postulates a purely physical force, such as the hypothetical ether, to explain the transmission of light, or the atoms, to explain chemical combinations, and in doing so often comes near to truth. The simple-minded man, on the other hand, uses a more radical method, in assuming, as often as he needs them, witches, devils, gods, or, as in our case, a separate individual soul standing behind the body, that is, a spiritual substance, or, to drop all circumlocutions, an actual "spirit." This completely effects the result he desires. All vexing problems are got rid of, once for all, completely, and at the same time in the simplest and most exhaustive manner. For us, however, our investigations yield us only the insight that man in truth as little conceals within himself a "spirit" or any spiritual substance, as that there are such "spirits" in haunted localities. As in the latter case a physical process

* This, by the way, is the origin of the notion of a god. In the doctrine of the Buddha, it therefore does not exist as used. According to the Buddha, the universe is without beginning as well as without end, and governed by iron laws which provide it with its exclusive and sufficient cause. Thereby, the postulation of an unknown cause of the universe, called God, becomes superfluous.

is hypostatized, so in our case a psychical one. What is real, what alone lies at the base of the notions of spirit and of spiritual substance, are only the so-called psychical or, more correctly, *sensual processes*. Thereby the mysterious "spirit" in man reveals itself as in reality only a simple collective term for the so-called mental or spiritual functions, as opposed to the corporeal ones. This alone is the true content of the notions of spirit and spiritual substance. Whatever else is usually thought to be within them, has no real foundation, and is therefore an empty creation of the brain.*

To understand the entire superfluity or even untenability of the postulation of a particular spiritual substance, a soul, as bearer of the mental functions, what follows is worth consideration. If a separate spiritual substance exercises the functions of seeing, hearing, smelling, tasting, touching and thinking, it cannot, in its functions, be dependent on the body, just because the functions are *its own* and not those of the body. Therefore the soul ought to be able to perform the act of cognition mentioned before with *every* organ of sense, just as it chooses; that means: if it liked, it might hear with the eye, or see with the ear; it would not even need to use any organ of sense, simply because it would be able to hear and see by force *of its own essence*. The organs of sense, on the contrary, would only make hindrances and difficulties for the functions of cognizing taking place only in the soul itself, in the same way that a keen-sighted man would only find his power of seeing interfered with, in using a pair of spectacles. But in reality it is just the reverse: the various psychical processes are exclusively bound up with the respective corporeal organs, the brain included,

* As remarked above, the expression "mind" also represents nothing but a collective term, designating the totality of the psychical processes in the direction of will and of thinking.

and in such a manner conditioned by these organs that every injury to these latter adversely affects the former, and the collapse of the bodily organs in death, brings about their definitive annihilation. From all this it accordingly follows that the act of cognition is exclusively the product of these organs, not that of an entirely superfluous soul standing behind them.

This reflection is also at the basis of the answer given to king Milinda by the wise Nāgasena on the question as to whether there is a cognizing soul-being:

"What do you mean, O king, by this cognizing soul-being?"

"That soul-being in the interior of man, sir, that with the eye beholds forms, that with the ear hears sounds, that with the nose smells odours, that with the tongue tastes flavours, that with the body touches objects of touch, and that with the mind perceives ideas. Just as we, sitting in this palace, may look through any window, as we like, be it through the eastern or the western, the northern or the southern one, just so, O Lord, this soul-being looks as it likes, through this one or that of the doors of the senses."

But the Thera said: "Those five doors of the senses I will explain to you, O king. Listen and pay good heed! If there was in the interior of man a soul-being perceiving through the eye, forms, just as we perceive through any window here, objects, then this soul-being ought to be able to perceive the forms just as well through the ear, through the nose, through the tongue, through the body or through the organ of thought. And it ought to be able to hear sounds, to smell odours, to taste flavours, to touch objects and to perceive ideas just as well through every single door of the senses."

"It is certainly not able to do that, sir."

"But then, O king, your last does not tally with your first nor your first with your last!—Just as we, O king, sitting in this palace, if we open the windows and put out our heads, in full daylight perceive objects more clearly, just so this soul-being within us, if the five doors of the senses were torn out, ought to be able to perceive objects better in full daylight."

"It is certainly not able to do that, sir."

"But then, O king, your last does not tally with your first, nor your first with your last.—If for example this Dinna should go out and take his place (before the open door) in the vestibule, would you, O king, know this to be so?"

"Certainly I should know this, sir."

"And if this same Dinna, O king, should come in again and take his place before you, would you, O king, then also know this to be so?"

"Certainly, sir."

"And if, O king, we should place a thing having taste upon the tongue, would this soul-being existing within us know, if this thing was sour, salty, bitter, sharp, acrid or sweet?"

"Certainly it would know this, sir."

"But if this thing were within the stomach, could this soul-being then recognize its taste?"

"Certainly not, sir."

"But then, O king, your last does not tally with your first, nor your first with your last."* [99]

To be sure, those who maintain the existence of a soul think they can meet these arguments with the following objection: "It is true, the functions of cognition are bound up with the organs of the senses, the brain included, but the purpose of the latter is only that of tools, of which the

* This means: If it were a soul that tasted the thing, thus affirming its own essence, it naturally ought also to be able to taste an object placed in the stomach instead of the mouth, in the same way that the king recognizes his servant Dinna just as well if he is standing in the open vestibule, as if he is standing immediately before him.

soul merely makes use." But whoever advances such an objection, forgets the principle hinted at above, that the principles of explanation must not be multiplied without necessity.* For if once the organs of sense form the necessary presupposition of every act of cognition there is no reason why they should not form its *only* condition. Then, however, they find themselves confronted with the following alternative: Either the assumed spiritual substance or soul must itself perish in death, inasmuch as then, after being robbed of the material organs of sense used by it till now, it is no longer capable of the act of cognition, and thus precisely that is wanting, to explain which it was postulated, and which forms its essential content; a soul which, together with its sensual activity, has also lost all activity of mind and of reason, being no soul, being nothing at all. Or else, the soul is still able to carry out its cognizing functions even after death, without the corresponding corporeal organs. In this case, it remains a puzzle why it cannot effect during life, when its organs are only impaired, what it may do after death, when they are completely gone. If it is able to cognize after death without any material organ, then it ought to be able to do the same in life much more easily when the organs are only impaired, since the instrument it is accustomed to handle is at least partially at its disposition. Thus it is here, as it is with every product

---

* This principle may be better understood from the following passage of *Du Prel, History of the Development of the Universe*, p. 180: "The subjective intellect desires to penetrate objective nature in a logical manner. As nature attains the object of her productions with the fewest possible means, those scientific hypotheses must also be the best which analyse phenomena conceptively according to the Law of Parsimony. The objectively smallest quantity of force in nature must be reflected in the minimum, but nevertheless sufficient, amount of logic present in scientific hypotheses. Of two hypotheses one explaining as much as the other, the simpler one is the better one. Accordingly, already in Plato's day, we find it prized as the first principle of science, that the principles of explanation must not be multiplied without necessity . . . . . . This is based upon the instinctive but firm conviction that simplicity is the mark of truth."

of phantasy; at last they break down before reality. Therefore the Buddha calls the dogma of the ego being constant and immutable in the form of an individual soul "an utterly and entirely foolish idea."[100]

But if thus the untenability of the soul-hypothesis is manifest in every direction, it only remains astonishing, how nevertheless men cling so tightly to such a hypothesis as to show themselves inaccessible to every other teaching. But the reason for this is not very difficult to find. The average man identifies his essence with the five components of his personality, thinking it self-evident that these components must stand in some essential relation to his real Self, and on this very account lives under the delusion that it is his essence which manifests itself in his personality and presents itself as such: "How, Venerable One, is there belief in personality?"—"Take, friend Visākha, the uninstructed man of the world, unperceiving of the Noble Ones, unacquainted with the Noble Teaching, untrained in the Noble Teaching, unperceiving of Good Men, unacquainted with the Teaching of Good Men, untrained in the Teaching of Good Men—this man looks upon body, sensation, perception, mentation, consciousness, as himself; or he looks upon himself as possessing body, sensation, perception, mentation, consciousness; or he regards body, sensation, perception, mentation, consciousness as being in himself; or else his regards himself as being in body, sensation, perception, mentation, consciousness."[101] But reality demonstrates to him, before his eyes, that all the five groups, and together with them also their product, personality, in death falls a prey to destruction. Accordingly there results for him a double conclusion: First, as a practical consequence, there arises in him an immense fear of death, as of the supposed annihilation of his essence. Only the reverse side of this fear is his boundless attachment to life, that is, to the Five Groups in action. This attachment generally maintains itself also in the face of suffering, to such an extent that men will even accept a life consisting solely of suffering, if only they may be allowed to live at all, and thus be saved from supposed annihilation for as long as possible. Here we come upon what is at once the deepest and last cause of all for this boundless attachment to life. This, as we have seen above, cannot reside in life itself being something worth desiring, but consists simply in the delusion that our essence consists in the five groups of personality, and thus is doomed to destruction together with them. Give a man the clear conviction that sickness and death cannot touch him in his real essence, and he will at once become perfectly indifferent in regard to them!

Besides this practical consequence of the fear of death, the belief in personality begets another, a theoretical one: In truth, man, as we saw above, does *not* consist in his personality, therefore death, being only the dissolution of the elements of this personality, cannot touch him. *But this he does not recognize*, being under the delusion that he consists of his personality. Thus he is blinded by a fatal error in regard to himself. But on the other hand, precisely because of this, he cannot with logical consequence carry through this error which is in direct contrast to his essence, but comes again and again into a conflict with it which reaches its culminating-point at the moment when death clearly reveals itself as the dissolution of the five components of his personality and thereby of this personality itself. For in consequence of his error, death presents itself to him as his own dissolution. But against this assumption his essence, as being in contradiction therewith, revolts. And so in despair he seeks for a way out of this conflict between his inner essence and his false apprehension of the relation in which he stands to his personality. But instead of, at least on this point, seeing correctly through this relation, he in a makeshift manner reconciles his false apprehension with himself through a fresh error whereby he deceives himself into believing in the continued existence of his personality after death, in spite of the *obvious* fact of its annihilation. This error just consists in the assumption of a soul, such an assumed bearer of the spiritual functions being not only a very easily assumed principle for the explanation of these, seeing that it is only postulated for this purpose, but also enabling man to believe, in spite of the opposing evidence of natural facts, that he himself is in no way touched by death as regards his spiritual functions, since the soul, being a simple substance, is not subject to death. To be sure, the fact that the body at least perishes, cannot be explained away even by the assumption of a soul. But because he dislikes the idea of going without his body for ever, he lets this body be placed again at his disposal, sooner or later, by the act of his almighty god. In such a manner, it is certainly not difficult to master all difficulties.

Thus also the assumption of a soul has its ultimate reason in the fundamental error of man that his personality is essential to him. But *we* who have clearly recognized from the course of our investigation that our essence cannot consist in our personality, regard its decay in quite another manner. Our real essence is as little touched by this decay as we are touched by the burning of wood that is felled in the forest and burnt before our eyes. Therefore we understand also the exhortation of the Master to let go, with tranquil mind, the five groups constituting our personality:

"What think ye, monks? Suppose that in this Jeta forest a man should come and gather together grass, twigs, leaves and branches and burn them up, or do with them whatsoever else he listed; should you think: 'This man is gathering together and burning or doing whatsoever else he lists with *us*'?"

"Nay indeed, Lord."

"And why not?"

"These things, Lord, truly are not our *I*, nor do they belong to our *I*."

"Just even so, ye monks, what is not yours, that surrender! Long will its surrender make for your happiness and well-being. And what is it that is not yours? Body, monks, is not yours; sensation is not yours; perception is not yours; the activities of the mind are not yours; consciousness is not yours. Give them up, one and all! Long will their giving up tend to your happiness and well-being!" [102]

Because we have now won the insight that the groups constituting our personality have nothing to do with our true essence, in order to banish our fear of being annihilated in death, we have no need to take refuge in such fantastic inventions as the hypothesis of a spiritual substance, a soul, by assuming which man, in contradiction to reality, deceives himself into believing in the duration of these elements of personality that are doomed to destruction. On the contrary, we may confidently trust ourselves to the further guidance of the Master on the path that really will lead us back to ourselves. For, though none of the elements constituting our personality nor a soul standing behind it can form our real essence, *Still We Are,* a fundamental fact which remains even in face of this result. And this, after all, is the main thing.

* * *

Still we are: But is this really true? Suppose that the whole of our personality, all mental functions included, before all, thinking and consciousness resulting from it, is dissolved in death, and behind this dissolved personality no substance nor soul of any kind remains. What shall I then be?

We may well be somewhat curious as to what answer the Buddha will give to this question; all the more so, that now we must gradually come to the point where the indirect path by which he has hitherto led us, namely that of pointing out to us wherein we do *not* consist, can no longer be followed. For nothing more seems to remain over wherein man might erroneously find his essence and so we ought soon to come upon the *positive* kernel of this our essence. For certainly we dare assume that the Buddha will not definitively lose himself in nothing but negations concerning what we are *not*, but will conduct us beyond them to a positive result, proceeding from this, that the method followed by him can only have for its object the pulling away more and more of the thick, alien covering that lies spread over our real essence, until that essence itself lies openly before us, like the kernel of a fruit that is gradually freed of its wrapping of leaves and husk, one after another. Let us therefore listen and examine what the Buddha has still further to tell us!

If he were himself standing before us, he would probably reply, smiling at our expectation: "Friend, take care that you do not lose that heedfulness with which you have followed me until now, for you are on the point of losing it, or rather, you have lost it already. You think, because you are, you ought also to be *something*, and this something you now wish to know. But now, just take pains to think clearly, and to analyse well all notions in regard to their content. For all evil comes from confused thinking.

"You want to be *something*, that probably means, you do not want to be *nothing*. But what is opposed to Nothing as its exhaustive contrary? Certainly *Everything*. For the most extreme and comprehensive alternatives you can set up are: Everything or Nothing. The Something you want to be ought therefore to belong to Everything, ought to be a part or element of it. Whoever has something, has not got everything, but only part of it; and whoever *is* something, is therefore just a part of everything. But what is Everything? 'Everything is what I want to show you, monks. What is Everything? The eye and forms, the ear and sounds, the nose and odours, the tongue and flavours, the body and objects of touch, thinking and ideas, this, ye monks, is called Everything.'[103] But I have just now shown you clearly enough that you cannot consist in anything of this. But behind all this, that is, behind Everything, there is only *Nothing*. Consequently you are no Something, but you are indeed—Nothing."

So then I am indeed fully summed up in the five groups constituting my personality, behind which yawns only Nothing! I am nothing but this personality; and personality is nothing but a heap of transitory processes without any abiding kernel. Accordingly, with the dissolution of this personality in death I have completely and radically come to an end, just as a carriage has come to an end, if it is broken up and its several constituent parts burnt! Why then all these long discussions about what I am not, if at last I am nothing at all? If this is the entire renowned wisdom of the Buddha, he might have given it in a much more simple and dignified manner. Trivial as is the saying, "Much ado about nothing," here it has become truth. That later disciple of the Buddha, Nāgasena, who enlightened king Milinda as to the nature of our essence, was quite another man. He openly confessed, he explicitly declared and made clear, that we are fundamentally nothing but a mere name, the foundations of which at death scatter to every wind. Look for yourself! Here is the famous dialogue:

"How is your reverence called? Bhante, what is your name?" "Your majesty, I am called Nāgasena; my fellow-monks, your majesty, address me as Nāgasena: but whether parents gave me the name Nāgasena, or Sūrasena, or Vīrasena, or Sīhasena, it is, nevertheless, your majesty, but a way of counting, a term, an appellation, a convenient designation, a mere name, this Nāgasena; for there is no person to be found."

Then said Milinda the king:

"Listen to me, my lords, ye five hundred Yonakas, and ye numerous monks! Nāgasena here says thus: 'There is no person here to be found.' Is it possible for me to assent to what he says?"

And Milinda the king spoke to the venerable Nāgasena as follows:—"Bhante Nāgasena, if there is no person to be found, who is it then furnishes you monks with the monkish requisites,—robes, food, bedding, and medicine, the reliance of the sick? who is it makes use of the same? who is it keeps the precepts? who is it applies himself to meditation? who is it realizes the Paths, the Fruits, and Nirvāna? who is it destroys life? who is it takes what is not given him? who is it commits immorality? who is it tells lies? who is it drinks intoxicating liquor? who is it commits the five crimes that constitute 'proximate karma?' In that case, there is no merit; there is no demerit; there is no one who does or causes to be done meritorious or demeritorious deeds; neither good nor evil deeds can have any fruit or result. Bhante Nāgasena, neither is he a murderer who kills a monk, nor can you monks, bhante Nāgasena, have any teacher, preceptor, or ordination. When you say, 'My fellow-monks, your majesty, address me as Nāgasena,' what then is this Nāgasena? Pray, bhante, is the hair of the head Nāgasena?"

"Nay, verily, your majesty."

"Is the hair of the body Nāgasena?"

"Nay, verily, your majesty."

"Are nails . . teeth . . skin . . flesh . . sinews . . bones . .

marrow of the bones . . kidneys . . heart . . liver . . pleura . . spleen . . lungs . . intestines . . mesentery . . stomach . . faeces . . bile . . phlegm . . pus . . blood . . sweat . . fat . . tears . . lymph . . saliva . . snot . . synovial fluid . . urine . . brain of the head Nāgasena?"

"Nay, verily, your majesty."

"Is the corporeal form Nāgasena?"

"Nay, verily, your majesty."

"Is sensation Nāgasena?"

"Nay, verily, your majesty."

"Is perception Nāgasena?"

"Nay, verily, your majesty."

"Are the activities of the mind Nāgasena?"

"Nay, verily, your majesty."

"Is consciousness Nāgasena?"

"Nay, verily, your majesty."

"Are then, bhante, corporeal form, sensation, perception, the activities of the mind, and consciousness unitedly Nāgasena?"

"Nay, verily, your majesty."

"Is it then, bhante, something besides corporeal form, sensation, perception, the activities of the mind and consciousness, which is Nāgasena?"

"Nay, verily, your majesty."

"Bhante, although I question you very closely, I fail to discover any Nāgasena. Verily, now, bhante, Nāgasena is a mere empty sound. What Nāgasena is there here? Bhante, you speak a falsehood, a lie: there is no Nāgasena."

Then the venerable Nāgasena spoke to Milinda the king as follows:—"Your majesty, you are a delicate prince, an exceedingly delicate prince; and if, your majesty, you walk in the middle of the day on hot sandy ground, and you tread on rough grit, gravel, and sand, your feet become sore, your body tired, the mind oppressed, and the body-consciousness suffers. Pray, did you come afoot, or riding?"

"Bhante, I do not go afoot: I came in a chariot."

"Your majesty, if you came in a chariot, declare to me the chariot. Pray, your majesty, is the pole the chariot?"

"Nay, verily, bhante."

"Is the axle the chariot?"

"Nay, verily, bhante."

"Are the wheels the chariot?"

"Nay, verily, bhante."

"Is the chariot-body the chariot?"

"Nay, verily, bhante."

"Is the banner-staff the chariot?"

"Nay, verily, bhante."

"Is the yoke the chariot?"

"Nay, verily, bhante."

"Are the reins the chariot?"

"Nay, verily, bhante."

"Is the goading-stick the chariot?"

"Nay, verily, bhante."

"Pray, your majesty, are pole, axle, wheels, chariot-body, banner-staff, yoke, reins and goad unitedly the chariot?"

"Nay, verily, bhante."

"Is it, then, your majesty something else besides pole, axle, wheels, chariot-body, banner-staff, yoke, reins, and goad which is the chariot?"

"Nay, verily, bhante."

"Your majesty, although I question you very closely, I fail to discover any chariot. Verily now, your majesty, the word chariot is a mere empty sound. What chariot is there here? Your majesty, you speak a falsehood, a lie: there is no chariot. Your majesty, you are the chief-king in all the continent of India; of whom are you afraid that you speak a lie? Listen to me, my lords, ye five hundred Yonakas, and ye numerous monks! Milinda the king here says thus: 'I came in a chariot' and being requested: 'Your majesty, if you came in a chariot, declare to me the chariot,' he fails to produce any chariot. Is it possible, pray, for me to assent to what he says?"

When he had thus spoken, the five hundred Yonakas applauded the venerable Nāgasena and spoke to Milinda the king as follows:

"Now, your majesty, answer, if you can."

Then Milinda the king spoke to the venerable Nāgasena as follows:

"Bhante Nāgasena, I speak no lie: the word 'chariot' is but a way of counting, term, appellation, convenient designation, and name for pole, axle, wheels, chariot-body, and banner-staff."

"Thoroughly well, your majesty, do you understand a chariot. In exactly the same way, your majesty, in respect of me, Nāgasena is but a way of counting, term, appellation, convenient designation, mere name for the hair of my head, hair of my body .. brain of the head, corporeal form, sensation, perception, the activities of the mind, and consciousness. But in the absolute sense is no person here to be found. Aud the nun Vajirā, your majesty, said as follows in the presence of the Blessed One:

> 'Even as the word of 'chariot' means
> That members join to frame a whole;
> So when the Groups appear to view,
> We use the phrase, 'A living being.'"[104]

As a matter of fact, not a few fall back precisely upon this dialogue when they wish to make out the goal of the Buddha's doctrine to be the absolute annihilation of man. Are they right? Let us again summon up the Manes of the Master. How would he speak on this question? "So then, after all, thou hast lost that heedfulness about which I particularly warned thee, hast indeed so completely lost it, foolish questioner, that now, at the end of all, thou rankest thy self with that class of men who, in philosophising, forget *themselves*. Formerly thou lookedst at them as at a curiosity, but now thou theyself hast lost all heedfulness, to such an extent that you even think it possible, that in searching for *what* I am, I myself might have forgotten *that* I am, that I must be, in some sense or the other; and that this fundamental, primordial fact remains, even if I perceive in regard to everything in the world that it cannot be my essence, that I cannot consist in anything within the world, that I therefore am *Nothing*. But with this little word *Nothing* you cannot come to terms; it embarrasses and perturbs you. But don't let it impose upon you; keep intact your heedfulness and your mental clearness in regard to it also, and very soon you will see how groundless was your perturbation, and how rash were the conclusions you drew from this little word."

Let us comply with this invitation of the Master. What is *Nothing?* As we saw, it is the antithesis of *Everything*. And what is *Everything?* As said above, the eye and forms, the ear and sounds, the nose and odours, the tongue and flavours, the body and tangibles, the mind (the organ of thought) and ideas. To whom is this not clear without further words? Who would not admire this astoundingly simple and nevertheless so extremely acute demarcation of being? Certainly our great philosophers also teach that everything that is, exists only with reference to *possible experience*, this statement as respects its contents coinciding with the definition given by the Buddha according to which the six senses, thought included, are the sole bearers of all possible experience. But how insipid thus abstractly given, does our formulation seem, when compared with the immediate obviousness of the Buddha's definition, the demonstrativeness of which cannot be surpassed!

But if we thus have such a self-evident definition of the notion of *Everything*, then the notion of *Nothing* also becomes completely luminous without further words: Because "*Nothing*" is only the antithesis of "*Everything*", therefore by *Nothing* we designate nothing more than the absence of all the elements out of which the notion of "Everything" is compounded. Hence, the answer to the question: "What is Nothing" is simply: "To see nothing more, to hear nothing more, to smell nothing more, to taste nothing more, to touch nothing more, to think nothing more: This is Nothing." Both questions: "What is Everything" and: "What is Nothing?" thereby have the same contents, the one in positive, the other in negative form. We find again the same thought in that other saying of the Buddha: "Here in consciousness everything is to be found"[105]. This means, as consciousness is the product of the respective activities of the senses: in visual consciousness, in auditory consciousness, in olfactory consciousness, in gustatory consciousness, in tactile consciousness, in mental consciousness, everything exists and is founded, and if you cease to see, to hear, to smell, and so forth, if you no longer see, hear, smell, taste, touch, think, then for you *everything* is annihilated, and only pure *Nothing* remains. But who would venture to assert that *this* Nothing was a real *Nothing*, absolute Nothing in every sense of the word, therefore no mere relative Nothing, no *nihil privativum*, but the veritable negative Nothing, the *nihil negativum?* Even this most complete Nothing that we are at all able to imagine, only expresses the annihilation of every function of sense, thinking included. Who does not feel without further saying that, as there are colours of which our eye is not susceptible, and which we therefore can only find out by way of chemistry, as for example, the ultra-violet rays; and as there are vibrations which we cannot perceive as sounds, so also there may be something lying behind all the activities of the senses, and of thinking, thus, something behind, or in, the so-called nothing? Indeed, if we again bring into play our heedfulness, if, in fact, we give close heed, we shall remember having already made the acquaintance of such a thing, as of the most evident thing in the world, namely, as *ourselves*. For we have learnt to know beyond doubt that ourselves, that is, our innermost essence, does not consist in the six sense activities and in their correlates, so that we must stand behind these; hence, there, where to our apprehension yawns Nothing.

This so much feared "You are nothing," thus ultimately only means what you know long since: You consist just as little in forms, sounds, odours, flavours, tangibles, and ideas, as in seeing, hearing, smelling, tasting, touching and thinking. You are nothing of all this, and therefore, since these are all the components of the world, of the universe, you are nothing belonging to the world. You are, in truth, beyond the world, beyond the universe; or, to express ourselves in the spirit of the Buddha: Everything is not your Self,—"the whole world is *anattā*."[106]

Of course Nāgasena also did not intend to tell king Milinda anything else. Both meet each other for the first time, and accordingly introduce themselves to each other. Nāgasena in a spirited manner makes use of the occasion to enlighten the king as to this entire representation being, like everything else in the world, nothing but illusion, and himself in truth, not to be found. For the king of course looked at him, according to the common opinion prevalent then the same as to-day, as at a *person*, that is, as at a substantial essence appearing in the fixed personality before him, as this personality or else as *in* it. The fundamental error of this view Nāgasena wishes to expose to him. Therefore he shows him that the real substratum of the notion of personality is nothing but a "heap of vital processes"—Saṅkhārā—appearing as a homogeneous organism, as the "body endowed with the six senses and with consciousness", just as the real substratum of the notion of carriage is formed by the several parts of the carriage put together in a certain manner, the entire content of the notion "person" on one side and "carriage" on the other, being thus in truth exhausted. If the "heap of vital processes," the "body endowed with the six senses and with consciousness" dissolves in death, then what was understood by the designation of "Nāgasena" has entirely and definitively come to an end, as the carriage has come to its end, when its component parts are burnt. Especially does no immaterial or spiritual substance, known to us so well as the soul, remain, but only—Nothing. But —and this is the chief thing, which Nāgasena, in his time, might assume to be understood, as self-evident, by the king, and therefore did not state expressly: *"All this am I not, this does not belong to me, this is not my Self."* Of his *real* Self Nāgasena says not a word in the dialogue. In exactly the same manner as the Buddha,—we shall soon see why—he always only explains to Milinda that what the king thinks to be his Self, is nothing but the unsubstantial ghost of Not-self, of *anattā*.

So I still exist, in spite of the expositions of Nāgasena, and though according to the Buddha himself, I am nothing, that is, *nothing belonging to this world.* For, as said above, we do not know any other Nothing, nay, we cannot even think of any other Nothing. Though already we may have a presentiment that this my real existence, is an existence of quite a different kind than that peculiar to the five groups. Accordingly, it is now evident how groundless was the embarrassment into which we let ourselves be flung, over the word *Nothing*; and that this embarrassment was only possible through want of heedfulness. On the other hand, it is evident how well-founded it was always to point out that by showing *what* I am not, the fact never can be denied *that* I am, that I must exist in some sense. Indeed, to state it for the last time: How confused a man must be who thinks it possible that a sound thinker—and this little will certainly not be denied to the Buddha even by his opponents—in a proof which ostentatiously confined itself to demonstrating to man what he is *not*, wherein he cannot consist, exhausting itself therefore in pointing out to him: "You are neither this nor that nor the other," in the end only wanted to prove: "Hence you are not at all, do not exist in any sense of the word!" For the whole argument proceeds on the self-evident assumption that he to whom it is addressed in reality must be present in some sense or another.*

But let us again bring proof of our contention by allowing the Buddha to speak for himself:

"There, ye monks, the instructed holy disciple, who has beheld the Noble Ones; is conversant with the Teaching of the Noble Ones, well trained in the Teaching of the Noble Ones; who has beheld Good Men, is conversant with the Teaching of Good Men, well trained in the Teaching of Good Men. Such an one does not regard body, sensation, perception, the activities of the mind, consciousness as himself; nor himself as similar to body, sensation, perception,

---

* This also is the literal meaning of *anattā*. The word does not mean "not *an* ego" but "not *my* ego"; therefore it presupposes the real existence of this my same ego. "What is transitory, is painful, what is painful, is *anattā, what is anattā, is not mine, this am I not, this is not my self.*" (Samyutta Nikāya, IV, p. 1.) The expression *anattā* is therefore an abbreviation, a symbol of this great formula. If we therefore wish correctly to understand the word *anattā,* we must always replace it by this great formula.

The essence of a thing is formed by that which may not be taken away from it without destroying it. In consequence of this, *every* reality has, of course, its own peculiar essence. So the plantain-tree, though having no *kernel,* has of course an essence in the given sense. This essence consists in the phyllodium sheaths rolled one over the other. Now man is also a reality, therefore an essence of man in the given sense must also exist. It is designed as the "*I*" as the "ego" or the "self." The question can therefore never be *if* there is such an *I,* such an ego or self, but only *wherein* this *I* or ego or self or human essence really *consists.*

the activities of the mind, consciousness; nor body, sensation, perception, the activities of the mind, consciousness as in himself; nor himself as in body, sensation, perception, the activities of the mind, consciousness."[107] Is it possible to read in these words that the whole essence of man is exhausted in these five groups? Do they not rather clearly illustrate the fact that the holy disciple *exists* as a self-evident presupposition, and only lay stress upon the fact that he is something essentially different from the five groups constituting his personality?

Perhaps this is expressed even more clearly in the following passage: "The earthy element, the watery element, the fiery element, the windy element, the element of space, the element of consciousness* I have conceived to be not the Self, and myself as not consisting in the earthy element, the watery element, the fiery element, the windy element, the element of space, the element of consciousness."[108] Is it not here expressly stated that the saint recognizes himself as standing beyond the five groups and thereby, beyond the world?

But if we want more proofs that the Buddha does not teach the nonsense of absolute Nihilism, proofs certainly not needed by any one who has recognized more or less within himself intuitively through deep contemplation that in his real essence he is not touched by the slow perishing of the five groups, and thus must be something essentially different from them, let us first turn to the following passage:

"The wandering ascetic Vacchagotta spoke thus to the Exalted One:

'How is this, dear Gotama: Is the *I* existent?'

Upon these words, the Exalted One kept silence.

'How now, dear Gotama? The *I* is not existent?'

Upon these words, the Exalted One again kept silence.

---

* The first five elements are the component parts of the bodily organism, *nāma-rūpa*, the six elements together constituting the "bodily organism together with consciousness."

Thereupon the wandering ascetic Vacchagotta rose from his seat and went away.

Not long after the wandering ascetic Vacchagotta had departed, the reverend Ānanda spoke thus to the Exalted One:

'O Lord, why did the Exalted One not explain himself upon this question of the wandering ascetic Vacchagotta?'

'If, Ānanda, I had answered to the question of the wandering ascetic Vacchagotta: 'Is the *I* existent?' 'The *I* is existent,' then, Ānanda, I had thereby sided with those ascetics and Brahmins who teach eternalism.* If, on the other hand, Ānanda, I had answered to the question of the wandering ascetic Vacchagotta: 'The *I* is not-existent,' then, Ānanda, I had thereby sided with those ascetics and Brahmins who teach annihilation.

'And if, Ānanda, I had answered to the question of the wandering ascetic Vacchagotta: 'The *I* is existent,' would this have been a means of causing to arise in him the insight: All phenomena are not the *I*?' **

'Nay, verily, O Lord.'

'But if, Ānanda, I had answered to the question of the wandering ascetic Vacchagotta: 'The *I* is not-existent,' then this, Ānanda, would have brought the confused wandering ascetic Vacchagotta into this still greater confusion: 'Formerly, my *I* was existent, but now it is not.' "*** [109]

In this passage, the Buddha expressly refuses to side with those ascetics and Brahmins who teach annihilation. He

* This means, the permanence of the Self *in time* as an individual soul.

** This alone is of value, all salvation consisting in being liberated from the component parts of Not-*I*.

*** Note that this passage is in the *Avyākata*-Saṃyutta, that means, in that part of the Canon which treats of what the Buddha has *not* revealed. He refuses also to reveal anything about the ego, especially whether it is correct to say:—"the ego exists" or—"the ego does not exist." He confines himself to explaining what in any case does *not* constitute our ego.

certainly knew why. For in his time too there was no lack of those shallow thinkers who are still so closely bound up with their personality that in their brains there is simply no room left for the idea of the ultra-mundaneness of their essence. Therefore, when they hear of the ultimate goal of the doctrine of Buddha being the definitive annihilation of the personality upon the death of the saint, they are only able to explain this as meaning the absolute annihilation of man. They only know the alternative of a personal *I* consisting in the five groups, or no *I* at all, and solve it in this way: The Buddha declares the five groups to be not the *I*, hence there is no *I* at all. Thus a saint would be a man who absolutely annihilates himself,—really, a curious kind of saint. Hence, each of them, hearing the Buddha's doctrine of salvation, must feel thus: "'Then I shall be cut off! Then I shall perish! Then I shall no more be!' And he grieves and mourns and laments and beats his breast in dire dismay." To make these confused brains harmless, the Buddha opposes to them the man who really understands his doctrine, who, confronted by the doctrine of the annihilation of personality "is not overcome by senseless trembling, not overcome by thoughts like this: 'Then I shall be cut off! Then I shall perish! Then I shall no more be!'"[110] He even in words of terrible earnest protests against the insinuation that he teaches annihilation: "To discover a monk the mind of whom is thus delivered, so that they could say: 'This is the substratum of the consciousness of the Tathāgata,' is impossible even for the gods, Indra and Brahma and Prajāpati included. And why so? Already even in this present life is the Accomplished One not to be found out, say I. And, monks, against me, thus teaching and preaching, many ascetics and brahmins falsely, groundlessly, untruly, in defiance of fact, bring accusation thus: 'A destroyer is this ascetic Gotama. He preaches the cutting off, the destruction.

the nullification of the present living being.' But for what I am not, for what I say not, for that these good ascetics and brahmins thus falsely, groundlessly, untruly, in defiance of fact impeach me. For, O monks, as before so also now, I preach only Suffering and the cessation of Suffering."[111] To these words he in another passage[112] appends the following: "In one connection, Sīha, whoso speaks the truth about me may say: 'Annihilation the ascetic Gotama teaches; for the purpose of annihilation he propagates his doctrine; and thereby he directs his disciples.' In what connection now, could a man telling the truth, thus speak about me? I teach the annihilation of craving, the annihilation of hatred, the annihilation of delusion, I teach the annihilation of manifold evil things that do not pertain to salvation." Certainly, one might add that we do not consist in craving, hatred and delusion, nor in those other manifold evil things; but this statement the Buddha, as speaking to reasonable men, may have thought superfluous.

Especially clear and beyond any misunderstanding is also the following dialogue wherein we find a summing up of all that we have hitherto been saying. In the mind of a monk called Yamaka the following wicked heresy had sprung up: "Thus do I understand the doctrine taught by the Blessed One, that on the dissolution of the body the monk, who is liberated from the influences, is annihilated, perishes and is no more after death."

"Say not so, brother Yamaka. Do not traduce the Blessed One; for it is not well to traduce the Blessed One. The Blessed One would never say that on the dissolution of the body the saint who is liberated from the influences is annihilated, perishes and is no more after death."

But, as nevertheless Yamaka persisted obstinately in adhering to his pestiferous delusion, the monks told the venerable Sāriputta, the greatest of the disciples of the

Buddha, "the disciple resembling the master, as it is said."[113] Sāriputta undertakes the correction of Yamaka in this way:

"Is the report true, brother Yamaka, that the following wicked view has sprung up in your mind: 'Thus do I understand the doctrine taught by the Blessed One, that on the dissolution of the body the monk, who is delivered from all influences, is annihilated, perishes, and does not exist after death?'"

"Even so, brother, do I understand the doctrine."

"What think you, brother Yamaka? Is the corporeal form permanent or transitory?"

"It is transitory, brother."

"And that which is transitory—is it painful or pleasurable?"

"It is painful, brother."

"And that which is transitory, painful, and liable to change—is it possible to say of it: 'This is mine; this am I; this is my Ego'?"

"Nay, verily, brother."

"Is sensation, perception, are the activities of the mind, is consciousness, permanent or transitory?"

"It is transitory, brother."

"And that which is transitory—is it painful, or is it pleasurable?"

"It is painful, brother."

"And that which is transitory, painful, and liable to change—is it possible to say of it: 'This is mine; this am I; this is my Ego'?"

"Nay, verily, brother."

"Accordingly, brother Yamaka, as respects all corporeal form whatsoever ... as respects all sensation whatsoever—as respects all perception whatsoever—as respects all activities of the mind whatsoever ... as respects all consciousness whatsoever, past, future, or present, be it subjective or existing outside, gross or subtle, mean or exalted, far or near, the correct view in the light of the highest knowledge is as follows: 'This is not mine; this am I not; this is not my Ego.'

"Perceiving this, brother Yamaka, the learned and noble disciple conceives an aversion for the corporeal form, conceives an aversion for sensation, conceives an aversion for perception, conceives an aversion for the activities of the mind, conceives an aversion for consciousness. And in conceiving this aversion he becomes divested of the influences, and by the absence of the influences he becomes free; and when he is free, he becomes aware that he is free.

"What think you, brother Yamaka? Do you consider the corporeal form as the Perfected One?"

"Nay, verily, brother."

"Do you consider sensation—perception—the activities of the mind—consciousness, as the Perfected One?"

"Nay, verily, brother."

"What think you, brother Yamaka? Do you consider the Perfected One as comprised in the corporeal form?"

"Nay, verily, brother."

"Do you consider the Perfected One as separated from the corporeal form?"

"Nay, verily, brother."

"Do you consider the Perfected One as comprised in sensation ... in perception ... in the activities of the mind ... in consciousness?"

"Nay, verily, brother."

"Do you consider the Perfected One as separated from sensation ... from perception ... from the activities of the mind ... from consciousness?"

"Nay, verily, brother."

"What think you, brother Yamaka? Are the corporeal form, sensation, perception, the activities of the mind, and consciousness unitedly the Perfected One?"

"Nay, verily, brother."

"What think you, brother Yamaka? Do you consider the Perfected One to be without body, without sensation, without perception, without activities of the mind, without consciousness?"

"Nay, verily, brother." *

"Considering now, brother Yamaka, that you fail to make out and establish the Perfected One *even in the present existence,* is it reasonable for you to say: 'Thus do I understand the doctrine taught by the Blessed One, that on the dissolution of the body the monk who is delivered from the influences, is annihilated, perishes, and is no more after death'?"

"Brother Sāriputta, it was because of my ignorance that I held this wicked view; but now that I have listened to the doctrinal instruction of the venerable Sāriputta, I have abandoned that wicked view and completely understood the doctrine."

"But if others were to ask you, brother Yamaka, as follows: 'Brother Yamaka, the monk, who is a saint and delivered from the influences, what becomes of him on the dissolution of the body, after death?' what would you reply, brother Yamaka, if you were asked that question?"

"Brother, if others were to ask me thus, then I would reply, as follows: 'Brethren, the corporeal form was transitory and that which was transitory was painful and that which was painful has ceased and disappeared. The sensation ... perception ... the activities of the mind ... consciousness was transitory, and that which was transitory was painful, and that which was painful has ceased and disappeared.' Thus would I reply, brother, if I were asked that question."

"Well said! well said! brother Yamaka. Come now, brother

* Of course the five groups, as long as we adhere to them, are qualities belonging to us, but not *essential* qualities. They have nothing to do with our real essence. Accordingly there results the following: As long as I adhere to them *I* am of course not without them, but if I let them go, I am thereby not touched in my essence.—Later on, we shall speak more at length about this.

Yamaka, I will give you an illustration that you may still better comprehend this matter.

"Suppose, brother Yamaka, there were a householder, or a son of a househoulder, rich, wealthy, and affluent, and thoroughly well guarded, and some man were to become unfriendly, inimical and hostile to him, and were to wish to kill him. And suppose it were to occur to this man as follows: 'This householder, or son of a householder, is rich, wealthy, and affluent, and thoroughly well guarded. It would not be easy to kill him by violence. What if now I were to ingratiate myself with him and then kill him? And suppose he were to draw near to that householder, or son of a householder, and say as follows: 'Lord, I would fain enter your service.' And suppose the householder, or son of a householder, were to admit him into his service; and the man were to be his servant, rising before him and retiring after him, willing and obliging and pleasant spoken. And suppose the householder, or son of a householder, were to treat him as a friend, were to treat him as a comrade, and repose confidence in him. And suppose then, brother, that when that man judged that the householder, or son of a householder, had acquired thorough confidence in him, he were to get him into some secluded spot and kill him with a sharp weapon.

"What think you, brother Yamaka? When that man drew near to that householder, or son of a householder, and said as follows: 'Lord, I would fain enter your service,' was he not a murderer, though not recognized as such?"

"And also when he was his servant, rising before him and retiring after him, willing and obliging and pleasant spoken, was he not a murderer, though not recognized as such?

"And also when he got him into a secluded spot and killed him with a sharp weapon, was he not a murderer, though not recognized as such?"

"Even so, brother."

"In exactly the same way, brother, the ignorant, unconverted man, who is not a follower of noble disciples, not conversant with the Noble Doctrine, not disciplined in the Noble Doctrine, not a follower of good people, not conversant with the Doctrine held by good people, not trained in the Doctrine held by good people, not disciplined in the Doctrine held by good people, considers the corporeal form as the Ego, or the Ego as of the nature of the corporeal form, or the corporeal form as comprised in the Ego, or the Ego as comprised in the corporeal form. He considers the sensation ... perception ... the activities of the mind ... consciousness as the Ego, or the Ego as consisting in them, or themselves as comprised in the Ego, or the Ego as comprised in them.

"He does not recognize the fact that the corporeal form is transitory. He does not recognize the fact that sensation ... perception ... the activities of the mind ... consciousness are transitory.

"He does not recognize the fact that the corporeal form ... sensation ... perception ... the activities of the mind ... consciousness are painful.

"He does not recognize the fact, that the corporeal form ... sensation ... perception ... the activities of the mind ... consciousness are not the Ego.

"He does not recognize the fact, that the corporeal form ... sensation, perception ... the activities of the mind ... consciousness are due to causes.

"He does not recognize the fact, that the corporeal form ... sensation ... perception ... the activities of the mind ... consciousness are murderers.*

---

* This means, in regard to the illustration given before, he takes the five groups of grasping to be his friend, whereas they are in truth his enemy, bringing death to him.

"And he seeks after the corporeal form, attaches himself to it, and makes the affirmation that it is his Ego. And he seeks after sensation . . . perception . . . the activities of the mind . . . consciousness, attaches himself to them, and makes the affirmation that it is his Ego. And these five groups of grasping, sought after and become attached, long inure to his detriment and misery.

"But the learned and noble disciple, brother, who is a follower of noble disciples, conversant with the Noble Doctrine, disciplined in the Noble Doctrine, a follower of good people, conversant with the Doctrine held by good people, disciplined in the Doctrine held by good people, does not consider the corporeal form as the Ego, nor the Ego as of the nature of the corporeal form, nor the corporeal form as comprised in the Ego, nor the Ego as comprised in the corporeal form. He does not consider sensation . . . perception . . . the activities of the mind . . . consciousness as the Ego, nor the Ego as consisting in them, nor themselves as comprised in the Ego, nor the Ego as comprised in them.

"He recognizes the fact, that the corporeal form . . . sensation . . . perception . . . the activities of the mind . . . consciousness are transitory.

"He recognizes the fact, that the corporeal form . . . sensation . . . perception . . . the activities of the mind . . . consciousness are painful.

"He recognizes the fact, that the corporeal form . . . sensation . . . perception . . . the activities of the mind . . . consciousness are not the Ego.

"He recognizes the fact, that the corporeal form . . . sensation . . . perception . . . the activities of the mind . . . consciousness are due to causes.

"He recognizes the fact, that the corporeal form . . . sensation . . . perception . . . the activities of the mind . . . consciousness are murderers.

"And he does not seek after the corporeal form ... sensation ... perception ... the activities of the mind ... consciousness, nor attach himself to it, nor make the affirmation that it is his Ego. And the not seeking after, the not becoming attached to these Five Groups of Grasping, long inures to his well-being and happiness."[114]

Thus in this dialogue, in complete harmony with our exposition, it is presupposed as self-evident that the delivered saint exists, in whatever way he may do so. But on the other hand it is also made plain wherein he cannot possibly consist, that is, in the five groups constituting personality. The definitive annihilation of these five groups happens in death. Hence, to the saint the process we call death is nothing but the annihilation of those things that are, because they belong to this world, transitory, painful, due to causes and therefore do not form his real essence, his true Ego. Only what is fundamentally alien to him has "come to annihilation." This relationship is fundamentally misunderstood by the ignorant, unconverted man, who brings the components of his personality into relation to his real essence, obstinately seeking them as if they were his Ego. But just thereby he loses himself completely in his personality, so completely as to be entirely absorbed into it. Hence he looks upon himself as doomed to death: personality in its five components becomes a murderer bringing death to him, more especially a murderer of the state alone proper to us, of freedom from these five groups, a state which, as we shall see later on, is one of inexpressible peace. This thought, by the way, finds expression in those other words: "Whoso, O brethren, does not taste of the insight into the body, truly does not taste the imperishable. He alone who tastes the insight into the body, truly tastes the imperishable."[115]

Finally, the two following sayings of the Buddha may be quoted in which he solemnly announces the existence of the realm of freedom from suffering, that alone in truth is proper to us, and must therefore be looked upon as our real home:

"*There is*, ye monks, something not born, not due to causes, not created, not originated. If, ye monks, this something not born, not due to causes, not created, not originated, did not exist, then a getting out of this born, this due to causes, this created, this originated could not be found. But because, ye monks, there is something not born, not due to causes, not created, not originated, therefore a getting out of the born, the due to causes, the created, the originated may be found.

"*There is*, ye monks, that realm where there is neither earth nor water, neither fire nor air, neither the realm of infinite space nor the realm of infinite consciousness, nor the realm of nothingness nor the realm of neither perception nor yet non-perception, neither this world nor the other one, nor both, neither moon nor sun. This, ye monks, I call neither coming nor going nor standing nor perishing nor originating. Without support, without progress, without basis is this; even this is the end of suffering.

"Verily, difficult to behold is the Non-ego; for not easy to behold is truth."[116]

Thus man exists, independent of his personality, and also after it is annihilated: This is the tremendous culmination of the doctrine of the Buddha, which may be won to on the basis of our own intuitive insight.*

Though this fundamental verity of the Doctrine of the Buddha stands out in the sharpest outlines, nevertheless from the passages in the Discourses, already quoted, we can see that the Buddha and his disciples obviously and deliberately evade making any positive statement as to the condition of

* It may be won by seeing through the realm of the Non-ego: "Difficult to behold verily, is the Non-ego," namely, in its quality as not our Ego.

the Perfected One after death, that is, after the personality is completely cast off, and thereby, as to our own essence independent of personality. Always and without exception they talk about it only in negative expressions; the Buddha even teaching that in a true monk not even the thought of the Ego should arise. This circumstance for people lacking understanding has become the chief argument for imputing to the Buddha the monstrosity of teaching the absolute annihilation of man upon the death of the saint, notwithstanding his repeated insistence that what perishes in death is only the components of the not-self. For him, however, who is able to follow the train of his thoughts, this declining of all and every positive definition of the real essence of man—what *we* name thus, is only the *apparent* man—is clear without further ado. The reason of this we already know. It lies in this, that the *true* man, as at the death of the saint he goes forth, entirely pure and liberated from all the stains of personality, is beyond the world and thereby in a realm forever inaccessible to knowledge. Thereby for knowledge he is nothing; but we must again lay stress upon his being nothing only for knowledge, that is, for seeing, hearing, smelling, tasting, touching and thinking, his nothingness being thereby reduced to his being nothing *knowable*. But where the veil of nothingness sinks down upon knowledge, there every positive definition, even that of being, comes to an end; yea, there is even no room left for the mere word "I" in its positive form. A little reflection will make this clear.

Here we must again remember the basic elucidation which Schopenhauer has furnished on the origin of notions. According to him, they are nothing originally real, but only an artificial product of reason distilled from perception. Therefore their contents are only of things given in perception, that is, of the world of the senses. Therefore they can and may only be immanently, but never transcendently, used. This is, as a rule, generally overlooked even by those who have gained this insight abstractly, as far as the fundamental notions of the *I* and of *being* are concerned. Especially in regard to the notion of being holds good what Schopenhauer blames the Germans for: "Before certain words, such as *right, liberty, goodness, being* (this insignificant infinitive of the copula), the German becomes quite dizzy. Suddenly he gets into a sort of delirium and begins to utter empty, high-sounding phrases, stringing the vaguest and therefore the hollowest notions artificially together, instead of fixing his eyes upon reality and looking at the real things and relations from which those notions have been abstracted, and which therefore constitute their only true content."

Let us therefore soberly formulate the contents of the notion "being."

To give a judgment, means, to give or to deny a predicate to a subject. This relation of the predicate to the subject is expressed by the copula "it is—it is not." In this manner, more particularly every verb may be expressed by means of its participle. Therefore the meaning of the copula is that the predicate should be thought of as connected with the subject, and nothing more. Now all predicates that can ever be attached to a subject are conditioned by experience, that means, every possible predicate is mediated through one of the six senses, and belongs to the sphere of one or other of these. For the six senses and their objects are, as we have seen, everything. The most general and ultimate predicates that may be given or denied to a subject are therefore seeing, hearing, smelling, tasting, touching and thinking. Only to these fundamental predicates, therefore, may the copula "to be" ultimately relate: I am a seeing, hearing, smelling, tasting, touching, thinking one. It makes no difference, if this is positively expressed, or if the copula seems to be used independently, thus: "I am, you are, he is," as it must be supplemented by "a seeing, hearing . . . thinking one." At least the copula must attribute the latter predicate, thinking, to the subject, as: I think, therefore I am, *i. e.* a thinking one. If I annul all these predicates, more particularly, thinking, then the copula "to be" loses every content; it becomes "a mere word within the brain," to which nothing corresponds, that means, it becomes itself nothing. Now, the holy one in death does indeed throw away, together with the six organs of sense, all seeing, hearing, smelling, tasting, touching and thinking. Accordingly it is senseless to declare him to be, simply because all being consists only in seeing, hearing, smelling, tasting, touching and thinking.

But it would be just as wrong to declare the delivered saint *not* to be. Certainly, he is no more in being in the proper sense of the word, he is no more a seeing, hearing, smelling, tasting, touching and thinking one, and thereby he has vanished so far as our powers of apprehension go, which are able to move only in this sixfold direction, and has become *nothing*. But as we saw above, this being which alone is comprehensible for us is not *being in itself*, but only a certain kind of being, just as our notion of Nothing is not an absolute, but only a relative nothing, only nothing for our apprehension. But man, from want of heedfulness identifying himself wholly and completely with that form of being, which consists in the six activities of the senses, is accustomed to take the notion of non-being not in its proper and correct meaning as a mere relative non-being, consisting in the absence of all sense activity, but as non-being in the absolute sense of the word, conceiving in the same manner the notion of nothing in its widest sense, as absolute nothing. Thus he extends the notions of nothing and non-being beyond the realm from which they are abstracted and for which therefore they only are valid. Instead of using them immanently, he uses them transcendently, and thus he arrives at the grave paralogism that with the ceasing of being consisting in the six activities of the senses, pure non-being, absolute nothingness takes place. To avoid this paralogism, we may not say that the redeemed saint is not, though he has become nothing to our apprehension.

The case, briefly, is as follows: The copula "to be" is the widest conception abstracted from experience, formed by reason for the purpose of giving or denying a predicate to the subject. Its application is therefore not permitted from the moment when a subject destitute of all predicates, that is, free from all seeing, hearing, smelling, tasting, touching and thinking, comes into question. Because here is no predicate at all that might be attributed to this mere subjective, even the copula "to be" which is merely meant to express that along with the subject some predicate must be thought, has no longer any meaning. But by becoming divested of its predicates, this subjective something, of course, does not itself become nothing, even though it may have ceased to exist as subject, that is, as bearer of these predicates, at least, not if, as here, all these predicates, as we have already seen, do not essentially belong to it and are therefore, at bottom, something alien to it. But we cannot any longer conceive it, because what we are able to conceive was nothing but these predicates from which it is now free.* Here, then, we find ourselves confronted by a kind of exis-

* The apparatus of our faculty of apprehension is only adapted to these predicates and therefore exclusively directed towards them, thus, towards the external, towards the components of the *not*-self. Therefore it is incapable of casting light upon our own essence which stands behind them: "Outwards the Self-Existent bored the holes, therefore man may look outwards but not into the inner self." (Kathaka Upanishad 4, 1.)—The same thought is expressed by Schopenhauer as follows: "The ego is the dark point in consciousness, as, on the retina it is exactly the entrance point of the optic nerve that is blind, as the brain itself is quite insensitive, as the body of the sun itself is dark, and as the eye sees everything with the exception of itself. Our faculty of apprehension *is wholly directed outwards* . . . Therefore everybody knows himself only as an individual . . . *But if he were able to become conscious of what he is besides and apart of this, he would willingly let go his individuality, and smile at the tenacity of his adherence to it.*"

tence that in *our* sense is no longer existence, we have arrived at the portals of the uncognizable, the transcendental: No eye can see it, no ear hear it, no nose smell it, no tongue taste it, no touching touch it, no brain think it any more; and because the subjective within us thus lies beyond all perception—"there is a refuge beyond this sensual world" [117]—therefore no conception and consequently no word, fits it. The Buddha himself expounds this train of thought in the Dīghanikāya XV as follows: First, he explains that we cannot in any way assert our true ego to consist in sensations, we cannot say that it is sentient in consequence of its inner essence, as sensations themselves again are conditioned through the sensual activities of the corporeal organism which obviously is alien to our essence, and are only generated through these activities, therefore only arise within us as something alien. After this, he speaks of the only possible assumption now remaining, namely, that our ego must be free from sensations, and then proceeds in this strain: "To somebody, Ānanda, who said: 'Not within myself is the sensation, free from sensation is my ego' it might be answered thus: 'But, brother, where there is no longer any sensibility, can there be an 'I am'?" To this question Ānanda answers: "Certainly not, Lord." Thus the Buddha here expressly declares that the copula "to be" possesses meaning only within the realm of sensations as within the realm of possible perception, the extremest, most comprehensive predicate that by its means can be brought into connection with the subject, being only sensation. If we have rid ourselves of sensation, it can no longer be said that our ego *is*.*

---

* As regards the details of this deduction, the following is to be noted: "Sensation does not belong to me, therefore I have to abandon it," this is correct. "Therefore I am without sensations," this is already wrong, as there is a touch of something positive concealed in this sentence, namely: I am, though without sensations. We are only able to say: I must *become* without sensations; or: The saint has made himself free from sensation.

But if thus even the most all-embracing conception man is at all able to form, that of being, cannot be applied to our true essence, then naturally *every* view pertaining to it is recognized as inapplicable, even as impossible: "If, Ānanda, a monk whose mind is set free, were asked: 'Does a Perfected One exist after death?'—that were a view and not becoming. Or: Does a Perfected One not exist after death?—that were a view and therefore not becoming. Or: Does a Perfected One exist and not exist beyond death?—that were a view and therefore not becoming. Or: Does a Perfected One neither exist nor not exist after death?—this were a view and therefore not becoming. And why so? So far, Ānanda, as a term reaches, so far as the path of this term reaches, so far as a discussion reaches, so far as the way of this discussion reaches, so far as a mutual understanding reaches, so far as the way of this mutual understanding reaches, so far as wisdom reaches, so far as the realm of wisdom reaches, so far as a circle extends, so far as the circle can exist: just so far can the circle exist.*—In

* This means: So far as the domain of views extends, so far can those views exist. Here, however, that domain is left behind.—Thus, especially unbecoming would be the view that the redeemed one remained at least identical with himself, thus, the conception of *identity:* Because of the redeemed one it cannot even be said, "He is;" therefore, still less can it be said: "He is something identical with himself." Neither is there anything at all identical with itself, within the world—personality, especially, is nothing of this kind—nor yet may my true essence be defined as such. For the conception of identity also, as abstracted from experience, presupposes a sequence of changes, and thereby at least two moments of time wherein something shall be identical with itself. But in the redeemed one all change, and therewith also, time, has been done away. As long as he is alive, certainly there is present the *appearance* of something identical with itself, because in his innermost depth he remains untouched by the succession of changes. But that this is indeed only seeming, and that, even during the lifetime of the Delivered One, in the strictest sense, there can be no talk of a persisting in itself, becomes clear at his death, from which time onward, because of the ceasing of all time, the very expression "to persist" has no more meaning. Thereby it is established that even in his lifetime also he cannot have been a persisting being in the strict meaning of the word, death not having touched him but only the component parts of his non-ego. Therefore also the conception of persistence or of identity is not to the point; the fact itself can always only be correctly characterized by negative expressions, such as "changeless," "deathless."

such insight the monk is delivered. But to say, of a monk, who has been so delivered by insight:—'He knows not, he sees not'—that were a view, and thus not becoming."[118] For the rest, there is only—silence:

"Om, Amitaya! measure not with words
Th' Immeasurable, nor sink the plumb of thought
Into the Fathomless! Who asks doth err,
Who answers, errs. Say naught!"[119]

Or, as it is said in the Canon itself: "As the flame swept away by force of the wind vanishes and cannot be designated by any word, just so the wise delivered from the organism (*nāmakāva*) vanishes, and cannot be designated by any word.

"For the vanished one there is no measure; that whereby he might be designated no longer exists; where all phenomena have ceased, there also all possibilities of naming are gone."*[120]

Very acute, and quite in the sense of the Buddha, are Schelling's remarks on this point: "In so far as the ego is eternal, it has no duration at all; for duration can only be thought of in relation to objects. We speak of the eternity of duration, of sempiternity, that is, of an existence lasting through all time, but eternity in its pure sense *(aeternitas)* is existence *outside of time. The pure and original form of eternity lies within the ego.*"

* If we consider that what is called god—at least in so far as this god is internally experienced, thus, apart from his character as a world-creating power—is nothing but our own innermost essence, as becomes especially clear in reading the Christian mystics, then without further ado we shall perceive the entire consonance of the following words of Schopenhauer with our foregoing exposition: "Of such a god we can have no other theology than that which Dionysius Areopagita gives in his Theologia Mystica, which consists merely in the explanation that about god all predicates may be denied, but not a single one may be affirmed, because he is beyond all being and all knowledge. Dionysius calls this 'the Beyond,'—the Buddha speaking of the 'other shore' - and describes it as something entirely inaccessible to our knowledge. This theology is the only true one, only it contains nothing at all. It expressly tells and teaches nothing, and consists only in the declaration that it knows this very well, and that it cannot be otherwise."

Compare, for the rest, the following words of Angelus Silesius:

"I am a blissful thing, a non-thing tho' I be;
To everything that is, 't is an unknown mystery,"

as also the passage from Merswin's *Book of the Nine Rocks:* "Tell me, my darling, how do they talk about these men, or how are these men called who have seen into their origin?"—"I will tell you. You must know that these men have lost their names and have become nameless, forever removed from the ocean of this world,"—the Saṁsāra.

"Is there, O Brother, anything left, after the six realms of consciousness have been annihilated and become extinguished without a remainder?"

"Just leave it alone, brother."

"Is there nothing left, O Brother, after the six realms of consciousness have been annihilated and become extinguished without a remainder?"

"Just leave it alone, brother."

"Is there, O Brother, something left and something not left, after the six realms of consciousness have been annihilated and become extinguished without a remainder?"

"Just leave it alone, brother."

"Or is there, O Brother, neither something left nor something not left, after the six realms of consciousness have been annihilated and become extinguished without a remainder?"

"Just leave it alone, brother."

"To my question 'Is there, O Brother, anything left, after the six realms of consciousness have been annihilated and become extinguished without a remainder' you reply: 'Just leave it alone, brother.' To my question: 'Is there nothing left, O Brother, after the six realms of consciousness have been annihilated and become extinguished without a remainder' you reply: 'Just leave it alone, brother.' To my question: 'Is there, O Brother, something left and something not left—or neither something left nor something not left, after the six realms of consciousness have been annihilated and become extinguished' you reply: 'Just leave it alone, brother.' But how, O Brother, shall the meaning of these words be understood?"

"To say: 'After the six realms of consciousness have been annihilated and become extinguished without a remainder, then there is something left,'—this, O Brother, would mean to explain something inexplicable. To say: 'After the six realms of consciousness have been annihilated and become extinguished without a remainder, nothing is left—something is left and something is not left—neither something is left nor something is not left,'—this would mean to explain something inexplicable. As far, O Brother, as the six realms of consciousness extend, just as far extends the expanse of the world *(papañca)*; and as far as the expanse of the world extends, just as far do the six realms of consciousness extend. With the annihilation and extinction of the six realms of consciousness without a remainder, O Brother, the expanse of the world is extinguished, the expanse of the world comes to rest." [121]

"Does, O Reverend One, the Perfected One exist beyond death?"

"The Exalted One, O Mahārāja, has not revealed that the Perfected One exists beyond death."

"Thus, the Perfected One does not exist beyond death, O Reverend One?"

"Neither this, O Mahārāja, has the Exalted One revealed, that the Perfected One does not exist beyond death."

"Thus, Reverend One, the Perfected One exists beyond death and at the same time does not exist beyond death—or neither exists beyond death, nor does not exist beyond death?"

The answer was always the same: "The Exalted One has not revealed this." *

"But what is the cause, Reverend One, what is the reason, why the Exalted One has not revealed this?"

"Your Majesty, let me now put a question to yourself," the nun answered, "and as it seems good to your Majesty, so do you make answer. What do you think, O Mahārāja, have you got a calculator or a mint-master or a teller, who might be able to count the sands of the Ganges, who might be able to say: 'So many grains of sand, or so many hundreds or thousands of grains of sand are there'?"

"That have I not, Reverend One."

* He only revealed that he is not touched by death.

"Or have you got a calculator, or a mint-master, or a teller who might be able to measure the water of the great Ocean, who might be able to say: So many quarts of water, or so many hundreds or thousands or hundreds of thousands of quarts of water are contained therein?"

"That have I not, Reverend One."

"And why not?"

"Because the great ocean is deep, immeasurable, unfathomable."

"Even so is it, O Mahārāja, if you wish to understand the essence of the Perfected One according to the predicates of corporeality, of sensation, of perception, of the activities of the mind, of consciousness. In the Perfected One, this corporeality, this sensation, this perception, these activities of the mind, this consciousness, would be extinguished, their root would be annihilated, like a palm-tree it would be cut off and flung away, so that it would not be able to develop again in future time. The Perfected One, O Mahārāja, is free from this, that his essence might be counted with numerals of the corporeal world: *he is deep, immeasurable, unfathomable like the great ocean.* That the Perfected One exists beyond death, does not apply; that the Perfected One does not exist beyond death, does not apply; that the Perfected One neither exists nor does not exist beyond death, neither does this apply."[122]

In short: Nothing in the world any longer applies. The Perfected One in his purity, rid of the dross of his personality, thus beyond death, is something uncognizable, is inscrutable; but he exists, he still is, namely, something inscrutable. Certainly, in attaining this result, the firm ground that supports all our knowledge, the apprehensible, seems to tremble and give way, just because it lies beyond this. Nevertheless it indicates to us the direction in which the thing apprehended lies hidden, the thing itself remaining veiled inasmuch as it does not enter apprehension, and therefore to this appears as nothing.

And because it appears to ordinary apprehension as nothing, therefore there is no longer any room left even for the mere *thought* of the *I* in its positive form. For thoughts may only be aroused by objects of apprehension, which latter are all not the *I*. But as a matter of fact, no thought oftener arises in us that that of *I*, nay, it accompanies all our thoughts as the logical *I*: *I* see, *I* hear, and so on. Therefore it is just as essential to become clear as to the origin and content of this thought of *I* as it was essential to come to clearness about the thought of *being*.

This is only possible, if we may at least temporarily reach the height of insight gained by a Perfected One, who enjoys the view of *anattā* in its entire purity. Let us imagine him sitting in deepest seclusion in some lonely place, having dismissed the entire outer world from his mind and in the highest degree of concentration holding it directed exclusively upon the machinery of his personality, thus remaining in contemplation of the origin and dissolution of the five groups of grasping: "Such is the body, such is the origin of the body, such is the dissolution of the body; such is sensation, such is the origin of sensation, such is the dissolution of sensation; such is perception, such is the origin of perception, such is the dissolution of perception; such are the activities of the mind, such is the origin of the activities of the mind, such is the dissolution of the activities of the mind; such is consciousness, such is the origin of consciousness, such is the dissolution of consciousness."[123] Where, in such contemplation, is room left for the *I*? From this standpoint the whole machinery of personality shows itself to be merely a whirl of processes, which to the spectator seem something so alien to his essence, that in regarding them, "temptations to think in the form of 'I' and 'My'"* no long arise, but within him, even in regard to his apprehending activity itself,

* *ahañkāra-mamañkāra-anusayā.*

the only thoughts aroused discharge themselves in the great formula: "This does not belong to me, this am I not, this is not my self."

In quite another manner does the "uninstructed man of the world" behave in regard to the machinery of his personality. He feels himself so intimately interwoven with it, or, as the Buddha says "the inclination to believe in personality adheres to him" to such an extent that he imagines himself to consist entirely in it. Therefore in observing the incessant origination and dissolving of the five groups, he imagines that he sees himself incessantly originating and dissolving; and accordingly he says: "*I* originate, *I* dissolve, *I* feel, *I* perceive," and so on.

Thus we arrive at the thought of our *I* only if we see ourselves bound up with the five groups of grasping, that is, bound up with our personality, and then lose ourselves in them, incapable of opposing ourselves to them with estranged regard:

"If, ye disciples, something is there, if we grasp something, if we are devoted to something, then this doctrine originates: 'This is my *I*, this is the world, and this my *I* will become permanent after my death, will be lasting, existing on, immutable.'—If, ye disciples, the body is there, if we grasp the body, if we are devoted the body, then this doctrine originates: 'This—[that is, the body]—is my *I*, this is the world, and this my *I*—[therefore the body]—will after my death become permanent, lasting, existing on, immutable.'

"If sensation, perception, the activities of the mind, consciousness are there, if we grasp sensation, perception, the activities of the mind, consciousness, if we are devoted to them, then this doctrine originates: 'This—[meaning sensation, perception, the activities of the mind and consciousness]—is my *I*, this is the world, and this my *I* will, after my death, become permanent, lasting, existing on, immutable.'

"What do you think, ye disciples: Is the body, sensation, perception, are the activities of the mind, is consciousness, permanent or transient?"—"They are transient, O Lord."—"But what is transient, is this painful or pleasureable?".—"Painful, O Lord."—"Now if we do not grasp what proves itself to be transient, painful, subject to all vicissitudes—may then this doctrine arise: 'This—[personality as the totality of the five groups]—is my *I*, this is the world, and this my *I* will become after my death permanent, lasting, existing on, immutable'?"—"Certainly not, O Lord." *

According to this, the *I*-idea is based upon a misunderstanding of our relation to our personality, having its origin ultimately in the fact that in the subjective—it will be

---

* The same idea as is also expressed in the following passage, often misunderstood: "If, monks, there were the Ego, would it not also be (possible to say): 'Belonging to my ego?'"—"It would, Lord."—"But since, ye monks, the ego, and anything belonging to the ego, is not to be found really and truly what of the theory: 'This is the world, this is the ego, this I shall become in death, permanent, stable, lasting, existing on, ever the same?' Is not such an idea an utterly and entirely foolish idea?" "How should it not be an utterly and entirely foolish idea?" (Majjh. N. I. p. 138.)

As results from this passage, the Buddha does not say: "The ego *is* not—this he positively declines to do (see above, p. 163)—; but he here again says that at all events the conception of being cannot be applied to the ego, for the reason that the ego cannot be *found out*. And because the ego cannot be found out, and therefore does not at all exist in the world, therefore of course it can neither be "permanent, lasting, existing, ever the same." For these conceptions also designate nothing but a certain state *within* the world.—The reality of the ego is further also fixed in the course of the quoted twenty-second Discourse of the Majj. Nik. with all emphasis, in the grand elaboration of the simile in wich the Buddha confronts us with our entire personality which he shows to be as entirely foreign to us as the branches and grasses of a forest are. (See above p. 149.)

The supra-mundaneness of the *I* is very clearly shown in the two following passages: "The empty world, the empty world, they say, Lord. But why, Lord, do they say so?"—"Because the world is empty of the ego and of anything belonging to the ego, therefore, Ānanda, they say, 'the empty world.'" [124] "It is impossible and cannot be that a correctly cognizing man should look upon anything as the ego,—such a thing cannot happen. But it is certainly possible that an average man should look upon something as the ego." [125]

noticed that this word also is only a term indicating *the direction* in which our transcendent ego may be sought—or in the inexplicable, or in the inscrutable, or in nothing—all merely tautologies—in a manner that will be treated later on, the psycho-physical process begins which we call personality, and therewith at the same time the illusion originates, that this process in its several activities, as seeing, hearing and so on, is essential to the subjective, and constitutes the activity of its own *essence.* This delusion makes the subjective, or our transcendent ego, the subject, more accurately the "subject of inherence," and, doing so, makes it the *empirical,* and thereby the *logical, I.* Now we never say, as we ought to do in harmony with truth, looking down upon all processes as upon something alien: "There arise movements of breath, there arises a sensation, there arises a thought", but: "*I* breathe, *I* feel, *I* think," meaning thereby, as expounded above: "I am *essentially* a breathing being, a feeling being, a thinking being." Our true ego, which really lies behind those processes, is thus at once regarded as consisting in them, they are thought to belong *essentially* to it, and we then have nothing but the conceptual *reflection* of this wrong *view* when it is itself made the subject, and thus the bearer of the predicates so erroneously attributed to it. Thus the ego thought of in the *I*-idea is our transcendent ego, in so far as it is made the subject, that means, the bearer of the predicates, and is regarded as consisting in them. If we come to the true view of recognizing everything as *anattā* and thereby denying every predicate to our ego, then in that moment the ego ceases to be the subject, ceases from its introduction by means of the *I*-idea into the world of experience. It vanishes again into nothing, in the sense sufficiently explained above.

But, of course, it nevertheless remains true that I am bound to my personality, and further, it remains true that I am using the machine of the six senses and thereby producing consciousness. In this sense, as of attributes *not essential* to us, a Perfected One also may certainly think and say: "*I* possess this body, *I* feel," and so on. But at the culmination of pure insight he has overcome the form of thinking with the *I* as subject, also in this justified domain, the case presenting itself to him as follows: First, he perceives the fact of his being coupled up with the components of his personality which are essentially foreign to him, and further, he definitely perceives that the totality of the processes of personality emanate from himself. For the rest, however, he perceives that, since he is not able to penetrate with his insight to his real self, neither can he definitely determine the nature of his coupling up with his personality, since this also takes place in those inscrutable depths. In these depths, no longer accessible to apprehension, *the actuation* of the machine of the six senses also goes on. Therefore we can neither perceive how we set the heart, the lungs or other organs in motion, nor even which nerves and muscles we use in hearing, seeing, thinking: the vegetative functions as well as the sensitive ones being performed below the threshold of consciousness, the light of consciousness lit up by the sensitive functions being thrown only upon the machine already in activity. From this it follows that thinking entirely adapted to reality neither troubles about the ego as such, nor about its connections with personality, because it is unable directly to apprehend anything of this. It occupies itself solely with the material processes of the personality as such, which alone may be apprehended. In short: thinking that is entirely adapted to reality does not occupy itself with *the subject* of cognition which is absolutely inaccessible to the faculty of cognition, but only with *the objects* of this cognizing faculty which alone may be cognized. But with these also, it only troubles in so far as their relation to this subject of cognition may be determined *from themselves*, which determining ultimately issues in this, that all these objects stand in no kind of *essential* relation to the *I*. On this height of insight we therefore only may think thus: "This originates, this perishes; this shall originate, this shall perish." That *I* am the one who is thinking and creating all this, never occurs to my consciousness as a self-evident thing, or at least only in the form of the *anattā*-thought, thus, only in the negative form that everything cognizable in no case has anything to do with my *essence*. We really have no *self*-consciousness, but only consciousness of what is *not* our self.*

Certainly, this perfectly objective thinking, strictly limiting itself to the *objects* of apprehension, in which therefore reflection does not go a hair's breadth beyond apprehension, can only be cultivated in hours of meditative contemplation. If we wish to share our insight with others, then we must again think and speak, in taking the *I* as subject, if only in order to distinguish our own experiences from those of others. Thus did the Buddha. For the time of meditative contemplation he taught entirely objective thinking, but for the rest, the form of thinking having the *I* for its subject, as far as this imperfect form of thinking is at least not directly contrary to reality. But even this last-named defect he had to accept into the bargain, since language has completely conformed itself to the fundamental error of mankind that we consist in the elements of our personality, in so much that we say for example: "I *am* a man, I *am* this one or that one."** But, once for all, he guarded his standpoint by

* Whereas the saint has lost the *I*-thought, the child has not yet come up to it. It calls itself as it hears itself called by others, which proves that it only recognizes its personality as an object. — If a saint with his full supreme knowledge should suddenly be transferred into the world, without fellow-creatures with whom he was forced to speak, and should form a language for himself, the word "I" would not occur at all in this language.

** The possibility of this delusion is based upon the inaccessibility of our true essence to apprehension: I may come to any view about myself, because all are equally wrong.

making this general reservation: "These are only current expressions, used also by the Perfected One, *but with due reserve.*"[126]

For the rest, as may be seen from the passage just given, and as we have repeatedly noticed, he calls the true man who has freed himself from the elements of his personality, and thereby from personality itself and so, from the entire world, hence, above all, himself—*the Perfected One*, Tathāgata. Hence, it makes no difference, if at first he remains in external connection with the elements of his personality, or if he throws them entirely away in death: in both cases he is the Perfected One, only, in the first case *before*, in the other one *after*, death. In the latter case, he is the Perfected One in his complete purity, entirely free from the taints of his personality which alone had made him visible to us, as pure glass is only made visible by the spots of dirt lying upon it. His death therefore has for sole consequence that, in completely divesting himself of his body, he becomes invisible to men: "As long as his body shall exist, gods and men will behold him; but after the dissolution of the body, after the end of his life, gods and men shall behold him no more. As, ye monks, when the stalk of a bunch of mango fruits is cut off from the tree, all the mango fruits hanging on the stalk will follow it, even so also, O monks, is it with the body of the Perfected One, whose will to live is annihilated. As long as his body still exists, gods and men will behold him; but after the dissolution of his body, after the end of his life, gods and men will behold him no more."*[127]

* * *

We shall now understand how right the Buddha was in

* Be it noted: The body of the Perfected One with its sensations and perceptions is compared to the bunch of mango fruits, his will to live to the stalk of this bunch, but the Perfected One himself to *the stem* of the mango tree, that is not touched by cutting

admonishing us to seek for our self,* his admonition being identical with the inscription of the temple at Delphi: "Know yourself!" For everything we took till now to be our I, proved itself in the "befitting search for the state beyond,"[128] shown to us by the Master, to be *not* the *I*. Thus at last there remained for our true *I* nothing of the world and thereby no possibility of understanding it in any way. Further meditation in this direction would therefore be stupid, hence the Master explicitly declares that no reasonable man "dwells in such contemplations."[129] Thereby we recognize the word *I* as the greatest equivoque existing, as Schopenhauer says. Everybody understands it to be something else; this one, as all the components of his personality; the other, as only the so-called spiritual elements of the same; a third, as consisting only of thinking; whereas we have recognized it to be transcendent in *every* direction.

In this manner we have, step by step, certainly come to an entire subversion of all conceptions. Before this, we regarded ourselves as belonging to the world, to the universe, consisting of its own elements. Hence, we felt at home in the world, and Nothing, as being the contrary of Everything, meant for us the total annihilation of the universe, as also of ourselves. We therefore shrunk back from it as from the abyss that would forthwith devour us. Now we have understood the world to be essentially foreign to our deepest self. We see ourselves in some inexplicable manner involved in it, so that it is to us in all its details an inscrutable riddle,

---

off the bunch. Compare Rigveda-saṃhitā X, 136,3: "The bodies only in our stead—ye sons of earth may there behold."—

To the question: "What shall I be, when once as a saint I have passed through the last death, have laid aside the last body?" we might reply thus: "Exactly the same as you are now. But what are you now? Can you tell me, since all the components of your personality are *not* your self, *anattā*? Only try to define yourself, bearing in mind this fact! It will be impossible to you, for even now you are something inscrutable."

* Compare above, page 120: "What may be better, ye youths, to seek for the woman, or to seek for your *I*?"

saving only the suffering it makes for us, which is the only thing we cannot doubt:

> "Mysterious is everything,
> Only one thing not, and that our pain."

This entire inversion of the manner of the saint of looking at the world, as compared with that of the average man, is hinted at by the Master himself, when he says: "What in the world is regarded as true, ye monks, that by the saints is regarded as false, as it really is, rightly, in accordance with perfect wisdom. What in the world is regarded as false, ye monks, that by the saints is regarded as true, as it really is, rightly, in accordance with perfect wisdom."[130]

To illustrate this inversion, we reproduce the beautiful simile wherein Du Prel in his "Enigma of Man" describes the situation of mankind, a simile which is true in a much deeper sense than its author himself suspected.

"Let us imagine the following case: On a ship sailing in the Pacific a sailor is put into hypnotic trance. It is suggested to him that he is to sleep till evening and then awaken without any recollection of his past. This suggestion having been strongly impressed upon him, the sailor is carried into a boat and landed upon a small island of the ocean, the ship sailing away at full speed.

"Upon awakening, this sailor would be entirely like a new-born babe, with this difference only that he would have come into his world as a full-grown and rational being. He would commence his existence as a man. In vain, however, would he think and meditate as to who he is and how he came into this environment so completely strange to him. Without the least memory of his past, he would thus be astonished, even terrified at himself and the place in which he had awakened, so that he might easily become a melancholiac.

"As far as his sight reaches, the ocean extends,—a sight he believes never to have beheld before. He turns inland in order to get some idea of where is on his island, but everything seems strange to him; he does not remember to have ever seen things of this kind: plants and animals, mountains, and the clouds flitting over them. At last he catches sight of creatures like himself; he hurries towards them to get some information, but they are all in the same inexplicable condition; they do not know who they are, nor whence they have come.

"A company of men in such a curious situation would be devoured with anxious pondering about themselves and their island; but all their thinking and mutual questions would never explain the inscrutable fate that had brought them there. With a mixture of keen admiration and deep astonishment they would see the sun sink down, as a spectacle never seen before, spanning the ocean with a luminous bridge of floods of gold, and boundless again would be their astonishment, when thousands of stars began to shine in the dark sky.

"By and by, of course, the wants of the body would draw them away from their meditations. Hunger and thirst, weariness and sleep appear; the inclemency of the weather compels them to look about for shelter, and thus on this island would begin the most curious Robinson Crusoe existence that can be imagined. For Robinson Crusoe brought memories of civilization with him to his island, whereas our colonists have had to think out and invent everything themselves.

"It is unnecessary to depict the situation further; and it is also immaterial, whether hypnotical emptying of the brain actually can go so far—but experiments of this kind have been made—that awakening out of trance may be fully the same as being newly born. Nevertheless I have not spoken of entirely imaginary things. The island of which I have told is called *earth*; the ocean surrounding it is called *space*; the creatures meeting each other on the island are called *men*; and the wearisome "Robinsonade" they go through is called *the history of human civilisation*.

"Indeed, if we reflect with any degree of heedfulness upon our own situation on earth, the comparison with those inhabitants of the island tallies at all points, with the exception of one: we do not awaken with a ready-formed consciousness as full-grown beings, but with undeveloped consciousness as helpless creatures. As this is the only difference, it depends only on this point that we behave quite otherwise than do these island inhabitants. These awaken as deep-thinking philosophers. For a philosopher is one who is able to wonder at his own existence and at that of the world. But during childhood we become so accustomed to the appearance of things and to our own existence that, far from perturbing us, they seem to us as self-evident things. And when our consciousness does attain to ripeness, through the blunting power of habit it is no longer capable of wonder, and so, through our whole life we go, entirely absorbed by practical occupations."

The Buddha, in teaching us to consider our situation with thoughtful heedfulness, has given back to us this capacity for wonder in fullest measure, so that we again feel ourselves as strangers in the world, as strangers even in our own body, as strangers in regard to everything we call our personality. He has given us, indeed, very much more, for as his disciples, even now we no longer share the fate of all the other inhabitants of the island who may perhaps feel themselves strangers on their island, but do not know who they are and where they came from. For we, even now, know at least this much, that the ocean flowing round the universe wherein we find ourselves placed, the ocean of *Nothingness*, contains "the island, the unique,"[139] from which we were driven out into the universe. For we have recognized in this nothing that we dreaded so much at first, the dark womb wherein our real essence, our eternal home, is hidden. *Attham̐ gata*, he who went home, the deceased saint is called.* Now we understand that in fearing this "Nothing" so much, we resemble children, who, though living in a comfortless region, look, full of fear and trembling, upon the immense dark forest that stretches out before them, and cannot be brought by any inducement to enter it, while, all the time, behind it, in the midst of green meadows, bathed in smiling sunshine stands their parents' house from which they set out at first. But if it has once become clear to these children that through this dark forest lies the way that leads to their home, then its hitherto uncanny stillness changes for them into mysterious silence, and the forest becomes for them the great hope of their life. So also for us, the *nothing* that we regarded so long as the measureless black pall spread over the abyss of absolute annihilation into which every living being must one day fall, now becomes the mysterious veil that lies over our own innermost essence. We only need to go behind it to escape the sufferings of Sam̐sāra for ever. Then we disappear for the world by becoming, as sufficiently explained, nothing cognizable, that is, nothing for it, but not nothing for ourselves. On the contrary we leave the world, in leaving behind the only thing still belonging to it, our corpse,—everything else we long before threw at its feet—and thus we proceed "to the glory of our Self," a word not used by the Buddha,** but this, not because of its being false, but because, according to what in our previous pages we

---

* Suttanipāta, v. 1076, whereas in the Dhammapada, v. 402, the redeemed one is called "he who crosses out of his fetters."

** It is taken from the Laws of Manu (12; 91), where it is said: "Thus he enters, lighting the sacrifice to the Self, to the own glory of his Self."

have been saying, it might give rise only too easily to misinterpretations, in consequence of its relation to personality. But as we have done our best to exclude the possibility of such misinterpretations, we may without fear make use of it. If understood, as we have learnt to take it, it tells us the same story as the Master's own words: "Liberated of what we call body, sensation, perception, mentations, consciousness, the Perfected One is deep, immeasurable, unfathomable, like the ocean." This his inscrutable essence the saint enters, to it he withdraws, in it he rests.*

Thus the great question, as to whether, having regard to our relation to suffering, it is not impossible to escape from it, is solved: It is possible. For suffering is rooted in the structure of the world, being as a whole, as well as in all its component parts, in an eternally fluid condition, subject to the great law of transitoriness. This world is the world of our six senses which we experience *in* our personality and *as* our personality. But personality in its elements is something alien to our true essence. From this alien thing we only need to free ourselves to become at the same time free from the whole world of suffering, and thereby from the suffering of the world, that is, from suffering altogether. The possibility of this liberation the Buddha expressly asserts in the following passage: "It is not, O disciples, as if liberation from corporeality, from sensation, from perception, from mentation, from consciousness, could not be attained, for then creatures could not liberate themselves from corporeality, from sensation, from perception, from mentation, from consciousness. But because there really is, O disciples,

---

* The words of Manu given above are, as to their contents, identical with the word dealt with later on, as spoken by Sāriputta, the greatest disciple of the Master: "Bliss is the Nibbāna, bliss is the Nibbāna." Instead of the words of Manu, we might say just as well, we enter the state of bliss.

liberation from corporeality, from sensation, from perception, from mentation, from consciousness, therefore creatures do liberate themselves from corporeality, from sensation, from perception, from mentation, from consciousness."[131]

But this insight, fundamental as it is, is not yet sufficient. For now the other great question arises: How can this liberation be realized? How can we vanquish our personality and the whole world and reach that realm, our own proper realm, "where there is neither birth nor sickness nor becoming old nor dying, nor woe, sorrow, suffering, grief and despair," and so, putting this statement to the test, by visible evidence prove ourselves to be beyond the world and all its suffering? It is clear that if the Buddha is able to answer exhaustively this question also, he has indeed bestowed upon mankind the greatest benefit that can ever be bestowed upon it.

Whether he succeeded, let what follows, show.

THE MOST EXCELLENT TRUTH OF THE ARISING OF SUFFERING

GENERAL INTRODUCTION

As we have amply shown, the problem of the annihilation of suffering coincides with that of the conquest of our personality through which alone we are joined to the world and thereby to suffering, nay, wherein alone we even experience the world and thereby suffering. In the same measure in which I succeed in liberating myself from my personality, in outgrowing it, I also outgrow the world and its sufferings; and after having entirely freed myself from the components of my personality, I look down upon it as upon something entirely alien to me, and thereby in the same manner upon the world and upon suffering. All of them, then, have nothing more to do with me, for I have withdrawn myself from them. I am indeed still *in* the world, but I am no longer *of* the world. I tower above it, and look towards the approaching decay of my personality with cool indifference. It affects me equally as little as it affects Himālaya, the king of mountains, when the wreaths of mist floating around him far beneath dissolve and vanish, whereby he, on the contrary, only stands out all the more clearly, in all his stainless purity. "Just as, O Brahmin, the blue, red or white lotus-flower, originated in the water, grown up in the water, stands there towering above the water, untouched by the water: just so, Brahmin, I am born within the world, grown up within the world, but I have vanquished the world, and unspotted by the world I remain."[132]

But in outgrowing my present personality, the problem of the annihilation of suffering is by no means yet solved. If it were only a question of the conquest of this my *present* personality it might rightly be replied that there really was no serious problem given, and it was therefore not worth the trouble of setting such a great apparatus of salvation in motion, since this personality of itself completely dissolves in death. But the important point lies in the hindering also of every new formation of such a personality in the moment of dissolution of the present one, since we have already learnt that at the moment of death we ever and again objectify ourselves afresh in one of the five realms. Herein precisely, for the Buddha also, lay the kernel of the problem. If it were only the suffering of this single fleeting present existence that was at stake, he, of course, would not, have troubled much about it either.

As this point is of decisive importance for clearly understanding the particular doctrine of the Buddha, we shall do well to keep the whole problem of the annihilation of suffering before our minds in direct pictorial form. This is all the easier for us, inasmuch as the Buddha himself describes most vividly, how it presented itself to him on the peak of insight as the first and second of the three great knowledges that arose within him on the night when he reached Buddhahood under the Bodhi tree near Uruvela, the third knowledge bringing to him the solution of the problem itself:

"And with thought thus fixed, cleansed, purged, and stainless; clear of all dross, supple, serviceable, firm, and unswerving, I turned my mind towards the recollection and recognition of previous modes of existence. And I called to mind my various lots in former lives: first one life, then two lives, then three, then four, then five, ten, twenty up to fifty lives; then a hundred lives; then a thousand lives;

then an hundred thousand lives. Then I recalled the periods of many a world-arising; then the periods of many a world-destruction; then the periods of many a world-arising and world-destruction. There was I. That was my name. To that family I belonged. This was my position. That was my occupation. Such and such the weal and woe that I experienced. Thus was my life's ending. Thence departing, there I came into existence anew. There now was I. This was my rank now. This was my occupation. Such and such the fresh weal and woe I underwent. Thus was now my life's ending. Departing once more, I came into existence again elsewhere. In such wise I remembered the characterics and particulars of my varied lot in previous lives. And this, O Brahmin, in the first watch of the night, was the first knowledge to which I attained, ignorance banished, knowledge gained; darkness dispelled, light won; abiding there as one, diligent, earnest, resolute.

"And then I directed my thought toward the perception of the disappearing and reappearing of beings. With the Heavenly Eye, the purified, the superhuman, I beheld beings disappear and reappear, low and high, beautiful and ugly, happy and unhappy, I beheld beings reappear according to their deeds. 'These precious beings, alas! are given to things evil in deeds, words, and thoughts. They revile the Noble Ones, hold perverted views; and following perverted ways, incur an evil lot. At the dissolution of the body, after death, they depart upon a sorry journey, downward to loss in the world of the hells. Those previous beings, however, are given to the good in deeds, words, and thoughts. They do not revile the Noble Ones; hold right views; and following righteous courses, earn a happy lot. At the break-up of the body, after death they fare forth upon a happy journey and come to the heaven-world. This, O Brahmin, in the middle watch of the night, was the second knowledge to which I attained, abiding there as one, diligent, earnest, resolute.

"And then I directed my mind toward the perception of the destruction of the Influences. 'Here is Suffering. Thus comes the Arising of Suffering. Thus comes the Cessation of Suffering. This is the Path that leads to the Cessation of Suffering. These are the Influences. Thus comes the Arising of the Influences. Thus comes the Cessation of the Influences. This is the Path that leads to the Cessation of the Influences.' All this I comprehended according to the truth. And thus perceiving, thus beholding, my mind was released from the Influence of Desiring, from the Influence of Craving for Becoming, from the Influence of Ignorance. 'I am delivered,' this knowledge came to me. 'Life is lived out, the holy goal achieved: done all that was to do; no more is this world for me.' This I fully comprehended. Such, Brahmin, in the last watch of the night, was the third knowledge to which I attained, ignorance banished, knowledge gained; darkness dispelled, light won; abiding there as one, diligent, earnest, resolute."[133]

Thus did the Buddha in direct vision look out over the endless chain of his bygone personalities, conditioned each time by a new birth, as well as upon the fact that all other creatures are ever and again conducted from death to renewed birth in an incessant round. This boundless circle of rebirths within the five realms he therefore understood by the third knowledge that arose in him, as the great suffering of man: "This is *the* suffering, I there understood."

How this circle of incessantly renewed objectification as personality—taking personality, of course, in its broadest sense, as individual existence of any kind—was to be brought once for all to a standstill, was therefore for him the great question. Its solution was given to him by the third knowledge, of which he says himself: "Then I saw and knew:

'Assured am I of deliverance; this is my final birth; never more shall I return hither.' "[134]

The Dialogues are full of passages which ever and again point to this getting out of the circle of rebirths, out of *Saṁsāra*, as the supreme goal of all sanctity. Only a few of them may here be quoted:

"Whatever there may be, brethren, of things created and not created, the highest of them is said to be ... the destruction of the circle (*saṁsāra*).[135]

"An enemy of birth is the ascetic Gotama, for the hindering of birth does he proclaim his doctrine, and thereby does he direct his disciples ... Through whom for the future, rebirth into another life is annihilated, as a palm tree is rooted up and destroyed, through whom it is brought to cease so that never in the future can it grow again, him I call an enemy of birth."[136]

"The saint who seeks peace bears his last body to the grave."[137]

"Through countless ages I have been devoted to the body:
This is the last of them,—this living conjunction.
The round of birth and death: there is now no more coming to be of it.
In the round of existence I came to the hell-world.
Again and again I came to the realm of the Shades.
In suffering born from the wombs of animals of various kinds, I lived for long.
Then a man I became, very well pleased. To the heaven-worlds I came now and again,
To the form-worlds, to the formless worlds, to the realm of neither perception nor non-perception.
All Becoming well seen as without substance, put together, unstable, changeable,
Having seen this complete Becoming of myself, heedful, I have attained to Peace."[138]

According to this, the case lies thus: I can only regard myself as definitely freed from suffering, when I reach the unshakeable, intimately assured certainty that I am not only something entirely different from the components of my present personality, and therefore something that cannot be touched by its fate, but also, that this my present personality will be the last to which I am chained, that therefore with my coming death, the last in store for me, I shall for ever depart out of the round of rebirths, *saṁsāra*, and never more be troubled by any of its elements. *This* is the problem.

But it is clear that if I am to cut short the endless chain of my personalities, if I am to be able to put a period to the eternal reappearing of such a personality, after the present one has dissolved in death, then before all else I must know how it comes about that such a personality ever and again arises anew. For only if I know the conditions of a process, can I undertake to guard against its initiation; or, in the Buddha's words: The annihilation of suffering I can only reach, if I know its arising. Hence it is only logical of the Buddha when, at the outset, in the second of the four holy truths he lays bare the arising of this endless chain of suffering.

Meanwhile, in this second holy truth he only gives the principal cause of this incessant and successive reproduction of personalities, as which we objectify ourselves from all eternity. In detail he points out the conditions of this process, incessantly repeating itself, in the famous formula of origination through dependence, *paṭiccasamuppāda,* with which therefore we have to deal first. This formula is generally regarded as the most difficult part of the doctrine of the Buddha, and has received the most various, and sometimes incredible interpretations, though, if only we are able to penetrate it, it is self-evident. In order to penetrate it, however, it is, first of all, necessary to be able to regard it in a purely objective manner, that is, without presuppositions, so that we may not proceed to its investigation wearing the spectacles of the philosophical views to which one is sworn. We must not start out, for instance, with the presupposition that the Buddha was teaching a purely idealistic world-view, in the modern sense of the word, and that the formula must therefore represent the Buddhist dianoiology. By such pre-conceived notions we render it impossible from the very first to understand the formula. The only correct thing is to place oneself in relation to it at the standpoint of a Perfected One, as far as one is able to do so. Already we have treated of this in detail. To state it precisely yet once more, it is as follows: The Perfected One is in such wise alienated from the five groups, out of which the complex called personality, representing the world, is built up, and is so far cured of the delusion that they are in any way an efflux of his *essence,* that in contemplating them, not even the thought of his ego arises in him. To him they are nothing more than processes restlessly heaving up and down, which at bottom have nothing at all to do with him. From the unmoving pole of his real essence lying beyond them, he looks down upon them as upon a phantasmagoria flitting before him; he perceives them as foreign elements rising incessantly from the realm of the uncognizable, or,—what, as we already know, means the same thing—from *Nothingness*, like bubbles rising out of the water of a swamp, on the instant to dissolve again and again. The idea of his ego does not even come to him to make him want to know the manner in which it is interlocked with those elements foreign to its essence. For the fundamental insight that all cognition is directed outwards, and that, accordingly, the essential and its whole domain are unattainable to it, has become so vivid within him that he only cultivates this kind of thinking that is perfectly adapted to reality.

If we are able completely to grasp this standpoint, then, even before we know anything at all about the formula of origination through dependence, it will be clear to us that it can only consist in showing us how these processes which yield the total impression of personality and world, are conditioned one by the other, how one arises through another, and we shall no longer think that there can be any talk of a person actuating these processes. In short: We already know beforehand that the formula of origination through dependence must be taken quite *impersonally,* since in the realm of the cognizable a person is not to be found, and the realm of the uncognizable, precisely as such, yields no ideas at all. And so, the formula of origination through dependence, in fact shows us nothing more than mere processes running their course against the background of *nothing,* as the domain of our innermost essence, withdrawn from knowledge, arising out of this "nothing" and always again disappearing into it:

"But who, O Lord, touches?"

"'The question is not rightly put,' the Exalted One replied. I do not say: 'He touches.' If I said: 'He touches;' then of course the question, 'Lord, who touches?' would be rightly put. But I do not say so. But if some one should ask me who do not say so: 'On what, O Lord, depends touch? then this question would be put rightly, and the right answer to it would run thus: 'In dependence upon the six organs of sense arises touch, and in dependence upon touch arises sensation.'"

"But who, O Lord, feels?"

"'Neither is this question rightly put,' the Exalted One replied. 'I do not say: 'He feels.' If I said: 'He feels;' then the question, 'Lord, who feels?' would of course be rightly put. But I do not say so. But if some one should ask me who do not say so, 'On what, O Lord, depends sensation?' then this question would be rightly put, and the right answer to it would be: 'In dependence upon touch arises sensation.'"[139]

Only because there is really no person, is there room left for a causal connection as conceived by the Buddha. For a person is thought of as a being to which sensation and perception are *essential*. If there were such a being, then of course every question as to the primary causes of sensations and perceptions would be meaningless, and every causal connection as conceived by the Buddha impossible. For to feel and to perceive would then be just the manifestation of my essence. These qualities would find their sufficient reason in the latter, so that no room would be left for any further cause, in the same way that the question, why a certain creature has wings, is sufficiently answered by pointing out that the said creature is a bird. But thereby any deliverance from sensation and perception, and thereby from suffering itself would be impossible. For it is impossible for me to annihilate myself.*

If now this peculiarity of the formula that it is an entirely impersonal conception, appears as self-evident, it will, for the rest, show itself to be of extreme lucidity, if only we always keep before our eyes the standpoint of the Buddha, as expounded above.

* See above p. 134.

OLD AGE AND DEATH — BIRTH AS IMMEDIATE CONDITIONS OF SUFFERING

Saṁsāra is an endless chain of single personalities strung one on to the other. Personality, as we know, consists in the interworking of the five groups of grasping in such a manner that the corporeal organism—the first group—represents the personality's substratum, the six senses-machine, that by means of the action of the organs of sense first rouses consciousness and then, in union with it, generates sensation, perception and the activities of the mind. Since, further, as we know, these five groups constitute at the same time all the elements and thereby the totality of all suffering, we might also well call the corporeal organism *the machine of suffering*.

With this, however, it becomes apparent that, if the endless chain of misery that is called Saṁsāra is to be shown as being causally conditioned, the corporeal organism,* the same machine of suffering itself, appears as the immediate cause of Suffering. It receives its character as a machine of suffering, as we saw above, in that it "ages and withers, worn out, becomes gray and wrinkled, vitality disappears, and the senses becomes dulled,"[140] until at last, in death, entire ruin and dissolution follow. These two fundamental qualities of the substratum of personality, old age and death, give at the same time to the whole process of personality and therewith to the whole of life in all its details and in every direction the stamp of transiency, and precisely in doing so, make life as such full of Suffering. In old age and death, therefore, suffering culminates; they are suffering's most pregnant expression. Precisely on this account, the first question that arose in the Buddha's mind, as in deep

* *nāma-rūpa.*

meditation he sought to discover the conditioned nature of the process of suffering, was: "Are old age and death dependent on something?" The answer, of course, was: "Yes, they are dependent."—"On what are old age and death dependent?"—"In dependence on *birth* arise old age and death."[141] Any one can see without further ado that this answer is correct. Because old age and death are nothing but the gradual decay and the final definitive dissolution of the corporeal organism, therefore they are inevitably bound up therewith, which means, they are conditioned by the same process whereby the organism itself arises with the accession of the element of consciousness: "Hence, Ānanda: Whatever is born, or becomes old, or dies, or perishes, or originates,—that is the corporeal organism together with consciousness."* This process of the arising of "the body endowed with consciousness" takes place within the maternal womb, extending from the moment of conception to the extrusion of the foetus from the womb. The whole process in its entirety is comprised by the Buddha under the expression "*birth*": "And what, ye monks, is birth? Of beings in this or that class of life the birth, the becoming born, the germination, the conception, the appearing of the groups, the grasping of the realms of sense,—this, ye monks, is called birth."[142]

From this insight that old age and death are by necessity of nature involved in birth that is to say, in the formation of "the body endowed with six senses," since they are only the external manifestation of the laws to which this body is subject, the first result for the Buddha was that liberation from old age and death to which was subject the body he at that time occupied, was proven to be impossible. With regard to this *present* old age and the death bound up with it, he was from the outset powerless. In

* See above pp. 77,78.

relation to *this* old age and *this* death, therefore, nothing remained but a calm, indifferent submission to these inevitable consequences of an already given cause, as expressed in the words: "With patience I wear out my body."[143] On the other hand there appeared the possibility of protecting ourselves in our inscrutable essence against a repetition of these processes in future time, that is, in a new existence, if only we succeeded in hindering every *new* birth, that is to say, the formation of any *future* new corporeal organism. The Buddha thus found himself here confronted by the new and unheard-of problem of finding out the secret in consequence of which, through the act of conception in a maternal womb, ever and again a new body endowed with senses is formed, with the result that in the same act consciousness comes down into it. Only if the solution of this problem could be effected, only then would it be at all possible to determine if the conditions of this act—birth, in the sense used by the Buddha—were such as it might be in our power to set up or to omit. The Buddha solved this problem also, and therewith, at the same time discovered the share that we ourselves have in our conception, so that every one is in a position to determine whether he shall be reborn or not. It is precisely this power of making a future rebirth impossible, together with the unshakeable certainty of having succeeded in doing so, which is the criterion of deliverance acquired and thereby of holiness gained. For he only has for ever escaped the circle of rebirth, thereby definitively passed beyond suffering, and thus become wholly delivered and perfectly sanctified, who can say of himself: "Rebirth is exhausted, lived out the holy life, done what was to do; no more is this world for me."[144] Or, as it is said in another passage: "Unshakeable is my deliverance, *this is the last birth,* there is no more becoming anew."[145]

Thereby the only moment when it is possible to depart

out of Saṁsāra for ever, is fixed as the same wherein a new birth takes place, namely, at the moment of death that is immediately followed by the new birth: "If one should die at this moment, he would be reborn as quickly as one throws off a load," is often said in the Canon.

THE CONDITIONS OF REBIRTH

It has already been said above, that the solution of the riddle as to how we come to be reborn again and again, shows itself to be astonishingly simple, as simple as only truth can be. Now we have reached the point of verifying that statement.

In the first place, of course, nobody can say from immediate ocular evidence how the event of his own birth takes place, though everyone has gone through it countless times. For the act of conception which led to his present birth took place, in the case of every being, in a night of the deepest unconsciousness, or, to speak in the spirit of the Buddha, in the deepest ignorance. But the idea might well occur to us of deriving the knowledge which the Buddha ascribes to himself on this point, from the second of the three great knowledges he had acquired, that is, from the faculty of cognizing "by means of the heavenly eye, the purified and supernatural, how creatures vanish and reappear." If the Buddha had really in this way arrived at establishing the conditions under which our rebirth takes place, this would be very unfortunate for us. For we, to whom this faculty of the heavenly eye is entirely wanting, would be limited to mere belief in his dictum, and thereby one of the strongest pillars of the colossal structure of his teaching, founded upon the possibility of our own immediate insight, would prove itself to be rotten. Nevertheless, this fear is unfounded, and for a very simple reason. By means of the faculty of the heavenly eye the Buddha could only register the mere fact that the beings—in our sensual world, within a maternal womb—always appear anew; but not the *cause* of this fact, which is not at all accessible to immediate ocular evidence. This cause he therefore had to find out in another way. And this way was as follows:—

The Buddha sought to comprehend the process of becoming born as the integral part of another, more universal process, in such wise that if he discovered the conditions of the latter, then those of the former at once became clear of themselves. And this more universal process he found to be *Becoming (bhava)*. Becoming is the most universal, nay, at bottom, the only process within the world. There is no real being in the sense of something persisting in any way, but everything is in a state of constant flow, developing from smallest beginnings, to dissolve again soon afterwards; everything is nothing but *Becoming*. In this manner also everything living *becomes* in every possible world, namely, in the world of desires, in the world of forms and in the formless world.* Thereby this Becoming, the Becoming of a new body endowed with senses, of a new corporeal organism,** happens always and exclusively in the way of being brought about by "conception, germination, becoming born." But according to this, the process described under these latter conceptions is only *Becoming* in its beginning itself. Therefore it is clear without further

* "These three (kinds of) Becoming exist, ye monks: Becoming in the world of desires, Becoming in the world of forms, Becoming in the formless world." 146—By "world of forms" those heavenly realms are understood wherein objectification is reached in corporeal forms, but free from sensual desire; the "formless world" comprises the realms of infinite space, of unlimited consciousness, of Nothingness and of Neither Perception nor Non-perception. We will discuss these later on.

** The expression "bhava," Becoming, is used exclusively in this sense in the Dialogues when in relation to the Paṭiccasamuppāda.

words that the latter conditions of birth in the sense given above, that is, *becoming* conceived and born, coincide with those of Becoming in general. If I give the conditions for the conception of a being, I thereby give the condition for its *Becoming*; and if I annihilate the conditions of all Becoming, I thereby also annihilate those of any birth. Therefore it is only a self-evident axiom when the Buddha says: "If, Ānanda, the question were put: 'Is birth dependent on something?' then it ought to be replied: 'Yes, it is dependent.' And if it is asked: 'On what depends birth?' then it ought to be replied: 'In dependence on Becoming arises birth.' "[147] That the Buddha in this saying really only means to express what has been expounded above, follows with all the exactness one could desire from the explanation he himself gives of it:

"I have said: 'In dependence on Becoming arises birth.' And this, Ānanda, that birth arises in dependence on Becoming, must be understood in the following sense: Suppose, Ānanda, that there was no Becoming at all of anything and in any sense, which means, no Becoming in the world of desires, no Becoming in the world of corporeality, no Becoming in the world of non-corporeality, if Becoming thus were entirely wanting, if Becoming were annihilated, could then birth be perceived anywhere?"

"Certainly not, O Lord."

"Here, then, Ānanda, is the cause, origin, arising, dependence of birth, namely, Becoming."

Thus for the Buddha the problem of birth led over to that of Becoming in general, inasmuch as now for him the question to be answered was: What is the sufficient cause of this unresting, unceasing Becoming in which we find ourselves involved? Again through deep meditation he obtained the answer that will, without trouble, solve the question, also for us.

I am walking on the street. A girl's form appears before me. I *grasp* it, in mind. As a consequence of this, I fall to considering how I can approach her. Plans are made. They are externally realized. I declare my love, and marriage ensues. Children are begotten; in short, the whole chain of happy and unhappy events, such as only family life can bring about, runs its course. All this is conditioned and effected through the sole circumstance that years ago I *grasped* in mind that girl's form on the street. It was this Grasping which then arose within me that effected all this Becoming, reaching through many years. If it had not arisen within me, if I had remained indifferent at the first sight of that female form, she also, like thousands of others, would have disappeared unnoticed from my field of sight, even as she had entered it, perhaps never again to cross my way of life, which, perhaps, thereby might have taken a diametrically opposite course. A young man who has to choose his life's profession *grasps* the thought arising within him, of becoming a merchant, an official, an officer, or an artist. "This thought he cherishes and cultivates, and cleaves to." The consequence is that the thought is translated into deed; *Becoming* sets in and remains in action until the young man has actually *become* a merchant, an official, an officer or an artist. In consequence of this Grasping he has become that which he grasped. If no such *grasping* had stirred within him, he would not have *become* anything of all this. We *grasp* some kind of food, with the effect that we eat of it and *become* ill; we *grasp*, in mind, the thought that a certain medicine may help us, in consequence of which we partake of it and *become* cured. We *grasp* a certain thing which somebody takes away from us, in consequence of which we *become* angry; we *grasp* a merry sight, and in consequence *become* glad. In short: As soon as some kind of *grasping* rises within us, *Becoming* begins; not merely *becoming* ill, *becoming* cured, *becoming* angry, *becoming* glad, but every kind of Becoming. Always and everywhere we *become* that which we *grasp*, by identifying ourselves at the same time with that which becomes in consequence of the grasping. Even my own body only *becomes*, if, and for as long as, I *grasp* food, and this, in consequence is incorporated into the body. If every *grasping* at food ceases, then there is no more *becoming* of the body as such, but it dissolves. The result therefore is this: If I *grasp* nothing more, then also nothing more can *become* in relation to me. Even a mere thought arising within me vanishes without foothold and dissolves, if I remain entirely indifferent towards it, that means, if no kind of grasping takes place: "If, Ānanda, the question were put: 'Is Becoming dependent on any thing?' then it ought to be replied: 'Yes, it is dependent?' And if it were asked: 'On what is Becoming dependent?' then the reply should be given: 'In dependence upon Grasping arises Becoming.'"

However convincingly, because drawn from immediate observation, this line of argument may demonstrate that all Becoming has its cause in a grasping, none the less, it —and with it, also its outcome—is entirely strange and unaccustomed to us, because so completely different from our so-called scientific method. For our natural science regards all Becoming simply and solely from the point of view of the incessant changes of matter caused by the laws dominating it. This matter and its laws for it are the only things given, through which, therefore, like everything else in the world, man also is to be wholly and completely comprehended. Therefore our investigators take it for granted in advance that matter and its laws must conceal within themselves the sole causes of all the phenomena of nature and thereby also of man. From this there results, as the only method of all aetiology, the completest possible exploration of nature within which man only represents a genus among many others. In consequence of this it is always only the *external* causal connection of phenomena that is recognized, but never the innermost principle from which they take their origin. This principle, called by us the force of nature, natural science, because of the nature of its method, leaves on one side as an unexplained and, for it, unexplainable residue. Hence we do not know how to behave at first when we suddenly find ourselves planted in the middle of the explanation of this force of nature itself. For it is nothing else but this explanation that is presented to us in the intuition that all Becoming proceeds from grasping. This grasping is the energetical principle resident in all the separate phenomena of nature, constituting therefore the essence of all natural forces. Of course we can thoroughly understand this only when, in place of the said *objective* standpoint of our natural science—called objective, because it proceeds from the object, regarding this as the primary thing, from which all other things, even the subject, are to be explained—we withdraw to the directly opposite one, the subjective standpoint taken up by the Buddha. According to him, as we already sufficiently know, the primary thing is not nature, not the world with its laws; but I myself am this primary thing; and the problem consists not in comprehending myself as a product of this world, thus in explaining how the world comes to me, but, on the contrary, in understanding how in my inscrutable essence I come to the world, to the realm of *anattā*, of non-ego; or what is the same thing, how I have got into this realm of *Becoming*. Precisely because of this, it can never be a question for the Buddha and for any one who from the Buddha's standpoint looks out into the world, as to how Becoming in itself, thus independent of me, is to be explained, but, just like the whole world, it becomes *a subjective pheno-*

menon of the individual; and consequently, from the very outset always and without exception, must have its ultimate and sufficient cause within the private individual. But from this there results a method the very opposite of ours, for discovering this ultimate cause. We shall never come upon it by external investigation, even if we search the entire universe through to the depths of starry space, just as little as we could ever find the subterranean inlet of a lake by exploring however closely its surface in every direction, with every possible kind of instrument. We must retire from the world back into ourselves, to the "centre of our vital birth" and by persistent introspection seek to find out how we have come into all this Becoming in which we find ourselves enmeshed. Under the Buddha's guidance, as we have seen, we shall be able without much difficulty, definitely to ascertain that whatever *becomes* in and about and for me, does so through an antecedent grasping that has arisen within me; nay, that it is precisely through this that I myself first become an *I*. Only when thus is discovered the source from which Becoming flows, may we with some hope of success turn our eye, in this manner rightly directed, upon other beings with a view to ascertaining if all Becoming, in regard to them also, is based upon a grasping,—in direct contrast to natural science which always seeks to comprehend the particular from the general.* As all the phenomena of life are obviously alike, we shall without further ado come to the insight that the axiom holds good to its full extent, for them also, as it is expressed by the Buddha: "I have said: 'In dependence on grasping arises Becoming.' And this, Ānanda, that in dependence on grasping arises Becoming is to be understood as follows.

* "Internally with body keeping watch upon the body, he becomes wholly calmed, wholly clarified, and because he is thus wholly calmed, wholly clarified, he is able wisely to maintain his gaze externally, upon other bodies." 148

Suppose, Ānanda, that there was nowhere and nowise any grasping of any being at anything, that is to say, no grasping at Sensuality, no grasping at Views, no grasping at Ceremonial Observances, no grasping at Doctrines about the *I*, thus if grasping were entirely wanting, if grasping were entirely annihilated, would then any kind of Becoming be perceived?"

"Certainly not, Lord."

"Thus, Ānanda, there is here the cause, origin, arising, dependence of Becoming, namely, grasping."

Indeed, if only we are able to look deep enough, at last even all forces in the vegetable kingdom and in the realm of inorganic matter, disclose themselves as expressions of grasping. Take a box of matches. As soon as a match is rubbed against the surface of the box, fire flames up. Whence does it come? Neither within the friction surface nor yet within the match, of course, is it contained; we may investigate both of these physically and chemically in every imaginable way, never shall we find in either a trace of fire or of anything like it. And yet, every time a match is rubbed against the surface, fire appears. Accordingly, friction-surface and match are nothing more than *conditions* —occasional causes—for a third factor which seizes upon these conditions, *grasps* them, and by their means becomes manifest as fire. This third thing really lies in wait for these conditions, in order to grasp them and by their means to come violently into manifestation. Wherever a match is rubbed against a friction surface, whether this happens in Europe or in America, upon the moon or on Sirius, it is all the same. Everywhere and always this mysterious power of nature will eagerly seize upon these conditions and by means of them force its way into existence. And yet, although it is always and everywhere, nevertheless again, it is nowhere, for nowhere can it itself ever be found. In short, it is for us something inexplicable and inscrutable; it ever arises anew for us out of the "nothing," into which it always again sinks back, on which account in the last analysis we can say no more about it than we can say about the manifestations of our own energies; only this, that it is a kind of *grasping* which comes to fruition, and which we then perceive as fire. And it is the same with every force of nature. As further illustration, the beautiful comparison in which Schopenhauer vividly depicts the essence of nature's forces, may here be given in Buddhist garb:

"Let us imagine a machine constructed in accordance with the laws of mechanics. Iron weights through their weight furnish the impetus to movement; copper wheels resist through their rigidity; they push and lift each other and the levers by means of their impenetrability and so forth. Here weight, rigidity, impenetrability are original and unexplained forms of *grasping*: merely the conditions under which they appear, and the manner in which they express themselves as dominating a given substance as well as time and space, are indicated by mechanical science. Now, for example, let a strong magnet act upon the iron of the weights and overcome their weight, at once the movements of the machine cease, and matter is immediately again the scene of some other kind of *grasping*, about which the aetiological explanation can tell no more than the conditions under which it happens, namely, magnetism. But if now the copper strips of this machine are laid upon zinc plates, and diluted acid is introduced between them, then at once the same matter of the machine falls prey to another kind of original *grasping*, that is, to galvanism, which now dominates it according to its laws, and reveals itself in it through its phenomena, of which aetiology can tell no more than the circumstances under which, and the laws according to which, they appear. Now let us raise the temperature, and introduce pure oxygen, and the whole machine burns up:

this means, again, that another kind of *grasping,* chemical action, now lays irresistible claim to this matter. Now let the metallic calcium thus produced be combined with an acid: a salt is produced; crystals shoot out; they are the phenomena of another kind of *grasping*, again quite inscrutable in itself, whereas the taking place of this phenomenon is dependent on conditions which aetiology is able to state. The crystals weather away and mingle with other substances, and a vegetation arises out of them: a new kind of *grasping*—and thus we might track the same persistent matter into the infinite . . . how now this, now that, species of *grasping* gains the right to it, and inevitably seizes it in order to show itself."

To be sure, the Buddha does not expressly teach that all Becoming in the vegetable kingdom and in the domain of inorganic matter also is conditioned by grasping; but not because this is wrong, but because here as everywhere with unequalled logical consequence he holds to his principle of dealing with nothing which does not serve to establish a truly holy life, but is only of use to satisfy our mere lust for knowledge. But Becoming in the vegetable kingdom and in the domain of the inorganic does not here concern us any further, at least as regards the original direction of our enquiries, since it can never become of practical consequence to us, inasmuch as we can never slip back again into these domains. If upon this account the Buddha does not expressly speak about the causes of Becoming in these realms, nevertheless, as we shall see later on, he assumes as self-evident that there also this cause always consists in some kind of *grasping.*

In the passage quoted above we also find a classification of the possible kinds of grasping, in so far as it may relate to sensual pleasure, to views, to ritual observances and to thoughts about the *I.* This classification also at first seems somewhat strange to us, as we should prefer to see this grasping classified according to the external objects to which it relates. But here again also we are influenced by our wonted objective standpoint which always wants, off-hand, to take the external world as its measure. But if we bear in mind the subjective standpoint of the Buddha, namely, that our inscrutable essence as something alien is opposed to the world which we only *grasp,* then it will become clear that this grasping ultimately has to do with sensual enjoyments, then with the views arising within us in regard to the world and our relation to it, then with the religious ceremonies through which we think we must effect our deliverance, as for example the worship of a personal god, but in particular, with the false idea that our essence is a positive quantity belonging to this world. Nevertheless, this classification is not the fundamental one. There appears another one, intelligible without further ado also to us, and known to us before. Its direct theme are the elements constituting our personality, within which, because in the latter we experience the whole world, all our grasping is summed up, to wit, body, sensation, perception, activities of the mind and consciousness, which, as the totality of everything which we can grasp, the Buddha calls the five groups of grasping, *pañcupādānakkhandhā.* The process of birth consists just in the working out, that is, in the *Becoming* of these five groups with the corporeal organism as their basis, which, accordingly, have the principal grasping as their antecedent condition. But before we look closer at *this* kind of grasping, it will be best first to make ourselves acquainted with the immediate *condition* of all grasping.

For grasping also is causally conditioned. Indeed, the essence of all aetiology, as we have seen above, consists in calling attention to those conditions under which grasping exists, and the nature and manner of its expression. Certainly, as we already know, aetiology, correspondent with its objective standpoint, is satisfied with the discovery of these *external* conditions, whereas from the Buddha we may again expect the *inner* reason, which he actually gives as follows: "If, Ānanda, the question were put: 'Is grasping dependent on anything?' then reply should be made: 'Yes, it is dependent.' And if it were asked: 'On what is grasping dependent?' then reply should be made: 'In dependence upon *thirst* arises grasping.'"

What this means, the Buddha himself explains to us: "I have said: 'In dependence upon thirst arises grasping.' And this, Ānanda, that in dependence upon thirst arises grasping, must be understood in the following sense. Suppose, Ānanda, that nowhere and nowise any thirst of any being for anything existed, that is to say, no thirst for forms, no thirst for sounds, no thirst for odours, no thirst for tastes, no thirst for objects of touch, no thirst for ideas,—if thirst thus were entirely wanting, if thirst were completely annihilated, would then any kind of grasping be perceived?"

"Certainly not, Lord."

"Here then, Ānanda, is the cause, origin, arising, dependence of grasping, namely, thirst."

According to this, by thirst, *taṇhā*, is to be understood every kind of desire or craving for anything whatever within the world, which, as we already know, is summed up in the objects of the six senses, from the slightest desire that arises within us to the most deeply rooted, apparently ineradicable passion. It is only the expression *thirst* which here is unfamiliar to us. Later on, we shall return to it, especially in its relation to the will. Here it is enough to say that it comprises within itself conscious as well as unconscious volition.

As soon as this thirst, this desire for some sensual object, arises within us, the natural, necessary consequence is, that a grasping also arises within us. To illustrate this, we need only go back to our examples given above. What was the cause of my grasping of the representation of the girl I met on the street, of my *attachment* to her with the result that this grasping itself in turn determined the Becoming that followed upon it, and therewith my whole life's fate? Unquestionably, the desire that arose in me to possess the girl. If this desire, this thirst had not arisen in me, then I should not have grasped, in mind, her form; I should not have become attached to it; and in turn all the effects of this grasping itself would have remained absent. And what is the cause of a man overcoming with iron energy every obstacle opposing itself to his plan to become a merchant, an official, an officer, an artist? What is the cause of his grasping with such force at these plans and ideas? Certainly his intense desire, his ardent *thirst*, his inflexible will to win this life-position. If he had no such desire, no such *interest*, which again, in itself, is nothing but a mode of thirst, then he would not grasp such thoughts and still less the means of their realization, and thereby nothing of all this would *become*. If I have no *desire* for food, no *thirst* for drinks that might make me ill, then I do not grasp them, I do not take them, and precisely thereby avoid becoming ill. And if, finally, I have not the least desire for my body and thereby no sort of wish to maintain it any longer, if, besides this, I am free from all desire to satisfy the hunger and thirst which announce their presence; in short, if I am entirely without any desire of any kind, then I grasp nothing and can behold with equanimity how this my body, through want of necessary food, declines and decays, until at last, together with the organs of sense, it entirely perishes. Thereby in immediate ocular evidence, I can confirm in myself how for me *all* Becoming little by little comes to rest.

All this is so clear that it needs no further proof; nay, at bottom, is even incapable of such a thing. That all grasping, all attachment, and thereby all Becoming is conditioned by thirst, by willing, is without further words, self-evident in itself to everyone who only once has understood the statement. It only remains to test it by practically trying on ourselves how, by the gradual killing out of the will, Becoming becomes ever less and less. And this dictum holds good not only for ourselves and those phenomena that are similar to us, the animals, but "continued reflection will lead men to recognize also the force—or to speak in the language of the Buddha, the grasping—that impels and vegetates within the plant, yea, even the force by which the crystal shoots forth, by which the magnet turns towards the north pole, the influence which strikes it from the contact of heterogeneous metals, that which appears in the elective affinities of substances as repulsion and attraction, separating and uniting, lastly, even gravity, which strives so powerfully within all matter, pulling the stone to the earth, and earth towards the sun,"[149]—to recognize all these kinds of grasping as conditioned by that cause which, there where it appears most clearly and unmistakably, in man, is called *taṇhā,* thirst, will. "No body is without craving and desire" says Schopenhauer in the spirit of Jacob Boehme as he expresses himself, and as we may venture to add, after what we have seen, not less in the spirit of the Buddha.

To come back once more to our simile of the fire. We have seen that the mysterious force that appears as fire, if a match is rubbed against a corresponding frictional surface, lies in wait, so to say, for these conditions of its becoming visible, ever ready, regardless of any restrictions of time or space, to lay hold of them with violence. Who will not recognize in this ever watching and waiting desire to grasp adequate conditions and thus to arrive at Becoming—as fire—the same *taṇhā, thirst,* notwithstanding the gradually increasing distance of this kind of existence from our own?

But thereby *taṇhā,* thirst, will, is shown to be the ultimate ground of all being, or—to speak in the enlightened mode of the Buddha who acknowledges in this world no Being but only an eternal Becoming,*—of all Becoming: "Where is craving of will, there is grasping."[150] "In dependence upon grasping arises Becoming."[151]

Our expositions thus far yield us this result: Our birth, as a part, that is, as the first stage of Becoming, in common with this latter, has the same fundamental cause, *grasping.* But all grasping is rooted in *thirst,* in willing. Thus the search for the cause of our ever repeated rebirth led the Buddha to the discovery of the fundamental cause of all Becoming, that is, in the language of ordinary speech, of all being. On the other side, however, precisely through this, the process that brings about our ever repeated rebirth is flooded with brightest light. How it presents itself in this light will now be the subject of our discourse.

THE PROCESS OF REBIRTH
THE LAW OF KARMA

Our true essence lies beyond our personality and its components, even beyond the world. But we do not allow ourselves to be satisfied with it. We have a longing, a thirst for something else, entirely alien to our innermost essence, namely, for the world, a world of forms, of sounds,

---

* Here again one has to complain of the inexactness of many translations from the Canon, which, instead of leading us to the height of insight attained by the Buddha, from which no Being is to be found in the world but only Becoming, and of purifying thus our own shallow views, do exactly the reverse. Contrary to the language of the original text, they force the clear insight of the Buddha into modes of expression current among ourselves, and thus degrade and obscure it, when they translate *bhava,* Becoming, always by *Being* or *Existence.*

of odours, of sapids and of things tangible. And because we long and thirst for it, we always eagerly seize any opportunity of coming into contact with it. But this is not directly possible. To bring about a contact with form, an eye is needed; for contact with sounds, an ear; for contact with odours, with sapids, with things tangible, a nose, a tongue, a body are necessary; but a brain is always needed as a central organ. In short: to obtain the contact with the world which we so eagerly strive for, we need the corporeal organism, the "body endowed with six senses," as the six senses-machine. And so great is our thirst for the world of forms, of sounds, of odours, of sapids and of things tangible, that we imagine this thirst to be the immediate manifestation of our own essence, and therefore "the corporeal organism together with consciousness" the present appearance of this our essence, which objectifies itself therein. Hence also our unexampled clinging to this organism so long as we possess it, and our boundless thirst for a new one the moment we lose it, thus at the moment of death, a thirst which then actually leads to the formation of a new organism of the same kind, of a new six senses-machine. The process of this formation, as given in the teaching of the Buddha, is as follows:

We now know that every kind of Becoming presupposes two things: first, that conditions are set up for its taking place, and secondly, that these conditions are attached to, that they are grasped. Let us bear in mind the simile of the fire. The rubbing of the match on the frictional surface constitutes the condition at which grasping occurs. Or, since this grasping, this attachment, follows out of apparent nothingness, so that is impossible to define it more closely in any way, more especially not as the action of a subject, we may still better and more briefly express it thus: The match in consequence of friction becomes the object of grasping.

From these two factors there results this new Becoming also which sets in with conception, or, keeping to the language of the Buddha, with birth. The two parents, by uniting in copulation the male sperm with the female ovum—a process analogous to the rubbing of the match on its frictional surface in the production of fire—provide the condition, or, what is the same thing, the object of grasping, in consequence of which the object grasped, that is, the ovum thus fertilized, becomes an embryo, and the Becoming of a new corporeal organism sets in. But this grasping was that which the thirst of a dying creature, unallayed notwithstanding all sickness and death agony, had produced for a new six senses-machine, as for the only possibility of remaining in contact with, and enjoying the world of forms, sounds, odours, sapids and tangibles. To speak concretely: Let us imagine ourselves beside the sick-bed of some man, for example, a mighty prince, who is about to meet with what we call death. This means, that he is forced to give up the foreign elements he retained till now in his body endowed with six senses which alone made him visible for others; and who, on that very account once more as so often before in the course of time, has again to experience the sensation of dying. The thirst for the world is not yet dead within him; but where is thirst, there is grasping. This grasping shows itself as long as life has not fled from the body, in this present body itself. But in the same moment when the body, after the faculty of life has vanished, ceases to be an object that may be used for this grasping—only a body possessed of life sufficing for the satisfaction of the thirst for life—the former body is abandoned and a new life-informed germ is laid hold of, and grasping made at it. And this germ is the same that has just been generated in a strange bed by a man and woman, perhaps by a couple of rough working people, in voluptous paroxysm, by uniting their sperm and ovum. And consciousness descends upon the germ thus seized upon in a maternal womb: the germ develops into an embryo, the fruit is born—and that once powerful prince finds himself in the light of this consciousness back again as a child of these working people, though without remembrance of his former existence. In consequence he is only insufficiently nourished, badly treated, often heartlessly maltreated, and in later years forced by his father to beg, in order to provide him the means of satisfying his craving for drink. The former prince has become a miserable beggar. But this is not yet the worst. In another man at the moment of death, grasping at a new germ, conditioned through thirst for new Becoming or existence, is realized in some animal body or it may be even in some hell-world, the deceased man finding himself back as a beast or even as a devil. On the other hand, it may happen that when the present body is abandoned, grasping may take place in a world of light, a heaven, so that he in whom this process of dying has run its course, sees himself changed to "a god or a divine being."

With this the question as to the "causal connection between my former death and the fruitfulness of an alien marriage-bed" is solved, the bridge between the fresh existence of a new-born creature and that of a perished one is shown: "Where, monks, three are found in combination, there is a seed of life planted. Thus, if a father and mother come together, but it is not the mother's period and the being to be born is not present, then no seed of life is planted. Or, if father and mother come together, and it is the mother's period, but the being to be born is not present, then again no seed of life is planted. But when, monks, a father and mother come together, and it is the mother's period and the being to be born is also present, then by the combined agency of these three, a seed of life is planted."[152] Since the Buddha teaches re-birth, any one can see at once that "the being to be born" must depart from somewhere.

Thus death and conception reveal themselves as two sides of the one same process: Every conception is only possible through the simultaneous death of another creature in one or another realm of Saṁsāra. What disappears here, reappears there. To the paroxysms of lust in the moment of coition thus stand opposed the pangs of death of the creature just conceived.

In this whole matter we must, of course, proceed from this, that, for a dying creature's thirst for existence leading to new grasping of a new germ, the laws of space and of time at that moment do not exist. All the germs in the world are therefore equally near to it. For thirst at this moment is without any substratum, since its former body, upon which it had concentrated itself, has been snatched from it.* It is in just the same condition as that other kind of thirst which we see manifesting itself as fire. As we know, it lies in wait in ghostly omnipresence for the conditions of its entry and seizes upon them with eagerness, no matter whether they are given here upon our own earth or upon Sirius.**

* * *

If the problem of rebirth is thus solved in the simplest imaginable manner, none the less this solution is not yet an exhaustive one. For the question—of such an immense

---

* At this moment, free from its former restrictions, it flames up out of the "Nothing," that is, out of our innermost essence, which is as boundless as the universe, as we shall see in the last chapter.

** In the "Milindapañha" this idea is expressed as follows:

"The king said: 'Master Nāgasena, if somebody dies here and is reborn in the world of Brahma, and another one who dies here is reborn in Kashmir, which of them would arrive first?'

'They would arrive at the same time, O King.'

'Give me a simile.'

'In which town were you born, O King?'

practical importance—still remains to be answered: How comes it, that one creature in dying grasps the ovum of a woman, another the ovum in an animal womb, another in a hell or in a heaven? Or more briefly: Through what is determined the different *direction* of grasping, upon a being's death? The answer is: Through the same factor which represents the cause of grasping in general, thirst, *taṇhā*. The special kind of thirst, or to put it otherwise, the main direction taken by will in a dying being, determines not only the grasping itself, but also its direction.

To understand this fully, we must before all else get a clear idea as to the condition of thirst or will at this decisive moment. We only grasp what is in harmony with our will, —this axiom holds good everywhere without exception, as we have had occasion to see in our investigations thus far, and as every one may experience at every moment in himself. But though of such unlimited validity, in normal life it must be completed by this other, that we do not always grasp

---

'In a village called Kalasi, Master.'

'How far is Kalasi from here, O King?'

'About two hundred miles, Master.'

'And how far is Kashmir from here, O King?'

'About twelve miles, Master.'

'Now think of the village of Kalasi, O King.'

'I have done so, Master.'

'And now think of Kashmir, O King.'

'It is done, Master.'

'Of which of these two, O King, did you think the more slowly and of which the more quickly?'

'Equally quickly of both, Master.'

'Just so, O King, he who dies here and is reborn in the world of Brahma, is not reborn later than he who dies here and is reborn in Kashmir.'

'Give me one more simile.'

'What do you think, O King? Suppose two birds were flying in the air, and they should settle both at the same time, one upon a high, and the other one upon a low tree,—which bird's shade would first fall upon the earth, and which bird's later?'

'Both shadows would appear at the same time, Master.'

'Just so, O King, both men are reborn at the same time, and not one of them earlier and the other later.' "

what is in harmony with our willing. This is the case when we recognize with sufficient clearness the injurious or deceptive nature of that for which we long. Indeed this recognition, if only it is complete enough, may entirely cure us of our desire for an object and thereby also from grasping at it. For instance, a man may be filled with hottest passion for a woman. The girl seems inclined to gratify his lust and bares her bosom which exhibits distinct symptoms of syphilis. His passion for this woman, and therewith his grasping at her, will probably in an instant vanish for ever. Thus our willing is generally modified by *cognition,* inasmuch as in its light we reject objects which in themselves are in complete harmony with our willing, but are known to us to have predominantly injurious consequences. Our will affirms itself unchecked only when, from one cause or another, the light of knowledge no longer shines, thus, when the will is blind. Then, without making any distinction we grasp at everything that is in harmony with it, regardless of the fact—just because we have no knowledge of it—that the object seized will, as outcome, involve us in the most serious suffering. Even if consciousness is merely dimmed, the longing for possession of a walking-stick will cause a man to grasp at a poisonous snake lying quietly on the ground. But still more eagerly will a sleeping man greedily swallow a sweet draught dripped upon his tongue, though it be a deadly poison, if only his willing is excited so far that it acts, though yet without consciousness.* In full consciousness, thus, in possession of the light of cognition, neither of them, of course, would do any such thing.

But in exactly the same situation are we, and all beings at the moment of death. For then *every* kind of consciousness disappears, since their supporters, the recent activities of the senses, have ceased. The thirst to maintain ourselves in

* That is: Only consciousness of taste is aroused, but not thought-consciousness.

existence, our will for new Becoming, then affirms itself, because devoid of any kind of cognition, in total blindness, and for this very reason without the least regard to the consequences resulting therefrom, it simply leads to a grasping at that germ among all possible ones, among the five courses, that is most in harmony with itself, to which, preciselv for this reason, it becomes chiefly attracted, all the same whether this germ is in a human female, in an animal womb, or even in some hell. Only *later*, when this germ has developed, and with the entry of sense-activity, consciousness again dawns, will the germ seized and adhered to, be illuminated by this same consciousness. *Then* we recognize ourselves as men, as beasts or as devils, just like the man who has laid hold of a poisonous snake under the delusion that it is a walking-stick, or the other who, almost wholly unconscious, has greedily gulped down the poisonous draught, and only with the restoration of the power of thought becomes aware what a trick his own will has played upon him.

Because the thirst for new Becoming at the moment of death, that is, upon the abandonment of the present body, thus acts entirely blindly, and for this very reason, in accordance with its innermost nature, therefore, to use a modern expression, we can say that at this moment it stands purely subject to *the law of affinity*. As a chemical substance forms a homogeneous combination only with certain other substances, but strives for this with all possible vehemence, while showing indifference towards all others, which is what we call chemical affinity, in exactly the same way there exists in every living creature at the moment of death a certain definite striving, called by the Buddha *taṇhā* or thirst, which striving stands in a relationship of affinity only with a certain kind of germ to which alone, therefore, it is led by grasping from which, thereupon, the new organism results. This is clearly to be seen in the animal world without further ado. The fundamental striving of every animal during its lifetime, when a gleam of knowledge is present, is restricted to its own kind, all animals having intercourse only with those of its own species. All the more exclusively will this concentration of the will to live upon its own species declare itself at the moment of death, when only a striving for grasping at a similar animal germ will be present, and, accordingly, only grasping at such a germ will take place. On the other hand, the determination of affinities among mankind will be much more difficult. For among men all sorts of directions of the will are represented. Alongside of men with the mind of an angel, there are others who stand far below the beast. "Man has reason, but he uses it only to be more beastly than any beast." * It will be all quite clear, then, without more ado, when the Buddha, as we have seen above, teaches that from the human realm, paths lead to all the five tracts of Saṁsāra: the thirst for existence of a man with an angel's mind will, when in death he abandons his former organism, draw him to a heavenly world and lead him to a grasping there, with the same necessity that the light, transparent smoke of burning precious wood by natural law mounts upward. On the other hand, the base inclinations of a degenerate man, if in the animal world they light upon a germ akin to themselves, will grasp this germ, but if they are still worse than any animal, then they will only find corresponding materials in a still lower realm, in one of the hells, and, accordingly, in their blindness cling to this, exactly as the thick heavy smoke of coal cannot rise upwards, but in accordance with its nature remains in

* Precisely because man possesses reason, it makes him sometimes appear much worse than a beast. First just because of this reason, man may, from a purely objective standpoint, act much worse than any beast. But then his actions, if the other conditions are equal, are, in relation to his reason, always worse than those of an animal. For it is clear that a man stealing or murdering in spite of his reason, ranks morally far below an animal doing the same without reason.

the depths. Thus the nature of our future rebirth depends upon the direction our desires take during the course of our life up till death. *Thirst is the leading string, bound to which beings are led on the long road of their rebirths through Saṁsāra, as an ox is led along the street with a rope.*

This idea finds its most pregnant expression in the fifty-seventh Discourse of the Middle Collection. Punna, a cow-ascetic, and Seniya, an unclad or dog-ascetic, two penitents who, Brahmin fashion, wished to secure a fortunate rebirth through exquisite self-torment, Punna leading the life of a cow and Seniya that of a dog, betake themselves to the Exalted One. Punna asks him the following question: "This unclad one, sir, this Seniya, the dog-ascetic, practises a heavy austerity: he partakes only of food thrown upon the ground. For long years he has followed and kept the dog-vow; whither will he go? What may he expect?" The Buddha at first refuses to answer the question, but at last, under Punna's urging he makes the following reply:

"Well then, Punna, as you do not give way, I will answer you. Suppose, Punna, that someone realizes the dog-vow, carries it out completely, realizes the dog's habits, carries them out completely, realizes the dog's mind, carries it out completely, realizes the dog's behaviour, carries it out completely. When he has realized the dog-vow, when he has carried it out completely, when he has realized the dog's habits, carried them out completely, when he has realized the dog's mind, carried it out completely, when he has realized the dog's behaviour, carried it out completely,—then when the body breaks up, after death, he will come back to existence among the dogs. If, however, he cherishes the opinion: "Through these practices or vows, self-castigation or abstinence, I shall become a god or a divine being,—then this is a false opinion. And this false opinion, I say, Punna, causes him to come either to this side or to that: either into a hell-world or into an animal womb. Thus, Punna, the dog-vow, if it is successful, leads to the dogs, and if it fails, into a hell-world."

Seniya now asks: "This Koliya Punna, the cow-ascetic, sir, for a long time has kept and practised the cow-vow: whither will he go, what may he expect?" To him also the Buddha only answers after having been urged several times:" Really, Seniya, since you insist, I will answer you. Suppose, Seniya, someone realizes the cow-vow, carries it out completely, realizes the cow's habits, carries them out completely, realizes the cow's mind, carries it out completely, realizes the cow's behaviour, carries it out completely. And having realized the cow-vow, having carried it out completely, having realized the cow's habits, having carried them out completely, having realized the cow's mind, having carried it out completely, having realized the cow's behaviour, having carried it out completely,—then, upon the dissolution of the body, after death, he comes again into existence among cows. But if he cherishes the opinion: 'By means of such practices or vows, self-castigation or abstinence I shall become a god or a divine being,'—then this is a false opinion. And his false opinion, I say, Seniya, causes him to come to this side or to that, either into a hell-world or into an animal womb. Thus, Seniya, the cow-vow, if it is succesful, leads to the cows, and if it fails, into a hell-world."

And how should it be otherwise? To what other grasping than of a dog-germ should the blind thirst of a dying human being to maintain itself in existence, lead, in accord with the law of affinity, if his whole striving and willing have become dog-like? At the worst, it may happen, that this striving, which in that decisive moment is entirely blind, may lead to grasping in yet greater depths, namely, in a hell, "if the dog-vow fails." Then, in one's blind willing, one has gone astray, somewhat like an animal that in its blind craving to satisfy its hunger comes upon poisoned food and swallows it.

So it is in every case. Always and without exception the striving for new Becoming, that is, to maintain oneself in existence, if it is forced, in consequence of the decay of the body inhabited till now, to search for a new germ, leads to such a grasping as corresponds with the direction already taken during the course of life, in the way that a stone that is thrown keeps to the direction given to it: "Suppose, monks, that a monk has won to confidence, virtue, experience, renunciation, wisdom. And he thinks: 'O that I might return, upon the dissolution of the body, after death, to the company of mighty princes!' This thought he thinks, on this thought he dwells, this thought he cherishes. These activities of his mind* and inner conditions, which he thus cherishes and promotes within himself, lead to his rebirth in such an existence. This, O monks, is the way, this is the transition that conducts to return thither. And further, O monks, if a monk has won to confidence, virtue, experience, renunciation, wisdom, and heard this saying: 'The thirty-three gods—the shadow gods—the blissful gods—the gods of boundless happiness—the gods dwelling beyond boundless happines—these live long and gloriously and happily.'** Such an one thinks within himself: 'O that upon the dissolution of the body, after death, I might return to the society of these gods!' This thought he thinks, on this thought he dwells, this thought he cherishes. These activities of the mind and the inner conditions that he thus cherishes and promotes within himself, lead to his

---

* Sankhārā, as the fourth group of grasping.

** Brahmā, who does not in the least belong to the highest spheres of the gods, exists for a hundred years, every day and every night of which constitutes a Kalpa, a world-cycle. Whoever is inclined to smile at this figure, may reflect that in comparison with our essence which stands above all time, it shrivels into a moment, yea, even to—nothing!

rebirth in such an existence. This, ye monks, is the way, the transition that leads to return thither."* [153]

According to this, man always becomes what he would like to become, that is, whatever he desires and thirsts after; for whatever we thirst after, that we grasp. Of course this is not to be understood as if it meant that a mere wish would be sufficient; but what has directing force, is the nature of our willing and of our desire in its innermost depth, that means, our innermost character, as it appears in action as blind impulse, without being guided by the light of knowledge. For according to the foregoing expositions, exactly in this situation is our will at the decisive moment of death, when it determines our grasping of a new germ. To know to what kind of grasping our will may lead us, we must dive into the depths of our animal life, as it reveals itself when the dominating influence of reason is eliminated, thus, in emotion, or still more, in a state of intoxication, or in dream. Hence it is not decisive, if a person in rational reflection does not murder nor steal, is neither unchaste nor heartless, but only if he is incapable of all this even in the height of passion, nay, even in his dreams. Only that which even in such conditions never more arises, never more *can* arise within us, of which therefore, as we can easily feel, we are absolutely incapable, only this is definitively eradicated from our will. Therefore it can never any more make itself felt when in death we have entirely abandoned consciousness, and precisely because of this, cannot any more as blind impulse determine our new grasping. If, for example, I know that I could not, under any circumstances, conceive the thought of killing, not even in a dream, then I am sure

* Compare also Angutt. Nik. I, p. 288, where the Buddha says in regard to Ānanda's enthusiasm about the former's immense realm of power at Udāyi: "If Ānanda should die without being liberated from desire, then in consequence of this inclination, he would rule seven times among the gods as a god, and seven times in the Indian continent as a king."

that this inclination no longer exists within me, thus also can no longer determine my new grasping at death. But if I must confess, after having carefully studied myself, that in a state of clear consciousness I am indeed incapable of killing, but might become a murderer in an excited or drunken state, then my will is of such sort that in the future, if unilluminated by any consciousness, it might cause a grasping of a germ and in a world where murders can be, and are, indeed, committed; and where perhaps also this capacity of will still asleep within me, under the appropriate external circumstances,—for instance, if I were born into a rude and uncultured family—might some time or other flame up again and make me a murderer. The fundamental condition for the certainty that after death I shall not become attached to a germ in a low-class, pain-laden world, is therefore this, that I know myself, at latest, in the hour of my death, to be definitively free from all bad inclinations. In so far as this is the case, in so far as a man has acquired confidence, virtue, experience, renunciation, wisdom, and thereby become nobler and purer and thereby more adapted to attachment in higher and purer spheres, he also has it in his own hands to bring about his rebirth in closely determined circles or spheres, be it in a powerful high-placed family, or in a world of gods. By incessantly and intensively occupying himself with thoughts relating to this, he may turn his entire striving in this direction, until he is quite absorbed, completely saturated with it, so that of itself the unshakeable certitude comes to him: After death I can no longer possibly sink into the depths, as little as coal-smoke, when cleansed, that is, freed from its heavier components, can settle in lower levels, but *must* rise upwards. Indeed, in this decisive unconscious condition, I can grasp no other germ but the one desired, because every other would be contrary to my innermost nature, that is, to the characteristic direction of my will, to my deepest thirst for a certain definite mode of existence, and therefore, without further ado, even though blind, would be rejected by it.

As a typical example of how it is the law of affinity that determines our grasping in death, the thirteenth Discourse of the Dīghanikāya may be cited, in which the way to union with Brahmā,* the highest aim of the Brahmin caste, is treated thus:

"Vāseṭṭha, what think you and what have you heard from old and elder Brahmins, who were your teachers or the teachers of your teachers, about this point: Is Brahmā interested in house and home, in wife and child, or not?"

"He is not, reverend Gotama."

"Is his mind spiteful or peaceable?"—"Peaceable, reverend Gotama."—"Is he ill-natured or good-natured?"—"Good-natured, reverend Gotama."—"Is he pure or impure of heart?"—"Pure-hearted, reverend Gotama."—"Is his will constant or not?"—"It is constant, reverend Gotama."

"Now what think you, Vāseṭṭha? Are the Brahmins knowing the three Vedas attached to house and home, wife and children, or not?"—"They are attached to them, reverend Gotama."—"Are they spiteful or peaceable?"—"They are spiteful, reverend Gotama."—"Are they ill-natured or good-natured?"—"Ill-natured, reverend Gotama."—"Are they pure-hearted or impure-hearted?"—"They are impure-hearted, reverend Gotama."—"Of constant will or not?"—"Of inconstant will, reverend Gotama."

"Vāseṭṭha, do these agree together: the Brahmins, knowing the three Vedas, but esteeming property and family, and Brahmā who is without property and family?"—"No, reverend Gotama, these do not agree together."

* Brahmā is the Christian god, existing within the world and therefore not eternal —see above p. 238**—but imagining himself eternal, because of the immense duration of his life. Compare Dīghanikāya XI.

16

"Very good, Vāseṭṭha. That therefore these Brahmins, knowing the three Vedas, but esteeming property and family, after the end of the body, after death should attain to union with Brahmā who is without property or family—this is impossible."

"Then, Vāseṭṭha, the Brahmins, knowing the three Vedas, according to your saying are spiteful, but Brahmā is peaceable; they are ill-natured, but Brahmā is good-natured; they are impure-hearted, but Brahmā is pure; they are of inconstant will, but Brahmā is constant. Do these agree together: The spiteful, ill-natured, impure-hearted, inconstant Brahmins knowing the three Vedas, and the peaceable, good-natured, pure, constant Brahmā?"—"No, reverend Gotama, these do not agree together."

"Very good, Vāseṭṭha. That thus these inconstant Brahmins knowing the three Vedas, after the end of the body, after death, should attain to union with constant Brahmā—this is impossible . . ."

Thereupon the young Brahmin Vāseṭṭha spoke to the Exalted One saying: "Reverend Gotama, I have heard that the Samana Gotama shows the way that leads to Brahmā and to union with him. May the reverend Gotama be pleased to show us this way and lead the Brahmins upwards."

"Listen then, Vāseṭṭha, and note well what I shall say."—"So be it, Lord," said the young Brahmin Vāseṭṭha assenting to the Exalted One. The Exalted One spoke, and said:

"There the bhikkhu (monk) with his loving mind penetrates one direction of space, and so he penetrates the second and so the third and so the fourth. And thus he penetrates upwards and downwards and horizontally the whole wide world everywhere, completely, with loving benevolent mind, all-embracing, great, beyond all measure, full of peace."

"Just, Vāseṭṭha, as a powerful trumpeter easily penetrates all the four regions with the sound of his instrument: even so there remains no restriction for the development of such a benevolent mind thus released. Vāseṭṭha, this is the way leading to Brahmā, to union with him."

"Vāseṭṭha, such a bhikkhu also penetrates with compassionate mind—with joyful mind—with equal mind one direction of space, and so the second and so the third and so the fourth. And thus he penetrates upwards and downwards and horizontally the whole wide world everywhere, completely, with all-embracing, broad, measureless, compassionate mind, with joyful mind, and with equanimity.

"Just, Vāseṭṭha, as a powerful trumpeter easily penetrates all the four regions with the sound of his instrument; even so there remains no restriction for the development of such a compassionate mind—joyful mind—with equanimity. Vāseṭṭha, this is the way leading to Brahmā, to union with him.

"Now what think you, Vāseṭṭha? Has the bhikkhu who keeps himself thus, any interest in the petty things of every-day life, or not?"—"He has not, reverend Gotama."—"Is he spiteful or peaceable?"—"Peaceable, reverend Gotama."—"Ill-natured or good-natured?"—"Good-natured, reverend Gotama." —"Pure-hearted or impure-hearted?"—"Pure-hearted, reverend Gotama."—"Constant or inconstant in his will?"—"Constant in his will, reverend Gotama."

"So then, Vāseṭṭha, you say that such a bhikkhu is without interest in the petty things of every-day life, and that Brahmā is without interest in the petty things of every-day life. Do these two agree together, a bhikkhu without interest in worldly possessions, and Brahmā without interest in worldly possessions?"—"Yes, reverend Gotama, they agree together."—"Very good, Vāseṭṭha! That such a bhikkhu uninterested in worldly things, after the end of his body, after death, should attain to union with Brahmā, who is untouched by worldly cares, this is possible."

"And so you say, Vāseṭṭha, that such a bhikkhu is, just like Brahmā, peaceable, good-natured, pure-hearted, constant in his will. Do these agree together: a peaceable, good-natured, pure-hearted, constant-willed bhikkhu, and peaceable, good-natured, pure-hearted, constant-willed Brahmā?"—"Yes, reverend Gotama, they agree together."—"Very good, Vaseṭṭha! That therefore such a peaceable, good-natured, pure and constant bhikkhu, after the end of his body, after death, may attain to union with unchanging Brahmā—this is possible.'" For he is by his thirst, his willing, "as it were, conducted" to the heaven of Brahmā, as it is said in the 153rd to the 162nd Discourse of the Book of Threes, in the Anguttara Nikāya.

But with this the law of affinity, as leading the will in its grasping, is not yet exhausted. It not only generally determinates the germ in which the new grasping takes place, in general as regards its belonging to one of the five realms of Saṁsāra, but it also indicates in minutest detail the guiding clue as to why a certain definite germ is seized and adhered to, why, for instance, within the human kingdom a grasping takes place just in the womb of a poor working woman, or of a noble lady, or at a germ already diseased from father or mother and endowed with but small vitality. This is expounded in detail by the Buddha in the hundred-and-thirty-fifth Discourse of the Middle Collection as follows:—

"What, O Gotama, may be the reason, what the cause, why also among human beings, born as men, depravity and excellence are found? There are, O Gotama, short-lived men and long-lived men, there are sickly ones and healthy ones, there are ugly ones and beautiful ones, there are powerless ones and powerful ones, there are penniless ones and well-to-do ones, there are such as are in high, and such as are in low position, there are stupid ones and acute ones;—what is the reason, O Gotama, what is the cause, that also among human beings, born as men, depravity and excellence are found?"

"Owners of their works, O Brahmin, are beings, heirs of their works, children of their works, creatures of their works, slaves of their works. Works discriminate beings, according to their depravity and excellence . . . .

"Suppose, O Brahmin, some woman or man kills living creatures, is cruel and bloodthirsty, accustomed to murder and homicide, without compassion for man and beast. Such action, thus performed, thus completed, upon the dissolution of the body, after death, causes such an one to go downwards, upon an evil track, into the depths, into a hell-world. Or, if he does not reach there, but attains to humanity, then, wherever he is re-born, he will be short-lived. This is the transition, Brahmin, that leads to a short life.

"Again, Brahmin, suppose some man or woman has rejected killing, abstains from killing, without stick and sword, full of fellow-feeling and compassion, and cultivates kindness and compassion towards all living creatures. Such action, thus performed, thus completed, upon the dissolution of the body, after death, causes his arrival upon a good track, into a heavenly world; or, if he does not reach there but attains the human state, then wherever he is reborn, he will be long-lived. This is the transition, Brahmin, that leads to long life."

In continuing his Discourse, the Buddha proceeds to explain, how the cruel, the angry, the envious, the miserly, the haughty, the man living without any interest in his future wellbeing, if they do not fall into a hell, but reach humanity again, will be reborn, the first sickly, the second ugly, the third powerless, the fourth poor, the fifth in a low position and the sixth a fool, whereas men who have cultivated the contrary qualities, rise up to heavenly worlds, or, if they are reborn as men, become respectively healthy, beautiful, powerful, well-to-do, of high rank or wise.*

* * *

Until now, we had proceeded chiefly on the assumption that the main striving of a man tends in a certain definite direction, and that in consequence of this, he develops certain quite definite and special qualities of mind, and in an outstanding direction. These, then, before all else, are decisive as regards the nature of his grasping at death. But, generally speaking, his thirst, or, as we are more accustomed to say, his willing at the moment of death is not at all homogeneous, but a summation of manifold, nay, even of opposed tendencies. In every man there dwells an angel and a devil. Therefore the question arises, as to what it is which in such a case determines the new grasping upon death. The answer again is very simple. It depends upon whether the good or the bad striving comes into activity at the moment of death and thus determines the new grasping.

---

* It is not difficult in all these cases also, to show the law of affinity as the regulator of the grasping of a new germ that occurs at death:

Whoso, devoid of compassion, can kill men or even also animals, carries deep within himself the inclination to shorten life. He finds satisfaction or even pleasure in the short-livedness of other creatures. Short-lived germs have therefore some affinity for him, an affinity which makes itself known after his death in the grasping of another germ which then takes place, to his own detriment. Even so, germs bearing within themselves the power of developing into a deformed body, have an affinity for one who finds pleasure in ill-treating and disfiguring others.

An angry person begets within himself an affinity for ugly bodies and their respective germs, since it is the characteristic mark of anger to disfigure the face.

Whoever is jealous, niggardly, haughty, carries within himself the tendency to grudge everything to others and to despise them. Accordingly, germs that are destined to develop in poor, outward circumstances, possess affinity for him.

It is, of course, only a consequence of the above, that a change of sex may also ensue. Thus it is related in the Dīghanikāya XXI, that Gopikā, a daughter of the Sakya house, was reborn after her death as "Gopaka, a son of the gods," because "the female mind had become repulsive to her, and she had formed a male mind within herself."

By this, however, it is not meant that the opposite direction of will lying latent at this moment, has become ineffectual for ever. On the contrary, it also somewhere and sometime will make itself felt, being decisive as regards some later birth, some "future return." For it remains, smouldering, so to say, beneath the ashes, and need not enter consciousness for a long time. To understand this thoroughly, we have only to reflect how very few men really know their own character, that is, the sum of the tendencies of their will. Either the outer motives are wanting which might wake the impulses and inclinations slumbering within them, or external circumstances, more especially the laws of the state, hinder *the expression* of an evilly disposed will, but not this will itself. "Hence it happens that it is only very rarely that a man sees his entire disgustingness in the mirror of his deeds. Or do you really think that Robespierre, Bonaparte, the Emperor of Morocco, or the murderers you see broken on the wheel, are the only men among all who are so bad? Do you not see, that many would do the same if only they were able? Many a criminal dies more peacefully upon the scaffold than many a non-criminal in the arms of his dear ones. For that one has recognized his will and changed it; but the other has not been able to change it, because he never was able to recognize it."[154] Thus it becomes apparent how some trait of character may slumber within us through whole existences, until all at once, suddenly it somehow becomes manifest and actively operative.* From this point of view we can also understand how an evil inclination may lead us upon our next death to grasp in a hell, whilst our good tendencies, possibly under the repeated influence of

---

* An analogy to this is to be found in hereditary physical germs of disease, which often only in the second or even the third generation lead to sickness, as is especially the case with mental diseases. These therefore are carried about by their bearers during their whole life, in the same manner, quite unconsciously.

our evil impulsions, may only determine a later grasping, after the efflux of our objectification in a hell-world, only then becoming effective, or *vice versa*. Of this the Buddha gives an example in the following case:

King Pasenadi of Kosala tells him:

"Sir, here in Sāvatthī a householder and master of a guild has died. He has left no son behind him, and now I come here, after having made over his property to the royal treasure. Sir, a million gold pieces, and what shall I say of the silver! But this householder and master of a guild, sir, used to eat alternately broken scraps of food and sour gruel. And thus he clothed himself: For dress he wore a robe of coarse hemp; and as to his coach, he drove in a broken down wagon with a worn-out sun-shade of leaves."

Thereupon the Buddha says:

"Certainly, O king, certainly, O king! In a former life, O king, this householder and master of a guild once gave alms of food to a Pacceka-buddha,* called Tagarasikhi. And as, after having said, 'Give alms of food to the ascetic!' he rose from his seat and went away, he repented having given the food saying within himself: 'It would be better, if my servants and workmen ate the food I gave for alms!' And besides this, he deprived his brother's only son of his life, for the sake of his property.

"And because, O king, this householder and master of a guild gave alms of food to the Paccekabuddha Tagarasikhi, in requital for his deed he attained seven times the good way, into the heavenly world. And in the same manner, as requital for his deed, he became seven times master of a guild here in Sāvatthī.

---

* An Awakened One for himself alone, who, in contrast with a completely Awakened One—a Sammāsambuddha—does not possess the power of sharing his knowledge with others.

"And because, O king, this householder and master of a guild repented of having given alms, saying to himself: 'It would be better that my servants and workmen ate the food;' therefore, as requital for this deed, he had no appreciation of good food, no appreciation of fine dresses, no appreciation of an elegant vehicle, no appreciation of the enjoyments of the five senses.

"And because, O king, this householder and master of a guild deprived of his life the only son of his brother for the sake of his property, as requital for this deed he had to suffer many years, many hundreds of years, many thousands of years, many hundreds of thousands of years of pain in hell. And in the same manner, as requital for this deed, he is without a son for the seventh time, and in consequence of this, has to leave his property to the royal treasury."

It is hardly necessary to point out particularly that the said deeds of the guild-master only brought about their later consequences as manifestations and extensions of the corresponding tendencies of will. According to the law of gradual becoming, that dominates everything, no one can commit a serious crime, unless his will for long before has travelled the roads on which it lies. The decision and the perpetration of the crime itself merely strengthen and set the seal on the tendency of will already existing. This tendency, of course, also remains after the deed is done, even if in the sequel it never breaks out again, nay, even if it remains unknown to the criminal himself—nobody will trust a man who has consciously killed another, even if many years have since gone by—by reason of which, precisely, this tendency of will, thus become latent, at the approaching death may determine the direction of the new grasping. It is not the externally visible deed as such, regarded from a purely objective standpoint,—for example, the killing of a man, done without intention—which determines the future fate of a man, but rather the mental disposition in which it is performed, that is, the direction of will upon which it has followed, whose strengthening is partly conditioned by the very deed. This is set forth by the Buddha in the fifty-sixth Discourse of the Middle Collection, where in a dialogue with Upāli the householder, an adherent of Nigantha Nathaputta, he deals with the following chain of thought: What is done without intention, is not so very bad. If, however, it is done with intention, then it is very bad. Thereupon, he thrice declares in solemn repetition, that of possible deeds in thoughts, words and deeds those done in thought, because created by a bad disposition, are the worst. In the sixth Book of the Anguttara Nikāya the Buddha directly identifies action with willing: "Willing, ye disciples, I call acting *(kamma)*; for if will is there, then one acts, either in deeds, in words, or in thoughts."*

According to this, every act of volition leads to certain quite definite consequences, not only consisting in those which manifest themselves in this very life, and called by the Buddha the "visible chain of suffering," but manifesting

---

* Compare also Milindapañha:

The king said: "Master Nāgasena, whose fault is greater, that of a man doing evil consciously, or that of another, doing it unconsciously?"

The elder said: "Whoso unconsciously does evil, O king, commits the greater fault." —"Then, master Nāgasena, we ought to punish our princes and ministers doubly, if they commit faults without knowing it?"—"What does your Majesty think about this: If someone, without knowing what he is doing, and another consciously, seizes an iron ball heated red-hot, which of these two men would burn himself more?"—"That one, master, who unsuspectingly seizes the ball."—"Just so, O king, is the fault of him greater who does evil unconsciously."—"Very good, master Nagasena."—How is this to be understood? Hardly otherwise than that in him who knows his deed to be detestable, very soon repentance ensues, and, in consequence of this, wickedness does not increase, whereas in him who without remorse may deceive his friend, who is able to murder a man or to torment a beast without feeling compassion, the inclination towards evil will grow through the hardening of his character. If another saying of the Buddha, on the contrary, declares a man who unconsciously does evil to be free from fault,—"*ajanantassa n'apatti:* without knowledge no fault"—then this "without knowledge" must be understood in the sense of an objective error *(error in objecto)* in opposition to the case of ignorance of the moral law or *karma* treated above, an

themselves also beyond death as the "hidden chain of suffering." For every act of volition determines by way of the *tendency* of will, conditioned or partly conditioned or strengthened by it, the grasping of one of our future rebirths and thus contributes towards our transference into the corresponding external circumstances. This effectuation of all willing, in accordance with law, called the law of Karma* in the Dialogues, is also called "the fruit of deeds," or simply the law *(dhamma)*:

"What, dear Gotama, may be the cause, what may be the reason, that many creatures, upon the dissolution of the body, after death, come upon the downward way, upon the evil road, to states of suffering, to hell?"

"Just because of their lawless behaviour, their wrong behaviour, O Brahmin, do many creatures, upon the dissolution of the body, after death, come upon the downward way, upon the evil road, to states of suffering, to hell."

"And what, dear Gotama, may be the cause, what may be the reason, that many creatures, upon the dissolution of the body, after death, come upon the good road, to the heavenly world?"

"Just because of their behaviour being in harmony with the law, because of their right behaviour, O Brahmin, many creatures, upon the dissolution of the body, after death, come upon the good road, to the heavenly world." [156]

Closely regarded, this law of Karma is nothing more than

---

ignorance always betraying a very low moral standard. This is illustrated by the following sentence from the Sutrakṛtanga, put into the mouth of a Buddhist: "If a savage throws his spear through the side of a corn-stack, believing it to be a man, or through a pumpkin, believing it to be a child, and roasts it, then he is guilty of murder, according to our view. But if a savage spears a man and roasts him, believing him to be a part of corn-stack, or a little child, believing it to be a pumpkin, then he is not guilty of murder, according to our view."

* The Sanskrit word *karma*, in its Pāli form *kamma*, means the effecting deed, or, briefer, the acting, therefore the law of acting, or,—since, according to what we have demonstrated, acting is the same as willing—the law to which all willing is subject.

the law of *causality,* not only in its formal meaning, as the law of cause and effect, but also in its material significance, according to which a certain quite definite effect always follows upon a certain definite cause. Only it is freed from any restriction to the physical world and shown to reign also in the domain of the moral, and therefore beyond death. In this its all-embracing sphere of validity it is that power, now marvelled at as benevolent providence, now feared as the dark fate, to which is subject every act of will, even the slightest in the faintest thought. The moment any kind of volition stirs, it stirs in harmony with the law of causality, or else not at all.

Hence we cannot escape from our deeds; they will inevitably find us at the proper time in the form of their effects:

"Not in the air, not in the depths of the ocean, nor in a distant mountain cave: nowhere in the world is there a place where a man can escape his own evil deeds."[157]

"That no fruit should arise from those evil deeds, the defiling, birth-producing, dreadful, sorrow-inflicting, leading anew to birth, old age and death,—this no one can effect, no ascetic nor priest, nor spiritual being, no god nor devil nor any one whatsoever in all the world."[158]

"He who after long absence safely arrives home from far-off countries, upon his arrival is welcomed by the crowd of friends and relatives; even so, he who has acted rightly on earth, is welcomed by his own good deeds in the next world, like a dear friend by his friends."[159]

First of all, of course, our present body, like every future one, together with all its sense organs and mental faculties, thus what we have called before the six-senses-machine, is exclusively a product of our previous action, inasmuch as this has brought about the grasping in the maternal womb:

"This is not, ye disciples, your body nor the body of

another, rather must it be regarded as the deed of the past, the deed that has come to fruition, the deed that is willing actualized, that has become perceptible."* [160]

"The eye, ye monks, is to be recognized and regarded as determined through former action.

"The ear, the nose, the tongue, the body, the mind, ye monks, is to be recognized and regarded as formed and determined through former action." [161]

In short: "My action is my possession, my action is my inheritance, my action is the womb that bears me, my action is the family to which I am related, my action is my refuge." [162]

If the consequences of all our willing are thus strictly regulated by the law, it is clear without further argument, that no good faith, no firm trust based upon religious dogmas as to the correctness of our mode of life can protect us from them. A man with weak lungs, who in a heated condition takes a cold drink, will get inflammation of the lungs, whether he has known the consequences or not, and even if he has an unshakeable conviction that the drink will do him no harm. And whoever climbs a glacier with an inexperienced guide, will tumble dawn into a crevasse, even if the guide has succeeded ever so well in convincing him beforehand of the infallibility of his acquaintance with the right track. For it is just a law of nature that a cold drink has bad consequences for heated lungs, and that a man who wanders towards a crevasse at last must tumble into it. It is exactly the same law that reigns in the realm of morality, nay, at bottom it is just the same eternal law as the law of nature just mentioned, that every action of will and, accordingly, every kind of grasping leads to its corresponding consequences

* This passage means: This body does not essentially belong to you, but is only produced through your former acting, and to this product you now see yourselves chained.

in the corresponding kind of Becoming. This idea is set forth by the Buddha in the hundred-and-twenty-sixth Dialogue of the Middle Collection, where, among other things, he says:

"Whoever, Bhūmija, being an ascetic or a Brahmin, cognizes wrongly . . . acts wrongly . . . and thus perhaps with hope leads the life of an ascetic, cannot possibly reach the goal, and thus perhaps without hope leads an ascetic life, cannot possibly reach the goal. And why not? Because, Bhūmija, he does not from the very foundation understand the reaching of the goal. Just as if a man, Bhūmija, who wants milk, who seeks for milk, who is in search of milk, should begin to milk a cow that had calved, by the horns: though he should exert himself full of hope, nevertheless he could not possibly get milk, and if he should exert himself without hope, he could not possibly get milk. . . . And why not? Because, Bhūmija, he does not from the very foundation understand how to get milk. In the same manner, Bhūmija, such ascetics or Brahmins cannot possibly reach the goal. And why not? Because, Bhūmija, they do not from the very foundation understand how to reach the goal."

* * *

Though the causality of all willing is thus beyond all doubt, it does not necessarily extend in *every* case beyond death into one of our future rebirths. This, on the contrary, is only the case, if the tendency of will, the outcome of which was a given deed, is present at all even though only in latent condition, *at the moment of death,* when the new grasping takes place. If at this moment it already again has been completely rooted out, then neither itself nor, of course, the deed resulting from it, can in any way be of causal importance for the new attachment and those that follow later on, just as little as a cold drink can be hurtful to a man, if immediately after he has taken it, before the effects of the inflammation of the lungs have set in, the pathological change in the lungs is again altered by corresponding medical treatment, and as little as an ignorant mountain-climber will fall into a crevasse, if in good time he turns back from the direction first taken:

"These three, ye disciples, will fall a prey to the abyss and to hell, *if they do not abstain from the following things*. Which three? He who lives unchastely and pretends to be a chaste-living disciple; he who accuses a chaste-living disciple of unchaste living; he who, believing and thinking that there is nothing evil in sensuality, falls a prey to sensual pleasure. These three, ye disciples, will fall a prey to the abyss and to hell, *if they do not abstain from these things*."[163]

The same is said in the Book of Threes:

"There, ye disciples, a certain person has only committed a small crime, and this brings him to hell. There, however, ye disciples, another has committed the same small crime, but this ripens even during his lifetime, and not even a small effect manifests itself, to say nothing of a great one." This means: In one man a certain willing, manifesting itself in a crime, acts beyond death in such wise that it may bring him directly to hell, whereas with another, it exhausts itself completely during his life-time, and does not exhibit even a small *post-mortem* effect.

"But of which kind, ye disciples, is the man whom a small crime which he has committed brings to hell? There, ye disciples, a man has not won insight into the body,* has not practised himself in virtue, has not developed his mind, not awakened knowledge, is narrow-minded, small-minded, and so has to suffer even in consequence of trifles. Such a man, ye disciples, even a small crime which he has committed may bring to hell."

* This means, he has not reached clearness about what we call personality, *sakkāya*.

"But of which kind, ye disciples, is the man in whom the same small crime which he has committed will ripen even during his life-time, and in whom not even a small effect (after death) ensues, to say nothing of a great one? There, ye disciples, a man has won insight into the body, has practised himself in virtue, has developed his mind, has awakened knowledge, is broad-minded, magnanimous, dwelling in the Immeasureable. In such a man, ye disciples, the same small crime which he has committed ripens even during his life-time, and not even a small effect manifests itself (after death) to say nothing of a great one."

"What do you think, ye disciples: Suppose a man throws a lump of salt into a small cup of water, would then the little water in that cup through this lump of salt become saltish and undrinkable?"

"Yes, Lord."

"And why so?"

"There is only very little water in the cup, Lord. So it would become saltish and undrinkable through this lump of salt."

"But what do you think, ye disciples: Suppose a man should throw a lump of salt into the river Ganges, would the water of the Ganges then become saltish and undrinkable through this lump of salt?"

"Certainly not, Lord."

"And why not?"

"There is, Lord, an immense quantity of water in the river Ganges. So, through that lump of salt, it would not become saltish and undrinkable."

"Just so, ye disciples, one man has only committed a small crime, and it brings him to hell. And another man has committed the same small crime, but it *ripens even during his life-time,* and not even a small effect manifests itself (after death), to say nothing of a great one."

As we see, the reasoning which demonstrates why the same deed leads one man to hell, while in another's case entirely exhausting itself during his life-time, is perfectly in harmony with our foregoing explanations. Whether the consequences of a deed shall extend up to the death-moment and thereby into the next existence, is exclusively determined by the extent to which the deed affects the will. A vain, narrow-minded man will even feel a slight insult as a serious assault upon his self-conceit, which he will be unable ever to pardon sincerely and from the heart, so that it will leave behind it inextinguishable traces within him. On the other hand, upon a noble-hearted man, thoroughly convinced of the worthlessness of all worldly things, the same insult will make no impression, or, if it does excite him, this excitement will only be momentary, and the influence upon his will brought about by this excitement will very soon *ripen* into bitter repentance, work itself out, and through the kindness and compassion dwelling within him,* will be completely dried up in the shortest time, will be clean taken out of him, root and branch, so that at his death nothing more will remain of it that might influence the next following grasping.

But thereby also the way is shown, not how we may escape from the consequences of our evil actions of the past,—for after what we have said above, this is impossible,—but how we can confine these consequences to our *present* life, or at least weaken their *post-mortem* consequences. We only need to annihilate or at least to weaken the evil dispositions of our will, the bad qualities of our character, which, as we shall clearly perceive later on, have grown out of our evil deeds, yea, which at bottom represent nothing but

* Kindness and compassion are the "Immeasurables" mentioned above, wherein all egotism is dissolved, as is a lump of salt in the river Ganges.—Of these "Immeasurables" we will say more in the last chapter of this work.

the sum of these, in which therefore, in some mysterious manner, we carry about with us the continuously active force of each former evil deed. Precisely because of this, in our heavy labours of soul for the entire annihilation or weakening of several, or of all, of our bad qualities, we also kill our former evil deeds themselves, "outlive them one after the other," as it is said in the "Book of Threes," so that in the same proportion that we are freed from a certain bad quality of character, we also are freed from the further consequences of the deeds related to this quality. Now the Buddha indicates with perfect clearness the way to the complete annihilation of our evil inclinations, from which it follows that, whoso follows this way, and in so far as he follows it, need have no further anxiety on account of the later fruits of his former evil life, or of his former evil lives. This goes so far that at last, full of inner happiness, he may cry out: "Escaped am I from hell, escaped from the animal kingdom, escaped from the realm of the shades, escaped from the evil track, escaped from the path of suffering, from the rejected world! I have entered the stream [that leads to "the Deathless"]. Sure am I never again to sink back to the abodes of misery. With unalterable resolve I turn my mind to making myself ripe for the knowledge that delivers." [164]

But, be it noted, this consoling confidence may only be reached by him who in real earnest and at the same time with success, therefore in the right manner as laid down by the Buddha, wages warfare for the gradual eradication, or at least the weakening, of his passions. Therefore it is not enough merely to be a good man in the sense of keeping in check one's bad qualities of character, and cultivating the good ones. For thereby the former still remain as bearers of our earlier bad deeds; there merely take place no *new* evil deeds, undesirable fruits, but only good actions which of course in time again will bear their good fruits. But because thus the evil actions of a former existence, manifesting themselves in present bad qualities of character, still remain in existence, it may well happen that a man who only in this sense has been good during his immediately past lifetime, that he has kept his bad qualities in check without annihilating them, or at least without appreciably weakening them, after death, in consequence of his former evil deeds, may pass to a hell-world. On the other hand, on like grounds a bad man, in consequence of his good actions in a lifetime previous to his present existence being saved up, so to speak, in his present latent and uncultivated, good qualities of character, at death may rise to a heaven-world, though only, upon his departure from this heaven-world, to rush straight down into a hell, in consequence of his bad actions during his last earthly existence now coming into effect.*

Both these cases are dealt with by the Buddha in the hundred-and-thirty-sixth Discourse of the Middle Collection. In the same place it is also shown, how also upon other grounds a good man may come into a hell, and a bad one into a heaven, namely, in that the former at the moment of death displays wrong, and the latter right, knowledge. The first case occurs, for example, if a man otherwise good during his life, in time loses patience in consequence of his last wearisome and painful illness, and becomes fretful and quarrelsome, as is not seldom the case in daily life; the latter, however, occurring when a criminal comes to his senses on the scaffold.** In both cases, strivings are called into life which are at work in the very moment of death,

* Like the fallen angels of the "Old Testament."

** In the "Questions of King Milinda" the example is quoted of a man who for a hundred years has been given to vice, but will be reborn among the gods, if, in the hour of death, he only devotes one serious thought to the Buddha or to his Doctrine.

and which *must* therefore determine the new grasping. But withal, the good or evil strivings latent at this dying moment and thereby ineffectual, though cultivated during the rest of the life, will determine a *later* future.*

According to this, the *harvest* of our doings is certain, but the course of Karma, in its details, is for most men very uncertain, because of its extreme complexity. This complexity is so great, that "the fruit of deeds," for this very reason, is one of the "four inscrutable things about which one ought not to brood, because who broods about them, will fall a prey to delusion or to mental disturbance." [165]

Such brooding, moreover, upon the probable condition of our future would also be highly superfluous. It is enough to know that we ourselves make this future, according to fixed norms. This knowledge we now possess: *We may become everything in the world, because we are nothing pertaining to this world.* I may become a king or a beggar, a nobleman or a vagabond; I may become a man, a ghost, a beast, a devil, and I can become a god. In itself, any one of these is just as near to me, because as essentially alien, as any other. It all depends upon my will, upon the innermost striving that I nourish and develop within myself, which will lead to its corresponding grasping.** Now only one thing is wanting, namely, a knowledge of the *material* contents of the norms, according to which this grasping takes place; that is to say, the answer to the question as to how our actions must be shaped in accordance with the law of Karma, if they are to bear us good fruit, lead us to a fortunate rebirth; or, otherwise expressed: What for us is wholesome

* The serious disciple of the Master is, of course, also protected against the worse of the above two eventualities, since already in days of health he has brought his mind completely or at least thus far under his power, that he is sure of not losing control over it in days of serious illness.

** "That influence, Brahmin, that would make me a spirit of the air, a ghost or a man, is extinguished within me." [166]

(kusala), and what unwholesome *(akusala)*? Thereby we come to the problem of good and evil. For good is just what is wholesome for us; and bad or evil is what is unwholesome for us.

* * *

In the passages from the Texts from which we have been quoting, we have learnt of the particular wholesome and unwholesome qualities. But now it is a question of the principle lying at their foundation.

We know that the law of Karma acts in the form of affinity, every rebirth taking place through a grasping within the five realms of the Saṁsāra, that are partly painful, partly pleasant, partly pleasant-and-painful, the grasping itself, however, being determined by the nature of tendencies of will prevailing at the moment of death, which in their totality give *taṇhā*, thirst. According to this, the action which creates those tendencies of will* that lead to grasping in a joyful world, is a wholesome or a good one; that which brings forth tendencies of will to which corresponds a grasping in a painful world, is an unwholesome or an evil one; and lastly, that which conditions rebirth in a world endowed with pleasures and pains, is at the same time wholesome and unwholesome, good and bad:

"There is, ye monks, bad action which bears bad fruits. There is, ye monks, good action, which bears good fruits. There is, ye monks, action partly good and partly bad, which bears fruits partly good and partly bad.

"But what, ye monks, is this bad action, which bears bad fruits? There, ye monks, a certain person practises pain-full action in deeds and words and thoughts. Practising pain-full action in deeds, in words and in thoughts, he comes back to existence in a pain-full world. Having come back to

* The possibility of creating such tendencies of will to our liking, thus the problem of free will, we shall discuss later on.

existence in a pain-full world, he is touched by pain-full things. But while touched by pain-full things, he experiences pain-full sensations and extremest woe, like the beings in hell. This, ye monks, is called bad action, which bears bad fruits.

"But what, ye monks, is good action, which bears good fruits? There, ye monks, a certain man practises pain-free action in deeds, in words and in thoughts. Practising pain-free action in deeds, in words and in thoughts, he comes back to existence in a pain-free world. Having come back to existence in a pain-free world, he is touched by pain-free things. But while touched by pain-free things, he experiences pain-free sensations and highest bliss, like the brightly shining gods. This, ye monks, is called good action, that bears good fruits.

"But what, ye monks, is action partly good and partly bad, which bears fruits partly good and partly bad?

"There, ye monks, a certain man practises action partly pain-full and partly pain-free in deeds, in words and in thoughts. Practising action partly pain-full and partly pain-free in deeds, in words and in thoughts, he comes back to existence in a world partly pain-full and partly pain-free. Having come back to existence in a world partly pain-full and partly pain-free, he is touched by things partly pain-full and partly pain-free. But while touched partly by pain-full and partly by pain-free things, he experiences sensations partly pain-full and partly pain-free, changing weal and woe, like men, certain spirits, and certain rejected beings. This, ye monks, is called action partly good and partly bad, which bears fruits partly good and partly bad."[167]

Now the outstanding feature of the pain-laden worlds, hell and the animal Kingdom, is that the creatures in them recognise in themselves no limit to the thirst for existence and wellbeing which animates them, and in its coarsest form. On the contrary, they so completely identify themselves with this thirst in its two main manifestations, namely, desire for everything corresponding to it, and hatred of everything opposed to it, that in order to satisfy it, they without further ado encroach upon the sphere of other creatures' interests.* In correspondence with this, the inhabitants of the joyful worlds, the heavens—the higher, the more joyful—are free from such desire and such hate, especially in their coarser forms. Above all, they do not satisfy their desires at the expense of other creatures, but on the contrary, they include these beings with an ever more comprehensive love in their own thirst for wellbeing, which thus in them takes a new direction. The reason for this is that in these realms the delusion in which all living beings are caught, namely, that our essence is identical with our personality, and that our thirst for wellbeing ought therefore to be concentrated upon it, is partly overcome, and thereby the partition-wall between ourselves and the other creatures is partly thrown down.** According to this, desire, hatred and delusion appear as the characteristics of the lower and woeful worlds; while, as those of the higher worlds, upon the path of an ever more expanding love, there is an increasing approximation to desirelessness, freedom from hatred, and right insight. Between both stands what is specifically human. Since we have seen that our present entrance into one of these worlds is determined according to which of our own qualities of character, of our own deepest aspirations, are most closely conformed, related to it, it follows that *desire (lobha), hate (dosa)* and *delusion (moha)* are unwholesome or bad for us, and that *desirelessness (alobha), freedom from hatred (adosa)* and *non-delusion (amoha)* are wholesome or good for us. In these fundamental qualities all virtues and vices are embraced.

---

* That creatures in hell find no objects corresponding to their desires, but only such as rouse their abhorrence, makes their state all the more woeful.

** About this, more will be said in the last chapter.

THE CONDITIONING OF THIRST

In what has gone before we have seen that our existence is conditioned through *the thirst* for existence which animates us, and that the shaping of the outer conditions of this existence may be traced back to *the character* of this thirst. We are in the world because we thirsted for it; and we are just in such a world as ours is, because we had a thirst which, according to the eternal laws, had to lead us just into this world. Thereby it might seem as if the problem of the arising of suffering were solved, as far as it is necessary for the practical purpose of the annihilation of suffering; and this alone had any interest for the Buddha. For we need only annihilate this thirst within ourselves, in order to prevent any future rebirth, and so, with our next approaching death, depart out of the world for ever. From the standpoint which we now occupy, however, such a conclusion would be somewhat over-hasty. For to the thinking man another question at once arises: Am I at all able to annihilate this thirst for existence within myself? Is it not rather a manifestation of my essence itself, and for that very reason just as little to be annihilated as this? Certainly the Master has already told us about this thirst also that it is not our self, since in it also can be observed an arising and a passing away.* But this criterion for the recognition of the sphere of *anattā,* of non-ego, cannot be accepted at once. For thirst for existence and wellbeing fills us from the first moment of our existence, yea, through all our repeated existences, so unceasingly and so powerfully, that even the great Schopenhauer came to the conclusion that in will, that is, in thirst, no arising and passing away was to be observed. Rather, as the thing in itself, thirst was

* See above, p. 125.

without cause or condition, and could never be the *cause* of anything else; everything besides it, more especially, our own personality, was not its *effect* but rather its *phenomenon.* In short, thirst he considered to be the immediate manifestation of our essence itself which in it became apparent. Or, in the language of the Buddha, thirst was our veritable, actual and true self, of which it held good that "This am I, this belongs to me, this is my self," a standpoint also practically taken up by mankind in its entirety from all times. But from this it is clear of what decisive importance in the doctrine of the Buddha is the proof that this thirst also is *nothing metaphysical*, but subject in every respect to causality, therefore conditioned, and therefore something *purely physical*, that is, *anattā, not-the-I.** For if it were not so, if thirst really were the essence of man, and thereby our self, then through all eternity no deliverance from it and thereby from suffering would be possible, since no one can annihilate himself, jump out of his own skin,** a consequence, which was actually drawn by Schopenhauer to this extent, that according to him, our intelligible character is unchangeable, and at bottom we can contribute nothing towards our deliverance.*** But if this were the case, then the doctrine of the Buddha would become meaningless from the outset, since its very heart consists precisely in pointing out a way to deliverance that may be trodden at all times and speedily lead to the goal, if the necessary intensity is applied to its treading. Accordingly, it is not at all, as is thought by some, against the spirit of his doctrine, when in it the reason why this thirst maintains itself in existence is definitely laid down; but on the contrary, the doctrine

---

* One sees that *anattā* and things physical are identical conceptions.

** See above pp. 119, 124.

*** Schopenhauer only leaves open the *possibility* that some time or other in the course of endless time our will may perhaps of itself and without our assistance, turn and renounce.

of the Buddha would in itself be absurd, if this were *not* so. And, as a matter of fact, it is so: "If, Ānanda, the question were put: 'Is thirst dependent on anything?' then it ought to be replied: 'Yes, it is dependent.'"

The question therefore now is: *On what* is this thirst for existence dependent, this thirst which shows itself chiefly at the moment of death, ever and again bringing about a grasping of a new germ? What fundamental antecedent condition must there be, that it is able to rise, to spring up in us?* The Buddha tells us this in the following words: "If it should be asked: 'On what is thirst dependent?' then it ought to be answered: 'In dependence on *sensation* arises thirst.'" This too is clear without further explanation. Without the stimulus of *sensation* there is no desire. When every sensation has vanished completely and for ever, then all willing, all thirst, of every kind, also is gone for ever. A man who is quite without sensation *wills* nothing more, has no kind of *thirst* for anything any more. And if he has become without sensation *for ever,* then this phenomenon of thirst can no longer show itself within him through all eternity. "I have said: 'In dependence on sensation arises thirst.' And this, Ānanda, that thirst arises in dependence on sensation, must be understood in the following sense. Suppose, Ānanda, that nowhere and nowise there occurred any sensation of anything, that is to say, no sensation resulting from eye-contact, no sensation resulting from ear-contact, no sensation resulting from nose-contact, no sensation resulting from tongue-contact, no sensation resulting from

---

* Precisely the same as with the other links of the chain it was not a question with the Buddha in the case of Thirst also, of firmly fixing its *absolute* general cause, but only of discovering the cause of *the occasion* that enables thirst to appear and to become evident. This finds expression in the very *form* in which the question is put: "On what is thirst *dependent?*" Here the Buddha completely shares the standpoint of Schopenhauer: "Every natural cause is only an *occasional* cause, nothing within the world having an *absolute* cause for its existence."

body-contact, no sensation resulting from mind-contact, if thus sensation were entirely absent, if sensation were abolished, would then any kind of *thirst* be perceptible?"—"Certainly not, Lord."

"Therefore, Ānanda, here is the cause, the origin, the arising, the dependence of thirst, namely, sensation."

But whence comes sensation? "If, Ānanda, the question were asked: 'Is sensation dependent on something?' then it ought to be replied: 'Yes, it is dependent.' And if it should be asked: 'On what is sensation dependent?' then it ought to be replied: 'In dependence on *contact* arises sensation.' And this, Ānanda, that sensation arises in dependence of contact must be understood in the following sense. Suppose, Ānanda, that there is nowhere and nowise contact of any (sense) with anything, no eye-contact, no ear-contact, no nose-contact, no tongue-contact, no body-contact, no mind-contact, if thus, contact were entirely absent, if contact were abolished, would then any sensation be perceived?"

"Certainly not, Lord."

"Therefore, Ānanda, here is the cause, the origin, the arising, the dependence of sensation, namely, contact."

But for any kind of contact to take place within me, my corporeal organism, as bearing the organs of sense, the six senses-machine, is necessary. "If, Ānanda, the question were put: 'Is contact dependent on something?' then it ought to be replied: 'Yes, it is dependent.' And if it should be asked: 'On what is contact dependent?' then it ought to be replied: In dependence on *the corporeal organism [nāma-rūpa]* arises contact."

That sensation, and perception inseparably connected with it,* are conditioned by contact, and this by the organs of sense of the corporeal organism, is already explained

* In Dīgha Nikāya I, therefore perception is given instead of sensation as the antecedent condition of thirst.

in the previous chapter on personality, an accurate knowledge of which is here, of course, assumed. There, by means of passages which are *the immediate continuation given here,* it is explicitly shown, how the corporeal organism is again dependent, namely, on consciousness, and this again in its turn, upon the corporeal organism, both in mutual dependence.* Thus the chain of dependences ultimately comes to its end in the "corporeal organism together with consciousness," wherewith, indeed, in the Māha-Nidāna-Sutta it reaches its definite conclusion. The reason of this can only be that therewith the circle of dependences is actually closed. And this is really the case.

We know that we can only escape from suffering for ever, when we succeed in leaving behind for ever Saṁsāra, the circle of rebirth, when, thus, we are no longer exposed to a future new birth, hence to no new formation of the "corporeal organism together with consciousness." For the moment the process through which this new formation is accomplished ("birth" in the phraseology of the Buddha) has merely begun,—through conception in a maternal womb—for the entire duration of the existence of this newly forming "body endowed with consciousness" we are again indissolubly bound to it: only at the moment of the ensuing death can we entirely step out of Saṁsāra. All suffering, thus, is founded in the *"corporeal organism together with consciousness,"* which we might therefore call, as we do call it the six senses-machine in general, the machine of suffering in particular. For this reason, at the very beginning of our task of showing all suffering to be naturally conditioned, we were forced to establish the cause of *birth,* that is, for the ever renewed formation of this "corporeal organism together with consciousness." As such a cause we discovered *the*

* This mutual dependence is, in Dīghanikāya II, 84, illustrated by saying that consciousness is bound to the body like a string that is threaded through a gem.

thirst for existence animating us, always causing in the moment of our death a new grasping of a new germ in a maternal womb and thereby *the Becoming* of a new organism. With this, however, we found ourselves confronted by the further question, as to whether this thirst also is conditioned, or, in other words, whether it is something physical, and not rather our metaphysical substratum, and therefore indestructible. But we found it also to be conditioned stage by stage, first by sensation, then by contact, and lastly, by—*"the corporeal organism together with consciousness."* With this, however, we have again got back to our starting-point. *The circle is closed:* All suffering is rooted in our "corporeal organism together with consciousness;" these two united as our present "body endowed with consciousness" are the consequence of our thirst for existence during the last existence *before our birth.* This birth, on its side again, had, as antecedent condition, "a corporeal organism together with consciousness," and so on backwards to all eternity.

If we remember that from the corporeal organism together with consciousness, thirst is always issuing in such a special manner that the former, as the six senses-machine is set in activity, and thereby in the immediately up-flaming consciousness sensation and perception are aroused, from which latter, then, thirst during the whole of our life up till the moment of death is always welling forth anew, and that we have summed up this whole process of activity of the six senses-machine together with consciousness, as it goes on from birth to the moment of death, as the machinery of *personality,* then the content of the formula of causality may be summed up still more pregnantly as follows: *Personality*—in both its main groups, the corporeal organism, together with consciousness as its real substratum—is conditioned by *thirst,* and thirst by *our bygone personality,* just as the hen is conditioned by the egg, and the egg again by the hen.

So astoundingly simple is the formula of origination by dependence.* But what all has not been made out of it!

With this result the root of suffering is fully laid bare; we have penetrated to the unwearied builder of our corporeal organism itself, through which, as through the machine of suffering, all suffering becomes primarily possible for us. At the same time, we have recognized this builder of the machine of suffering as a fellow who has nothing at all to do with our true essence, to whom therefore we need only hand his passports in order to be free for ever from any new reincarnation. Hence, if we wish, with the Buddha we now can exclaim:

The changing state of rebirth always new,
By pain and sorrow chased, I wandered through.
In vain I often looked around for him,
Who once did build this house of suffering.

Builder, I know you now, and laugh at you.
You'll never build for me a house anew.
My spirit has from sensual action fled,
All thirst is killed, suffering at last is dead.[169]

Now also we are ready to understand the second of the four holy truths in all its depth: "This, ye monks, is the most excellent truth of the origination of suffering: It is thirst generating rebirth, thirst accompanied by pleasure and lust, now here and now there taking delight, thirst for sensual pleasure, thirst for Becoming (for existence), thirst for annihilation."** [179]

---

* Certainly, if we combine the formula with the *anattā*-thought, then on its side the formula also becomes deep as an abyss. Then too we understand the words of the Master upon Ānanda remarking that the formula now seemed to him easy to understand: "Speak not so, Ānanda, speak not so! Deep is this origination by dependence, it contains a deep revelation." [168]

** The thirst for annihilation arises in consequence of the wrong view that personality is our essence. For if we recognize at the same time that this personality as such is

We said above that the formula of origination in dependence is closed in the Mahā-Nidāna-Sutta with the link "corporeal organism together with consciousness." The same is the case in the Mahāpadhānasutta, where the Boddhisattva Vipassī, after having followed the origination of dependence up to the two factors "corporeal organism and consciousness" and having recognised both as mutually conditioned, expressly declares: "The series goes no further." But in many other passages of the Canon the formula of causality is nevertheless extended still further. For after the causal nexus, in entire unison with the links presented up till now, has been traced back to the corporeal organism—*nāma-rūpa*—and further, this latter declared to be conditioned by consciousness, this consciousness itself is not again represented as conditioned by the corporeal organism, but the text runs on thus: "In dependence upon the Sankhārā, ye monks, arises consciousness.... In dependence upon ignorance, ye monks, arise the Saṅkhārā." It is clear that this conclusion of the formula can tell us nothing fundamentally new, if it is not to contradict what we have hitherto been learning,—and such a possibility may safely be exluded from the outset, in view of the importance of the Paṭiccasamuppāda. For, since the conclusion as we have been learning to know it, turns back again to the beginning, a further continuance of the dependences beyond it, is thus quite impossible. This somewhat different formulation of the last links of the chain at most can only be a matter of a more detailed explanation of the conclusion of the formula as we have hitherto learned to know it. And this is actually the case, as will now appear.

---

full of suffering, then the further notion arises that we can free ourselves from suffering only by the annihilation of our personality and thereby of our own essence. Accordingly, *the thirst* for annihilation springs up. (Concerning this thirst for annihilation [*vibhava*]- see Itivuttaka, 49.)

THE SAṄKHĀRĀ

Like the chain of causality in general, the conception of Saṅkhāra in particular has received the most widely different interpretations at the hands of European Scholars. Some translate it by "dispositions," others by "differentiations," or "formations," or "syntheses." And yet this conception also is as clear and simple as the chain of causality itself.

Saṅkhāra is derived from *samskar,* to put together, which latter is therefore the equivalent of the Latin *"conficere."* Hence the *participium praeteritum,* Saṅkhata, fundamentally means "put together," "formed." According to the Canon, it can be used of anything in the world: "All phenomena are *saṅkhata.*" But how is this to be understood? What does it mean: Everything is created or formed?

We know that, according to the Buddha, there is no *Being,* but only an eternal, ceaseless *Becoming.* This implies that in the world there is no such thing as an unchanging subject that might create or form anything; but that everything is purely the product of the *entirely impersonal processes* of eternal Becoming. Everything created or formed is only created or formed *through these processes;* has been put together, compounded because of them; that is to say: it has *arisen, become;* under which conceptions more particularly the result of the creating and forming of these impersonal processes is to be conceived.* According to this, therefore, *saṅkhata,* in the language of the Buddha, means "arisen" or "become," ** as is always without exception borne out by every passage wherein the word occurs.***

---

* See above, p. 208.

** In the same manner, the passive form of the Latin *conficere, confieri,* has the meaning "to become, to happen."

*** The explanation in the Dhammasangani: "Everything resting upon an antecedent condition is *saṅkhata*" is, of course, in entire agreement with this. For everything originated or become is *conceptionally* conditioned, being a product of the processes of nature.

With this, however, the meaning of the word Saṅkhāra is established without further ado. For *saṅkhāra* is the substantive verb of *saṅkhata;* that is to say, the *Saṅkhārā* it is which produces the *saṅkhata:* "Bhikkhus, the *Sankhārā* derive their name from this, that they *produce* what is *saṅkhata.*"[171] What produces *saṅkhata,* however, we have just heard: It is just those impersonal processes, those activities, procedures, occurrences, which we recognized in the foregoing as the cause of all that has become, that has arisen. Accordingly, the word *saṅkhāra* means *process, activity, procedure, occurrence,* and exactly like *saṅkhata,* can be used about everything in the world. For since everything is comprehended in the stream of the eternal Becoming, everything, on one hand, is something that has *become, arisen,* and, on the other hand, it is itself again a causal *activity,* a causal *process, procedure,* or a causal *occurrence.** It is in this all-embracing sense that the expression *saṅkhāra* is used, for instance, when, in the thirty-fifth Dialogue of the Middle Collection, it is said: "*sabbe saṅkhārā aniccā,*" all processes or all occurrences are transitory. Certainly this mode of expression in the sense in which it is used by the Buddha, namely, as meaning there are nothing else but transitory processes in the world, may not seem acceptable to us at once, since *to us* everything by no means without further discussion seems a mere process, or a mere occurrence. But a very little reflection here again will make clear to us that the reason for this lies exclusively in ourselves. For our conception of nature, in spite of all the progress made in natural science, is not yet as purified as that which he possesses who has learned something of the mode of thought of the Buddha. For, in spite of everything, we still speak of a *Being* within Nature and correspondingly of *things* of nature, in which conception we include the idea of some sort of duration. We are so imbued with

* Or: it is at once *conditioned* and *conditioning.*

this mode of thinking that we think it strange, even though our own natural science has dissolved everything in the world into incessantly changing processes, to hear everything actually spoken of as mere *processes,* and no longer to hear of any kind of persisting *things*. To the Buddhist, however, the conviction that within the world there is no *Being,* but only a ceaseless *Becoming,* and accordingly also, no *things,* but only natural *processes,* procedures, occurrences, has entered into his very flesh and blood, so much so, that it finds immediate expression in the language. Moreover, we also possess a word which takes in the content of the conception *saṅkhāra*, as established above, even if not in such conspicuous fashion, and nevertheless does full justice to our feeling. This is the word *phenomenon,* taken literally, as that which appears in the course of eternal Becoming, only soon to disappear again, so that we can translate the above sentence "*sabbe saṅkhārā aniccā*" in entire accordance with our style of speech, by saying: "all *phenomena* are transitory." For all Saṅkhārā are nothing more than sections of the general Becoming. This close connection between the conception of *saṅkhāra* and that of *bhava* (Becoming) as part of the latter, becomes strikingly clear from the following saying which occurs very often in the Canon: "All phenomena (*saṅkhārā*), alas, alternately are subject to arising and passing away."

"What is born, must disappear; blessed is the end of Becoming; 'tis Peace."*

* That we have not yet come so far as to look at all things in the world as simple processes, is the reason why we have no perfect equivalent for the conception of *saṅkhāra,* but are forced to render it now by *process,* now by *activity, occurrence, procedure, phenomenon* or similar expressions, though all these words stand for the same thing. — The conception of *Dhamma* is wider than that of Saṅkhāra. In it, the characteristic mark of transitoriness and flux is *not* thought along with the others. Therefore, contrary to *saṅkhāra,* it is used to designate Nibbāna. Nibbāna also is *dhamma, paramattha-dhamma,* absolute *dhamma.* Hence a subtle distinction is to be found in the phrase: "*Sabbe saṅkhārā aniccā, sabbe saṅkhārā dukkhā, sabbe dhammā anattā.*" For these *dhammā* — but of course not the *saṅkhārā* — embrace also Nibbāna. — *Dhamma* also is impossible to translate adequately. It designates every *reality.* At best we may use the word "thing" in its widest and least determined meaning.

Clearly evident stands out the meaning of *saṅkhāra* in its widest sense, particularly in the following passages:

"Not to be measured, ye monks, is the circle of rebirth, not to be perceived is the starting-point of the beings confined by ignorance, fettered by thirst, hurrying and wandering incessantly.

"In former times, ye monks, this mountain Vepulla was called Pācīnavaṁsa, and in those days, ye monks, the men here were called the Tivara. And the Tivara men, ye monks, lived for forty thousand years. In four days, ye monks, the Tivara men climbed the mountain Pācīnavaṁsa, and in four days they come down again.

"And in those times, ye monks, there appeared in the world Kakusandha as the Exalted One, as the Master, as the Perfectly Awakened One . . .

"Look, ye monks; That name of this same mountain has perished, those men have perished, and that Exalted One has gone to the highest deliverance.

"Thus impermanent, ye monks, are the Saṅkhārā [occurrences]; thus transitory are the Saṅkhārā; thus untrustworthy are the Saṅkhārā. And this, ye monks, is enough to be weary of, it is enough to be estranged from, it is enough to be set quite free from the Saṅkhārā."[172]

In the seventeenth Dialogue of the Dīgha Nikāya,[173] the Buddha tells about the glories of the king Mahāsudassana, about his cities, treasures, palaces, elephants, horses, carriages, women, in the possession of which he led a wonderful life, about the undertakings he carried out, and finally about his death in holiness, from this again to draw the conclusion:

"Behold, Ānanda, how all these Saṅkhārā [occurrences] are now past, are ended, have vanished away. Thus impermanent, Ānanda, are the Saṅkhārā; thus transitory, Ānanda, are the Saṅkhārā; thus untrustworthy, Ānanda, are the Saṅkhārā. And this, Ānanda, is enough to be weary of, it is enough to be estranged from, it is enough to be set quite free from the Saṅkhārā."

The Aṅguttara Nikāya,[174] finally, gives examples of the transitoriness of great things of nature that are called Saṅkhāra, thus the same that we call processes (of nature).

If thus under the designation of *Saṅkhāra,* everything in the world is characterized as mere occurrence, mere process, nevertheless before all else in importance to the Buddha stood out that "heap of processes"—*saṅkhārā*—which we call *man.* For at bottom it was with man only that he had to do, in that he showed *him* the way to deliverance, and only to him alone could show it. Therefore the chief problem was, to find out the nature of man, and to make it clear to every one, who at all might want to know, that also his supposedly persistent personality, in entire agreement with the rest of the happenings of the world, in truth is nothing more than a collection of ceaselessly changing processes. "By whom is the person created? Where is the creator of the person? The person which there arises, where is it? Where is the person that passes away?" thus Māra, the Evil One, asks the nun Vajirā, who thereupon answers him: "Do you think, Māra, that there is a person? You cling to a wrong doctrine. *Only a heap of changing processes*—Saṅkhārā—is this, no person may be found here."[175] Since therefore, at bottom, for the Buddha only *this* "heap of processes" is of any moment, in speaking of the Saṅkhārā, if not expressly stated otherwise, he only means the Saṅkhārā constituting what we call person or personality, in contradistinction to the all-embracing sphere of the conception of which we have learnt hitherto. This therefore only is referred to, when a division of the Saṅkhārā into parts is given, as by the nun Dhammadinnā to the adherent Visākha: "How many in number are the Saṅkhārā, Venerable One?"—"Three in number, friend Visākha, are the Saṅkhārā, these namely: the

Saṅkhāra of body, the Saṅkhāra of speech and the Saṅkhāra of mind."—"What, Venerable One, is the Saṅkhāra of body, what the Saṅkhāra of speech, what the Saṅkhāra of mind?"—"In-breathing and out-breathing, friend Visākha, are the Saṅkhāra of body, cognition and reflection are the Saṅkhāra of speech, perception and sensation are the Saṅkhāra of mind."—"Why, Venerable One, are in-breathing and out-breathing the Saṅkhāra of body, why are cognition and reflection the Saṅkhāra of speech, why are perception and sensation the Saṅkhāra of mind?"—"These things, in-breathing and out-breathing, inhere in body, are bound up with body, therefore, friend Visākha, are in-breathing and out-breathing the Saṅkhāra of body. What is previously cognized and reflected upon, afterwards comes forth in speech, therefore are cognition and reflection the Saṅkhāra of speech; and these things, perception and sensation, inhere in mind, are bound up with mind, therefore are perception and sensation the Saṅkhāra of mind."[176] Since with this subdivision is evidently summed up the whole heap of processes yielded by the machinery of "the corporeal organism together with consciousness" which we are wont to designate as our personality, it is clear without further words, that by the Saṅkhāra of body is to be understood the corporeal process, that is, the totality of corporeal processes, such as the circulation of the blood, digestion and so on. That the process of breathing is specially mentioned as *pars pro toto,* is because it represents, as already mentioned, the basis and centre of all somatical processes.* The same is the case with the Saṅkhāra or process of speech. It also not only consists in cognition and reflection, but comprises the totality of inner emotions rising within us because of our sensation and perception of a certain object. Thus it comprises the

* See above, p. 141. According to Schopenhauer, the motion of life must be regarded as proceeding from the process of respiration.

whole complex of the course of willing and representation outlined above and comprised under the expression of "activities of the mind," which takes place, when a certain object of sense is felt and perceived. The Sankhāra of speech is thus the same as the activity of the mind. Certainly this activity is *concentrated* in "cognition and reflection," in the same manner as the corporeal processes are concentrated in the process of respiration: "It has been said: 'The doctrine of the eighteen mental considerations, ye monks, I have promulgated, the doctrine free from objection, free from faults, not blamed by ascetics, priests and reasonable men.' But in relation to what has this been said? If a form is perceived with the eye, then one dwells in mind upon the form giving occasion for joy, the form giving occasion for sadness, the form giving occasion for indifference. If a sound is heard with the ear, if an odour is smelt with the nose, if a flavour is tasted with the tongue, if an object of touch is felt with the body, or if a representation is entertained in mind, then one dwells in mind upon the representation giving occasion for joy, the representation giving occasion for sadness, the representation giving occasion for indifference. If therefore it has been said: 'The doctrine of the eighteen mental considerations, ye monks, I have promulgated, the doctrine free from objection, free from faults, not blamed by ascetics, priests and reasonable men,' then in relation to this was it said."[177]

Because thus, cognition and reflection constitute the focus of all mental processes, Dhammadinnā in setting forth the latter, could be content to enumerate only the two former, in the same way, that in alluding to the corporeal Saṅkhāra, only the process of respiration is given.* Thereby, without

---

* Also otherwise in the Canon, definitions are often given by the method of part for the whole: "'Perception, perception,' is said, friend; but according to what measure does one say: 'Perception'?"—"One perceives, one perceives, friend, therefore does one

further ado, the reason adduced by her for calling these processes Saṅkhārā of speech, becomes clear. For language chiefly serves these mental processes which are essentially rational as "their first product and at the same time necessary tool;"* on which account it is only natural, that they should receive their designation from the same.

Thereby another riddle is solved, which has produced much confusion in the doctrine as to the Saṅkhārā. As we already know, the mental processes figure among the five Groups of Grasping in the form of the fourth group as the Saṅkhārā, albeit, from what we have just said, sensation and perception also, the second and third Group of Grasping are Saṅkhārā. We now know how this is meant. The *Group* of Grasping formed by the Sankhārā, Saṅkhāra-*khandha*, if closely looked at, represents *vacī*-Saṅkhāra, the Saṅkhāra of *speech*, just as Rūpakkhandha is in truth *nāma*-Rūpakkhanda.** The processes, Saṅkhārā, beginning in mind in dependence on a concrete sensation and perception, because of their twofold direction towards willing and thought taken together as activities of the mind, form *the* Saṅkhārā, just as criminal processes are, in Europe, called *the* processes among all other processes. Saṅkhāra-*kkhandha* is, hence, a special class of Saṅkhārā in general.

Now also we understand, why as cause of the Saṅkhārā, at one time *contact* is given, and another time, as we shall see, *ignorance*. In the latter case, the Saṅkhārā of life in general are meant, but in the former, the special group of activities of the mind, Saṅkhārā-*kkhandha*, that, as broadly expounded in the chapter on personality, is always aroused through *contact*, taken along with sensation and perception,

---

say: 'Perception;' and what does one perceive? One perceives blue, one perceives yellow, one perceives red, one perceives white. Thus does one say: 'Perception.'"178

* Schopenhauer. Otherwise he says further on: "Word and language are the indispensable means for clear thinking."

** See above p. 77*.

that is, through contact between one of our organs of sense and one of its objects:

"What is the cause, what is the reason, that the group of sensation can appear? What is the cause, what is the reason, that the group of perception can appear? What is the cause, what is the reason, that *the group of the Sankhārā—the activities of the mind*—can appear?* "Contact, monk, is the cause, contact is the reason, that the group of sensation can appear; contact is the cause, contact is the reason, that the group of perception can appear; *contact is the cause, contact is the reason, that the group of the Saṅkhārā can appear*."[179]

Thus we may distinguish three classes of Saṅkhārā: Saṅkhārā as *processes* of nature in general—*everything* being, according to the Buddha, a process of nature; then Saṅkhārā forming the "heap of processes" constituting our personality; and thirdly, *the* Saṅkhārā, *saṅkhārakkhandha*, the mental processes, which must be regarded as a separate class of the Saṅkhārā of the second kind. We already know, that the Buddha fundamentally has only to do with the totality of the Saṅkhārā of the second kind which we have briefly called the processes of personality, wherein after what we have just said the Saṅkhārā of the third kind are, of course, always contained.

These processes of personality in their totality, have their focus in the *sensation*, and therewith, in the *perception* of the outer world, in the same way that the corporeal processes culminate in the function of breathing, and the mental ones in "cognition and reflection," for it is precisely to this end, as we have already seen above, that the machine of the six senses has been put together. We had thirst to come into contact with the world of forms, of sounds, of odours, of sapids, of things tangible and of ideas. In consequence of this thirst, grasping within the womb of our mother took

* Note that the term "*the Group*" of the Sankhārā, Sankhāra-*kkhandha* is used.

place upon the opportunity of the act of our conception, and thereby the *Becoming* of our "body endowed with the six organs of sense," came about which is therefore fundamentally nothing but an apparatus for sensation and perception. Thus all the processes — Saṅkhārā — maintained by this apparatus have this sensation and perception of the world for their special purpose, the corporeal processes (*kāyasaṅkhārā*) and the mental processes (*vācīsaṅkhārā*) not less than the activities of our organs of sense themselves *immediately* directed towards generating sensation and perception (*cittasankhārā*), since the corporeal processes are intended for the maintainance of the six senses-machine, and the mental processes serve to work up the *results* of the activities of sensation and perception, with the object of leading to new sensations and perceptions. Since thus the whole heap of the processes of personality is subsumed in this sixfold activity of the senses leading to sensation and perception, therefore we find the Buddha often summing up together the whole processes of personality simply as sensation and perception, or, what is the same thing, as *the six activities of the senses.* Because these are the real purpose of the whole corporeal organism together with consciousness, therefore it is even the rule that, when the Canon speaks of the Saṅkhārā, it means the processes of personality, especially in the form of *the activities of the senses,* thus, as seeing, hearing, smelling, tasting, touching and thinking. That, for example, is the case, when it is said: "Monks, that I said that everything that is felt is suffering, this was done because of the transitoriness of the Saṅkhārā;"[180] or, "The ceasing of the Saṅkhārā is blissful;"[181] further: "Whatever suffering may arise, all has the Saṅkhārā as its antecedent condition: this is one consideration (that must be entertained); if, however, the Saṅkhārā are annihilated without a remainder, so that one wishes to have no more to do with them, then there is no more arising of suffering: this is the second consideration (that must be entertained);"[182] and finally: "When one has penetrated this misery, that suffering depends upon the Saṅkhārā, then the end of suffering comes in consequence of the coming to rest of all Saṅkhārā, *the abrogation of perception*."[183] Whoso, for all that, doubts that here the processes of the senses especially are meant, may compare the hundred-and-second Discourse of the Middle Collection with these passages. There the theme discussed is that all the states a man may reach in life, or that he can imagine at all for the period after death, is always *saṅkhata, become,* and therefore transitory. This holds good even of the highest state that may be attained in the world: "There, ye monks, an ascetic or a Brahmin has left off investigating the past, has left off investigating the future, has entirely thrown off the chains of desire, has overcome the joy of solitude, has overcome the blessedness of selflessness, has overcome the feeling that is without joy or sorrow, and observes within himself: 'Peaceful am I, extinguished am I, no more a grasping one am I.' But now, ye monks, the Perfected One recognizes: 'Certainly this venerable one has spoken of the path leading directly to Nibbāna . . . But that he *cognizes* within himself: 'Peaceful am I, extinguished am I, no more a grasping one am I,' this must be called grasping in this dear ascetic or Brahmin. And this also is *saṅkhata* (become, produced); but there is a dissolution of the Saṅkhārā [producing the *saṅkhata*]. "Only this complete annihilation of all Saṅkhārā is the great final goal. As this dissolution of the Saṅkhārā it is finally and solemnly proclaimed: "There, ye monks, the Exalted One has opened the incomparably high path of peace, that is to say, the understanding as they really are, *of the six realms of sense,* of their arising and passing away, their comfort and misery and the way of escape from them and to be free without grasping."[184]

And in the 105th Discourse of the same Collection the six inner realms, that is, the six organs of sense, are compared to a wound that must be closed. According to this, all suffering is produced by the actions of these organs of sense; *they are the Saṅkhārā creating suffering.*

With this, we have arrived at the point where we may now proceed with the formula of the causal nexus, which we left at the close of the last chapter at the following link: "In dependence on the Saṅkhārā arises consciousness." After what we have just seen, this will now become clear at once. It simply means: In dependence *on the activities of sense* arises consciousness.* The truth of this dictum, however, has already been seen by us in the chapter on personality, where it was pointed out to us: "Through the eye—which is just the activity of the eye directed towards seeing—and forms consciousness arises: 'visual consciousness' accordingly is the term applied. Through the ear and sounds consciousness arises: 'auditory consciousness' accordingly is the term applied. Through the nose and smells consciousness arises: 'olfactory consciousness' accordingly is the term applied. Through the tongue and flavours consciousness arises: 'gustatory consciousness' accordingly is the term applied. Through the body and objects of taction consciousness arises: 'tactile consciousness' accordingly is the term applied. Through the organ of thought and ideas consciousness arises: 'mental consciousness' accordingly is the term applied."**

* This might be concluded already from the following passages[185]: "But what is consciousness? What its arising? What its ceasing? What the way that leads to its ceasing?"—"Of consciousness, friends, there are six kinds: *eye*-consciousness, *ear-, nose-, tongue-, body-mind*-consciousness. The arising of the Saṅkhārā conditions the arising of consciousness; the ceasing of the Saṅkhārā conditions the ceasing of consciousness." From this, it results quite evidently, that these Saṅkhārā forming the conditions for the origination and annihilation of consciousness are nothing but the activities of eye, ear, nose, tongue, body, mind,•the sixfold division of consciousness being therefore made according to the cause *of its origin.*

** Compare above p. 54.

Thus the saying: "In dependence on the Saṅkhārā arises consciousness" at bottom means nothing else but this: Consciousness is the product of the physiological processes of our body in general, and of the functions of the senses in particular. Or, to speak in the spirit of Schopenhauer: Consciousness is a secondary phenomenon, conditioned by the functions of the cerebral nervous system, based upon the somatic life of the individual; "only by means of organic life is consciousness possible," dicta which are almost verbally identical with the lapidary apophthegm of the Mahāpadhāna-sutta: "*Retroactively, consciousness depends on the corporeal organism (nāma-rūpa); the series goes no farther.*"

This is nothing new to us. We saw before and indeed more closely, that consciousness is dependent on the corporeal organism, and that the latter also again as regards its maintenance is dependent upon the accession of this same consciousness. Thereby, however, our presumption proves to be justified—at least as far as the Saṅkhārā are concerned—that the continuation of the causal nexus beyond the "corporeal organism together with consciousness" to the Saṅkhārā and to ignorance, at bottom could tell us nothing new, but only represent a closer explanation of the conclusion of the formula dealt with by us before, the continuation of the formula up to the Saṅkhārā making specially clear the *manner* in which consciousness is conditioned by the corporeal organism; consciousness being conditioned by the setting in of the activities of the senses of the corporeal organism.

It now remains only to show how *ignorance* also as the cause of the Saṅkhārā fits in harmoniously with the formula of causality treated above.

IGNORANCE
SUMMARY OF THE CHAIN OF SUFFERING

"In dependence on ignorance arise the Saṅkhārā" this means, according to the foregoing: In dependence on ignorance arise the activities of the senses. With this we have come to the last link of the formula of the causal nexus, also in its amplified form. From this placing of ignorance at the extreme end of the chain of causality alone we may judge it to be of fundamental importance; and this really is the case.

First, it is clear that in this dictum the Buddha wishes to say that the activities of the senses are the outcome of the ignorance of something, *and would not come about, if this something were known.* What now may this something be, with respect to which this unknowingness, this ignorance exists? The Buddha tells us in the following words: "To be ignorant as regards Suffering, to be ignorant as regards the arising of Suffering; to be ignorant as regards the ceasing of Suffering, to be ignorant as regards the path leading to the ceasing of Suffering—this, friends, is what is called ignorance."[186] In the first of the four most excellent truths we saw what this suffering is. It is the great misery of the world, transitoriness, to which everything is subject, so that the whole world is only one great world of suffering. *Everything* is transitory, and thereby painful; the eye and forms, the ear and sounds, the nose and odours, the tongue and sapids, the body and tangibles, the organ of thought and the thinkable. This the "average man" does not cognize according to truth. He is not able to understand that ultimately, ever and always, the inevitable collapse of all the enjoyments and satisfactions of sense of every kind, even of the highest and most ideal kind, must ensue, and that these, either in this present life or in some later form of existence, perhaps even in the animal kingdom or in some hell-world, must flow into a measureless ocean of woe. And so "he delights in the eye and in forms, in the ear and sounds, in the nose and in odours, in the tongue and in sapids, in the body and in tangibles, in the organ of thinking and in thoughts," as it is said in the 149th Discourse of the Middle Collection. This means: he cultivates the activities of sight, hearing, smelling, tasting, touching and thinking, in short, the activities of the senses, the Saṅkhārā. In consequence of this, the whole chain of suffering runs its course again, inevitably leading the careless creature in the course of time, as so often already during the immeasurable past, down again into all the abysses of existence. For just because of these renewed activities of the senses, consciousness ever and again flames up anew, and thereby new sensation, and there-with new thirst for the world of forms, sounds, odours, flavours, tangibles and thoughts; whereupon that factor again is actualized which at the next approaching death again must lead to a new grasping exactly corresponding to the quality of this thirst. This quality of thirst, however, is expressed in the *kind* of activities of the sense, more especially the kind of *thinking*, in which all the activities of the senses unite as in their focus. Therefore the 120th Discourse of the Middle Collection, with which we dealt above, is called "Rebirth according to the Saṅkhārā," that is, according to our respective processes of mind or thought. The activities of the senses, on their part, are in themselves as well as in the direction they take, only the self-evident consequence of our not being clear, or, at any rate, not sufficiently clear, about their evil consequences; which just means, they proceed from ignorance. With this it at once becomes apparent, why the Buddha, in the formula of the causal nexus did not confine himself to the *objectively* last link, "the corporeal organism together with consciousness," but carried it on to the Saṅkhārā and ignorance. For him it was a question of laying bare the definitive cause of the thirst that is ever and always breaking forth anew and forming the source of continually repeated rebirth. Not only had the *objective* cause to be found out, as the Mahānidānasutta, we dealt with above, has done in concluding that it is "the corporeal organism together with consciousness;" but in correspondance with his practical purpose directed towards the annihilation of this thirst, he had, if at all possible, to penetrate to its final *subjective* condition, dependent upon ourselves, which condition he found to be the activities of the senses, but ultimately lack of knowledge of the real character of the world, and thereby, of the perniciousness of entering into connection with it by means of the six organs of sense, thus *ignorance*. This ignorance, even in the maternal womb, where, in the absence of a developed brain and thereby of thought-consciousness, it is complete, gives rise to the first and lowest activities of the senses, and also after birth during the whole life constitutes the real cause of every activity of the senses. We make unceasing use of the organs of sense, because we do not recognize, in accordance with truth, the consequences of these activities. Hence ignorance is the *basis* of the whole chain of suffering. It is the deep night, wrapped in which, beings from beginningless time have used their six senses-machine, with the result that ever and again new thirst for more of such activity arises, which thirst, then, in its turn, upon the break-up of the six-sense apparatus in death, effects the constant upbuilding anew of the same: "Ignorance is the deep night, wherein we here so long are circling round."[187]

But according to this, it is not only established beyond all doubt that thirst is *conditioned* as the immediate cause of the circle of rebirth and thereby is a purely physical phenomenon, but also its final fundamental conditioning is recognized as being something, the removal of which is entirely in our power: If ignorance is abolished, thirst and, together with it, all causality is uprooted for ever. "Those who have vanquished delusion and broken through the dense darkness, will wander no more: *Causality exists no more for them.*"[188]

With this, we now know the whole formula of origination through dependence, and may well also have seen that in all its parts it is lucid to the utmost degree. No one can shut his eyes to the insight that one link hooks with logical necessity into the other, the whole chain of conditionings being thus not only correct, but also exhaustive. In particular it has been shown to us that ignorance as well as the Saṅkhārā, join on harmoniously to the conclusion of the formula treated above, which had the "corporeal organism together with consciousness" for its final link. Neither of them go beyond this last link, this being impossible according to the foregoing. For together with it, especially together with the corporeal organism which begins to take form at the moment of conception, there is given immediate linking up with the *former* "body endowed with consciousness" that had immediately proceeded conception. As the Saṅkhārā cleared up the *mode* in which consciousness was conditioned by the corporeal organism, so ignorance gives us the key to the understanding of how we have come to shape the germ, seized in consequence of our former thirst in a maternal womb, into a six senses-machine and to make use of this machine.

Now we only need to run through the whole formula in its totality:

"Inasmuch as that is, this is. Through the arising of that does this arise. Thus, namely:

"In dependence on ignorance—*avijjā*—arise the processes," that is, the organic processes, especially those of the senses, the Saṅkhārā.

"In dependence on the processes [of life, especially on the activities of the senses] arises consciousness, *viññāṇa*.

"In dependence on consciousness arises the corporeal organism—*nāma-rūpa.**

"In dependence on the corporeal organism arise the six organs of sense—*salāyatana.***

"In dependence on the six organs of sense arises contact —*phassa.*

"In dependence on contact arises sensation—*vedanā.*

"In dependence on sensation arises thirst—*tanhā.*

"In dependence on thirst arises grasping—*upādāna.*

"In dependence on grasping arises Becoming—*bhava.*

"In dependence on Becoming arises birth—*jāti.*

"In dependence on birth arise old age and death, sorrow, lamentation, pain, grief and despair.

"Thus comes about the arising of this entire sum of Suffering."[189]

What, until now, has made the understanding of this formula so very difficult for us, was, among other things, the circumstance that it was generally thought to be an

---

* Compare our disquisitions on pp. 72, 73, above. There we saw that only a corporeal organism endowed with consciousness is able to develop and to live, that even the very first development of the fecundated germ is conditioned by consciousness being aroused by means of its organized matter, though this consciousness is at first only plant-like.

** Salāyatana is generally translated by "sixfold realm," Ayatana signifying "residence, realm, cause."

The sixfold realm is divided into "the six inner and six outer realms." Whereas the six outer realms represent the totalities of the objects corresponding to the several organs of sense, as forms, sounds *etc.*, the six inner realms mean the six organs of sense themselves.

Here, in the chain of causality, first of all, of course, the six inner realms, that is, the organs of sense, are meant, since it is the explanation of the five Groups of Grasping in form of the machinery of the personality that is in question.

This link of the six organs of sense that we see here and elsewhere inserted is, however, wanting in the chain of dependencies, as we know it until now according to the Mahānidānasutta. The reason is clear: it is essentially given by the corporeal organism, *nāma-rūpa,* the fourth link, and therefore is really superfluous.

The links Saṅkhārā, Consciousness, corporeal organism together with organs of sense, are *mutually* conditioned, representing only the further explanation of the two links "corporeal organism" and "consciousness," *conditioning each other,* with which in the Mahānidānasutta the formula is closed. See above p. 268.

exposition of several links of the causal nexus simply in their *temporal* sequence. We saw the wrongness of this point of view from our foregoing explanations of the chain, given in accordance with the Buddha's own statements. According to these, the correct train of thought of the formula, and thereby the key to its understanding, is rather as follows: The Buddha in it wishes to show the relation of the single links in a *purely abstract* manner, in the way in which they condition themselves internally and in themselves, that is, as follows: Old age and death, sorrow, affliction, pain, grief and despair are only possible in and with a corporeal organism, as a six senses machine. Such an organism must be born, therefore it presupposes *birth*. But birth is nothing but a special case of *Becoming*. Every Becoming is conditioned by a *grasping* and grasping is conditioned by the *thirst* for Becoming (*bhavataṇhā*). Such thirst can appear only, where *sensation* is. But sensation is the consequence of *contact* between the senses and an object; therefore it presupposes *organs of sense*. Organs of sense, of course, presuppose a *corporeal organism* for their supporter. Such an organism unquestionably can only exist, even, only develop, if *consciousness* is added to it. But consciousness is only known to us as the result of *the organic processes*, especially of the activities of the senses. But these are only set going, where *ignorance* exists as to the unwholesomeness of their results.

Taken in reverse series, and at the same time having regard to their actual realisation, these general dicta take shape as follows:—

In the maternal womb, in the night of deepest *ignorance*, because of complete unconsciousness, the *activities*—Saṅkhārā—begin in the seized and fertilized germ, which gradually increase until they reach the stage of the *processes of the senses*, and then continue on during the whole subsequent life in consequence of the continuance of ignorance. These activities in the seized organic matter, which include, the activities of the senses, constitute the necessary antecedent condition for the arising of *consciousness.* But consciousness, on its side, again constitutes the necessary condition for the development of the organism itself even in the maternal womb and for its continued existence after birth, so that it is only in dependence upon consciousness that the *corporeal organism* with the *six organs of sense* can come to maturity and continue maintaining itself. The organs of sense, on their side, again represent the necessary presupposition of every *contact* and thereby of every *sensation.* Out of sensation* in due sequence there ceaselessly springs forth *thirst* for the world of forms, sounds, odours and so forth, which on its side constitutes the *sine qua non* of *grasping.* With this, however, the immediate cause of all *Becoming* is laid bare: whatever becomes, becomes in consequence of such grasping. This grasping in particular is the cause of the becoming of a new organism, which is brought about by *birth,* that is, by conception and the corresponding following development in the maternal womb. With this the circle is again closed, and thus once more the antecedent conditions are provided for the arising of old age and death, of sorrow, lamentation, pain, grief and despair.

If thus we see explained in the formula of the causal nexus only the *inner* dependence of the several links of the chain of suffering, one upon the other, thus, how they are conditioned *in themselves,* none the less, as we might expect, the Buddha on the other hand also furnishes the formula as it takes shape from the point of view of the *actual effectuation* of the Saṅkhārā, of the processes of the senses:

"In dependence on the eye and forms arises visual consciousness; the conjunction of these three is contact;

* Reciprocally, out of perception that is always inseparably associated with it.

in dependence on contact arises sensation; in dependence on sensation, thirst; in dependence on thirst, grasping; in dependence on grasping, Becoming; in dependence on Becoming, birth; in dependence on birth arise old age and death, sorrow, lamentation, pain, grief and despair.

"In dependence on the ear and sounds arises auditory consciousness; in dependence on the nose and odours arises olfactory consciousness; in dependence on the tongue and sapids arises gustatory consciousness; in dependence on the body and tangibles arises tactile consciousness; in dependence on the organ of thought and objects of thought arises mental consciousness. The conjunction of these three is contact; in dependence on contact arises sensation; in dependence on sensation, thirst; in dependence on thirst, grasping; in dependence on grasping, Becoming; in dependence on Becoming, birth; in dependence on birth arise old age and death, sorrow lamentation, pain, grief and despair." [189]

From this reading of the formula it becomes at once apparent, how ignorance, not mentioned here, as constituting the cause of the activity of the senses, is also the immediate cause of the thirst for existence, that ever and again gushes forth anew from sensation. For at the moment when the senses come into activity, thus, when the eye meets a form, the ear a sound, and so on, *consciousness* also flames up, and therewith sensation, and therewith thirst, desire. Thus, it is not the case, as it is often said, that thirst by means of a series of intermediate links separated in time is artificially traced back to ignorance; but it is because I am ignorant "in respect of corporeality"* as of something fraught with suffering, that I therefore continually use my six senses, with the immediate consequence that *as soon* as I use them, ever new sensation arises, and therewith again thirst immediately makes its presence known. The processes of the senses,

* See the following third reading of the formula.

the Saṅkhārā, as cause, and thirst as effect, thereby meet in the act of sensation. Hence they do not lie apart in time; on which account precisely, if thirst is to be modified or annihilated, this is only possible by applying the lever to the primary cause of the activities of the senses, namely, to Ignorance.

Still a third way of looking at the formula of the causal nexus is possible. We may follow its course in a single concrete case, beginning with the first arising of the six senses machine, as the machine of suffering, at its conception in the maternal womb, then on through the time when this machine is in activity, up till the formation of a new one in a new conception. As the matter is of fundamental importance, it is only natural, that the Buddha gives the formula also from this point of view:[191]

"When, monks, a father and a mother come together, and it is the mother's period and the being to be born is also present, then, by the combined agency of these three, a seed of life is planted.

"And now for nine or ten months* the mother bears in her womb this seed of life, with much anxiety, a weighty burden; and when the nine or ten months have run their course, the mother brings forth that weighty burden with much anxiety, and this that is born she now nourishes with her own blood. 'Blood,' monks, is what mother's milk is called in the Order of the Exalted One.

"And now this boy, with the growth and development of his faculties, takes part in all sorts of games and sports appropriate to youth, such as ploughing with toy ploughs, playing tip-cat, turning somersaults, playing with toy windmills, toy measures, toy carts, and toy bows and arrows.

"And this boy, with the continued growth and development of his faculties, *now lives his life open to all the five incitements*

---

* Lunar months are meant.

*to desire,** namely, Forms cognisable through the organ of sight, Sounds cognisable through the organ of hearing, Odours cognisable through the organ of smell, Flavours cognisable through the organ of taste, and Tangibles cognisable through the organ of touch—all longed for, loved, delightful, pleasing, bound up with desire, provocative of passion.

"And now, through the eye sighting forms, through the ear hearing sounds, through the nose smelling odours, through the tongue tasting flavours, through the body encountering tangibles and through the mind discerning ideas, he is enamoured of pleasing forms, pleasing sounds, pleasing odours, pleasing tangibles, pleasing ideas, and shuns unpleasing forms, unpleasing sounds, unpleasing odours, unpleasing flavours, unpleasing tangibles, unpleasing ideas; ** being void of Recollectedness as respects corporeality, bounded and limited of mind, knowing naught, in accord with truth, of the Deliverance of the mind, the Deliverance by wisdom, whereby all that is evil and insalutary totally ceases to be.***

"So, with such likes and dislikes, when he experiences any kind of sensation, pleasant or unpleasant, or neither pleasant nor unpleasant, he greets, welcomes and clings to that sensation, and in him, thus greeting, welcoming and clinging to that sensation, there arises delight; the which delight in

---

* Of course, he has already before this exercised the five powers of desiring, that is, seeing, hearing, smelling, tasting and touching, and thereby set going the Saṅkhārā, beginning with their slightest stirrings in the maternal womb on to their full unfolding, to which the Buddha here introduces us.

** To be enamoured and to shun, are the two fundamental directions of *Thirst.* Note that this thirst above is the direct consequence of the activity of the senses. As soon as this latter sets in, at the same moment there comes about sensation and perception, and therewith also thirst.

*** "Being void of Recollectedness as respects corporeality, bounded and limited of mind": this is *Ignorance.* "Knowing naught, in accord with truth, of the Deliverance of the mind, the Deliverance by wisdom, whereby all that is evil and insalutary, totally ceases to be": by this is meant *Knowledge,* which he does not possess, and about which he does not exert himself. It is precisely this whole attitude of mind which determines his sense-activity.

sensation is Grasping.* Then, in dependence upon that Grasping, there arises Becoming,** in dependence upon Becoming, there arises Birth, and, in dependence upon Birth it is, that Growth and Decay, Death, Sorrow, Lamentation Suffering, Grief and Despair come to be. Thus comes about the arising of the entire Sum of Suffering."[192]

If the Buddha thus has pointed out to us, "how ever and again a new being arises," and thereby suffering is perpetuated, precisely thereby he also has put into our hands the key as to how we can prevent the arising of a new being or a new corporeal organism, and thereby of a new personality, and thus break through the chain of suffering, and be able for ever to pass out of the circle of rebirths. With this, accordingly, we now shall have to deal.

---

* Hence only a grasping *bound up with delight* is a grasping in the Buddha's sense of the word. The Saint, *also,* still satisfies his hunger and thirst. "Be so good, Ānanda, as to bring me some water; I am thirsty and would fain drink," says the Master to Ānanda shortly before his death; but there arises no more *delight* in drinking.

** As we have already seen, upon every grasping there immediately follows a Becoming: as soon as I grasp, something becomes. At the moment when I no longer grasp, for me also nothing more becomes. As already previously stated, however, *this* Becoming is not what the Buddha means here, but the Becoming of a *new personality,* of a new existence which begins with conception. In the above cited passage the Buddha describes how the ignorant man spends his *whole* life from youth to the grave. During this whole period he practises grasping in all its forms, so that *this* grasping—namely, what he has practised precisely *up to the moment of death*—effectuates itself in a new germ just at the death-moment, and so brings about the becoming of a new personality. That it is only *this* Becoming that is meant follows indeed from the fact that only of it does the further sentence hold good: "In dependence upon Becoming arises Birth," since *this* Becoming is brought about precisely by conception—Birth in the Buddha's sense—but not that Becoming which still *during* life arises in consequence of grasping. Precisely on this account, up to the very moment of his death, man has it in his own hands to put a stop to *Becoming*,—that is, of a new personality—since it suffices that in this last moment he has no more thirst for life, and thereby possesses the assurance that he will grasp no more at any new germ. (Cfr. also above p. 214**.)

THE MOST EXCELLENT TRUTH OF THE ANNIHILATION OF SUFFERING

NIBBĀNA

THE MOST EXCELLENT TRUTH OF THE ANNIHILATION OF SUFFERING

NIBBĀNA

Everything is Anattā, not the *I*, and does not belong to my innermost essence, the whole external world as little as my corporeal organism together with consciousness. I am beyond all this, beyond the world. This was one of the truths which the Buddha had to tell us.

The second was this: All these alien things in which I see myself involved, for me are nothing but one endless chain of misery. Hence, the best thing I can do, if at all possible, is to free myself from them again.

From this, however, followed the necessity of getting a clear idea of the relationship in which we stand to these alien things, above all, of how we have come to them, and of how we ever and always keep on coming to them. This we now know. Taken as a whole, the case presents itself thus.

We grasp the world; we thirst and desire to remain in unbroken contact with it. This end alone is served by our "body endowed with six senses" constituting the apparatus for *contact* with the world of forms, sounds, odours, sapids, tangibles and ideas, on which account precisely, we could call it the six senses-machine. This apparatus works in such fashion, that, when an organ of sense encounters a corresponding object, consciousness is immediately aroused, and reciprocally, consciousness already aroused is affected. In this consciousness we, then at first of all, and in fact, in the form of sensation and perception, are brought into *contact* with the object and thereby with the world.

Because thus our corporeal organism is the apparatus enabling us to come into contact with the world, therefore all our thirst is concentrated on maintaining and using this organism, as well as on replacing it, at the moment of its dissolution in death, by a new one. This is attained by a grasping of a new germ taking place in consequence of this thirst, which germ then develops again into a new organism.

Thus it is now; thus it has been through all the long past; and thus it will be on through all the future. Ever and again in our inscrutable essence, or what, as we know, is the same thing, out of the "Nothing" in consequence of the activity of the six senses-machine there flames forth "consciousness, invisible, infinite, all-penetrating,"* in which we experience every single effect of the world and thereby the world itself in its entirety, just by its coming into our consciousness. Everything, "water, earth, fire, air, long and short, small and big, the beautiful and the ugly,"[193] for us is present only with and in this our consciousness, which it enters by means of the organs of sense. In exactly the same way, particularly the bearer itself of these organs of sense, the vital body, enters into the consciousness, and in this way we receive our earliest knowledge also of it.**

By means of this consciousness at the same time is determined the direction in which the further activity of the six senses-machine shall run its course.

But from all eternity consciousness has not sufficed to

---

* With this passage we shall deal later on.

** According to this, the element of consciousness stands between us and the world, or, as Schopenhauer says, imperfectly cognizant of the psychical processes: "Between things and ourselves there always stands *the intellect*." The element of consciousness is thereby as different from *me*, as from the *phenomena*; it stands *in the middle*.

enlighten us as to the real nature of the processes, the bare knowledge of the existence of which it transmits to us. On the contrary, it becomes for us a direct instrument of delusion, inasmuch as we hold the corporeal organism to be our true essence, and its activity as the six senses-machine to be the only adequate expression of this our essence, so that we regard ourselves as belonging to this world, and everything that is agreeable to our senses and in harmony with them, as furthering our true welfare, but everything repugnant to them as a hindrance to this true welfare. The immediate consequence of this is, that as soon as, through any organ of sense, an agreeable object in the form of an agreeable sensation, is presented to us, immediately craving for this object arises. If, however, the object presented evokes a disagreeable sensation, with equal promptness, detestation arises in us; thus precisely that which the Buddha understands as thirst. According to this, precisely in consequence of the state in which it finds itself, namely, of ignorance, our consciousness incessantly perpetuates itself. For the thirst, ever born anew from this ignorance, in our approaching death, brings about a fresh grasping and thereby creates new organs of sense, which have as their consequence the new up-flaming of consciousness.*

In another manner our relation to the world admits of being made as vividly evident:

We are nothing of what we appear to be, therefore we are in the most complete sense *without quality*, and thereby

* But why do I know nothing of the *immeasurable duration* of this process of consciousness? A curious question indeed! Why do you not know anything about the time you spent at the beginning of your present existence in the maternal womb? Why do you not know anything of your earliest childhood, or of your own existence every night, while you are lying in deep sleep? Why do you preserve in memory only the main events of your present life, so that a thousand scenes are forgotten for one that is remembered, and of the course of your own life you hardly know any more than of a novel you once read? Why, the older you grow, do events more frequently pass by without leaving a trace in your memory? Why is extreme age, an

for knowledge, which can only have qualities for its object, we are *nothing* at all. But we are nothing only *for knowledge;* in ourselves we are the most real thing of all, for we are the very opposite of everything we have seen arise and pass away for countless milliards of years, yea, for eternities.

In the heavenly clearness of this "Nothing," from immemorial time and still to-day, consciousness flames up, as symptom that a something is disturbing this heavenly clearness, that *a contact* with something alien has set in. For only in consequence of irritation by some foreign body is consciousness aroused; where nothing is of what we might become conscious, there is also no ground for the arising of a consciousness.* "And of what does he becomes conscious? He becomes conscious of pleasure, and he becomes conscious of pain, and he becomes conscious of the absence of both pleasure and pain."[194] This means, the becoming conscious happens in the form of *sensation.* We feel something, a sensation, which immediately takes the form of *perception;* we perceive what is felt through sensation, as this corporeal organism which at bottom is nothing but a collection of activities of will, and the external world made known to us through it. And because thus in the light of consciousness, what stirs within us and arouses consciousness, is recognized as a collection of motions of will, all of which have for their object, connection with the world, therefore we imagine

injury to the brain, or madness, able to take the memory entirely away? Because originally we do not possess the faculty of cognition and especially of memory, but have to acquire and learn them with much effort. Indeed, these faculties are even so essentially strange to us, that, despite the beginninglessness of our world-pilgrimage, we have not been able to develop them beyond the modest degree in which we possess them at present. For, on account of the trouble of developing them, we have always been content to possess just as much of them as was needed for the maintainance of our life. But if we display the same energy with which one who wishes to master the piano, every day for hours, through many years, practises at his instrument, and pursue the right method, then we also, like the Buddha, may recover the back-going memory of our countless existences in the past.

* "To be conscious means: There are Objects for me." (Schopenhauer).

ourselves to consist in them and express this in the sentence: I am nothing but will.

In truth, I am will just as little as I am consciousness. So far as the latter is concerned, as sufficiently follows from the foregoing, it is only the consequence of the former, and therefore inseparably bound up with it. It flames forth, as often as a piece of willing in the form of one of the six activities of sense manifests itself in me, and only then. As regards this willing, however, it is a mere emotion, a mere craving for something alien, which rises within my inscrutable essence, not because this kind of activity is peculiar to this my essence, so that it is *forced* to act in this way, but it is only able to rise, because the aroused element of consciousness is not giving clear light, and in consequence hangs over me like a dim cloud, so that objects do not appear to me as they really are. As soon as this state of *ignorance* is removed by the rise of knowledge in consciousness, and the cloud of ignorance thereby dispersed for ever, the motion of willing *cannot* rise any more. Whoever as a child, ignorant of the effect of heat, once has put his hand on a heated stove and burnt himself severely, in future, as long as the remembrance of this lasts—and probably it will remain alive during his whole life—*cannot* any more will to touch a heated stove; *this* motion of will is extinguished in him for his whole life. Of course it follows, precisely from this example, as, moreover is self-evident, that mere abstract knowledge of the evil consequence of willing is not sufficient to remove it, but that direct actual knowledge of this must be obtained. I may explain to a child the pain which results from touching a hot stove as minutely as I please; curiosity will nevertheless at last lead it to touch the stove. Only after, in this way *directly* for itself, it has experienced the consequences of this its willing, does it possess actual knowledge in this direction. This direct, immediate knowledge of the perniciousness of a certain act of willing is thus the unfailing grave of the same. To this, there is no exception. To him who might answer that he knows very well the evil consequences of a certain direction of will, but notwithstanding is not able to crush it out, the reply must be made that in that case his knowledge is not yet sufficiently strong and direct. The stronger an inclination is, all the more, precisely through this its intensity, is real and complete cognition of its perniciousness made difficult. *The will falsifies cognition*, finding always new resources against confuting arguments, thereby overcoming them, let the resource appear ever so destitute of foundation to any third party. In short: Man makes a fool of himself. He does not *want* right insight when he is admonished to fight his passions. If this holds good, generally, during the times when these are slumbering, when the passions really break over him, the little morsel of insight he actually possesses, wholly disappears before his desires. Then these bury all reason beneath them. "To these five enjoyments of sense, o Brahmin, has the Brahmin Pokkharasāti, the Opamañña from Subhagavana, abandoned himself; enticed and blinded, he has fallen a prey to them, without seeing their misery, without thinking to escape from them. That he might understand or recognize or realize the supramundane deliverance, the highest *knowledge*,—this is impossible."[195] Thus the generally known impossibility of changing one's will, that is, one's character, only proves our lack of knowledge of the way by which may be overcome the turbidity of cognition produced by the violence of willing. But if there is such a way—and there is one, which the Buddha points out to us in his Excellent Eightfold Path, as we shall see in detail later on—then we can translate ourselves into a state wherein our attitude towards our whole willing is as estranged and objective, as, for instance, that of a man who loves his life, towards a cup full of poison set before him, or to a poisonous snake shut up in a box. Then, just as clearly as this man perceives all the consequences of a drink from the cup, or of grasping the poisonous snake, we perceive the abysses into which our thirst for existence and welfare will inevitably lead us, if we yield to it. And then it is as impossible that this thirst should rise any more within us as that this man can will to drink from the cup of poison, or to lay hold of the poisonous snake:

"Just as if, Sunakkhatta, there were a drinking-vessel, with fine, aromatic contents, of pleasant taste, but impregnated with poison, and there came a man, who wants to live and not to die, who desires wellbeing and abhors woe. What do you think, Sunakkhatta? Would the man empty the vessel, of which he knows: 'If I drink this, I must die or suffer deadly pains'?"

"Certainly not, Lord."

"Even so, Sunakkhatta, that a monk who bewares of the six domains of the senses and has discovered that *Grasping is the root of Suffering* .... might bring his body near to grasping, and let his mind cleave in any way: such a possibility there is not.

"Just as if, Sunakkhatta, there were a poisonous serpent, hissing angrily, and there came a man who wants to live and not to die, who desires wellbeing and abhors woe. What do you think, Sunakkhatta? Would the man stretch out his hand or his thumb towards the serpent, the poisonous, angrily hissing one, of which he knows: 'If this bites me, then I must die or suffer deadly pains'?"

"Certainly not, Lord."

"Even so also, Sunakkhatta, that a monk who bewares of the six domains of the senses and has discovered that *Grasping is the root of Suffering* .... might bring his body near to grasping and let his mind cleave in any way: such a possibility there is not."[196]

Thus all willing is unfailingly, of itself, killed by knowledge, by insight. Accordingly, the possibility of all willing is actually conditioned by the absence of this knowledge or insight, that is, by ignorance. But what is united with my essence only *conditionally*, what clings to me only *conditionally*, what only *conditionally* can rise out of me, that, for this very reason, I can also lose without myself being hurt thereby in my real constitution. It is nothing *essential*, but merely a quality adhering to me only *under certain conditions*, which falls off from me, when the condition is removed under which alone it is able to exist. Though thus on one hand, willing is self-evidently a quality of mine, as rising within me, on the other hand, it is equally clear that it represents only an *inessential* quality, which I can cause to disappear from me by removing its condition.

But if willing is not essential to me, then, of course, neither is my organism, which only arises in consequence of grasping caused by this willing, and fundamentally is nothing but the tool thus formed for the satisfaction of my willing. And just as little is this the case with my consciousness, which on its part only flames up, following upon the activity of the organism, and so, just as little, sensation, perception and the activities of the mind, which only become possible for me as consequence of the activities of the senses and of the element of consciousness aroused by them.* Thus, these also are mere *inessential* determinations of mine. Thereby, however, everything cognizable in me is recognized as inessential, and therewith also, from this point of view, the truth of the Buddha's words is confirmed: "This does *not* belong to me, this am I *not*, this is *not* my

* They are especially conditioned by the corporeal organism, as, "conditioned by a tree, a shadow might originate." Compare above p. 76*.

Self." Thereby, of course, he only wishes to say that the five groups constituting my existence are *indeed qualities of mine, but no essential ones.* Therefore they may easily be removed. In my deepest essence I am in no wise affected thereby; I am then indeed *poorer,* but not *less,* yet once more to repeat this much-used word. I then become without qualities, and so, without will, consciousness, sensation, body? By no means. That would not be quite correct. For we connect expressions like "being without qualities, without will, consciousness, sensation or body," with the idea of something defective or insufficient, quite in harmony with the remark just made, that whoever becomes thus, becomes poor, inexpressibly poor, utterly poor; he indeed loses *everything* in the widest sense of the word. But this poverty, closely regarded, as we also already know, is only poverty in—*suffering!* In giving up will, body, consciousness, and sensation, we become inexpressibly poor in *suffering.* For all will, all corporeality, all consciousness, all sensation, as already sufficiently explained, are only directed towards contact with the world. We strive for this contact by means of our will, achieve it by means of our corporeal organism, and experience it in the form of sensation and perception. This world, however, is the world of transitoriness, of decay, and thereby of suffering. Accordingly, all will, all consciousness, and all sensation are only a will for, and a consciousness and a sensation of, *suffering,* and thereby themselves full of suffering. The annihilation of all willing, all consciousness, and all sensation, is therefore not the loss of anything good, but the getting rid of a burden, of an immense burden, as least for him who has penetrated the whole truth.* The holy disciple as it is said in the Saṃyutta-Nikāyạ,[197] penetrates *contact,* that means, he

* In the Saṃyutta Nikaya, III, XII, 22, it is said: "What now, ye monks, is the burden? The five Grasping groups, ought to be replied. Which five? They are the body-

looks upon it as a fostering soil, like the body of a flayed cow, that is still alive, which, wherever it may be, near a wall, near a tree, in the water, in the field, everywhere, with its bare flesh provides an object for the attacks of flies and mosquitoes, worms, and whatever crawls and flies. Whoso thus has penetrated contact, has penetrated all sensation; for him nothing more remains to be done; he wants no more contact with the world, and thereby, since there is no willing for any other object, he wants nothing more at all. Above all, he wants no more consciousness, since all consciousness consists only in becoming conscious of this painful contact in the form of sensation. Herein especially he recognizes the truth of the words: "To be conscious is to be sick, to be conscious is to be pain-stricken."[198] He recognizes only too clearly how just it is to designate consciousness as an evil, which in its intensity may well be compared with the punishment of the criminal who receives a hundred blows every morning, midday and evening as described in the Samyutta-Nikāya.[199] Thus having reached the insight that here *"naught else but suffering perishes,"*[200] he wishes to become perfectly *free* from will, from consciousness, and thereby from sensation, in short, from all qualities whatsoever. Our only fit and proper state, is therefore that of *freedom* from all these qualities and determinations, with which we find ourselves encumbered at present, and which thus are not only inessential, but, at bottom, even unnatural to us.*

---

grasping-group, the sensation-grasping-group, the perception-grasping-group, the mentation-grasping-group, the consciousness-grasping-group — this, ye monks, is called the burden."

* It follows from the foregoing, that it is one and the same thing "to renounce the transitory phenomena of the world" and "to renounce sensation once for all." For only in relation to these transitory phenomena can sensation at all take place, which, just because of the transitoriness of what is felt, must, in the end, be always painful. Hence we may establish the following equation: capacity of sensation = capacity of suffering; and: real sensation = real suffering; we experience suffering, or we experience nothing at all. When, therefore, we wish to maintain at least our capacity of sensation or of consciousness, we wish nothing more or less than to maintain our capacity to suffer.

Only now, for the first time, do we know in its full content what the word *liberty* means.

Liberty is a negative conception, not a positive one. It indicates only that we are set free from something, more exactly, from some hindrance or limitation, but not what we then are, when in this manner we are freed. The highest liberty, "holy liberty" consists in being liberated from *all* limitations, not only from those imposed upon us by the external circumstances surrounding us, but, above all, from those that are by law of nature given together with, and in, our personality, thus, from the limitation of ever and again being born, of being ever and again subjected to illness, old age and death; in short, from being ever and again entangled in this unwholesome *Becoming*. Only when we have shaken off from us *these* limitations, are we really free. Now these limitations, as in general all others, are nothing but the consequences of our willing, which precisely in order to attain its sole object, contact with the world, is directed, and must be directed towards our organism built up from the matter of this world and therefore subject to its laws, therefore also builds up this organism by the bringing about of *grasping*, and then uses it as its tool. Liberty is therefore fundamentally nothing but liberty from willing. Whoso is able to free himself from his will, in the very act frees himself also from his organism, together with consciousness. For in his approaching death, since will is wanting, no new grasping is brought about, and thereby no new organism endowed with consciousness is built up. Thereby all the five groups at which grasping can take place, for him have disappeared for ever, so that the entire truth of the sentence becomes clear to us: "The five groups of grasping, monk, are rooted in willing."[201] According to this, the problem of freedom in general coincides with that of the freedom of the will in particular. *This* problem, however, after the foregoing, solves itself in the most simple manner: because we *are* not will, but only *possess* will, which consists in innumerable, single motions of will rising incessantly, and since this will, in addition, is something that is not essential to us, because only present within us under a certain condition, therefore we can not only change it as we please, by modifying or annihilating this condition, namely, that of ignorance, but also completely remove it. To be sure, this in practice is not quite as simple as perhaps it may seem when thus put in words, since it can only be realized in a certain quite definite manner, which we shall deal with later on; but it is not this that is in question here, but only that it is possible to realize it at all.

With this, however, we have already disposed of the third excellent truth, which therefore, will be intelligible to us without further ado:

"This, ye monks, is the most excellent truth of the annihilation of Suffering: it is the entire and complete annihilation of this same thirst, its abolition, rejection, putting away, extirpation." [202]

But since in the second as well as in this third of the excellent truths, *thirst* is always named as the positive cause of the circle of our rebirths, while we, instead, in what has gone before, have repeatedly spoken of *will* or *willing*, it will be convenient at this point to determine the exact relation in which these two concepts stand to one another. To begin with, it is clear that both mean fundamentally the same thing, as in fact we find in the Suttanipāta, [203] in the exposition of the causal nexus, where instead of thirst, as elsewhere, *will* is said to be conditioned by sensation, and to proceed from it. But on the other hand, every one will feel that the two conceptions are by no means exactly identical. They therefore must represent nuances of the same fundamental thought; and such really is the case.

If we closely look at our will,* we see it acting in a twofold manner. On one side, it acts as willing determined by consideration and reflection, and then, on the other hand, as *inclination* making itself felt in spite of consideration and reflection. Our whole willing, almost, is more or less the outcome of such inclinations within us. Thereby it takes a quite definite direction, and is, from the outset, more or less determined, so much so, that the will of every man, taken as a whole, represents a summation of certain dispositions of will, called his qualities of character, or, in their totality, as simply his character. It is just this kind of willing manifesting itself as inclination peculiar to each man, which the Buddha in the most vivid manner designates by the expression, *thirst*. Just as physiological thirst is not dependent on our arbitrary choice, in the same way we see the thirst for existence and wellbeing that animates us, ever and again welling up out of us with irresistible might, so much so, that instead of its being subject to the domination of our reason, that is, of our cognition, without ceremony it forces this latter into its own service.**

It is this willing manifesting itself as inclination in particular, which at the moment of death ever and again drives us to a new grasping of a new germ, brings about another such new grasping and thus ever and again chains us to a new organism. Hence it is this which must be completely

* That we are at all able to look at it, is of itself a proof that it has nothing to do with our true essence. For, what in us is cognizable, is *anattā*, not the I (see above p. 177*). Will, like all our other determinants, is closely cognizable, therefore it also is *anattā*!

** The word *taṇhā*, thirst, is identical with what Schopenhauer designates as will, thus consciously amplifying the normal content of this conception, where only "will led by cognition .... and expressing itself under the guidance of reason," is understood. Thus the Buddha already had penetrated "the identity of the essence of every striving and operating force in nature whatever with will." Therefore he created a special word "to designate the conception of this genus," in contrast to the species of volition in its narrower sense. To us who have not recognized this identity, such a word is wanting.

eradicated, root and branch, during our present lifetime, if at death we want to get out of the circle of rebirths. Motions of pure willing rising on account of a certain sensation or perception, thus, such as involve neither attraction nor repulsion, both characteristic of every inclination, cannot lead to any such grasping, since, the same as during the lifetime, they also vanish at the moment of death along with the respective sensation and perception which aroused them, without leaving a trace. We must therefore become quite *free from inclinations,* or, what, as we saw above, amounts to the same thing, entirely *free from character,** and thereby *from qualities.*

Now, however, the question arises as to how it comes about that our willing has developed to inclinations and thus has become determined, or, how we may have acquired our individual character. For it is clear that this also must be based upon a purely natural process, since, as we have seen, all willing of any kind, as in general *all* determinants within us, have nothing to do with our essence which is not subject to the laws of arising and passing away, but this willing also is *anattā*, that is, inessential, and thereby subject to the said laws.

In order to understand the change from pure willing to the impetuosity of an impulse, and thereby to a quality of character, we must first of all look closely at the fact that we may gradually become slaves of our will even in domains where this will before had no power over us. One who before was free—take notice of this word!—from the passion for smoking tobacco, allows himself to be determined by another's example to try it himself. He smokes once, and still feels himself entirely free to repeat it or to leave

* Here again distinction is made between being *without* character, and being *free* from character. A man without character has not yet got one; whereas the man free from character has one no longer.

it alone in the future. He smokes a second time and already feels the temptation to do it again at the next opportunity. He must already put forth his strength to withstand this temptation, though this is not yet difficult. But instead of resolving to exert his strength, he yields and goes on smoking. With each repetition, his inclination becomes stronger, until at last it becomes a proper passion, to fight against which seems entirely hopeless. Or a boy belonging to an industrious family may early lose his parents, under whose guardianship he was orderly and diligent. He is brought to depraved relatives. Instead of being given the opportunity of learning some proper trade, he is taught to beg and to steal. There can be no doubt that in time he will become a lazy fellow; nay, this distaste for work will later on become a deeply rooted inclination. In both cases it cannot be said that the disposition to this later and seemingly ineradicable inclination was born with the child. On the contrary, the germ of it has only been sown in this life and then, as the result of *habit,* developed into a permanent disposition of will. How many young people through bad example, through enticement, or in consequence of unfavourable external circumstances have come upon the path of lying, or stealing, or a dissolute life, and in consequence of long-continued activity in these directions have become habitual liars, thieves, debauchees, who under contrary circumstances would have become decent people, and therefore were *not* bad by nature! They also had not brought into the world with them these later characteristics of their willing, but on entering life were still *free* from them, they being only the result of a gradual habituation to them. This power of habit gradually to create irresistible inclinations, everyone will find at work in his own daily life; the emptiest trifles, the most wretched relationships, in consequence of the power of habit may force us completely under their spell, so that at last we foolishly break out into lamentations over the invincibility of our willing, and make the excuse that we were unable to act otherwise for want of another kind of will, instead of remembering that we ourselves by our thoughtless yielding to its first motions, have given ourselves over into bondage to this will.

"Suppose, Udāyī, a quail, bound with a strip of rotten bast, precisely thereby comes to sorrow and death: If now, Udāyī, someone said: 'But the band of rotten bast, with which this quail is bound, and through which it comes to ruin, sorrow and death, this for it is no strong band, but a weak band, a rotten band, a brittle band,'—would this man speak rightly?"

"Certainly not, Lord. For the band of rotten bast, Lord, with which this quail is bound, and through which it comes to ruin, sorrow and death, this is for it a firm band, a sound band, a tough band, no rotten band, but a heavy fetter."

"Even so also, Udāyī, many a fool, admonished by me to abstain from this and that, has said: 'Why trouble about this and that small trifle? Too punctiliously exact is this ascetic!' And he does not desist from it, and makes the monks diligently training themselves, distrustful of me. To him, Udāyī, this becomes a firm band, a sound band, a tough band, no rotten band, but a heavy fetter!"[204]

Thus it is *habit* that leads willing during the course of life upon certain paths, and creates certain definite dispositions of will. These dispositions, thus originated, later on determine the nature of the new grasping in death, with the result, that the creature which grows out of the newly laid hold of germ *corresponding to these dispositions,* brings with him into the world those habits which he developed in the former existence, as a present predisposition, as a particular trait of character. This habit which has become *a trait of character* is further yielded to in the new life, whereby it grows still stronger. This goes on through a series of existences following each other, until the peculiarity of character at last attains such strength, seems so intimately interwoven with us, that we no longer see any possibility under normal circumstances of liberating ourselves from it. On the contrary, on this ground we imagine ourselves to consist in it, and then, also on this ground, we coin the phrase: "I am will, through and through,"—a saying, which, after what we have been considering in our previous pages, is only correct in the same sense that a piece of cloth also may be wet through and through, but nevertheless does not consist of water.

That our characteristic peculiarities originated in this way, is expressed in the words already known to us: "Owners of their deeds, Brahmin, are beings, heirs of their deeds, children of their deeds, creatures of their deeds, slaves of their deeds. Deeds cut off beings, according to their depravity or their excellence," as the Buddha explains in the following example:

"There, O Brahmin, some woman or man has met an ascetic or a priest, without asking him: 'What is wholesome, Sir, what is unwholesome? What is right and what is wrong? What may be done and what may not be done? What, in doing it, may long time make for my suffering and misery? And what again, in doing it, may long time make for my joy and welfare?' There such action, thus performed, thus carried out, causes him when the body is dissolved, after death, to go downwards, upon the evil track, into the depths, into a hell-world. Or, if he does not come there, but reaches mankind, he will be lacking in understanding, where he is newly born. This is the transition, Brahmin, which leads to lack of understanding. . . . . There again, O Brahmin, some woman or man has met a priest or an ascetic and asked him: 'What is wholesome, Sir, and what is unwholesome? What may be done and what may not be done? What, in doing it, may long make for my suffering and misery? And what again, in doing it, may long make for my joy and welfare?' There such action, thus performed, thus carried out, causes him, when the body is dissolved, after death, to go upwards, upon the good track, into a heavenly world; or if he does not come there, but reaches mankind, then he will be intelligent, wherever he is reborn. This is the transition, O Brahmin, which leads to knowledge." [205]

By way of habit repeated through endless time the fundamental error in particular of mankind also has reached its granite-like strength, the error namely, that at least the mental capacities must be the immediate efflux of our essence: "Also an inexperienced, average man may well become weary of the body built up from the four chief elements. But what is called 'thought' or 'mind' or 'consciousness,' of this the average inexperienced man cannot get enough, he cannot break loose from it. And why not? *For a long time the inexperienced average man has held fast to it, has cherished and cultivated it,* thinking: 'This belongs to me, this am I, this is myself,' in correspondence with which fundamental error, egoism is the most prominent fundamental property of will. It is only the consequence of this correct insight into habit as power forming the character, that, where *we* speak of character or the characteristic directions of will, the Buddha knows only of "habitual attitude," "habitual longing," "habitual obstinacy, obduracy, irritability." [206] In its contents, however, this habitual attitude represents willing that has become impulse, thus, thirst in its sixfold activity as thirst for forms, sounds, odours, sapids, tangibles and ideas. [207] Venturing a bold expression, we might say that the thirst filling us and gushing forth anew in every new sensation is willing grown petrified in consequence of habit. For this reason exactly, is its eradication so very difficult, and the share which habit has in our willing, must have had a decisive influence upon the outlining of the Path established by the Buddha for the annihilation of thirst, as we shall see later.

After this elucidation of the relationship in which thirst stands to will, the third of the four excellent truths, to which we may now return, is entirely clear: *In thirst, our will must be annihilated, as far as it has won power over us.* With this annihilation, the chain binding us to the world and thereby to suffering, is finally cut through: we are delivered. For, to repeat it once more: If I have no will, no more thirst for the world, then in coming death, for want of a will, no grasping of a new germ will take place, and thereby also the six senses-machine as the apparatus serving for contact with the world will not be built up again. But where there is no contact, there is also no sensation,* and thereby no more suffering. The whole chain of suffering that we have come to know in detail as the chain of causal nexus, the *paṭiccasamuppāda,* is abolished for ever.

"Suppose, ye monks, the light of an oil lamp is burning, generated by oil and wick, but no one from time to time pours in new oil and attends to the wick; then, ye monks, according as the old fuel is used up, and no new fuel added, the lamp for want of nourishment will go out. Even so, ye monks, in him who dwells *in the insight into the transitoriness of all the fetters of existence,* thirst is annihilated; through the annihilation of thirst, grasping is annihilated; through the annihilation of grasping, Becoming is annihilated; through the annihilation of Becoming, birth is annihilated; through the annihilation of birth, old age, sickness, death, pain, lamentation, suffering, sorrow and despair are annihilated. Such is the annihilation of the whole chain of suffering."[209]

Here we see again, how thirst is annihilated, namely, by means of *insight.* Whoso recognizes ever more clearly and

* "It would be nonsense to assume that they would have sensation without contact." 208

clearly, that everything in the world at last must perish, and hence that only suffering can result from its possession, will find ever fewer objects adapted to the activities of sense, until at last he reaches the general insight that "nothing is worth relying on,"[210] that nothing in the world deserves to be seen, heard, smelt, tasted, touched or thought, but that all seeing, hearing, smelling, tasting, touching, thinking, are in themselves activities full of suffering, because all these functions fundamentally bring only suffering to us. He recognizes: "To whom the eye is pleasing, to him suffering is pleasing. To whom the ear, the nose, the tongue, the body, the organ of thought is pleasing, to him suffering is pleasing."[211] Whoever has recognized this, really recognized this, is seized with disgust for everything, "he is disgusted with the eye, with forms, with visual consciousness, with visual contact, with sensation, with thirst; he is disgusted with the ear, the nose, the tongue, the body, the organ of thought; he is disgusted with sounds, odours, sapids, tangibles, thoughts; he is disgusted with auditory consciousness, with olfactory consciousness, with gustatory consciousness, with tactile consciousness, with mental consciousness; he is disgusted with visual contact, with auditory contact, with olfactory contact, with gustatory contact, with tactile contact, with mental contact; he is disgusted with sensation; he is disgusted with thirst."[212] Thus thirst also is definitively extinguished. For what should he long who has recognized as full of suffering all actual and possible objects that can ever offer themselves to his six senses? who, therefore, wherever in the world he may look, sees streaming towards him only an ocean of suffering? Suffering *cannot* be desired, for suffering we *can* have no longing, because, this, indeed, would be against our real essence, "which craves wellbeing and shuns woe." Hence every kind of thirst, as soon as the full insight has dawned upon us that everything that can ever become an object of our will, is only masked suffering, must unfailingly be extinguished simply *for want of proper nourishment.*

But if complete insight is followed by the extinction of every kind of thirst for existence, and therefore also by the impossibility of any further grasping upon the approaching death, then with this extinction, *eternal* deliverance also is secured, and the chain of suffering is not merely for an interval severed at death. For the organic processes, the Saṅkhārā, come *definitively* to rest in death, without being able to begin again in a new body. Thereby consciousness also is for ever abandoned, that is only able to exist in consequence of the Saṅkhārā, especially of the sense-processes, since it has its seat in them. And together with consciousness, the corporeal organism also disappears for ever. But if thus every kind of body endowed with senses is annihilated for all eternity, then also the six senses themselves are annihilated, and together with them every possibility of further contact with, and sensation of, the world.* In this eternal freedom from sensation, and thereby from perception, however, lies the garantee that in my inscrutable essence through all eternity no new thirst for the world can arise again, thus also, never again a grasping take place, and thereby never again the Becoming and birth of a new organism set in, so that the attainment of perfect knowledge, in consequence of the complete annihilation of the thirst for existence dwelling within me, immediately brought about by this same knowledge, will be followed by *eternal* liberation from old age and death, from sorrow, lamentation, pain, grief, and despair. Hence the formula of the

* "Broken is the body, extinguished is perception, all sensation has disappeared. The organic processes have found rest, consciousness has gone to rest," the Buddha says at the death of one of his holy disciples; whilst upon the death of holy Godhika to the question: "Where has the consciousness of noble Godhika found its seat?" he answers: "The consciousness of noble Godhika has nowhere found a seat."[213]

causal nexus, without further words, is intelligible in its second part also, when it tells us:—

"Inasmuch as that is not, this is not. If this is removed, then that disappears. Thus, namely:—

"By the entire and complete annihilation of ignorance, the organic processes, [especially the activities of the senses], the Saṅkhārā, are annihilated.*

"By the entire and complete annihilation of the organic processes, consciousness is annihilated.

"By the entire and complete annihilation of consciousness, the corporeal organism is annihilated.**

"By the entire and complete annihilation of the corporeal organism, the six senses are annihilated.

"By the entire and complete annihilation of the six senses, contact is annihilated.

"By the entire and complete annihilation of contact, sensation is annihilated.

"By the entire and complete annihilation of sensation, thirst is annihilated.

"By the entire and complete annihilation of thirst, Grasping is annihilated.

"By the entire and complete annihilation of Grasping, Becoming is annihilated.

---

* When it is said: "Through the annihilation of ignorance the Saṅkhārā are annihilated," then, of course, as we said above, and wish to emphasize once more only because of the importance of the problem, this does not mean that the acquisition of knowledge is *immediately* followed by the annihilation of the Saṅkhārā, but in dependence on the annihilation of ignorance as *immediate* consequence, the *actual* thirst for existence is abolished and so every new grasping upon the coming death is made impossible; therefore when the latter happens, *new* organic processes and with them new consciousness and a new corporeal organism are no more able to arise, and so on, as said above.

** If the formula of the causal nexus is to be *completely* understood, in its first as well as in its second part here dealt with, we must look at it from *the standpoint of the being entering the world, as also from that of the saint leaving it.* For the latter, first of all, the organic processes cease; in consequence of this, consciousness; therewith also for him disappears his body, and so on.

"By the entire and complete annihilation of Becoming, birth is annihilated.

"By the entire and complete annihilation of birth, old age and death vanish, together with sorrow and affliction, pain, grief and despair.

"Thus comes about the annihilation of the entire Sum of Suffering."[214]

Because thus the whole circle of rebirths within the world, upon the next approaching death, is broken through for ever in consequence of the impossibility of a new birth, therefore the saint has also escaped for ever the consequences of all his former evil deeds, in so far as these deeds would only mature after his death, let them have been ever so bad. For in leaving the world, he of course also escapes from the law of Karma, which dominates it. Thus the 294th verse of the Dhammapada says:

> "Though mother, father he has slain,
> Though he has murdered Khattiya kings,
> Though he has crushed out land and folk,—
> The saint is faultless and without blame."

But on the other hand, of course, he remains subject to the consequences of his former deeds as long as he still tarries in the world, that is, up to the time of his death. An example of this is furnished by Aṅgulimāla, in the 86th Discourse of the Majjhima Nikāya. "Once a robber, cruel and bloodthirsty, wont to kill and murder, without compassion for man and beast," he was converted by the Buddha and later became a saint. One day, while begging for food, he was set upon with sticks and stones, and came back to the Buddha, streaming with blood. And the Buddha speaks thus: "Only bear it, saint, only bear it, saint! The requital of deeds, for which you would have to suffer many years, many hundreds of years, many thousands of years, many hundred-thousands of years of torment in hell,—this requital, O saint, you find now during this lifetime." Thereby the Buddha says that this maltreatment of Aṅgulimāla is causally connected with his earlier wicked life, even though this connection is not apparent in its separate links, but comes under the caption of *"the hidden chain of suffering."*[215] For the rest, however, his words mean that Aṅgulimāla ought to be glad that he, as a saint, had only to undergo these slight consequences occurring now during his life, being meanwhile liberated from the other dreadful consequences, that would have matured after his death, *if he had not become a saint.**

* * *

The dawn of complete insight, and the extinction of every kind of thirst for the world effected thereby, not only at death entirely annihilates the chain of suffering, but also during the lifetime brings about a radical change in it: deliverance becomes *manifest* even during life. Together with the extinction of thirst, as we saw above, aversion from every further activity of sense sets in, wherein thirst only manifested itself, and from which, on the other hand, it always drew new nourishment. Thereby, however, we also get weary of our own body, which we only love as bearer of the organs of sense, as the six senses-machine. Whoever really does not wish to see any more, is not in the least concerned if everything in his body perishes that makes possible the activity of seeing; and whoever does not want any more to hear, smell, taste and touch, clings to his body

---

* That these consequences which followed during his lifetime, were so very slight, was mainly due to the views prevalent in Angulimāla's time, in accord with which, government did not call to account even a robber or murderer, if he was treading the holy path as an ascetic.[216]

If Aṅgulimāla had lived in our days, his sanctity would not have availed to shield him from the condemnation of the judge who could have done no other than sentence him to the death penalty. In this case also, the Buddha would have called out the above exhortation to him, even at the foot of the scaffold.

only so far as it is the necessary tool for thinking that alone is still held to be indispensable. But whoever, in addition, becomes weary of all thinking, has lost all interest in the continuous existence of his body, which is now of no more use to him; the six senses-machine in its entirety, has become superfluous for him. It is with him as with a painter who has become weary of painting and lost all pleasure in it. As such a painter for this reason becomes indifferent towards his brush and palette, and carelessly casts them aside, since now they are even a nuisance to him, in the same way, to him who has become weary of all the activities of sense on account of their pain-producing character, the organs of sense and thereby the entire corporeal organism becomes a nuisance; he regards them as a burden, yea, as the burden of which to get rid is deliverance. This is all the more true in that he resembles the said painter in this point also, that just as the painter in his pure entity is not touched by his abandonment of the profession, that has become distasteful to him, but on the contrary, only now for the first time becomes fully and undisturbedly conscious of his entity; in the same way the more he cuts himself loose from all activities of sense, to his own surprise he directly recognizes that thereby he is in no way impaired in his essence, but merely gets free from disturbing accessories. It is a mere *turning away*, a mere *getting free* from the body endowed with the six senses, that happens within him: "Disgusted he turns away; turned away he delivers himself," the passage from the Majjhima Nikāya quoted above[217] goes on. If, nevertheless, he again takes up activities of the senses, then he immediately feels the sensations aroused through them as not belonging to him, as something that he can omit, unhurt thereby in his integrity; he feels them as a *delivered one*. "If now a pleasant sensation is felt, then one recognizes: 'It is transitory,' 'it is unappropriated,' 'it is unpleasant.' If a painful sensation is felt, then one recognizes: 'It is transitory,' 'it is unappropriated,' 'it is unpleasant.' If now a sensation neither pleasant nor unpleasant is felt, then one recognizes: 'It is transitory,' 'it is unappropriated,' 'it is unpleasant.' If now a pleasant sensation is felt, then one feels it as a *delivered* one. If now an unpleasant sensation is felt, them one feels it as a *delivered* one. If now a sensation neither pleasant nor unpleasant is felt, then one feels it as a *delivered* one." [218]

Because one thus confronts one's own sensations as a delivered one, therefore they cannot take one captive any more. "Through the eye and forms sight-consciousness arises; the conjunction of the three gives contact; through contact arises a sensation of pleasantness or unpleasantness, or of neither pleasantness nor unpleasantness. If struck by a pleasant sensation, one experiences no joy, no satisfaction, no attachment, and feels no motion of desire. If struck by an unpleasant sensation, one neither grieves nor mourns nor laments, he does not beat his breast all distraught, feels no motion of aversion. If struck by a sensation neither pleasant nor unpleasant, one understands the arising and passing away of this sensation, its comfort and misery and overcoming according to truth, and feels no motion of ignorance."* [218]

In consequence of the activities of sense, consciousness also, of course, still continues to flame up, but only so that it looks down with equanimity upon the things through which it was aroused. Yea, because we have become entirely estranged from our own sensations, and can as with a searchlight illuminate the objects arousing them with the light of pure cognition, according to which they *all,* at bottom, conceal within themselves corruption, and thus, are disgusting, therefore we have it in our power to turn pleasant and

* The like, of course, holds good, as there is further set forth, with regard also to the sensations aroused through the activity of hearing, smelling, tasting, touching and thinking.

unpleasant sensations arising within us into their contrary and thus, especially, to experience pleasant sensations as unpleasant ones. Or we may behave with complete indifference, thus, with absolute equanimity towards all sensations, according as we allow cognition to play upon the objects arousing sensation.

"But how, Ānanda, may a saint dominate his senses? There, Ānanda, a monk has seen a form with the eye, has heard a sound with the ear, has smelt an odour with the nose, has tasted a flavour with the tongue, has touched something touchable with the body, has thought an idea with the organ of thought, and thus he is moved pleasantly, is moved unpleasantly, is moved partly pleasantly and partly unpleasantly. And if he wishes: 'The repugnant, I will perceive unrepugnant,' then he perceives unrepugnant. If he wishes: 'The un-repugnant, I will perceive repugnant,' then he perceives repugnant. If he wishes: 'The partly repugnant and partly un-repugnant, I will perceive un-repugnant,' then he perceives un-repugnant. If he wishes: 'The partly un-repugnant and partly repugnant, I will perceive repugnant, then he perceives repugnant. If he wishes: 'The repugnant and the un-repugnant; both I will banish from me, and I will remain with equal mind, thoughtful and clearly conscious,' then he remains with equal mind, thoughtful and clearly conscious. Thus, Ānanda, does a saint dominate his senses."[219]

Thus sensations are still felt, but they have lost all power over us. We are not indeed yet free *from* them, but stand *towards* them as *free men*.

"This is a monk, who bears cold and heat, hunger and thirst, wind and rain, mosquitoes and wasps and vexing crawling things. Malicious and spiteful words, painful feelings of the body striking him, violent, cutting, piercing, disagreeable, tedious, life-endangering, he patiently endures. He is entirely free from greed, hate and delusion, disjoined from misconduct. Sacrifices and gifts, service and greetings he deserves, as the holiest state in the world." [220]

Of him hold good the impressive words: "Those who cause me pain and those who cause me pleasure, towards all of them I behave in the same way; affection or hate I know not. In joy and sorrow I remain unmoved; in honor and dishonor; everywhere I am the same. This is the perfection of my equanimity." [221]

Nothing is able to arouse in him a motion of desire or of repulsion; only totally pure willing remains. For through what might such a saint still be influenced, after he has become free from all former determinations and independent of all external impressions? Whatever motion of willing he wishes to arouse, that he allows to arise, and whatever again he wishes to subside, that he allows to subside. He has realized *the most perfect freedom of will.**

It may even happen, that such a delivered one, during his lifetime, may realize not only freedom *in* willing, but also perfect freedom *from* willing, and thereby absolute freedom from consciousness and from sensation, to be sure, not at once, in a moment, but in successive upward stages, as a man climbs the steps of a ladder,—so powerful are the influencing elements of the world, that stream in upon us through the five external senses, that even the delivered one can only completely stop them one after the other, though, as we have seen, even if they press in on him, in each case they fall off from him without leaving a trace. This way of the delivered one, leading to perfect liberty *from* volition also, and thereby at the same time from the whole world, is as follows.

Willing effectuates itself in the activities of the six senses.

---

* Accordingly, a saint may also be defined as a man who has realized freedom of will, or, what is the same thing, simply as a *free man.*

Of these, the delivered one may, according as he pleases, entirely stop those of the five external senses, and to this extent abolish all willing. He is then, on the outward side, entirely blind and deaf, insensible to every smell, every taste, every touch, thus, in so far, has already left this world.

"At that time, Pukkusa, the prince of the Mallas, a disciple of Āḷāra Kālāma, was travelling on the highway from Kusinārā to Pāvā. Now Pukkusa, the young Malla, saw the Exalted One sitting under a tree. Having seen the Exalted One, he came near, saluted the Exalted One respectfully and sat down aside. Sitting aside, Pukkusa, the prince of the Mallas, spoke to the Exalted One thus:—

'Astonishing, sir, extraordinary it is, sir, how deep, sir, is the peace in which pilgrims may abide. One day, sir, Āḷāra Kālāma was wandering along the road, and had turned aside from the way and sat down under a tree near by, to stay there till evening. There, sir, about five hundred carts came past Āḷāra Kālāma. Now, sir, a man, who was following the traces of this caravan of carts, came to Āḷāra Kālāma and asked: 'Sir, did you see about five hundred carts come past?'—'Nothing have I seen, brother.'—'But surely, sir, you heard their noise?'—'No noise have I heard, brother.'—'Then you were sleeping, sir?'—'I did not sleep, brother.'—'How then, sir; and were you conscious?'—'Certainly, brother.'—'So then, sir, conscious and with waking senses, you have neither seen the five hundred carts that came past you, nor heard their noise; but your mantle, sir, is quite covered with dust.'—'So it is, brother.' Thereupon, sir, this man thought thus within himself: 'Magnificent it is, incredible, indeed, how deep is the peace in which pilgrims are able to abide, since one, conscious and with waking senses, needs neither to see five hundred carts passing by him, nor to hear their noise.' And having thus made known his great admiration for Āḷāra Kālāma, he went on his way."

"Now what think you, Pukkusa: Which may be more difficult to carry out, which more difficult to effect—that a person, conscious and with senses awake need neither see five hundred carts passing right by him, nor hear their noise, or that one, conscious and with senses awake, in a thunderstorm, in a whirling hurricane, while the lightnings are flashing forth, and the thunderbolts are crashing, need neither see, nor yet hear the noise?"

"How, sir, could five hundred carts be compared with that, or even six, seven, eight or nine hundred, even a thousand or a hundred thousand carts? Much more difficult would it be to carry out this, to effect this,—that one conscious and with senses awake in a thunderstorm, in a whirling hurricane, when the lightnings are flashing forth, and the thunderbolts are crashing, need neither see, nor yet hear the noise!"

"Now at one time, Pukkusa, I was staying near Ātumā, in a barn. Just then in a thunderstorm, in a whirling hurricane, when the lightnings were flashing forth and the thunderbolts were crashing, not far from the barn two peasants, brothers, were struck by the lightning, and four draught-oxen. Then, Pukkusa, a great crowd of people came from Ātumā, and stood round the two peasants, brothers, and the four oxen, killed by the lightning. Now, Pukkusa, I had come out of the barn, and was pacing up and down in front of the threshing-floor under the open sky. And a man out of this great crowd of people came towards me, bowed and stood aside. And to the man, who stood there, Pukkusa, I spoke thus: 'Why, brother, has that great crowd gathered there?'—'Just now, sir, in the hurricane, amidst the rain pouring down with flashes of lightning and crashes of thunder, two peasants have been killed, brothers, and four draught-oxen. Therefore this great crowd has assembled. But you, sir, where have you been?'—'Just here, brother, I have been.'—'Then surely, sir, you have seen it?'—

'Nothing, brother, have I seen.'—'But, sir, you have surely heard the noise?'—'Nothing, brother, have I heard of the noise.'—'Then, sir, were you sleeping?'—'No, brother, I was not asleep.'—'How now, sir; were you conscious?'—'Certainly, brother.'—'Then, sir, conscious and with senses awake in the hurricane, amidst the rain pouring down with flashes of lightning and crashes of thunder, you neither saw, nor yet heard the noise?'—'Certainly, brother.'—Then, Pukkusa, the man began to wonder: 'O, how strange, how wonderful, how deep indeed must be the peace wherein pilgrims are able to abide, since one of them, being conscious and awake, here in the hurricane, amidst the rain pouring down with flashes of lightning and crashes of thunder, need neither see, nor yet hear the noise!' And having thus shown his great admiration for me, he turned round and went off." [222]

But *internally* he has not yet entirely come to rest. For the organ of thought is still agitated and unable at once to come to peace, in the same way that a pendulum set swinging, still for a time goes on swinging. But as the man who has his senses under his control, is able to think whatever he pleases,—"whatever thought he wishes to think, that he thinks; and whatever thought he does not wish to think, that he does not think," [223]—already, as soon as he has retired from the outer world, he has, "so to say, bound" his mind to a certain definite thought, concentrating it, for example, on the idea of 'earth,' taking up the idea 'earth,' as his sole object. "In the idea 'earth' his mind is elevated, rejoiced, becomes appeased, delivered." [224] This deliverance has especially also for result that soon he contemplates the idea 'earth' with complete equanimity, and thereby can dismiss it from his consciousness as the last reflection of the material world, while he immerses himself in the idea of '*boundless space.*'

"And the things of the sphere of boundless space, perception of the sphere of boundless space, and concentration of mind, contact, sensation, perception, thought, consciousness, will, resolution, energy, reflectiveness, equanimity, recollectedness,* all these things, one after the other, he has brought into order, these things he knowingly causes to arise, knowingly causes to continue, knowingly causes to disappear. And he recognizes: 'Thus these things, not having been, come to appear; and having been, again disappear.' And he is not inclined towards these things, and not disinclined towards them; not adhering, not attached, he has escaped from them, has fled from them, without allowing his mind to become restricted. For he knows that there is still *a higher freedom;* and as he develops it, he notes that it exists.

"And again, ye monks, Sāriputta, after having entirely overcome the sphere of boundless space, in the idea 'Boundless is the sphere of consciousness,' has won to the realm of boundless consciousness. And the things of the sphere of boundless consciousness, perception of the sphere of boundless consciousness, and concentration of mind, contact, sensation, perception, thought, consciousness, will, resolution, energy, reflectiveness, equanimity, recollectedness, all these things, one after the other, he has brought into order, these things he knowingly causes to arise, knowingly causes to continue, knowingly causes to disappear. And he recognizes: 'Thus these things, not having been, come to appear; and having been, again disappear.' And he is not inclined towards these things, and not disinclined towards them; not adhering, not attached, he has escaped from them, has fled from them, without allowing his mind to become restricted. For he knows that there is still *a higher freedom;* and as he develops it, he notes that it exists.

"And again, ye monks, Sāriputta, after having completely overcome the sphere of boundless consciousness, in the idea

* All these functions have, of course, only the idea of infinite space for their object.

'Nothing (more) is there' has won to the sphere of Nothingness;* and the things of the sphere of nothingness, perception of nothingness and concentration of mind, contact, sensation, perception, thought, consciousness, will, resolution, energy, reflectiveness, equanimity, recollectedness, all these things, one after the other, he has brought into order, these things he knowingly causes to arise, knowingly causes to continue, knowingly causes to disappear. And he recognizes: 'Thus these things, not having been, come to appear; and having been, again disappear.' And he is not inclined towards these things, and not disinclined towards them; not adhering, not attached, he has escaped from them, has fled from them, without allowing his mind to become restricted. For he knows that there is still *a higher freedom;* and as he develops it, he notes that it exists.

"Again, ye monks, Sāriputta, after having completely overcome the sphere of nothingness, has won to the boundary of possible perception.** And from this conquest thoughtfully he returns. And when he has thoughtfully returned from this

---

* On this height, the delivered one has only the consciousness of being quite alone and loosened from everything. Not only nothing of the noisy unrest of the corporeal world comes to him, or perhaps rather, into him, but internally he is now entirely absorbed by being conscious of the most lofty and sublime loneliness, and thereby of the most majestic peace. He has shaken off everything, and thereby also his own corporeal organism, which he uses only in his organ of thought, and even in this, only for the recognizing of the immense voidness in contrast to which he sees himself. This brings to him the further sublime insight: "I am not anywhere whatsoever, to any one whatsoever, in anything whatsoever; neither is anything whatsoever mine, anywhere whatsoever, in anything whatsoever." 225

** In connection with the realm of nothingness, it is said in the 9th Discourse of the Dīgha Nikāya: "As soon, Poṭṭhapāda, as the monk has obtained perception *within himself,* he is able to proceed further, step by step, to the boundary of perception. If he has reached the boundary of perception, he says to himself: 'To suffer thoughts is worse for me, not to suffer thoughts is better for me. If I should now go on thinking and acting, then this perception would perish within me, and another, grosser perception would arise. How now, if I should try to think and to act no more?' And thus he thinks no more and acts no more. Because he thinks no more and acts no more, also this perception perishes and another, grosser perception does not arise."—This state is described in the 106th *Discourse* of the *Majjhima Nikāya,* as follows: "There, Lord, a monk has proceeded thus: 'What is, what has become, shall not be, shall not be for me, shall not become, shall not become for me: I put it away; thus he wins

conquest, he perceives the things that are overcome, dissolved and transformed: 'Thus these things, not having been, come to appear; and having been, again disappear.' And he is not inclined towards these things, and not disinclined towards them; not adhering, not attached, he has escaped from them, has fled from them, without allowing his mind to become restricted. For he knows that there is still *a higher freedom.* And as he develops it, he notes that it exists.

"And again, ye monks, Sāriputta, after having completely overcome the boundary of possible perception, has won to the *dissolution of perception and sensation,* and having by wisdom sighted this, the influences upon him are at an end.* And

---

equanimity." With this he also ceases to think at all, just perceiving: "Peaceful am I, extinguished am I, *no more a grasping one am I.*" The activity of perception, taking place even now *in full consciousness,* is thereby reduced to the smallest possible residue, namely, to the perception that there is no perception left! This state is therefore called the realm of "neither perception nor non-perception"—nevasaññanasaññāyatanam, translated by Neumann "the boundary of possible perception."

* The Pāli term designating this state is *nirodha-samāpatti,* attainment of annihilation, and *saññavedayitanirodha,* annihilation *(nirodha)* of perception and sensation. It may last for full seven days. In the 43rd Discourse of the Majjhima Nikāya it is said: "In the case of a man dead, expired, and in the case of a monk attained to the ceasing of perception and sensation—what is the difference between these two?"—"In the case of a man dead, expired, the processes of the body—Saṅkhārā—are perished, come to an end; the processes of speech are perished, come to an end; the processes of mind are perished, come to an end. Vitality is exhausted, heat extinguished, the senses shattered. And in the case of a monk attained to the ceasing of perception and sensation the processes of body, speech and mind are perished, come to an end; but vitality is not exhausted, heat not extinguished, the senses are not shattered."—In the 50th Discourse of the Majjhima Nikāya, this state, as it appears from without, is described as follows: "The venerable Sañjīva was in the habit of resorting to the forest or to the foot of a tree or to some solitary place, and with but little difficulty there attained to the ceasing of perception and sensation. Now it happened once that the venerable Sañjīva was seated beneath a certain tree absorbed in the attainment of the ceasing of perception and sensation, and some cow-herds and goat-herds and husbandmen wayfarers happened to see the venerable Sañjīva where he sat beneath the tree, and, seing him, they cried: 'Wonderful indeed, extraordinary indeed! That ascetic is sitting there dead! Come, let us give him to the fire!' And those country folk gathered together some grass and sticks and dried cow-dung, and, heaping the stuff over the body of the venerable Sañjīva, set it alight and went their way. And when night was gone, rising from his absorption, the venerable Sañjīva shook his garments, and,

from this conquest he thoughtfully returns. And having thoughtfully returned from this conquest he perceives the things that are overcome, dissolved and transformed: 'Thus these things, not having been, come to appear; and having been, again disappear.' And he is not inclined towards these things, and not disinclined towards them; not adhering, not attached, he has escaped from them, has fled from them, without allowing his mind to become restricted. For he knows that *there is no higher freedom*." [227]

Such an one has thus, already in this present life, actually realized complete deliverance from everything that is *anattā*, not the *I*, that means, from the components of his personality, and thereby from the world. He has completed the gigantic task, he has burst all the fetters, "whether refined or gross." [228] He has completely annihilated all the activities of the senses, for *they* are the fetters, hence, all seeing, hearing, smelling, tasting, touching, thinking, and thereby for a time completely thrown aside the six senses-machine. He has gained the highest, the holy freedom. To be sure, later on these activities of the senses, the Saṅkhārā, rise again, since the capacity of life of the six senses-machine still remains, and call him back again into the world. But now he stands entirely estranged from both his own sense-activities as well as the world. For now in the most immediate manner imaginable, he has directly experienced that he does not consist in them. For it goes without saying that after having freed himself from every kind of sensation, he had not become nothing—taking this word in the sense of *absolute* nothing—and then again arisen anew; but he had remained what he is from all eternity, while

---

suitably attiring himself, took mantle and alms-bowl and entered the village to go the usual morning round for alms of food. And those cow-keepers and tenders of goats and farmers and passers-by, observing the venerable Sañjīva upon his begging-round, exclaimed: 'How wonderful, how extraordinary! There is that ascetic we saw sitting dead; he has come alive again!'" [226]

these phenomena which run their course on him or before him or in him, or whatever we like to call it, and continually arouse his consciousness in the form of sensation, incessantly "not having been, come to appear, and, having been, again disappear." Yea, it is he himself who "*knowingly causes them to arise, knowingly to remain, and knowingly again to perish,*" and thus, if it is permissible to use such a humble comparison, he plays catchball with the world, which he can make disappear and rise again before him according as he chooses. He has experienced in himself the full truth of the famous words of the monk Assaji, in which the doctrine of the Buddha seems to be summed up:

> "The [painful] phenomena arising from a cause,
> Their cause the Perfect One has told,
> And their annihilation too.
> This the great ascetic teaches."[229]

From this standpoint he now of course knows immediately that he himself will die just as little as in truth he ever has arisen. What is to perish and die, are only these phenomena which as the machinery of his personality, not having been, come to appear; and having been, again disappear; and are only the components of *anattā*, of not-the-*I*. His ostensible, up to the present moment ever repeated new dying during the endless Saṁsāra which soon will come finally to rest, now reveals itself as a gigantic and incessant self-mystification, resting upon the delusion that his real essence has something in common with the components of his personality. This delusion he now has entirely destroyed; yea, he has discovered that every kind of reflection of a positive content about himself or his relation to the world, by natural necessity must be illusionary, thus, a mere imagination, a mere opinion, since his own essence does not enter into this thinking, but is only realized, when this thinking also, in the state of the annihilation of perception and sensation, is completely abrogated, as darkness only becomes apparent, when the light is extinguished. Further, he has discovered that, as soon as this thinking, as a mere imagining, begins anew, we again find ourselves plunged into the domain of the laws of arising and passing away, and thereby of death, thus, of self-mystification. From his own experience he understands the truth of the description of this perpetual self-mystification, as it is given in a significant legend of the Saṃyutta-Nikāya.[230]

The demon Vepacitti, together with his legions, is vanquished by the gods in battle, and bound in fivefold fetters. As often as he thinks: "The gods are right, and the demons are wrong," he finds himself free from the five fetters, and enjoying heavenly pleasures; and as often as he again thinks: "The demons are right, and the gods are wrong," he again finds himself bound in the fivefold fetters and deprived of the heavenly pleasures. "So feeble," it goes on, "are the fetters of Vepacitti, but far more feeble still are the fetters of death. To imagine, causes us to be bound by death; not to imagine, causes us to be freed from the Evil One." "'I am,' is imagination, 'I am not,' is imagination, 'I shall be,' is imagination, 'I shall not be,' is imagination; 'I shall be possessed of form,' is imagination, 'I shall be without form,' is imagination; 'I shall be conscious,' is imagination; 'I shall be unconscious,' is imagination; 'I shall be neither conscious nor unconscious,' is imagination." Thus a monk, who once has experienced the annihilation of perception and sensation and thereby the total ceasing of all imagination, imagines nothing more, even after having returned from this state to the world: "This, ye monks, is a monk who does not imagine anything, does not imagine anything of anything, does not imagine anything about anything."[231] He only cherishes the one purely negative thought, because rejecting *every-*

thing: "This does not belong to me, this am I not, this is not my self."*

For the rest, deliverance is not dependent on our being able to effect at will the annihilation of perception and sensation during our lifetime, and thereby to leave the world entirely—to realize this, requires extraordinary faculties of concentration, as we shall see later on — but deliverance is exclusively conditioned by this, that in consequence of the advent of the complete knowledge that all is full of suffering and conditioned by thirst, this same thirst is completely destroyed. Everyone who has attained to this, already during his lifetime takes up this position towards his own personality, especially towards the activities of the senses, and therewith towards the world, like him who has attained to the annihilation of perception and sensation. For, just because he has no longer any kind of desire for sense-activity and the world, thereby the chain is broken that bound him to these, and ever and again caused to arise in him the delusion that in some way they belonged to him, were it only in the sense that he himself in himself truly is not touched by their loss, but at least he needs them for his happiness; in consequence of which delusion he is unable to win to the full, pure view of Anattā, and to take his stand as a complete stranger, and thereby as a free man over against the world, including the elements of his own personality. And because he has now recognized as such the chain that fetters him to his personality and to the world, that is, the thirst for them, and broken it, he knows just as well as he who is able to win the annihilation of perception and

* Compare also Majj. Nik. I, p. 40: "Of the many different teachings, Cunda, that appear in the world and deal now with the contemplation of the self, now with the contemplation of the world, everywhere holds good, wherever they appear, arise, spring up, the following truthful perfectly wise judgment: 'This does not belong to me, this am I not, this is not my self.' Thus are they to be got rid of, thus are they to be put from you."

sensation, that in the moment of his coming death, through the absence of this thirst and the grasping conditioned by it, no more rebirth will lie before him, but eternal deliverance from the world, *absolute freedom from sensation* for ever will supervene. "And thus he recognizes: 'These six senses will come to perfect, complete and entire annihilation, and nowhere, in no place, will other six senses arise.[232] "Within the delivered one the knowledge of his deliverance arises: 'Rebirth is annihilated, fulfilled is the holy life; done, what was to do; no more is this world for me,' thus he knows."[233]

According to this, we did not at all need here the special case of a delivered one who already during his lifetime has been able to free himself from sensation. If, nevertheless, we have dealt with it, this has happened because it is precisely in such an one that the effects of deliverance, already during his lifetime, stand out with special clearness and distinctness.*

* * *

Now many a reader will perhaps wonder to himself that in what has passed in our previous pages, in the course of our exposition of the Buddha's doctrine of deliverance, we have not devoted a single word to the concept *Nibbāna,*

---

* Besides this, the state of the annihilation of perception and sensation may be attained not only by a perfect saint, thus, by one who has annihilated for ever every kind of thirst for existence (Becoming), in every possible form so that he faces everything with the most perfect equanimity, more especially his own capacity for realizing this last and highest state of the annihilation of perception and sensation during his present lifetime; but it may be reached also by him who has lost all thirst for existence, *with the exception* of that final residue whereby he still feels "love and joy and inclination" towards the perfect equanimity he has won thereby, and to the capacity for the annihilation of perception and sensation thereby arising within him. Such a person, in the latter state, may attain a transitory or temporary deliverance; but as long as this last residue of thirst, thus, the satisfaction felt over this all-embracing equanimity he has won, is not yet annihilated, he does not yet possess *eternal* deliverance, since even this last residue of thirst at death must manifest its consequences, that is to say, it must lead to a new, even if a "best grasping."

which yet, as everybody knows, constitutes the final goal of his teaching. "Nibbāna is the kernel of the holy life, brother Visākha, Nibbāna is its purpose and its goal."[234] But this surprise is unfounded. For in dealing with the state of the perfectly delivered one after death, and even during his lifetime, we were speaking about nothing but Nibbāna. For Nibbāna and eternal deliverance are synonymous concepts which in so far coincide, that they have no sort of positive, but only a purely negative content. As by *deliverance* we simply think of *freedom,* without thereby giving any definition of what the delivered one really is after his deliverance, so Nibbāna literally only means *extinguishing*. And as we recognized deliverance to be liberation from the thirst dwelling within us for the five groups of grasping, as for the painful components of our personality, and precisely therefore, as the final complete liberation from these groups of grasping themselves, occurring in death, and thereby from the whole world, even so Nibbāna means nothing else but the extinguishing of this thirst, and thereby, ultimately, the extinguishing of our personality and of the world at the death of the saint. "Nibbāna, Nibbāna, so they say, friend Sāriputta; what now means Nibbāna, friend?" "That which is the vanishing of desire, friend, the vanishing of hate, the vanishing of delusion; that, friend, is called Nibbāna."[235] Only we must keep clear in mind, that desire, hate and delusion represent the three modes of manifestation of thirst.*

* Thirst arises always out of sensation, to wit, out of a pleasant sensation as desire, out of an unpleasant one, as hate or detestation, and out of a sensation neither pleasant nor unpleasant, in this manner, that one indeed approaches the object arousing sensation, but only to find that it has no relation to our will. So also the objects neither pleasant nor unpleasant, in our *delusion* are exclusively regarded from the point of view of thirst, instead of our making clear to ourselves that they too are *anattā*, and therefore need not concern us at all. "To the pleasant sensation, the inclination to desire adheres, to the unpleasant one, the inclination to hate, and to the sensation neither pleasant nor unpleasant the inclination to ignorance."[236] Thus in the Canon the regularly recurring tripartite division "Desire, Hate and Delusion," represent the three possible modes of manifestation of thirst.

Accordingly in the Canon we find frequent, direct mention of *taṇhā*-nibbāna, *thirst*-extinction.

Because thus Nibbāna is nothing else but deliverance, like this, it becomes equally evident during the saint's lifetime.

"Visibly present Nibbāna, they say, dear Gotama; how now, dear Gotama, is Nibbāna visible and present, inviting to come and see, leading to the goal, intelligible to the wise, each for himself?"

"Inflamed by desire, evil-disposed by hate, confused by delusion, overcome, entirely influenced internally, O Brahmin, we think of hurting ourselves, we think of hurting others, we think of hurting both ourselves and others, and feel mental pain and grief. But if we have abandoned desire, abandoned hate, abandoned delusion, then we do not think any more of hurting ourselves, nor of hurting others, nor of hurting both ourselves and others, and we do not feel mental pain and grief. Thus, O Brahmin, Nibbāna is visible and present, inviting to come and see, leading to the goal, intelligible to the wise, each for himself.

"In so far, O Brahmin, as a person experiences the complete and entire disappearance of desire, the complete and entire disappearance of hate, the complete and entire disappearance of delusion, so far, O Brahmin, is Nibbāna visible and present, inviting to come and see, leading to the goal, intelligible to the wise, each for himself."[236]

Thus also according to this, at the death of the saint, nothing of his self is extinguished, for in spite of his entry upon extinction, Nibbāna, he still continues to live on here below. Only desire, hate and delusion are extinguished, of which no thinking man will maintain that they constitute his essence. All that is extinguished, as their epitome, is the flaring flame of thirst to remain in contact with the world.*

* That this extinction is nothing more than the extinction of *will*, is beautifully expressed in v. 283 of the Dhammapada, where instead of *nibbuta*, extinguished, *nibbāna*, devoid of will, is the expression used.

We know of course, that in consequence of the extinction of this thirst, in the approaching death, the body also endowed with the six senses, must definitively perish, without a new one being formed; but this *complete* extinction, this *Parinibbāna,* touches the saint just as little as Nibbāna, the extinction that happened during the lifetime. If thirst for the world were something he could lose without any hurt to himself, as being something alien to his deepest essence, very much more does this hold good of his corporeal organism, this mere "*fabrication* of thirst."[237] Parinibbāna is nothing else but the final extinguishing of *all* the components of *anattā*, of not-the-*I*. It is the *anupādisesanibbāna,* the extinguishing without any remainder of accessories, in contradistinction to extinction happening during the lifetime, the *sa-upādisesa-nibbāna,* Nibbāna with a remainder of accessories.*

Even in this manner does the saint, from the moment of entry of Nibbāna, penetrate his whole relation to the world—it is surely clear without further argument that to the world also belong all the components of his own personality—he *awakes* out of the long dream of life, dreamt during Saṁsāra and maintained by the activities of the senses, in which he imagined himself to belong to the world,** and remembers that this state is the only one becoming to him, the ceasing of all these activities of sense, and with them, of all organic processes, which thereby is the eternal peace, the eternal rest. "This is the peaceful, this is the exalted: the coming to rest of all organic processes, the becoming free from all accessories, the drying up of thirst, the unattractiveness, the dissolution of causality,*** Nibbāna."[238]

* The remainder of accessories—*upādi*—is, of course, formed by the five groups of grasping appearing as our personality.

** Therefore Gotama calls himself the *Buddha,* the *Awakened One,* or the *Sammā sambuddha,* the *Perfectly Awakened One.*

*** Nirodha. That this term means indeed the dissolution of *causality* is expressly said in the Itivuttaka, 72.

Parinibbāna, thus, may also be defined as the final ceasing of all the activities of the senses by the abandonment of the six senses-machine which on this very account has now become superfluous. "When thou hast recognized the passing away of the organic processes—Saṅkhāra—then doest thou know the Un-become."[239] Nibbāna, however, may be defined as the most complete *independence* of these activities of the senses, and thereby as their complete mastery in the absence of all further attachment to them, in certain circumstances up to the point of being able at will to put a complete stop to all of them even during the present lifetime.*

* * *

With this, we have arrived at the point, where each may decide for himself, whether he wants to stay on in the world, or prefers to take up the struggle for its overcoming and for separation from it. For this is how the problem presents itself, not at all as the "ordinary person" pictures it, who imagines death to have as its inevitable consequence the annihilation of the world for him, and who therefore knows no higher aim than to prolong the duration of his stay in the world as much as possible. But the case is just the reverse. Life is assured to us through all eternity, as long as we only will it; for the saying of Schopenhauer, that "life is assured to the will for life," holds good, as we have seen, to its full extent with the Buddha also; and the problem is not how to remain in the world as long as possible, but how to escape from it as soon as practicable. Therefore the true alternative, which always stands open to everyone, is this: Either we do *not* renounce the activities

---

* Whoever is able to realize this temporary annihilation of perception and sensation, reflects in his consciousness this state, and thereby that of Parinibbāna, by means of the three sensations, with which he again awakes to life. These are, the sensation of emptiness, the sensation of being free from the impressions of the senses, and the sensation of motionlessness.[240]

of the senses, but accept it in the bargain that we must ever anew let ourselves be subjected to the process of birth, ever and again fall a prey to the troubles and sorrows of life, all possible diseases, lastly to old age and death; yea, and with the certainty, in the course of endless Saṁsāra through immeasurable spaces of time, of sinking down again into the abysses of existence, the animal realm and the worlds of the hells; or else we renounce all activities of sense for ever, thereby divesting ourselves of the body for ever, and in requital therefor, escape for ever from all sorrow of no matter what kind.

But clear as these alternatives may be, the "ignorant worldling" may not yet be able to come to a definite decision. For there still remains for him, in so far as he tries to keep to a standpoint of pure cognition, one great objection which he does not find refuted in the foregoing exposition. He knows himself as a being "that desires weal and shuns woe."[241] Now in what has gone before he indeed sees a possibility of escaping evil, but it would seem to him, only at the price of all wellbeing also coming to an end for him for ever. He has a feeling as if such a state could not possibly be agreeable to him, certainly not as agreeable as residence in this world, where beyond doubt there is also some pleasure for him, as the Buddha himself admits: "It is not, ye disciples, as if the joy of corporeality, of sensation, of perception, of mentations, of consciousness were not there; for then beings would not let themselves be swept away by corporeality, by sensation, by perception, by mentations, by consciousness."[242] Certainly, this pleasure at last, ever and always is changed again to pain: "If pleasure has arisen, pain arises, say I, Punna,"[343] and certainly at the end of all, it is always pain that predominates: "Suffering predominates."[244] Yet, nevertheless, that other side of our nature which craves wellbeing, to some extent at least, is taken into consideration.

The Buddha does not mistake the weightiness of this objection. He even concedes that despite all our recognition of suffering, it would be impossible to overcome the thirst for the world, if the desire for wellbeing could only be satisfied in the world and by its means, if therefore this same desire were not taken into account, and even to an incomparably higher degree, in the striving for release from the world. "Unsatisfying are sensual enjoyments, full of torment, full of despair, misery is predominant in them;—if, Mahānāma, the noble disciple, wholly wise, thus rightly sees according to truth, in perfect wisdom, but outside sensual enjoyments, outside evil, finds no happiness, nothing better, then he certainly does not turn away from these sensual enjoyments. But when, Mahānāma, the noble disciple with true wisdom thus rightly perceives: 'Unsatisfying are sensual enjoyments, full of torment, full of despair, misery is predominant in them,' and outside sensual enjoyments, outside evil, finds happiness and something better, then, verily, he follows no longer after sensual enjoyments. I also Mahānāma, before my full Awakening, being incompletely awakened and still only striving for awakening, clearly thus perceived: 'Unsatisfying are sensual enjoyments, full of torment, full of despair, misery is predominant in them,' but not finding happiness or aught better outside sensual enjoyments, outside evil, I knew not to turn away from following them. But when, Mahānāma, with true wisdom I thus clearly perceived: 'Unsatisfying are sensual enjoyments, full of torment, full of despair, misery is predominant in them,' *and outside sensual enjoyments, outside evil, had found happiness and something better,* then I knew to turn away from sensual enjoyments."[245]

To what an extent the Buddha acknowledges the justice of the desire for wellbeing, together with the unfoundedness of the fear that it might not be satisfied in deliverance from the world and on the way thereto, may be seen in more precise form, especially from the following passage:

"Poṭṭhapāda, I preach to you the doctrine that shall release you from the possession of the material, the mental, the bodiless self—[meaning, the *assumed* possession of such a self]*—through following which, all defilement shall fall from you, your purity increase, and even here on earth you shall behold the fulness and perfect unfolding of wisdom through your own knowledge, and attain to enduring possession thereof. Now, Poṭṭhapāda, it may be that you are thinking: 'Defilement certainly may vanish, purity may increase, and even here on earth one may see the fulness and perfect unfolding of wisdom through one's own knowledge, and attain to enduring possession thereof, but that must be a very dreary life.' But the matter is not thus to be regarded, Poṭṭhapāda; rather will all that I have mentioned happen, and *then only joy, pleasure, quietude,* earnest reflection, complete consciousness *and bliss* ensue."[247]

The climb upwards to the heights of deliverance, to Nibbāna, the nearer we come to the goal, brings all the greater bliss in its train, a bliss of whose depth the worldling can form no conception. Here we give the special description of that blissful state entered by the aspiring disciple, when in time he succeeds in liberating his mind from all the disturbing influences of the external world, and thereupon enters into the four absorptions, of which we shall speak later on.[248]

---

* "Poṭṭhapāda, if others should ask me: 'But what, friend, is the possession of the material, the spiritual, the bodiless self, from which you wish to liberate us through your doctrine?' then I should answer: 'Friend, it is only from the by you *assumed* possession of the material, the spiritual, the bodiless self that I seek to free you by preaching my doctrine."[246] Thus here again the Buddha wishes to liberate us from the *delusion* of the existence of a self either corporeal (coarsely material), spiritual (subtly real), or having its abode in the world of non-corporeality,—see above, p. 67—in which self we might consist, in short, from the delusion of thinking ourselves to consist of anything at all belonging to the world.

"Endowed with these things not to be found in the average man: the treasure of moral discipline, of watchfulness over the senses, of thoughtful and complete consciousness and contentedness, the monk chooses out for himself some solitary spot—the foot of a forest tree, a cleft in the rocks, a mountain cave, a place of burying, a thicket or a couch of straw in the open field. And having returned from his begging round and partaken of his meal, he sits down with legs crossed under him, body held upright, and deliberately practises Recollectedness. Putting away worldly craving, he abides with thoughts free from craving; he cleans his mind of craving. Putting away anger and ill-will, he abides benevolent-minded. Kindly and compassionate towards everything that lives, he clears his mind of all anger and ill-will. Putting away sloth and torpor, he dwells vigilant and alert. Wholly conscious and recollected, he clears his mind of sloth and torpor. Putting away inner unrest and anxiety, he dwells in quietude. His inward thoughts quieted, he clears his mind of inner unrest and anxiety. Putting away doubt, he dwells delivered from doubt. No longer questioning what things are good, he clears his mind from doubt.

"With this, O king, it is the same as (with the abandonment of the following burdensome things): Suppose that a man, having borrowed a sum of money, should engage in business, and that his ventures should succeed, so that he should be able to wipe out his original debt, and with what remains over take to himself a wife. Such a man would rejoice thereat and be glad in mind, saying: 'I that aforetime borrowed money to engage in business have succeeded in my affairs and have cancelled my debt, and, over and above, have got me a wife.'

"Or suppose, O king, that a man has been sick, in great pain, seriously ill, unable to partake of food, exceedingly weak of body; and that after a time he recovers from that sickness, takes his food again, and becomes strong of body. Such a man would rejoice thereat and be glad in mind, saying: 'I that aforetime was sick, suffering and weak, behold! I now am cured of that illness again, and strong in body!'

"Or suppose, O king, that a man who has been bound in prison, after a time is released safe and sound, without loss or damage to any of his property. Such a man would rejoice thereat and be glad in mind, saying: 'I that aforetime was bound in prison am now restored to liberty with all my property intact!'

"Or suppose, O king, a man to be a slave, not his own master, at the beck and call of another, unable to go about at will. And suppose that after a time this man is free from servitude, becomes his own master, is no more thrall to another, is a freedman, able to go whithersoever he will. Such a man will rejoice thereat and be glad in mind, saying: "I that aforetime was slave and servant of another now am a freedman and can go whithersoever I choose!'

"Or suppose, O king, that a man with much goods and wealth is upon a long desert journey, and that after a time, safe and sound, he leaves the desert behind without having suffered the loss of any of his goods. Such a man would rejoice thereat and be glad in mind, saying: 'I that aforetime was toiling through the desert am now returned in safety with all my goods untouched!'

"Even thus, O king, as a debt, as an illness, as imprisonment, as thraldom, as a desert journey, does the monk regard these Five Impediments while as yet they are not banished from within him. But, like a cancelled debt, like recovery from illness, like release from prison, like being a freedman, like safe soil—even so does the monk regard the banishing of these Five Impediments from within him.

"As soon as he perceives them to be eradicated from his internal nature, joy and pleasure are awakened within him, his body comes to rest, in possession of this rest, he feels happiness, and when he feels at ease, his mind also reaches concentration. Being sundered from desires and all things evil, but exercising energetic thinking and contemplation, in the joy and bliss that are born of detachment, he attains to the First Stage of Absorption, and this body he soaks, saturates, fills and penetrates with the joy and bliss that are born of detachment, so that there is no single part of the body that is not penetrated with the joy and bliss that are born of detachment.

"Just as, O king, a competent bath-attendant sprinkles the soap-powder upon a platter, and kneads and works the water into it, until the entire lump of soap is thoroughly blent and pervaded with moisture without and within, so penetrated with the moisture that not a drop falls—even thus, O king, does the monk completely soak, saturate, fill and penetrate the body with the joy and bliss that are born of detachment.

"Again, O king, stilling thinking and contemplation, through deep inward quietude the mind emerging sole, having ceased from thinking and contemplation, in the joy and bliss that are born of concentration, the monk attains to the Second Stage of Absorption, and this body he soaks, saturates, fills and penetrates with the joy and bliss that are born of concentration, so that there is no single part of the body that is not penetrated with the joy and bliss that are born of concentration.

"Suppose, O king, that there is a pool of water over a spring, with no inlet of water from any other quarter whatsoever, east, west, north, or south, and suppose that never a cloud in the rainy season unlades its burden into it; then that pool with the cool spring-waters welling up beneath will be soaked, saturated, filled, penetrated with these same cool waters, so that there will be no part of the pool that will not be penetrated by the cool spring-waters—even thus does the monk completely soak, saturate, fill and penetrate the body with the joy and bliss that are born of concentration.

"Again, O king, joyous, freed from passion, even-minded, the monk dwells collected of mind, clearly conscious, and in the body tastes the bliss of which the Noble Ones say: 'The man of even and collected mind is blest,' and so he attains to the Third Stage of Absorption, and this body he soaks, saturates, fills and penetrates with a bliss apart from active joy, so that there is no part of the body that is not penetrated with that bliss apart from active joy.

"Suppose, O king, that there is a pond of lotuses, blue and red and white, all growing and thriving in the water, immersed in the water, deriving their sustenance from the covering waters; from head to root those lotuses will be soaked, saturated, filled and penetrated by the cool water; there will be no part of them that will not be penetrated by the cool water—even thus does the monk completely soak, saturate, fill and penetrate this body with a bliss apart from active joy.

"Again, O king, pleasure and pain left behind, with the fading away of all past joy and sorrow, in the painless, pleasureless utter purity of a mind wholly calmed and collected, the monk attains to the Fourth Stage of Absorption; and he seats himself and envelops this body in cleansed and purified thought, until there is no single part of the body that is not enveloped in cleansed and purified thought. Just as a man might sit down and envelop himself, head and all, in a clean white cloth, so that no part of his body remains uncovered by the clean white cloth, so the monk sits down and completely envelops this body in cleansed and purified thought."[249]

Certainly, this wellbeing is of quite another sort from sensual wellbeing. It is "the welfare of renunciation, of solitude, of quietude, of awakening," the welfare that is followed by no kind of suffering, on which account, of it the words hold good: "It is to be cultivated, and cherished and increased. One has not to guard oneself against such wellbeing, say I."[250] Who once has enjoyed this wellbeing, has, "apart from sensual enjoyments, apart from evil, found happiness and what is better." For him "sensual weal becomes filthy weal, vulgar weal, unholy weal,"[251] which, in face of that "heroic weal" he can easily renounce, yea, which for him, stands opposed as a miserable caricature to that real wellbeing in his innermost nature. "What do you think, O Brahmin? If a fire were kindled, fed with hay and wood, or if fire were kindled and fed with hay and wood soaked with rain,—which of these two would possess flame and splendour and light?"—"If it were possible, Gotama, to kindle fire by means of hay and wood soaked with rain, then this fire also would possess flame and splendour and light."—"But it is impossible, O Brahmin, it could not be that fire should be kindled, fed with hay and wood soaked with rain, except by magical might. As if, O Brahmin, fire should be kindled, fed with hay and wood soaked with rain, just so, Brahmin, appears to me a happiness fed with the five enjoyments of the senses."[252]

But this "perfect wellbeing" is not yet everything. "There are, Udāyī, still other things, that are better and more excellent, for the attainment of which the monks who stay with me lead the holy life."[253] For above this "visible wellbeing," stands the "blissful tranquillity"[254] which supervenes when the striving disciple, leaving the whole corporeal world far below him, enters that sublime state of mind, where to his mental eye only the realm of boundless space, then that of the infinity of consciousness remain, which opens out into direct knowledge of the immense void he then alone sees around him: "Empty is this of the *I*, and of aught pertainiug to the *I*." Upon these lonely heights, inexpressible peace comes over him—"here is no suffering, here is no vexation"[255] until at last, with the annihilation of every kind of perception and sensation, he has become tranquillity itself. Whoso once has experienced this state within himself, is lost to the turmoil of the world, even if he again awakes to it: "His mind inclines to solitude, bends towards solitude, sinks itself in solitude."[256] The only longing of which such an one is still capable, can only be to let this state of absolute peace become eternal, fully to realize Nibbāna. For to him, this is highest blessedness.

Thus Nibbāna shows itself to be *eternal rest*, „eternal stillness,"[257] the "GREAT PEACE"[258] whose realm the delivered one enters even during his lifetime, which he completely realizes at death, and in which he has taken possession for ever of everything "that is true and real."* This Great Peace stands above all "perfect wellbeing," above all "blissful rest" that can be won here below. All this is "insufficient,"[259] for it has the defect that is has "become," is "compounded;" but "what has in any way become, what is compounded,—this is changeable and must perish."[260] Therefore it does not definitely lead beyond transitoriness, and thereby beyond suffering; *eternal*, because unchanging, rest alone, is the state free from suffering. For where no change occurs, nothing more, not even the redeemed one himself, any longer, through grasping, can arise. "And because he does not arise, how

* Like a stone out of place, a hint of this eternal rest, this eternal peace, is also to be found in the Catholic church, when we hear, quite contrary to its doctrine of eternal *life*, its prayers before the open grave: "Lord, give him eternal rest."—Here also it becomes apparent, that the opposite of life is not death. Death belongs to life, just as much as birth. It is nothing but the actual *moment* of our great life in all the worlds, in which the corporeal organism hitherto used, is let go, and grasping of a new germ of new life takes place. The opposite to life is really *rest*—since life is movement—namely, rest from the unceasing motion of the five groups. But this rest is only definitively reached with holiness, from which the self-deception involved in such expressions as "rest of the grave," "rest of the dead," becomes at once evident.

should he pass away? Because he does not pass away, how should he die? Because he does not die, how should he tremble? Because he does not tremble, for what should he long?"[261] He has "become still." But "having become still, he does not incline; not inclining, he neither comes nor goes; neither coming nor going, he neither appears nor disappears; neither appearing nor disappearing, there is no here nor there nor between; this is the end of suffering,"[262] yea, it is pure blessedness. "Bliss is Nibbāna, bliss is Nibbāna," Sāriputta exclaims;[263] and even more, it is the highest bliss: "Hunger is the worst disease; the activities of the senses* are the worst suffering. Having recognized this, verily one reaches Nibbāna, *highest bliss*."[264] For rest, peace, and blessedness, are fundamentally the same: "Whoso is impregnated with goodness, the monk cleaving to the doctrine of the Buddha, he turns towards the land of *peace*, where transitoriness finds *rest*, to *bliss*."[265]

But here once more "normal" understanding will again be inclined to protest. How can bliss exist, where absolute rest reigns of such sort that nothing more of any kind is even felt? Thus it will question, in entire agreement with that contemporary of Sāriputta, who in reply to the latters exclamation 'Bliss is Nibbāna, bliss is Nibbāna,' full of astonishment, asked: "How can there be bliss, where there is no sensation?" And like this questioner, the modern sceptic also will probably at first not understand the reply of Sāriputta: "This, precisely, O friend, is bliss, that here there is no sensation."[266] Therefore we will briefly deal with this.

Everything occurring to us and in us, is willing. We will to see, to hear, to smell, to taste, to touch, to think—of course, pleasant things only,—or what is the same thing, we wish to generate within us a pleasant consciousness in the form of the sensation of pleasant objects, which consciousness is the sole object of the activities of the senses. But consciousness aroused in the end always disappoints expectation: Suffering ultimately predominates every time; the painful impressions of consciousness are far more numerous and also more intense than the pleasant ones. Thereby new willing is excited within us, namely, the desire or will to know the causes of those unpleasant impressions of consciousness, and how to eliminate them, so that only the pleasant ones may remain. This willing also always remains unsatisfied; we never succeed in finding out beyond question the cause of suffering. This is shown in the history of medicine in respect of the suffering associated with disease, no less than in the history of religions and philosophy with regard to suffering conditioned by the laws of nature. The answers given by the religions to the question as to the cause of suffering, are nearly all of the same kind as that with which the Bible solves the problem: We suffer, because our ancestress Eve was so thoughtless as to take a bite at the apple against the bidding of a god, whereby, of course, every possibility of freeing ourselves from suffering is cut off in advance. Hardly more satisfactory are the answers given by the philosophers of the older and later times. Only two men have discovered the true and ultimate cause of all suffering, the Buddha and Schopenhauer, though the latter, only in a manner purely theoretical. Both say: Thou sufferest, because thou willest. For everything that thou canst ever will, thus all objects of seeing, hearing, smelling, tasting, touching, thinking, yea, even the organs of this willing, in their innermost nature are transitory, hence, do what thou wilt, always inevitably perish. If therefore thou wishest to do away with suffering, thou must altogether do away with willing. But this is impossible, Schopenhauer proceeds. For it is precisely in this willing that your real essence consists, which in it manifests itself, in it appears. As long as this your essence does not one way or another change of and by itself, you thus will be abandoned to suffering. You cannot flee from yourself.

This is quite wrong, the Buddha says. You *are* not will, but in you there arise merely motions of will as in the darkened heavens flame forth lightnings. And just as those flashes of lightning, though arising in space, have nothing in common with it, so the motions of willing that arise in you have nothing in common with your true self. For this very reason not only can you cause new willing to arise within yourself, but you can also annihilate old willing, yea, every kind of willing, and thereby every kind of suffering, by especially developing within yourself the will to insight into the painful nature of all that has arisen. When this will is fully satisfied, and thus complete insight attained, then no other further willing of any kind can possibly exist within you; it is killed by this insight.

In harmony with this declaration, my striving for insight and the removal of the cause of suffering, already roused and active in me, now takes this direction pointed out to me by the Buddha. More and more do I understand the correctness of his explanations, for which very reason, the Buddha for me far outshines Schopenhauer, and at last appears to me as the highest of gods and men. But this insight, being not yet perfect, and, above all, not always present to me, is not sufficient to kill my willing grown to the intensity of thirst. At first I rather behold, as fruit of this partial insight, only a new kind of volition growing out of me, directed towards the overcoming of the former willing, thus, towards *renunciation*. Thereby the unconcern with which up till now, I had abandoned myself to those motions of willing that affirmed the world and myself, has disappeared, and in its stead there has entered what is called the *self-division* of the will, with all the inward dissension which this brings with it, the motions towards renunciation waging unremitting warfare with those of desire. And only by incessant, and hard, and painful resistance to the latter, can we help the former to victory. But if we follow the latter, then as a new kind of suffering, there now enters *remorse of conscience*,—conscience, according to what we have been considering in our previous pages, being nothing but the struggle of our innermost essence against what we have already understood as bringing about suffering and as therefore unwholesome for us.* But if we do not yield in this struggle, if at all costs we deepen the insight we already have gained, then with its growth, the new will risen in us directed towards the overcoming of the thirst that animates us, will be more and more realized, the thirst will become weaker and weaker; we notice that it is less and less able to overcome us; yea, there may even be times, when temporarily it goes entirely to sleep, and we are rid of its fetters. Then we experience a hitherto unknown feeling of relief, the highest and purest bliss of life, as Schopenhauer calls it, which we have just learned to know as the wellbeing of renunciation, the wellbeing of appeasement. As to its contents, from what has just been said, it is the feeling of being independent of the world and of our own inclinations: "At such a time, ye monks, he is neither dependent on himself, nor on others; being neither dependent on himself nor on others, at such a time he only experiences a feeling of independence. Independence,

* Just because conscience is nothing but the reaction of already acquired knowledge as to the wholesomeness or unwholesomeness of a deed, contemplated or already carried out, it is different in nearly every man. There may even be men, within whom there is no stirring of conscience at all. These are those within whom there is no living insight into the law of Karma. One may also have a *false* conscience, namely, when that insight is a false one, when one holds as unwholesome something that in truth is wholesome; or the reverse. Thus the convinced adherent of one religion, in the face of a deed he has carried out, may be pricked by a bad conscience, whereas the same deed, committed by an adherent of another religion of opposite teachings. in the latter arouses a good conscience.

ye monks, I say, is the highest comfort of feeling."[267] To whomsoever this comfort has once been given, such an one henceforth knows no other kind of willing than to obtain this independence for ever. That is to say, the will for the overcoming of his will as it presents itself in the form of thirst, becomes at last so strong that it takes complete possession of him, even as formerly did this thirst. He goes on living only for the sake of *its* realization. Certainly, he thereby gives himself over again into the servitude of the will, he sacrifices everything to it, as before to thirst. But this new will, in an essential point, is distinguishable from the thirst still dwelling within him. The latter can never hope to be satisfied,—'thus do I stagger from desire to enjoyment, and midst enjoyment for desire I starve,'[268] holds good of him—for which reason we can never escape from suffering. But this new will, directed towards the overcoming of all willing, the will for *holiness*, and it alone, can ever be fully satisfied, and is fully satisfied in the delivered one, who in Nibbāna experiences that mighty triumph of that complete and eternal satisfaction of his will, *the no longer having any will*, and thereby the highest bliss.

For if happiness, as we saw at the commencement of this work, is nothing but satisfaction of will, if happiness and satisfaction of will are identical concepts, then the complete, perfect and permanent satisfaction of the will for holiness which alone predominates in the striving sage, that is, the will for will-lessness, precisely for this reason must be purest bliss. *He alone of all the milliards and milliards of beings, who since ever the world began, have striven in vain for the ideal of all happiness, "has got all his will."* * This idea must be thought out to the end, to obtain at least a glimpse of the immense and unparalleled idea lying within it.

Now we may completely understand the powerful words:

* "Who has got all his will and his desire, has got peace." (Master Eckhart.)

"For the denying of the will (*chandapahānattha*), is the holy life lived under the Exalted One: *chanden' eva chandaṁ pajahati*, just through will is will denied: for if through will holiness is reached, then the will for it is satisfied."* [269]

According to this, will-lessness, absolute freedom, inexpressible peace and purest bliss, are merely synonymous expressions descriptive of the state of Nibbāna, in contradistinction to the complete lack of liberty, the continual unrest and thereby the ceaseless suffering of man, who still tarries in the world. Further, Nibbāna is also called the state of *health*, in contradistinction to the state of sickness wherein *we* still tarry. Yea, personality, with its five elements, is compared by him who has reached Nibbāna to a knacker's shirt, blackened with oil and soot, which only a totally blind man could take for a white garment he supposed himself to have put on.

"As if, Māgandiya, there was a man born blind and unable to see things black or white, blue or yellow, red or green, unable to see smooth and rough, unable to see sun and moon and stars. And he heard the words of a man able to see: 'Truly decent, my good man, is a white garment, very fine, without spots and clean.' And he tried to get one. And then another man should deceive him with the shirt

---

* The bliss of absence of will may also be paraphrased thus: Certainly there is no longer any happiness for me, if I have no longer any willing, since every happiness consists precisely in the satisfaction of will. But then I no longer miss this happiness, because I no longer have any kind of will requiring to be satisfied. Which is in the happier state: He who in drinking cool water enjoys the happiness of quenching his thirst, or he who is not at all troubled by any thirst requiring to be quenched? In addition, from this idea it follows that happiness and peace are synonymous conceptions: Peace is reached by the pacifying of will, for which very reason we speak of the "pacification" of will. On the other hand, pacification of will means happiness; therefore peace is the same as happiness; and thereby the highest peace, attained through extinguishing all tormenting desires, is the highest bliss. With this, the negative character of all happiness also is established, since it consists merely in the removal of the disturbance caused by the non-satisfaction of our will. This removal is experienced as all the more happy, the more intense was the unsatisfied will, and along with it, the disturbance conditioned thereby.

of a knacker, blackened with oil and soot, saying: 'There, good man, you have a white garment, very fine, without spots and clean.' And he should take it and put it on, and thus clad he should with pleasure utter the joyous words: 'Truly decent is this white dress, very fine, without spots and clean.' And his friends and comrades, relatives and cousins should call for an expert doctor, who should give him a remedy, make him void upwards and downwards, and use ointments, balsam and sneezing-powder. And he should undergo this treatment, and then his eyes should open, and become cleared. And as he begins to see, his joy and pleasure in the knacker's shirt, blackened with oil and soot, should vanish, and he should take that other man for his enemy, and perhaps wish for his death as expiation, saying: 'For a long time, truly, I have been deceived by this fellow, defrauded and cheated with this knacker's shirt, blackened with oil and soot.' In exactly the same way, Māgandiya, I should like to expound to you the doctrine, as to what is health, what is Nibbāna. And you might behold health, and see Nibbāna, and as you were beginning to see, joy and pleasure in the five groups of grasping would vanish from you, and you would think: 'For a long time I have really been deceived, defrauded and cheated by this mind.* For I was in attachment grasping the body, I was in attachment grasping sensation, I was in attachment grasping perception, I was in attachment grasping mentations, I was in attachment grasping consciousness.' "[270]

But not only our personality, as existing on this earth, looks to the delivered one like a knacker's shirt, blackened with oil and soot. *Every* personality, even such as exists in the highest heavens of the gods, is for him who has withdrawn to the purity of his innermost self, nothing but—filth! For, according to the Aṅguttara Nikāya, even a form

* Because it did not allow me to recognize the true state of affairs.

of existence reduced to the very smallest residue is still as such, evil, just as even the smallest residue of filth or pus still smells badly. Though this remainder of existence has, in the pure gods, become as small as possible, nevertheless they appear to the ascetic only as the immeasurable vault of heaven with its golden fires appeared to the Prince of Denmark, that is, as "no other thing than a foul and pestilent congregation of vapours," not as a thing one wants to return to. For this very cause, the delivered one on no account turns back to the world. "And even, Sāriputta, if I should only be reborn among the Pure Gods, I do not wish to return to this world."[271] Herein precisely, the bliss of the peace he has won becomes especially clear. The saint who has completely mastered his willing, has it in his power to bring about through all the eternities, only re-embodiment in the highest worlds of light, by generating within himself only so much and such a kind of thirst, that at the moment of death it always brings about a grasping in those worlds of light. But even this he despises. How could he who has experienced in himself the "stainless"[272] bliss of eternal peace, once more choose filth, when in death he lays aside the stain of his present personality? Thus then for him the stain of the world vanishes for ever, and he vanishes for ever for the world.* There is no longer any bridge between the two. He is *extinguished,* but, to repeat it once more, only for the world, as we expounded in detail, in speaking of the state of the perfected one after death,** with which the present chapter is thus immediately connected. Only, to what has been said before concerning the expression "extinction," which only now has become completely comprehensible to us, we may in conclusion add a few words.

---

* From the standpoint of the saint, it is not he who disappears, but the world. To us the process presents itself as just the reverse.

** See the chapter on the subject of suffering!

The term "extinction" was chosen by the Buddha in relation to fire which also may be extinguished. But fire, as we know,* *is* in some way or other, even when it is extinguished; it is nowhere and everywhere. For nowhere can it be found, and yet everywhere it is lying in wait for the conditions of its entry into this world, and, consequently, can flame up every moment and in every place, where these conditions are provided, greedily seizing the food offered it, be it here with us, or on far-off Sirius. In exactly the same way the totally extinguished delivered one is nowhere and everywhere. For nowhere can he any longer be found, but everywhere, here upon our earth, even in our very midst, or again, in any other place in the infinity of space, he might now, just as well as at any time in the infinitude of the ages, re-enter the world, if only he *wished*, if only the slightest desire for such a thing should arise within him, and thereby a grasping take place. But contrary to the greed with which fire ever and always presses into the world, he has lost all desire of this kind for all eternity. Safe and secure he reposes in the boundlessness and infinitude of his own highest essence. This the Buddha sets forth at length in the 72nd Discourse of the Majjhima Nikāya, when the wandering ascetic Vacchagotta asks him what becomes of the delivered one after death.

"Vaccha, this subject is difficult to fathom, to perceive, and to think out; it is peaceful and exalted, not to be reached by mere abstract thinking, sublime and only to be understood by the wise . . . What do you think, Vaccha? If a fire were burning before your eyes, would you then know: 'There, before me, a fire is burning?'"—"Yes, reverend Gotama."—"But, Vaccha, if someone should ask you: 'Through what is the fire before your eyes burning,' what would you answer him?"—"Reverend Gotama, I should answer: 'The

* See above p. 220.

fire before my eyes is burning, because it is fed with grass and wood.'"—"If now the fire before your eyes should go out, would you then know that the fire had gone out?"—"Certainly, reverend Gotama."—"But, Vaccha, if you were asked: 'Towards which region of the world has the fire departed, that has gone out before your eyes, towards the east, the west, the north or the south?' what would you then answer?"—"Reverend Gotama, this question is wrongly put. The fire that before was burning because it was fed with grass and wood, now that it has consumed the fuel and received no fresh fuel, and thus finds no more food, has gone out. 'Gone out,'—this is only a concept."—"Exactly the same is it with the Perfected One, Vaccha. His body, his sensation, his perception, his mentations, his consciousness, that might be thought of when speaking of him, are done with, are entirely annihilated, beyond all possibility of their ever again arising in the future, and the Perfected One is *exalted above all comprehensibility* by means of the form of apprehension we call body, sensation, perception, mentations, consciousness. *He is indefinable, inscrutable, immeasurable, like the great ocean.* It were false to say: '*He is;*' it were just a false to say: '*He is not.*'"* And now, all is said

* Compare Udāna VIII, 10. "Just as of the fire that flames up under the strokes of the smith's hammer it cannot be said where it has gone, after it is extinguished, so just as little can be discovered the abode of the truly delivered ones who have crossed over the stream of the bonds of the senses, have reached the unshakeable bliss."

In the passage of the Majj. Nik. cited above in the text, a perfected one, that is, one who has entirely freed himself from his personality, in his inscrutability is compared to the great ocean, whereby it is expressed as clearly as possible, that he is something immeasurable, inapprehensible for knowledge, of which one cannot even say: 'It is.' [Compare the words of the nun Khemā, quoted above p. 183.] But the question may be raised as to how the saint attains a knowledge of this immeasureableness of his essence, since beyond his personality all knowledge too comes to an end. But it is precisely this latter circumstance which points the direction in which we must look for the answer. The saint gains a knowledge of the immeasureableness of his essence, as also of his essence in general in an *indirect* manner, by penetrating the realm of *not-the-I.* In the first great knowledge that arises in him—see above p. 203—the whole that can be said as to the nature of our eternal destiny. He whose mind thereby feels "aroused, rejoiced, pacified, relieved,"[273] or, "who longs after the *unnameable*, laid hold of in his innermost,"[274] such an one with good prospect of success may tread the way to realizing Nibbāna for himself, and thus with his own eyes behold the truth of that which hitherto he has only known as the experience of others.

---

beginningless chain of rebirths, revolving through countless millions of Kalpas, unveils itself before him, the endlessness of time thereby becoming the mirror of his own essence. Later, like every dying person, if he wished it, he would have the opportunity of grasping in death at any germ in infinite space, were it distant, trillions of light-years,—each of them measuring thirty-one billions of miles—so that hence he is also unaffected by the boundlessness of space. According to this, however, the world in all its temporal and spatial infinity is "only the measure of his own grandeur, always surpassing it." (Schopenhauer) But by this, be it well noted, again, at bottom, nothing positive is affirmed, but only his unlimitedness, thus, something purely negative.

THE MOST EXCELLENT TRUTH OF THE PATH LEADING TO THE ANNIHILATION OF SUFFERING

A. THE EXCELLENT EIGHTFOLD PATH IN GENERAL

That most men live their lives as carelessly as they do, has its ground in this, that they do not rightly know the condition in which they find themselves. Either they persuade themselves that they have emerged out of absolute nothingness into this world, and at their death, will again disappear, equally without leaving a trace; or they regard themselves as productions of a creator who will take them after their death into his heavenly kingdom, having no doubt about it that the hell which of course exists along with it, is destined only for others. Hence the result that for unbeliever as well as for believer it seems the highest wisdom to make themselves as comfortable as possible on this earth; for the former, because it were the height of foolishness not to make the utmost possible use of this so fleeting existence; for the latter, however, because his stay in this world is a gift from his god, not to enjoy which thankfully were the height of ingratitude. If only they would look into their real position and thereby recognize with sufficient clearness, that since beginningless time, aimlessly and without plan, they wander through the world in all its heights and depths, now as gods, then as men, now as beasts, then as devils, and that this wandering without end or aim, under perpetual self-delusion, will go on to all eternity; if, further, they would recognize the possibility of escaping forever from this circle of suffering, and of withdrawing to a place wholly devoid of suffering, to "a hiding-place, an island," then they would surely seize the proffered hand that will lead them to that place devoid of suffering, with the same eagerness that a drowning man seizes the hand that is ready to pull him to the shore. In such a situation, however, we are at present, if we have at all understood what has been said in our past pages, on which account the last of the four excellent truths, that which deals with the path leading to the removal of suffering, must appear to us as the most sublime revelation ever given to this world, and particularly as the highest of the four excellent truths themselves. For the three others with which we are now acquainted, despite their sublimity, without this fourth would be a gift of the Danaides of the worst kind, since, enlightened precisely through them as to the whole horror of the situation in which we find ourselves, they would only make us all the more unhappy. The last of the four excellent truths thus constitutes the cap-stone and crown of the mighty structure of the Buddha's teaching. He himself takes this point of view, when he designates a possible dissension as to the content of the path as the gravest misfortune that could happen to his disciples. "It would matter little, Ānanda, if there were dissension as to the necessities of life, or about the rules of the Order; but as to the Path, Ānanda, as to the Way, if dissension should arise among the monks in regard to this, then such dissension would cause misfortune and loss to many, ruin to many, misfortune, and suffering to gods and men."[275] And his monks have expressed their feeling of the decisive importance of the last of the four excellent truths by praising the master especially as "the discoverer of the undiscovered path, the creator of the uncreated path, the explainer of the unexplained path, the knower of the path, the acquainted with the path, the expert in the path."[276]

1. The outlines of this way are already given together with the three other verities. Every kind of thirst for the world, as being the real and deepest source of all suffering, must be brought to disappearing without residue. But this thirst is rooted in ignorance, hence it can only be removed by the entry of knowledge. Therefore, before we know the way itself, so much is clear, that it must issue in the killing within us through *knowledge*, of all thirst for the world. From what has gone before it follows further on, that this knowledge, in correspondence with the nature of the ignorance from which this thirst proceeds, must be twofold. On one side, we must see clearly that our entire personality in all its constituent parts, and therewith, the whole world, at bottom is something alien to us, to which we cling merely because we think that we must possess these things that are fundamentally alien to us, in order to be happy. Then, next, we must see the components of our personality, like everything in the world, as a possession that brings *suffering* to us, and thereby recognize as delusion the belief that this personality, and therewith our stay in the world, are necessary to our happiness. If we have attained real insight in these two directions, then we no longer *can* have any desire, any thirst for personality and the world, just as little as we can have desire to receive every day a hundred lashes with a whip. For "we are beings craving weal and shunning woe." Of course, this knowledge, as we already know, must be real and not merely abstract. That this latter is not enough, we may experience in ourselves every day, when, in a *general* and therefore *abstract* manner, we recognize some passion to be clearly injurious to ourselves, but nevertheless are unable to summon up the resolution to fight it. Mere abstract knowledge therefore provides no motive force, on which account morally it is entirely valueless. A positive ground for the determining of our actions is only provided

by *direct actual* knowledge, wherein the object desired, as also the consequences of its possession are vividly presented before our bodily or our mental eye. If I know how to lay before a certain person the pleasant consequences of a deed suggested to him so convincingly and vividly that he is able to form for himself a concrete representation of the same, then he will invariably commit the deed, if he is in a position to do so, and if there are no serious reasons against it. In the same manner, desires arisen within him will speedily vanish again, if the injurious consequences their satisfaction will have for him or for others are vividly present to him. "And when now in me, thus earnest, strenuous and resolute, a Consideration of Craving arose, I forthwith said to myself: 'Behold, this thought of Craving seeks foothold in my mind, and verily it will lead to my own hurt, will lead to the hurt of others, will lead to the hurt both of myself and of others. It is destructive of wisdom, leagued with pain, not conducive to deliverance.' And so reflecting, that unwholesome thought died away from within me."[277]

If, further, I bring a sensual man to such deep penetration of the human organism, that he comes to see in every woman only a "skeleton covered with skin that is filled with filth and pus,"[278] then his passion beyond question will vanish, as surely as a hungry person will lose all appetite, if, when he removes the cover from an inviting dish, instead of the dainty food expected, he finds snake carrion.[279] This direct vivid knowledge thus provides the motive force, which, so far as it is correct, that is, as far as it points out to us that all real and possible objects of our thirst must ultimately always bring us suffering, manifests itself in this manner, that in exactly the same degree that this knowledge enters, thirst disappears, so that when it has become complete and all-embracing, all thirst thereby is destroyed. Correct ocularly evident knowledge therefore finally turns, to use the words of Schopenhauer, into the *quieting* of all willing, or, to use those of the Buddha, "holy wisdom, *able* wisdom, *powerful* wisdom."[280] Thus this correct view is the very first element of the path constructed by the Buddha for the annihilation of suffering. He himself calls it *sammādiṭṭhi, Right View*: we must win the right *view* of things, we must not take them as they appear to the superficial observer, but must penetrate them to the very bottom, see them as they really are, namely as transitory, pain-producing and precisely on this account, fundamentally unsuitable for us. To bring about this correct view, therefore, the way has been laid down.*

2. Next, it is clear that it can only be reached by continual and deep contemplation: "Two occasioning causes, friend, give rise to Right Seeing—the voice of another, and deep reflection."[281] But this deep reflection does not without further ado lead to the goal. The "ignorant worldling" may look at the things that give him pleasure, especially at the elements of his personality, as intensely as he likes, he will always come to the conclusion: "I cannot find anything horrible in them."[282] For the mind must be in a quite definite condition, if it is to perform the task the Buddha suggests to it. He calls this mental condition *samādhi*, literally, "bringing together," a conception which is defined more closely in the 43rd Discourse of the Majjhima Nikāya as "oneness of the mind." "The coming of the mind to oneness *(citt' ekaggatā)*, this friend Visākha, is *samādhi*."[283] To understand what is meant by this, we must first see, why the normal mode of contemplation, be it as deep as it may, cannot lead us to the goal, *samādhi* consisting pre-

* In the Aṅguttaranikāya X No. 104, *View* is represented as the basis of action. From an evil view, evil action results; from a right view, right action, in the same way that the seed of the gall-tree changes all the juices drawn out of the earth into bitterness, the seed of the sugar-cane, all juices into sweetness. In No. 121 of the same work, Right View is also compared to the dawn which precedes the sun of Right Action.

cisely in elimination of the sources of error adhering in the former.

Within us lives the thirst for the world, which is a thirst for forms, sounds, odours, tastes, tangibles, and ideas. Our body endowed with the six senses represents nothing else but an apparatus for the satisfaction of this thirst, as it is also its handiwork. The average man, during his whole life, holds it as self-evident that the apparatus of the six senses is to be used exclusively for this purpose, being caught in the delusion that in this his thirst, his own innermost essence is asserting itself. And so he uses his sense organs, especially in their quality as organs of knowledge, exclusively for the satisfying of this thirst, that is, for the discovery of the objects corresponding to it, forms, sounds, and so forth, and further, the devising of the means of obtaining them, and avoiding those repulsive to him. This single end above all else is served by that central faculty of knowledge, intellect. This is used merely for the satisfaction of our inclinations, be they refined or vulgar, and thereby of our thirst, in the completest possible manner. Everything we look at, is looked at exclusively from this point of view. "Intellect is the servant of (instinctive) will," Schopenhauer says. Of course, from this point of view also we might come to abandon something in itself corresponding to our thirst, having regard to the predominating suffering which we recognize follows upon its possession, but this always and only, because such satisfaction of thirst is not the best possible. Therefore we generally select for its satisfaction only such objects as promise to provide this satisfaction in the highest possible degree, causing to us the greatest pleasure with the smallest possible accompaniment of pain. Since thus all the faculty of knowledge in the average man stands exclusively at the service of his thirst, the justification of which seems to him as unquestionable as his own existence with which he considers it to be identical, therefore he will never understand the dictum that *all* things are to be renounced, because they are all transitory and therefore ultimately bringing about suffering. To renounce everything, for him would be synonymous with renouncing every satisfaction of his will altogether; and this again would mean to him to remain incessantly and totally unsatisfied in his whole being, thus to hunger and thirst incessantly in every direction as long as he existed, hence, through countless ages, since "to the will to life, life is assured." But this represents such a horrible, nay, such an impossible supposition, that on no account can it enter into the question for him. Let the objects of his thirst, singly and collectively, be ever so perishable, and on this account, from their seizing let what may of new suffering ever and again break forth for him, nevertheless, they ever and again bring him at least a passing appeasement of his tormenting desires and thereby at least a temporary tranquillization of his being; in the same way, a man dying of hunger will finally take disgusting food, and a person dying of thirst drink filthy water. Still less will a man who shares this view understand the suggestion to give up his body endowed with the six senses; to him that would be identical with this other, to give up himself, which he immediately recognizes as impossible. Thus the doctrine of the Buddha becomes to him a book with seven seals.

As we see, the mistake a man makes in looking at things in this way consists in his identifying his essence with his thirst for the world. The direct consequence of this is, that his *faculty* of *knowledge or cognition* is always under the influence of this thirst; therefore it is unable to act purely independent of the inclinations, in which this thirst manifests itself: "The eye, ye friends, and forms, both are present; and through their being present, knowledge is chained to them by the craving of will. The ear, ye friends, and sounds, the nose and odours, the tongue and sapids, the body and the touchable, the organ of thought and ideas,—both are present; and through their being present, knowledge is chained to them by the craving of will," thus it is said in the 133rd Discourse of the Majjhima Nikāya, which passage is thus paraphrased in the 138th Discourse of the same collection: "If, ye friends, with the eye a monk has perceived a form, cognition follows the trace of the form, is enticed by the attractive trace of the form, is caught by the attractive trace of the form, is entangled by the attractive trace of the form . . . If with the ear he has heard a sound, if with the nose he has smelt an odour, if with the tongue he has tasted a sapid, if with the body he has touched a tangible, if with the organ of thought he has recognized an idea, then cognition follows the trace of this idea, is enticed by the attractive trace of the idea, is caught by the attractive trace of the idea, is entangled by the attractive trace of the idea." From this the correct point of view may be gained, namely, that we detach our cognition from the service of our inclinations, that is, of our thirst; that we refuse to allow it to be taken captive, and thus in advance, darkened, blinded by the attractive traces of forms, sounds, odours, and so on, but with this our cognitive faculty, confront in a manner entirely objective all these influences of the senses; in short, that we maintain an attitude of *pure* cognizing. How this is possible, will be seen from the following.

Every act of cognition rests upon an act of willing, that is, upon an activity of the senses, since, as we know, only through such a thing is it aroused.* Indeed, all willing at first is nothing but a will *to cognize*, and only after this, a will *to possess*. In the first place, we want to see, to hear, to smell, to taste, to touch, to think, that is, to *cognize*, with the eye, the ear, the nose, the tongue, the organ of touch,

* Compare the chapter on personality.

the organ of thought, what corresponds to our inclinations, to our thirst, and then to possess it, by finding out with the help of our faculty of cognition the means of obtaining it, and thus compelling the world to grant us our wishes. Thus the cognitive faculty as consciousness, is not only the medium by means of which alone we are connected with the world —"here in consciousness stands the All" * —but it is also the light which shows us our way through the world, in the gleam of which we control it, *make it serve* our purposes. "By what, Lord, is the world controlled, to what is the world bound, to the power of what is the world subjected?"— "Very good, friend, very good! Noble is your profound thought, good your penetration, excellent your question! You therefore wish to know: 'By what is the world controlled, to what is the world bound, to the power of what is the world subjected?'"—"Yes, Lord."—"By *cognition*, friend, is the world controlled, to cognition is the world bound, to the power of cognition is the world subjected."[284] To this power of cognition the world is particularly subject in so far as, by its light, and with its help, in face of the fact, made known to us precisely through it, that despite all our foresight we ever and always find ourselves surrounded by suffering, there arises in us the will to cognize the causes of this suffering, and then, by the removal of these causes, to this extent shape the world to our will. But *this* will, as far as all suffering conditioned by nature, especially death, is concerned, generally remains entirely unsatisfied. Therefore at last the insight arises, that the problem of suffering in its whole extent is not to be solved in the way generally taken. From this insight there finally springs up an entirely new kind of willing—as we see, every kind of willing is the fruit and consequence of a preceding right or wrong cognition—this namely, to seek for the deepest and last cause of all suffering

* See above p. 158.

no longer outside but inside ourselves; that means, to ascertain whether this last cause may not be contained in our *former* willing itself, which in its totality exhibits itself as the thirst for the world that fills us. *This* will for cognition, which very soon takes possession of the whole apparatus of cognition, is thus quite unique. It is not, like our previous will for cognition, acting *in the service* of thirst, by seeking to satisfy it, but it opposes itself to it, by making it its task to analyse it in all its innumerable manifestations of desire and disinclination, of painful and pleasant emotions, as they incessantly whirl through our mind, and to penetrate into its causality. Hence, it itself no longer stands in any kind of immediate relation to things, since its object of investigation is just the thirst for them, so that it takes up an attitude of entire disinterestedness towards them, of absolute objectivity. But just for this reason, the cognition acting in *this* manner is entirely pure, *harmonious in itself*, no longer a cognition darkened by anxiety for the satisfaction of our inclinations. *This* is what the Buddha means, when he says: "The eye, ye monks, and forms, both are present; but while they are present, cognizing is no more attached to them by desire of will, and because cognizing is not attached to them by desire of will, we take no pleasure in them; and because we take no pleasure in them, we are not overcome by things present. The ear, ye monks, and sounds, the nose and odours, the tongue and sapids, the body and tangible things, the organ of thought and ideas, both are present; but while they are present, cognizing is not attached to them by desire of will; and because cognizing is not attached to them by desire of will, we take no pleasure in them; and because we take no pleasure in them, we are not overcome by things present."[285] And further: "But how, ye monks, is cognition designated as being outwardly not dispersed, not scattered? If, ye monks, a monk with the eye has cognized a form, cognizing does not follow the trace of the form, is not enticed by the attractive trace of the form, is not caught by the attractive trace of the form, is not entangled by the attractive trace of the form. If with the ear he has heard a sound, if with the nose he has smelt an odour, if with the tongue he has tasted a sapid, if with the body he has touched a tangible thing, if with the organ of thought he has cognized an idea, cognizing does not follow the trace of the idea, is not enticed by the attractive trace of the idea, is not caught by the attractive trace of the idea, is not entangled by the attractive trace of the idea. Outwardly, it is said, cognition is not dispersed, not scattered."[286]

This cognizing activity, withdrawn from the service of thirst, is, so to say, posted at the extreme end of the world, that is supported for us by our thirst for it. Only thus, looking down upon it as from afar, have we got the right distance for the cognizing, not only as before, of the relations of the world to the thirst for it that animates us, but also of the relations of this thirst and of its "handiwork," the body endowed with six senses, to ourselves. It is to this relation the Buddha refers, when he says: "How, if now I dwelt with mind broad and deep, having overcome the world, [to which, of course also the corporeal organism belongs] standing above it in mind?"[287] Further, it is very vividly expressed in the Aṅguttara Nikāya, that the holy disciple who thus recognizes is compared to a fighting man *who hits from afar*: "Just as, Sāḷha, the fighting one hits from afar, in the same way, Sāḷha, the holy disciple possesses right concentration. And whatsoever there is of body, whatsoever there is of sensation, whatsoever there is of perception, whatsoever there is of mentation, whatsoever there is of consciousness [cognition] in the past, in the future and at the present moment, our own or a stranger's, gross or subtle, mean or exalted, remote or close at hand—all this, Sāḷha, the rightly concentrated holy disciple according to truth, in perfect wisdom recognizes thus: 'This belongs not to me, this am I not, this is not my self.'"[288]

Because thus from this standpoint we clearly see that our personality, and with it, our thirst for the world which is realized therein, has not the least to do with our true essence, the problem no longer consists in the question as to how in this thirst we can satisfy our essence, but in this: whether the satisfaction of our essence might not be attained precisely by freeing ourselves from this thirst. Adopting this point of view, we will look at things now, only from this side. We no longer look at them, identifying ourselves with our thirst for the world, to see if they are suitable objects for the satisfaction of the same, but only as to whether these words of the Buddha do not much more apply to them: "Nothing is worth adhering to,"[289] and thereby, whether also every desire, every kind of thirst for such things is not itself foolish. The result of this cognizing activity cannot long remain in doubt. Everything in the world and of the world, the components of our own personality included, is subject to incessant change, a ceaseless change felt by us, if we chain ourselves to the world, equally unceasingly in the form of birth, old age, sickness, death, sorrow, lamentation, pain, grief and despair so that we are never able to free ourselves completely from painful sensations; whereas, if we let go *everything*, renounce *everything* in the world, and thereby the world itself, we enter the sublimest, profoundest, holiest peace, which is no more disturbed by sensation of any kind. In the face of such cognition, thirst for the world *can* no longer exist, in it is realized the entire truth of the words of the Master: "To the power of cognition is the world subjected." For it kills thirst for the world, thereby annihilating the world itself for me. Cognition thereby becomes a parricide, since it was just this thirst which aroused it by the activity of the organs of sense. But simultaneously with its creator, it itself dies; for it was only supported by the will to cognize this thirst, a will that is now satisfied, makes its presence known no more, whereby also cognizing itself goes to rust, just as the flame goes out when the wick is burnt up—Nibbāna is realized! *

According to this, *Samādhi*, or the unity of mind, shows itself to be cognition entirely uninfluenced by the motions of our inclinations or of our thirst, and thereby quite pure, or, as we might call it, *concentrated*. Thus the best translation of Samādhi is *concentration*, in the sense of *concentration of the mind* [*cetosamādhi*]. Only we must accustom ourselves to associate with this word the conception of a concentrated mind or concentrated thought, in the same way that we speak of a concentrated liquid. That thereby thinking is exclusively directed towards the chosen object, which meaning, in Europe, is generally attached to the word "concentration," is only a self-evident consequence.

We designate this concentrated form of cognition, from which, by analogy with a chemical process of analysis, all motions of thirst are eliminated, as the mode of contemplation pertaining to *genius*. But here it is to be noted that this mode, if it is to coincide with Right Concentration in the sense described above, must be used for the purpose given, that is, for the cognition of the objectionableness of all thirst. Otherwise, it is a wrong kind of concentration, under which heading falls every mode of contemplation peculiar to genius which, though in itself free from thirst, nevertheless indirectly

* Cognition dies simultaneously with its creator, thirst. The latter, however, works on for some time still in the vital process of the six senses-machine it has set going, even after having itself perished, namely, until this six senses-machine has broken up at the death of the saint, in the same way that the potter's wheel still for a time keeps on turning, after the force that had set it in motion has ceased to operate. Equally as long, naturally, is *cognition* still demanded. But after having brought about the annihilation of thirst, it sees all its work done, and only waits for its complete dying away, upon the coming to a complete standstill of its last after-effects.

serves this thirst, inasmuch as it has not thirst itself for its object, but some problem serving for its satisfaction under condition of a merely temporary elimination of its disturbing influence on thinking. Wrong concentration, in the Buddha's sense of the word, is therefore practised by all those men of genius to whom the state of pure cognition only serves for the solution of problems of one kind or another *within* the world.*

Right Concentration consists in liberating cognition, or consciousness, or mind, or thinking—all synonymous expressions**—from the service of thirst. Therefore it always

---

* As we see, according to the Buddha, the possibility of cognition free from thirst, *not free from will*—there being no cognition really free from will, since *every* kind of cognition presupposes a corresponding kind of will for its support—or the possibility of the mode of cognition of genius, is a self-evident consequence of the fact that we *are* not will, but merely *have* a will which in itself is composed of innumerable single motions of willing. These motions of willing, led, and ever and again aroused anew, by the cognition accompanying them, incessantly heave up and down in us chiefly in the form of activities of the mind, on which account the Buddha compared man to an ant's hill in which the same restless motion prevails. But as they all have as little to do with our true essence as the air with the space it fills, we may, in principle let any kind of willing arise within us, even motions of willing of contradictory contents, even if this in practice is made difficult by the fact that most of these motions, in the course of time, have assumed the form of thirst, that is, of iron-like habits. Therefore we may especially let a kind of will arise within us that is directed towards the cognizing of the totality of these motions of inclination, by putting cognition at the service of this new kind of willing.

** "What is called Citta (mind), Mana (thinking), Viññāna (consciousness or cognition)" we read in the Dīghanikāya, I 13.

As we saw above pp. 143*, 58***, the word "mind" is a mere collective term denoting the *so-called* mental functions of the six organs of sense, arousing, in the manner described in the chapter an personality, the element of cognition (Viññāna), and thus affecting sensation and perception. Therefore the Pāli expression, *citta,* mind, also designates the totality of these so-called mental functions, as may be gathered from the definition of the *cittasaṅkhāra* quoted above, p. 277. "Perception and sensation inhere in mind, are bound up with mind," (Citta) [meaning what is 'called' Citta in the sense of the definition just given] "therefore are perception and sensation the mental process *(cittasaṅkhāra).*"

But because the element of cognition (Viññāna) can only be aroused in consequence of the activities of sense, comprised in the conception of mind *(citta)*—the element of cognition by itself alone being as little able to become actual as fire without the friction of two bodies—therefore the word "Citta," mind, also serves to designate the

includes, as far as it is attained, a *freeing* in itself of our cognitive activity, and thereby of the element of cognition itself. For the slavery of the sixfold cognitive activity just consists in this, that ever and again it must become active in the service of our inclinations or of our thirst for the world. Accordingly, it is only a self-evident consequence, that the Buddha calls the higher degrees of *cetosamādhi* or mental concentration, also mental *liberations* or mental *deliverances*. In so far as this independence of our cognitive faculty of the service of our inclinations has become a fact, we ourselves also have become delivered. For, as we know, we are bound up with the world and tied to it only by means of the element of consciousness or cognition. Therefore when we liberate *entirely* our cognitive activity from the service of our inclinations, or from the thirst dwelling within us, which happens, if, by means of this same cognitive activity *every* inclination, and therewith all thirst, in particular for further cognitive activity itself, is brought to perfect silence, then, because nothing more impels us to further cognitive activity, we can in absolute freedom also cease from this itself, and thereby bring about the complete extinction of the element of cognition.* Along with this, however, *everything* vanishes for us, our sense-endowed body also, since everything was only made accessible to us with and in this "all-penetrating element." "An invisible, infinite, all-

---

element of cognition itself. On the other hand, the concept, *cognition*, not only serves to designate the element of cognition (consciousness), but also to designate the activities of sense directed towards arousing it, and thereby the activity of mind.

Because further, all cognitive or mental activity in *thinking*, or in the activity of the sixth sense, flows together as into the collective basin,—compare above, p. 52—the expressions "cognition", (*viññāna*) and "mind" (*citta*) always and *before all else* imply that of "thinking" (*mana*). Nay, the terms cognition, mind, and *thinking*, are always, also in our text above, directly used as synonyms, because all cognitive or mental activity culminates in thinking, as in their focus.

* We shall be glad to do this, because in the light of this pure cognitive activity, we already have cognized everything as transitory, leading to suffering, and therefore unsuitable to us.

penetrating consciousness (cognition): there earth, water, fire, and air no more find ground; there long and short, great and small, beautiful and ugly, there the body endowed with senses *(nāma-rūpa)* entirely cease. By the annihilation of consciousness (cognition), all this ceases."[290] If these profound words of the Master have thus become perfectly clear for us, we now will also understand why, with the advent of the perfect deliverance of the mind *(cetovimutti)*, our own eternal deliverance also is realized. With the extinguishing of all thirst, through all eternity no more occasion exists for our ever again developing any mental or cognitive activity, and thereby allowing the element of consciousness to arise once more, in order further in its light to enjoy the delusive spectacle of the world. For this very reason, in death we build up no more new *apparatus* for the activity of mind in the way of grasping a new germ. And thus with the final liberation of our cognitive activity or our mind from the service of thirst, such as comes about with the annihilation of the latter, already *eternal* peace makes its entrance into us, being crowned by our *last* death which follows upon this, since this to us signifies nothing more than the final throwing away of the *apparatus* of cognition, which has now become quite superfluous to us.* Thereby we also understand those other words of the Master: "More and more, ye monks, let the monk exercise himself, so that, as he exercises himself, cognition does not become dispersed and dissipated within himself, but is unshakeable because of his having turned away. If cognition is not dispersed and dissipated, then, unshakeable because of his having turned

* For the rest, *cetovimutti,* if used in the latter sense, in the Canon is always more closely defined as *paññavimutti,* deliverance *through wisdom,* in order to distinguish it from the above-mentioned merely partial and temporary deliverances of mind. For the eternal deliverance of the mind, or of our consciousness, and thereby our own eternal deliverance, after what we have explained in regard to right, direct, actual cognition, can only take place in consequence of holy wisdom.

away, an arising and a going on of birth and old age, death and suffering, in future will no more be found."[291]

3. As we perceive from the foregoing, *Sammā Samādhi* or Right Concentration is nothing more than pure cognition in itself, free from thirst and therefore not dimmed by any other disturbing motion of mind. Right Concentration of itself, therefore, is only to be understood as a purely *formal* condition of cognitive activity, whereby to be sure, its content is already thus much determined, in that it is specially occupied with thirst and its objects, and more closely, with their unsuitability for us. For the rest, however, in order really to understand this unsuitability we, of course, need yet closer lines of guidance for this cognitive activity. If a specialist shows a layman a complicated mechanism for him to examine and appraise by himself, if his naked eye is not sufficient, he must not only allow him to equip himself with a powerful lens—to which in our case, concentration of mind, or concentrated thinking would correspond—but must also direct his attention to the smallest details of all parts of the mechanism, and to the manner of their mutual interworking. Thus it is also of decisive importance for the success of the concentrated activity of cognition, as prescribed on the way to the annihilation of suffering, that its materials are laid before it in a perspicacious manner, and under a correct light, in order that they may be contemplated accordingly. It is therefore only self-evident, that this material content of Right Concentration is thought of as a fundamental condition of success, in a separate link of the path that otherwise would be quite incomplete. This link, because of its quality as embracing everything towards *which* Right Concentration should be directed, is called *sammāsati*, Right Recollectedness. The materials embraced under this heading consist, of course, in the first three excellent truths already dealt with, inasmuch as Right Concentration ought to lead us to the penetration

of the same. The Buddha has put together their chief contents in a manner most serviceable for direct consideration, in one of the most important Discourses of the whole Canon, which on this account bears the title of "The Four Foundations of Recollectedness," *cattāro satipaṭṭhānā*, where the material for concentrated thinking is not only schematically enumerated, but at the same time brought into the form of concentrated contemplation itself. The Discourse, with the wording of parts of which we are already acquainted,* is based upon the fundamental cognition that our whole thirst for the world is summed up in our personality, in and by which, as we know, we alone experience the world, for which very reason, in penetrating the components of our personality and seeing them as *anattā* and full of suffering, our thirst for the world is itself extinguished. According to this, the Buddha dissolves the "heap of processes" forming our personality into its several items, showing in the most vivid manner imaginable, how everything in it and about it, the noblest emotions included, nay, even the penetration of the four holy truths itself, are nothing but transient processes, phenomena, which we behold running their course, with which, for this very reason, we cannot possibly be identical. He divides this contemplation into four parts, dealing with the body, with sensation, with thoughts, and with another group of processes which he simply calls "objects" *(dhammā)*.** Because thus, in these "Four Foundations of Recollectedness" are embraced the most important and essential parts of all objects of meditation, to the question of the adherent Visākha, "What, Venerable One, are the mental images that pertain to Concentration?" in accord with the definition which Right Recollectedness receives

* See above p. 126 *et seq.*

** As, for instance, "the appearing of the six inner and outer realms," see above, p. 129.

elsewhere, the nun Dhammadinna makes answer: "The Four Foundations of Recollectedness are the mental images that pertain to Concentration." * [292]

4. After this, the situation, regarded from the highest standpoint, presents itself thus:

By allowing to arise within us the will to penetrate the machinery of our personality as a heap of painful processes, kept going by our thirst for the world, we retire to this pure will for cognition as to the point from which we may lift our personality, and therewith the world, off their hinges. From this point, representing, so to say, an island in the ocean of thirst wherein we swim, we observe the machinery of our personality in all its component parts, and its causal conditionedness so long and with such undivided attention, that we come to penetrate it as through and through, entirely different from ourselves, full of suffering, and on that account, also unsuited to us; and therewith recognize the thirst for it as a dimming of the heavenly clearness of our essence, whereupon it is extinguished. Along with it, the island also to which we had retired, may then vanish too!

Here, to be sure, the question arises as to how it is possible to scale this height of pure cognition, how with such wholly alienated eye, continuously and entirely concentrated, look

---

* For everyone who wishes to obtain an insight into the practice of contemplation, the study, word by word, of the Discourse on "The Four Foundations of Recollectedness" is indispensable.—Right Concentration and Right Recollectedness, after what we have seen, in practice always constitute an undivisible whole of which the former represents the form, but Right Recollectedness its material content. As long as Right Recollectedness is present, we are also rightly concentrated; and reverse-wise, as long as we are rightly concentrated, we are rightly recollected. From this it becomes clear why Right Recollectedness is so frequently spoken of in place of Right Concentration, as, for instance, in the 32d Discourse of the Majj. Nik.: "But now hear from me, what sort of monk adds to the glory of Gosinga Wood. The monk, Sāriputta, having returned from his begging-round and partaken of his meal, sits down with crossed legs under him, body held upright and brings himself to a state of recollectedness: 'I will not rise from this spot,' he resolves within himself, until, freed from clinging, my mind has attained to deliverance from being influenced by (desire for) Becoming (existence)." [293]

upon our pseudo-self until it is vividly realised as such. This is a question which he alone knows how to appraise in all its difficulty who once has tried to contemplate himself, undisturbed only for a few minutes. Again and ever again consciousness is taken captive by the motions of willing which restlessly rise within us, and by the thoughts that incessantly run through our mind, so that before we know, we have always lost ourselves in them again. How then shall be possible this quiet, and in addition, intense contemplation undisturbed by any other motion of the mind, such as is included in Right Concentration? It is clear that with this we come to the really practical part of the problem. The Buddha, in his Holy Path, solves it in the simplest manner imaginable. The Key-word to the riddle is *gradual* progress. What cannot be attained all at once, may be reached little by little, as the top of a high mountain, from which an enchanting view offers itself, must be gained only by gradually climbing upwards:*—"Just as, O Gotama, in this terrace of Migāra's mother gradual onsetting, gradual progress, gradual ascension may be noticed, from the lowest step upwards, certainly also, O Gotama, among our priests gradual onsetting, gradual progress, gradual ascension may be noticed, that is, in devoutness; certainly also, O Gotama among our archers gradual onsetting, gradual progress, gradual ascension may be noticed, that is, in archery; certainly also, O Gotama, among us accountants, living by accountancy, gradual onsetting, gradual progress, gradual ascension may be noticed, that is, in counting. For, O Gotama, when we take pupils, we first make them count one, the unity, two, the duality, three, the trinity . . . . and thus, O Gotama, we make them count up to a hundred. Now, is it possible, O Gotama, also to show in this Doctrine and Order, in about the same manner, *gradual* onsetting, *gradual* progress, *gradual*

* Compare above p. 25.

ascension?"—"It is possible, O Brahmin, also in this Doctrine and Order to show *gradual* onsetting, *gradual* progress, *gradual* ascension."[294]—"Just as, ye monks, the great ocean gradually becomes deeper, gradually steepens, gradually becomes hollowed out, and there is no abrupt fall, in exactly the same way, ye monks, in this Doctrine, in this Discipline, the training is *gradual*, the working is *gradual*, the path is *gradual*, and there is no sudden advance into full knowledge."[295] Withal the inner structure of this training for winning direct insight into truth shows itself to be so very adequate, that it caused Ānanda, the disciple who was always with the Master, to exclaim: "Astonishing it is, Lord, extraordinary it is, Lord: stage by stage, I see, the Exalted One has set before us escape from the realm of the flood."[296]

If we look closer at these stages, they show themselves to be a *methodically arranged exercise* of Right Concentration. According to the Buddha, exercise makes everything possible; it is even almighty. Especially may it liberate our cognition from serfdom to the motions of the mind dwelling within us, which, after all, is only natural, for it was only *habit* that put it in the fetters of these motions. When they appeared within us for the first time, we adhered to them with our cognition, without knowing their pernicious consequences, and continued so doing until they were able to gain such strength that they could appear as *characteristic* motions of ours, to serve which therefore became for our cognizing faculty an understood thing. Now exercise is, so to say, habit reversed; it means the *disaccustoming* of our cognitive activity from the service of those motions, in such a way that they themselves become the object of our cognizing faculty, and in this manner are more and more recognized as pernicious for us, and especially hindering to our further moral progrèss, with the result that our cognitive activity becomes, in the same measure that this happens, more and more independent of them, less and less yields to them, until at last, precisely for lack of food, they undergo complete decay. Through the freedom from them which thus supervenes, our cognizing faculty becomes capable of devoting itself ever more exclusively and undisturbedly to penetrating with its vision our whole personality, which activity itself again is more and more strengthened by continuous exercise, thereby generating an ever stronger and purer cognition in the said direction. After this, we cannot wonder that the whole way to deliverance is really nothing but a continuous, methodically progressive exercise of concentrated thinking, with the object of bringing about thereby Right Views, and thus freeing our cognizing, and thereby ourselves, at first for a time, and then enduringly, from the service of our accustomed motions of mind. Accordingly, the Buddha directly signalises methodically followed exercise —in concentration—as the *formal content of his doctrine.* "Now, Bhaddāli, by means of the simile of the young horse, I will expound to you *the Doctrine.* Hearken, and give good heed to what I shall say! Just as an expert horse-tamer, Bhaddāli, if he has received a beautiful and noble horse, first has it perform exercises with the bit. In performing exercises with the bit, it shows all kinds of unsubduedness, of uncurbedness, of untamedness, because it never has performed such exercises before. But after having repeated the exercises, after having gradually repeated them, it becomes content therewith. As soon, Bhaddāli, as the beautiful, and noble horse has become content therewith, by repeated exercise, by gradual exercise, then the horse-tamer causes it to perform other exercises, and puts it into harness. And while performing exercises in harness, it shows, just in the same way, all kinds of unsubduedness, of uncurbedness, of untamedness, because it never has performed such exercises before. But after having repeated the exercises, after having gradually repeated them, it becomes content therewith. As soon, Bhaddāli, as the beautiful, noble horse by repeated exercise, by gradual exercise has become contented, the horse-tamer causes it to perform other exercises, to pace and gallop, to race and jump, teaches it royal walk and royal bearing, makes it the swiftest and fleetest and most reliable of horses. And whilst thus performing exercises, it shows all kinds of unsubduedness, of uncurbedness, of untamedness, because of its never having performed such exercises before. But by repeated exercise, by gradual exercise, it becomes content therewith. As soon, Bhaddāli, as the beautiful and noble horse by repeated exercise, by gradual exercise, has become contented, the horse-tamer gives to it the final combing and currying. These, Bhaddāli, are the ten qualities that make a beautiful and noble horse appear suitable to the king, useful to the king, and therefore as belonging to the king." In the same way also the Buddha offers everyone who submits to his guidance, by the methodical exercise of concentration, therefore by pure thinking, to free him from all his passions, and to make him "the holiest place in the world."[297] That the Buddha in the passage given, by exercise really means exercise of *concentration,* follows from the whole construction of the way of deliverance; besides this, it is expressly stated in the 125th Discourse of the Majjhima Nikāya which has concentration of mind for its immediate theme, by means of the kindred simile of the elephant, and also confirmed by the following passages: "More and more, ye monks, let the monk *exercise* himself, so that, as he exercises himself, cognition does not become dispersed and dissipated within himself, but is unshakeable, because of his having turned away."*

"Nothing know I, ye monks, that without exercise would be more inflexible than the mind.

---

* Compare above p. 380.

"Nothing know I, ye monks, that by being exercised would become more flexible than the mind.

"Nothing know I, ye monks, that without exercise leads to such distress as the mind.

"Nothing know I, ye monks, that by being exercised leads to such prosperity as the mind.

"Nothing know I, ye monks, that without exercise, without being developed, generates such suffering as the mind.

"Nothing know I, ye monks, that by being exercised and developed, generates such bliss as the mind." [298]

In the excellent path itself, this methodical exercise of Right Concentration of the mind, or of thinking independent of our inclinations, appears as Right Effort, *sammā-vāyāma.*

5—8. In cultivating Right Concentration, two main stages may be distinguished, first, the "separating" of our cognizing "from the enemy," meaning, from the motions of thirst dwelling within us—it will be noted that an expression frequently used during the late war applies here also—in such a way that, first, one gradually becomes *"disaccustomed* to the body and wishes," [299] and then, when our cognizing, in the form of pure thinking, is thus enabled more and more to penetrate with its vision, undisturbed and continuously, the whole machinery of our personality, in which all our thirst for the world is summed up, as the second main stage, just this penetration itself, and therewith, the radical complete annihilation of every kind of thirst, "so that it can never sprout again, never more can raise its head." [300] This second part constitutes concentration of mind in its narrower sense, to which the first only supplies the necessary antecedent condition, on which account we may call it *preparatory* concentration. Now our thirst for the world acts in a threefold manner, first, in the form of all those inner motions, the results of which appear as our present resolutions; second, in what we say; and third, in what we do; in short, in the form of our thoughts, words, and deeds. In these three directions therefore concentration must be continually cultivated. This means, it must have Right Resolution, *sammā-saṅkappa,* Right speaking, *sammā-vācā,* and Right Acting, *sammā-kammanta,* for its goal, which is only possible if a right mode of life, *sammā-ājīva,* is present. Corresponding to the two principal stages of Right Concentration, these their four fields of action also are of a double kind. At the stage of preparatory concentration, Right Speaking means "to avoid lies, to avoid calumny, to avoid harsh words, to avoid gossip;" right acting means "to avoid killing living beings, to avoid taking things not given, to avoid unchastity;" but Right Resolution means the disposition of mind directed towards realizing those fundamental principles: we have always to "think of renunciation, never to cherish anger, never to foster rage," while the right mode of life is that which enables us to live according to these principles.[301] At the stage of real concentrative activity, however, correspondent with their task of killing out all thirst without leaving a remainder, Right Speaking, Right Acting, Right Mode of life, mean: "what turns off, turns away, turns aside, averts from the four kinds of evil talk, the three kinds of evil action, and a wrong mode of life," that means, the eradication of the *inclinations* towards them, in which direction, of course, here again, Right Resolution comes into play.[302]

With this, we now know all the eight members of the path leading to the annihilation of suffering, which the last of the four excellent truths has for its object: "This, ye monks, is the most excellent truth of the path to the annihilation of suffering. It is this excellent eightfold path, that is called: Right View, Right Resolution, Right Speaking, Right Acting, Right Mode of Life, Right Effort, Right Recollectedness, Right Concentration."[303]

If we look it over once more, we see that its eight members are not joined to one another like beads on a string, but coalesce into an organic unity. The way of deliverance consists in a constant *effort* after continued *concentration* of the mind, for the purpose of incessant objective contemplation of all our *thoughts, words,* and *actions,* as also of our whole *conduct of life* in general, by following the directions given by the Buddha in right *recollectedness* in order thus to win right *view*, in the end, in the form of holy wisdom.*

"Holy, Right Concentration, ye monks, I will show you, together with its conditions, together with its requisites. What now, ye monks, is Holy, Right Concentration, together with its conditions, with its requisites? It is, Right View, Right Resolution, Right Speaking, Right Acting, Right Mode of life, Right Effort, Right Recollectedness: a unity of mind, accompanied by these seven members, this is called Holy, Right Concentration together with its conditions, together with its requisites."** It would not be in the spirit of the Buddha, if we did not also pass in review before us in direct, vivid form, this organic unity into which the eight members of the Path merge, thus, as they present themselves in practice.

---

* If right view or right direct cognition is thus the *goal* of all moral striving, nevertheless, after what has gone before, it must on the other hand *precede* all striving of this kind, since it only furnishes the motive, and therefore only makes effort for right concentration possible, on behoof of an ever greater deepening of itself, as is set forth in more detail in the 117th Discourse of the Majj. Nik. As hinted above, —comp. p. 21—it is the same, as if someone, using a traveller's hand-book, were pressing along the highroad towards a distant goal. At first, he only sees the road that is before him, but takes it, in the consciousness that he is on the right way. The farther he goes, the more of the various places he has to pass, according to his hand-book, come into view, which gives him an ever higher degree of certainty, until at last the goal itself rises above the horizon.

** Majjh. Nik. 117th Discourse.—That Right Effort in particular goes along with Right Concentration, which itself again is inseparably bound up with Right Recollectedness, becomes clear from the fact that in the 44th Discourse of the Majjhima Nikāya, Right Effort, Right Recollectedness, and Right Concentration, taken together, are called "part of Concentration."

For this purpose, we need only turn to the 61st Discourse of the Majjhima Nikāya, in which the Buddha expounds to his son Rāhula this practical formation of the Way:—

"What do you think, Rāhula: what is a mirror for?"

"To look at oneself, Lord."

"Even so, Rāhula, we ought to look and look at ourselves, before we do deeds, look and look before we speak words, look and look before we cherish thoughts."

"Whatever deed, Rāhula, you wish to do, at this same deed you ought to look thus: 'How if this deed I wish to do should be grievous to myself, or grievous to another, or grievous to both? This would be an unwholesome deed, that produces suffering, breeds suffering.' If, Rāhula, in looking at this you observe: 'This deed I wish to do might be grievous to myself, might be grievous to another, might be grievous to both; it is an unwholesome deed, that produces suffering, breeds suffering,'—then, Rāhula, you certainly have to abstain from such a deed. But if you notice, Rāhula, while looking at it: 'This deed I wish to do can neither be grievous to me nor grievous to another nor grievous to both; it is a wholesome deed, producing welfare, breeding welfare,'—then, Rāhula, you ought to do such a deed.

"And *while* doing a deed, Rāhula, you ought to look thus at this same deed: 'Because I am doing this deed, is it grievous to myself, or is it grievous to another, or is it grievous to both? Is it an unwholesome deed, producing suffering, breeding suffering?' If, Rāhula, while looking at it you observe: 'This deed I am doing is grievous to myself or grievous to another, or grievous to both; it is an unwholesome deed, producing suffering, breeding suffering,'—then, Rāhula, you ought to abstain from such a deed. But if you notice, Rāhula, while looking at it: 'This deed I am doing is neither grievous to me, nor grievous to another, nor grievous to both; it is a wholesome deed, producing welfare, breeding welfare,'—then, Rāhula, you ought to promote such a deed.

"And if, Rāhula, you have done a deed, you ought thus to look at this same deed: 'Because I have done this deed, is it grievous to myself, or grievous to another, or grievous to both? Is it an unwholesome deed, producing suffering, breeding suffering?' If, Rāhula, you notice while looking at it: 'This deed I have done is grievous to myself, or grievous to another, or grievous to both; it is an unwholesome deed, producing suffering, breeding suffering,'—then, Rāhula, you ought to communicate, to discover, to expose such a deed to the Master, or to experienced brethren of the Order; and after having communicated, discovered and exposed it, you ought in future to guard yourself against it.* But if you notice, Rāhula, while looking at it: 'This deed I have done is neither grievous to myself, nor grievous to another, nor grievous to both; it is a wholesome deed, producing welfare, breeding welfare,'—then, Rāhula, you ought day and night to cultivate this blissful, joyous exercise in doing good."

The Buddha then proceeds to say the same as regards every word that is said, every thought that is entertained.

From this also it again becomes clear, how all members of the Way meet as in their focus in Right Concentration, that is, in unbroken, meditative contemplation of all motions of will arising within us. Every good, that is, renouncing, thought, every good word, that is, proceeding from self-mastery, every good deed, presupposes it, since they are all conditioned by Right View. But this Right View, on its side, is only possible as the fruit of that pure cognizing, standing

* Compare also Majj. Nik. 65th Discourse: "It is a progress, Bhaddāli, in the order of the Holy One, to look upon a transgression as a transgression, to confess it properly, and in future to be on one's guard against it."

behind the motions of thirst and showing itself in the form of contemplative meditation. In so far as it penetrates the perniciousness of these motions, it does not allow them to become prominent, because of which, thoughts, words and deeds born of this state of mind must be free from thirst, and therefore good. Because thus, concentration of mind is the indispensable presupposition of everything good, even the most insignificant good thought, it becomes clear precisely from this, that it must become a *constant*, that is to say, in the form of an unbroken *thoughtfulness*, it must more and more become the dominant factor of the whole life, if real moral progress is at all to be possible. As true as it is, on one hand, that the killing out of the motions of our passions is only possible by direct cognition of their perniciousness, just as certain is it on the other hand, that this direct cognition must always be a *present* one. For certainly each of us has had moments when the perniciousness of some passion has come before his eyes with terrifying clearness, so that he has not been able to understand how he could ever have given himself over to it. And yet, in spite of this right direct cognition, ever and again we fall back into the same old fault. The reason of this is that it always immediately vanishes again. At most, we retain a weak reflex of it in memory; but this reflex is much too weak to be of any lasting effect. If direct cognition is to be effective, it must be present at every moment, in everything we think, speak, or do. But this again presupposes that that contemplative meditation resulting from concentration of mind, is always at its post as constant organ of control, and confronts all motions of volition arising within us, as reservedly and acutely observant, as a sentinel at the gate a stranger who wants to enter. And as the watchman only gives free passage after having recognized the stranger as beyond suspicion, so meditation only gives passage to any motion of mind when it has recognized it to be harmless. Only in this manner is the purifying, and ultimate annihilation, of our character, in the complete extinguishing of our thirst for the world, possible: "For whosoever, Rāhula, of ascetics and Brahmins in times bygone has purified his deeds, purified his words, purified his thoughts, each of them has thus and thus contemplating and contemplating purified his deeds, contemplating and contemplating purified his words, contemplating and contemplating purified his thoughts. And whosoever, Rāhula, of ascetics or Brahmins in times to come will purify his deeds, purify his words, purify his thoughts, each of them thus and thus contemplating and contemplating will purify his deeds, contemplating and contemplating will purify his words, contemplating and contemplating will purify his thoughts. And whosoever, Rāhula, of ascetics or Brahmins in present times purifies his deeds, purifies his words, purifies his thoughts, each of them thus and thus contemplating and contemplating purifies his deeds, contemplating and contemplating purifies his words, contemplating and contemplating purifies his thoughts. Therefore, Rāhula, take notice of this: Contemplating and contemplating we will purify our deeds; contemplating and contemplating we will purify our words; contemplating and contemplating we will purify our thoughts. Thus, Rāhula, you ought to exercise yourself."* [304]

It cannot be otherwise. For we know from the foregoing, that our thirst for the world ever and again wells up anew out of our thoughtless taking part in the activities of the senses, wherein precisely ignorance consists. As soon as we behold a form with the eye, hear a sound with the ear,

---

* Why should not I enter upon this, at all times accessible path to the *changing of character?* In time might it not equally well be that, as result of a given perception, instead of, as now, always vulgar movements arising with me, there should be aroused only noble movements such as renunciation, mildness, patience, nay, at last, none at all?

smell an odour with the nose, taste a sapid with the tongue, touch something touchable with the body, encounter an idea with the organ of thought, immediately "being void of Recollectedness as respects corporeality" we are "enamoured of the pleasing phenomena and shun the unpleasing." Thirst, therefore, can only be annihilated on the opposite track. In every activity of sense, by means of collected thinking we must penetrate the objects of the same and see them as transient, indeed, at bottom, repulsive, and therewith also, every rising motion of willing in relation to them, as harmful to us, and thus no longer act *unknowingly*, but *knowingly*.

Thus the way of salvation shown by the Buddha reveals itself as the way of *cognition*, that is, of cognition of the perniciousness of thirst for the world that dwells within us. It is fundamentally nothing but an exhortation to *constant*, *right*, and, as far as possible, *acute* thinking. Thinking is *right*, if everything in the world, the five groups of our personality included, is scrutinized in respect of the three characteristics, *tīni lakkhanāni*: transitory *(anicca)*, painful *(dukkha)*, and therefore unsuitable to us *(anattā)*. This way alone can lead us to the goal, all the more exclusively in that all suffering has its ground in our thirst for the five groups of our personality, and thereby, for the world, and that this thirst is conditioned by our ignorance as to its pernicious consequences.

But with this the two other, still much frequented, ways to salvation are equally obviously shown to be byways, namely, the way of trying to effect one's salvation by means of religious ceremonies and usages, and the way of self-mortification, as practised so much in India, and often also in Christianity during its better days. "I do not, ye monks, grant holy life to a monk, to a wearer of the robe just because he wears the robe, nor to an unclad one, because he is unclad, nor to a man smeared with dirt, because he is smeared with dirt, nor to one who sprinkles himself with water, because he sprinkles himself with water, nor to a hermit in the forest, because he lives in the forest, nor to a fasting one, because he fasts, nor to a man well versed in sayings, because he is well acquainted with sayings* . . . If through the wearing of the robe, through nakedness, through being besmeared with dirt, through sprinkling with water, through living as a hermit in the forest, through fasting, through acquaintance with sayings, the greed of the greedy, the hate of the hateful, the anger of the angry, the hostility of the hostile could vanish, then the relatives and friends of a newborn babe would bring the robe to him, would prescribe to him nakedness, smearing with dirt, sprinkling with water, hermitage in the forest, fasting and acquaintance with the sayings, and with this they would endow him saying: 'Come, you lucky child, be a wearer of the robe, be unclad, be smeared with dirt, be sprinkled with water, become a hermit in the forest, fast and become acquainted with sayings, then, if you are greedy, your greed will vanish, if you are full of hatred, your hate, if you are angry, your anger, if you are hostile, your hostility.' But, ye monks, I see here many a wearer of the robe, many an unclad one, many a man smeared with dirt, many sprinkled with water, many a hermit in the forest, many a fasting one, many a man acquainted with sayings, who is greedy, hateful, angry, hostile, and so I do not grant holy life to any one of them for such a reason."[305]

But whoso treads the path shown by the Buddha, walks upon a holy way. For "on his track we become seeing and knowing."[306] And where knowledge is, there one *can* no longer do homage to passion. For no one knowingly can

---

* Knowledge of the holy scriptures of the Brahmins is meant, Christians would say "well versed in the Bible."

plunge himself into an ocean of pain. He alone can do so who does not "see the upshot," that is, the unknowing man. That is why in the moral teachings of the Buddha there are, at bottom, no good and bad men in our sense of the words, but only wise men and fools. Therefore in it there is also no contempt for the wicked, but only boundless compassion for them, who, even as ourselves, "cherish the desire, the wish, the intention: 'Oh, might the undesired, the unwished for, the unpleasing decrease, and the desired, the wished for, the pleasing increase.' But for them 'the undesired, the unwished for, the unpleasing increases, and the desired, the wished for, the pleasing decreases.' And why so? Because even thus it must happen, if a man is ignorant."* [306]

B. THE SEVERAL STEPS OF THE PATH

1. THE GOING INTO HOMELESSNESS

The more exalted anything is, all the less is it generally understood, because it exceeds the mental capacity of the average man; and all the more is it exposed to misinterpretations. Indeed, because the cause cannot be removed, it is also quite impossible to meet these misinterpretations successfully. Hence it has always been the fate of the highest verities not only to be misunderstood, but also, in so far

---

* We do many things which we would not wish a being beloved by us to do. Why is this? As soon as we use our cognizing apparatus in our own interest, our cognizing activity is forced into the service of the inclinations that fill us. These falsify cognition, hence we then act in a state of ignorance. But if the welfare of a beloved being is at stake, then our own inclinations are silent; we remain *purely cognizing*, and accordingly see much more keenly and clearly. If therefore we wish to know how to behave in any particular case, we need only ask how we would wish the loved being to behave. What we then and thus cognize, represents the high-water mark of our capacity for cognition.

as in their practical effectuation they attract the attention of the average man, to be ridiculed. It is therefore nothing astonishing that the doctrine of the Buddha also, the highest truth ever communicated to mankind, has frequently met this fate, especially in the countries of the West. This has been the case to a quite particular degree, from the fact that in its full, practical realization, it issues in monachism, an institution against which the ordinary man of the world instinctively revolts, because, if it were concordant with truth, it would mean the severest condemnation imaginable of his own way of living, which is entirely given up to the pleasures of the senses. There are even in Europe "Buddhists," in all seriousness believing themselves to be such, who consider this institution of the Buddha superfluous! Of course they thereby only prove the truth of the old Indian proverb: "Even in the ocean, more than its own measure a jug cannot hold." But to us it will have become clear merely from what we have heard up till now about the way of salvation taught by the Buddha, that it cannot possibly be trodden in its entirety in the world. It demands nothing more and nothing less than the cultivation of the deepest contemplation and ceaseless watchfulness with regard to every single act, even the most insignificant, in the activity of the senses, so as at once to recognize as such every motion of thirst for the world in all its perniciousness, and thus allow no kind of grasping any more to arise. But how should such unceasing control of all and every impression of the senses be possible within the world? It is impossible, because in the world these impressions are far too numerous for us to be able to maintain complete watchfulness over every single one of them. In the world, it is only on the rarest occasions, and then only for a brief period that we attain thoughtfulness, to say nothing of unbroken watchfulness. "If I really understand the doctrine expounded by the Exalted One, it is not possible, living the household life, to carry out point by point, the perfectly purified, perfectly stainless holy life," says Raṭṭhapāla to the Master, after having heard him.[307] Not even the fundamental precepts can be constantly kept. "Who lives at home, is much busied, much occupied, much concerned, much harassed, not always wholly and entirely given to truthfulness, not always wholly and entirely restrained, chaste, devout, renouncing."[308] Certainly, also in the world, we may restrict our relations to it as much as possible; for instance, we may enter no profession, found no family, but these relations will never allow of being cut off entirely. For to live in the world just means to maintain relations with the world. So far, however, as these relations extend, to that extent we are occupied with worldly things; to this extent, therefore, we are cultivating and strengthening the fetters that chain us to the world. In so far, therefore, the ties cannot be definitively severed; and hence, to this extent, complete deliverance is impossible. For, wholly delivered he only is who "has cut through every tie."[308] On this point there can be no reasonable doubt. And thus it is really only a self-evident thing when the Buddha expressly asserts the impossibility of reaching Nibbāna while living the ordinary life of the world. "Is there, O Gotama, any householder, who, not having left off household ties, upon the dissolution of the body, makes an end of suffering?" "There is no householder whatever, O Vaccha, who, not having left off household ties, upon the dissolution of the body, makes an end of suffering?"[309]

Precisely in consequence of this his point of view, the Buddha has founded the *Saṅgha,* as the Society of all those who have left home for the life of homelessness, in order, under his guidance to strive as monks towards the great goal of complete departure out of the world. In this Saṅgha, therefore, not less than in the Buddha and in his

Doctrine itself, as in the Three Jewels, *Tiratana,* must those take their refuge who wish to tread the most direct road to deliverance, as it is expressed in the formula of confession which up to the present day constitutes the actual confession of faith of all Buddhists.

"To the Buddha I will hold in clear faith.* He, the Exalted One, is the highest, holy Buddha, the knowing one, the learned, the Blessed One, who knows the worlds, who tames man like a bull, the teacher of gods and men, the exalted Buddha.

"To the Doctrine I will hold in clear faith: well expounded by the Exalted One is the Doctrine. It has visibly appeared; it is independent of time; it is called, 'Come and see;' it leads to salvation; *in his own interior it is recognized by the wise.*

"To the Order—Sangha—I will hold in clear faith. In right conduct lives the community of the Buddha's disciples, in true conduct lives the community of the Buddha's disciples; in straightforward conduct lives the community of the Buddha's disciples; in correct conduct lives the community of the Buddha's disciples; the four pairs,** the eight classes of men: ** this is the community of the disciples of the Exalted One, worthy of sacrifices, worthy of donations, worthy of gifts, worthy of raising the hands to in veneration, the highest state in the world in which man may do good."[311]

After this, the utter folly will probably be apparent of all those who think they must advocate a Dhamma without

---

* Faith (Saddhā) means, in the doctrine of the Buddha of course, as we have sufficiently gathered from the foregoing, no blind believing. "Saddhā is nothing but perfect trust in the Buddha, as in the best spiritual guide, won by insight and confirmed by the experiences and the facts of life; trust in the Dharma, (the Sanskrit form of *dhamma,* doctrine,) as in the expression of eternal truth; and in the Saṅgha, as supporter and proclaimer of the exalted doctrine of salvation."

** The four kinds of saints—see below!—as well as those who are on the way to it. 310

a Saṅgha. For they take away the blade from the knife; or, what is the same thing, they would have us believe that a bather might become dry before he has got out of the water. Such a standpoint, of course, they can only adopt because they are unable to grasp the kernel of the Buddha's doctrine, and with it, their own eternal destiny. That is to say, they are unable to comprehend that "the whole world is really a burning house, from which we cannot save ourselves quickly enough."[312] For if they did understand this, then it would be simply impossible that, instead of speaking contemptuously of "flight from the world," they should not draw a breath of relief every time they saw yet another person flee out of this burning house, and only regret that they themselves cannot find the courage to do the same.

From the foregoing it will probably also be clear what is to be thought about those complaints which culminate in the objection, that, according to this, all men ought to become monks and nuns, and that the world will thus be in danger of dying out.* Such complaints amount just to this, that one would regard it as a calamity if all men were to be cured of their bodily ailments because then there would be no more hospitals. Certainly, the world would cease to exist, if all beings could be brought to realize their eternal destiny; but thereby it would only be *Suffering* that would reach its definitive end. However, those who are so intensely concerned about the continuation of the world may console themselves, since this will not happen, and probably never will happen. For there will always be those who far from

* Such complaints were already current in the Buddha's own day. "But at this time well-known young people from the noble families of Magadhā under the guidance of the Exalted one led the life of purity. Thereby the people were perturbed, became ill-disposed, and grumbled: 'The ascetic Gotama has come to make us childless; the ascetic Gotama has come to make women widowed; the ascetic Gotama has come to cause families to die out'."[313]

leaving the world themselves, will even throw stones at those who set them the example.*

Assuredly, certain scruples are difficult to set aside, even for earnest strivers, namely, as regards the so-called collision of duties brought about by the way into homelessness —*pabbajjā*—as it affects one's own relatives, especially wife and children. Though the Buddha does not permit it to any one who has not got the permission of his parents —"the Perfect Ones do not accept a son without the permission of his parents," he tells Raṭṭhapāla who was asking to be accepted into the community of the monks[313]—nevertheless he is not opposed to a man's leaving wife and children, in order to effect his eternal salvation. This standpoint comes out most clearly in the following narrative.

"Once upon a time, the Exalted One was staying at Sāvatthī, in the Jeta forest grove of Anāthapiṇḍika. At the same time, the reverend Saṅgāmaji had come to Sāvatthī, in order to see the Exalted One. Now the former wife of the reverend Saṅgāmaji had heard that the reverend Saṅgāmaji was said to have arrived in Sāvatthī. Thereupon she took up her child and went to the Jeta forest. Now at this same time the reverend Saṅgāmaji was seated at the foot of a tree, in order to spend the afternoon there, sunk in meditation. Now the former wife of the reverend Saṅgāmaji went where the reverend Saṅgāmaji was staying, and spoke thus to the reverend Saṅgāmaji: 'Look here, O ascetic, at your little son and support me!' At these words, the reverend Saṅgāmaji remained silent. For a second time, the former

* The question as to whether all beings will reach deliverance, was not answered by the Buddha, because it is without value for the practical work of the deliverance of the individual. In the Aṅguttara Nikāya it is said: "As the guardian of the gate of a fortress does not know, how many persons enter the gate, but knows that nobody can enter otherwise than through the gate, in the same way it does not concern the Perfected One, whether the whole world or a half or a third part of it has won to freedom on this Way (taught by him), or gets there, or will get there."

wife of the reverend Saṅgāmaji addressed the reverend Saṅgāmaji thus: 'Look here, O ascetic, at your little son and support me!' And for the second time the reverend Saṅgāmaji remained silent. Now for the third time the former wife of the reverend Saṅgāmaji addressed the reverend Saṅgāmaji thus: 'Look here, O ascetic, at your little son and support me!' And for the third time the reverend Saṅgāmaji remained silent. Thereupon the former wife of the reverend Saṅgāmaji laid down the child before the reverend Saṅgāmaji and went off, saying: 'This is your son, O ascetic, support *him!*' But the reverend Saṅgāmaji neither looked at the child, nor did he speak a word. As the former wife of the reverend Saṅgāmaji now turned round from afar, she saw how the reverend Saṅgāmaji neither regarded the child nor said anything. Thereupon she thought: 'Not even for his child does this ascetic care.' And so she turned back, took the child and went off.

"But the Exalted One, with the heavenly eye, the purified, the supramundane, saw this meeting between the reverend Saṅgāmaji and his wife. And the Exalted One perceived the meaning (of this meeting) and on this occasion uttered the following verse:

'The coming does not make him glad,
The going does not make him sad;
The monk, from longings all released,
Him do I call a Brāhmaṇa.' "* [314]

---

* To the same effect is the following saying af the Christ (Matth. X, 34—37): "Think not that I am come to send peace on earth: I came not to send peace, but a sword. For I am come to set a man at variance against his father, and the daughter against her mother, and the daughter-in-law against her mother-in-law. And a man's foes shall be they of his own household. He that loveth father or mother more than me is not worthy of me: And he that loveth son or daughter more than me is not worthy of me." Of course the first part of the passage also refers exclusively to the conflict between the "rights" of the relatives and the moral obligations to which the adherent of the Christ is subjected.

There are many who are honest friends of the doctrine of the Master, but nevertheless are unable to understand this standpoint. And yet it is perfectly clear, if only it is envisaged from the heights of pure cognition.

If the Buddha is right in this, that the eternal destiny of every being lies in his outgrowing the world, and at last leaving it entirely, then from the nature of this destiny also must be taken the criterion for the evaluation of every action from a moral point of view, since good, or moral, in the highest sense can only be what serves for the reaching of this ultimate goal; bad or immoral, however, being everything that hinders this or directly makes it impossible. If this indubitably correct principle is taken as basis, then he is certainly not acting immorally who for the sake of his eternal welfare leaves the world and therewith also, wife and child. What he does is good for him, for it lies in the line of his eternal destiny; it is even extraordinarily good, for it lies upon the nearest way to it. But if, on his side, it is something extraordinarily good that he wishes to do, then just because of this, every obstruction of this step, from whatever side it may come, appears as something immoral, —this word used, of course, from the highest standpoint now adapted by us. In short: it is not he who wishes to become a saint who acts immorally; but those who act immorally are his wife and his children who out of selfishness wish to hinder him from achieving this his eternal salvation. In order clearly to recognize this distribution of the guilt, the following points ought to be considered. He also is moved by love of wife and child, perhaps more than those who condemn him, for he is unquestionably a noble man. But with the severest mental struggles he opposes this love as well as every other inclination leading back to the world, and presses forward to do the most difficult thing a man can ever do, to take up the struggle against himself to its full extent, a struggle, compared with which, every other is mere child's play,* for he aims to learn to renounce the satisfaction of every motion of will, yea, in time to become entirely free from willing. But all that the others want is not to lose their supporter. They are unable to master their inclination towards him who is leaving them, which presents itself in the guise of love; in a word, they are the slaves of the thirst that dwells within them. Who now is great, and who small? But is the great to abandon his goal for the sake of the small? May a warrior going to battle allow himself to be kept back by the complaints of wife and children? Would not the whole world cry out at him: "Weakling!"?

From this, it obviously follows that it is not advisable to neglect to do something morally good out of regard for the lack of understanding of others. For it is nothing else but lack of understanding that here stands obstructively in the way. During their endless pilgrimage through the world, some few persons have found themselves together for a brief time in one family, to be separated again very soon in death, and then, each for himself, to continue the pilgrimage alone, perhaps on through a terrible future. Looked at from this point of view, is it not unreasonable if one of them wishes to hinder another from putting an end to this unhappy wandering through the worlds only in order that *he* may enjoy this present fleeting existence as free from care and pain as possible, unconcerned about his own fate or about the future fate of the other? Is not this at bottom really irresponsible? Who is here the egoist,—he who wishes radically to annihilate everything that makes him something

* "Not who ten hundred thousand men
Has vanquished on the battlefield,
But he who vanquishes himself,
The greatest hero true is he." Says the Dhammapada.

positive, that is, an ego existing in the world; or the other who, not satisfied merely with the affirmation of his own ego, desires also to force the other into his service?

Since, therefore, the going into homelessness is moral, every impediment to the same is an immorality; hence none can claim treaty-rights as impediments against it. For every claim to such a restriction by treaty-right of the other party would itself mean an immorality, inasmuch as the character of the action that is immoral in itself cannot be altered by a claim to its being reserved to the person against whom it is to be committed, moreover under conditions quite different from those at present prevailing. In the same way that public law takes precedence of private law, and thus a private claim must give way to a public one, in the self-same way, every claim derived from a contract or from some other legal ordinance must give way to the demands of ethics, if law is not to become an instrument for the triumph of immorality.*

By this, however, we do not mean that the claim to go into homelessness is one that is free of all conditions. Rather does it find its limits in the very moral demands out of

* The possibility of a conflict between right and morality arises from their having in themselves nothing to do with each other. According to Schopenhauer the State also is not a means to morality. Of course, every law-giver will try to bring right into harmony with morality, since the state is not allowed to be an ethical wrong in itself, if it wishes to consist of just men. Therefore under *normal* circumstances, right and morality will be generally identical. But even here exceptions may occur; as for example, in the case of laws issued against any religion. Contradictions between formal right and morality are especially inevitable, when the morality of an individual outgrows the moral conceptions to which law pays heed. A soldier arrives at the moral conviction that killing in every form is reprehensible, also in war; a husband in time finds himself no longer able to reconcile the performance of his marital duties with his more purified moral feelings, whereas the wife continues to claim her "rights." Lastly, as in our case, a man discovers that worldly life is in itself detrimental to his eternal welfare, but his relatives do not wish to let him go, making appeal to his so-called "duties." In every case of this kind, before the judgment seat of the conscience of the individual, "right" must retire in favour of the demands of morality, though the state "rightly" takes the opposite view of things.

which precisely it arises. Whoever aims to effect his own eternal welfare, may not endanger the true welfare of others.* Of course, the sorrow he causes to those belonging to him without further ado may be excluded as regards him who leaves home; for it is not he who is the cause of this, but their own ignorance simply; accordingly, he has not to bear the consequences of the same. For the rest, however, it is, of course, only a question of the *true* welfare of those belonging to him, not what these themselves hold to be their welfare. Hence it is of no great moment if now they should lose that care-free, perhaps comfortable life they have hitherto been leading. For such a life, regarded from the highest standpoint, is more to be regarded as a misfortune than a blessing, since, as a rule, it only strengthens attachment to this world, and thereby, future suffering. "If, householder, you will do what I advise, then you will put this heap of gold and jewels on carts and have them taken out of town and thrown into the middle of the Ganges. And why so? Surely, househoulder, you will experience through them woe and sorrow, grief and pain and despair," Raṭṭhapāla tells his father who tries to persuade him to renounce monkhood, by calling his attention to his great wealth.[315] It does not matter even that those left behind lose their supporter, if only they are just able to support themselves, even though only with the help of others. For this, regarded from the highest standpoint, is rather a blessing than a misfortune, since it is particularly well adapted to make men think about their true relation to the world. Hence there remain only as cases demanding consideration of him who wishes to become a monk, those where without him even the minimum amount of support necessary to his relatives, or even their eternal salvation, would be jeopardised, as example of the

* This dictum, as, in general, those that follow, will later on be given its final justification.

latter, if his children were in danger of being morally neglected. The former standpoint is adopted by Ghaṭīkāra the potter, in the 81st Discourse of the Majjhima Nikāya, where in reply to the exhortation of his friend Jotipāla to enter the Order of the Master, he says: "Don't you know, dearest Jotipāla, that I have to support my old and blind parents?" But that in no case may a man put in jeopardy the *eternal* welfare of those he leaves behind through going into homelessness, becomes clear precisely from the story from the Udāna quoted above, where Saṅgāmaji maintains a passive attitude only towards the demand of his former wife that he shall *support* her and her child. If her *eternal* welfare had been in question, that pity for all beings, dwelling in him as in every saint, would have determined him to save her. To be sure, this pity, in the case before him, would probably have been confined to the "miracle of instruction"[316] as the only means promising real success.

To bring under one principle, in harmony with the intentions of the Buddha, the cases in wich the going into homelessness had better not be undertaken out of regard for others, we may say: Whoever wants to enter the Order of the Master, his relations towards those belonging to him must be of such a kind that his step would be approved by them, if they stood upon the same high moral level as himself. If, after having carefully examined himself, he finds these relations to be of this sort,—in other words, if, their rôles being exchanged, he could say that he, in their place, would consider himself obliged to give his consent, then, if now he actually goes away, he acts in entire harmony with the moral law that is decisive for him, and therefore cannot be doing anything in any way blameworthy. For the real cause of all the suffering entailed upon those belonging to him through the step he takes, lies, not in him but in their own lack of understanding or defective cognition. Thus, rightly regarded, the blame is not his but their own, and by them must be borne. If they were on the same level as he, instead of *their* making the event a source of suffering, it would be followed by the most wholesome consequences for them also. "If, Dīgha, the family whence have come these three well-born ones who have left home behind and vowed themselves to the homeless life shall think upon them with hearts fulfilled of faith, long will it make for the welfare and happiness of that family," it is said in the 31st Discourse of the Majjhima Nikāya, with reference to three youths who had followed the Buddha. The question, therefore, is, whether, for example, the wife, instead of complaining, should speak to her departing husband, if she was abreast of the situation, with the necessary changes, in the same manner as did the wife in the Aṅguttara-Nikāya to her husband who was seriously ill: "Don't die with sorrowful thoughts; such a death the Exalted one does not praise. Are you afraid that, after your death, I may not be able to support our children? But I am a clever cotton-spinner, and I shall have no difficulty in keeping up our household. Or do you think that after your death I shall leave off longing for a sight of the Buddha and his monks? That peace shall be wanting to my soul? That I shall not stand firm without wavering, in knowing the Doctrine of the Master and in trusting it? But if ever any uncertainty should come upon me, why, then he is staying near us, the exalted, holy Buddha, and I can go to him and put my question to him."[317]

If thus there may be external circumstances detaining one from going into homelessness,* the chief hindrance generally lies in the man himself. The man must be *ripe* for this, that

* From being received into the Saṅgha is also excluded: 1. one who suffers from certain diseases, 2. one who is in the King's service, 3. one who is not free, 4. one who has not yet paid his debts. We see that all these exceptions are based upon purely utilitarian grounds. The three latter exceptions evidently had in view the avoiding of conflicts with the power of the state. To similar considerations,—we must

is to say, his entire willing must already be so ennobled that nothing within this world is able any longer entirely to satisfy him, so that the eternal, as soon as in any comprehensible fashion it enters his range of vision, powerfully attracts him and causes all his earthly possessions to appear to him as empty and insipid, no further able seriously to fetter him. "Just as if, Udāyī, there was a householder or the son of a householder, rich, greatly endowed with money and valuables, in possession of many heaps of gold, in possession of many masses of corn, in possession of many fields and meadows, in possession of many houses and farms, in possession of many multitudes of women, in possession of many a crowd of servants, in possession of many a crowd of hand-maids. And he should see in a grove a monk, with clean-washed hands and feet, cheerful of countenance, after having taken his meal, sitting there in the cool shadow, giving himself to exalted heedfulness. And he would feel thus: 'Blissful, truly, is holy life! Free from suffering, truly, is holy life! O, that I were such a man who, with hair and beard shorn, clad in yellow garment, might go forth from home into homelessness!' And he should be able to leave the many heaps of gold, the many masses of corn, the many fields and meadows, the many houses and farms, the many multitudes of women, the many crowds of servants, the many crowds of handmaids, and to go with hair and beard shorn, clad in yellow garment, from home into homelessness .... These for him are no strong fetters, but weak fetters, rotten fetters, fetters unable to hold."[318]

But on this height stand only the very tiniest minority of men. The immense majority still cleave so tightly to the world, that the message of a supramundane happiness and

---

bear in mind the extensive power of parents over their children in ancient India—the unconditioned respecting of the guardianship of parents over their children is evidently also due, as expressed in making the consent of parents necessary for entrance into the Order, even a parental prohibition dictated only by ill-will being effective.

peace is at best only able to arouse in them, even if they live in the most miserable circumstances, a feeble and indefinite feeling of the unworthiness of their present situation, which of course can furnish no motive to corresponding action. "As if, Udāyī, there was a man, poor and neither free nor independent, and owning but a single hut, decayed and dilapidated, open to the crows, not at all beautiful, a single resting-place, decayed and dilapidated, not at all beautiful, a single bushel of corn-seed, not at all beautiful, a single woman, not at all beautiful; and in a grove he would see a monk, with clean-washed hands and feet, cheerful of countenance, after having taken his meal, sitting in the cool shade, giving himself to exalted heedfulness. And he should feel thus: 'Blissful, truly, is holy life! Free from suffering, truly, is holy life! O, that I were such a man who, with hair and beard shorn, clad in yellow garment, might go forth from home into homelessness!' And he should not be able to leave his one single hut, decayed and dilapidated, open to the crows, not at all beautiful, his one single resting-place, decayed and dilapidated, not at all beautiful, his one bushel of corn-seed, not at all beautiful, his one woman, not at all beautiful, and go forth, with hair and beard shorn, clad in yellow garment, from home into homelessness .... These are strong fetters for him, tight fetters, tough fetters, no rotten fetters, but a heavy clog."[319]

According to this, the Order of the Master comes into question only for very few men, for so very few, that the Buddha, after having come to full awakening, doubted if he ought to communicate to the world the whole truth that had unveiled itself before him, since it was a truth "going against the stream, deep, intimate, delicate, hidden, not to be reached only by mere reasoning, imperceptible to those delighting in desires."[320] But at last, consideration for those few "noble beings who would be lost if they heard not the Doctrine," determined him to found the Saṅgha. So very few minds of the highest order did the Buddha thus find even in his own favoured age when care for their eternal welfare exerted an influence over the actions of men as at no other time.* How many, then, in our "evil age" and moreover, in the Occident, may be ripe to walk the highest path on to its end!

The question therefore arises as to what all those are to do who in consequence of their previous, chiefly their antenatal, action, *Kamma*, for external or internal reasons are not ripe for the Saṅgha, in whom, however, on the other hand, more or less a "divination of the truth" has arisen, and thereby "trust in the Perfected One and in his Doctrine has become rooted and sent forth shoots."[321] To them also, as we know, the Buddha shows the way and precisely in the excellent eightfold path, points out to them also the only possibility of moral progress. Even in the world they may live in accordance with it in the measure of their capacity for doing so, and so far as the conditions under which they have to live, permit, be it that they have to confine themselves merely to creating the conditions for a favourable rebirth,** be it that they also may strive towards the great final goal of the complete overcoming of the circle of rebirth. Though they do not reach this, the highest goal of

* In the Dīghā-Nikāya XXVI, it is said in one passage that the Buddha was the leader of a body of disciples of a few hundreds, whereas the next Buddha will be the leader of a body of disciples numbering several thousands.

** This will probably always remain the standpoint of the multitude, as far as it is at all capable only of this minimum of forethought, to some extent to feel a little anxiety about the future after death.—To secure a favourable rebirth, according to the Buddha, the following five fundamental ethical precepts must be kept, which therefore apply also to all lay adherents: 1. Not to kill any living creature, whereby it is also forbidden to illtreat any creature. 2. Not to take things not given to us under any form, thereby neither in form of any imposition in business, or of direct fraud. 3. In the domain of sexual relations, always to keep within the bounds of the allowed, of course also in thoughts. To this it belongs especially not to enter into sexual relations, not only with the wife of another man, but also with no female who is still under the guardianship of her parents or other persons, and therefore not yet independent.

holiness in *this* life—in *this* embodiment Nibbāna according to what we have said above, can only be attained within the Saṅgha—nevertheless they may thus far curb and refine their passions and thereby their thirst for the world, that even in them the inner certainty may arise that at the moment of their approaching death they will never again attach themselves to a germ below the human kingdom; so that with every existence still in store for them, they come nearer to their eternal salvation. They, "having entered the stream, are safe from torment in the lower worlds and sure of the Full Awakening." They may even completely cast off "the Five Fetters of the low earthly life" that ever and again lead back to this our world of the five senses, namely, inclination towards sensual desire, towards ill-will, towards belief in personality, towards faith in the efficaciousness of ritual ceremonies and customs, and towards doubt,* so that after death they will no more return to this world, but in one of the highest worlds of light, attain Nibbāna.**

4. Not to tell knowingly an untruth, nor to make use of unpleasant modes of speech against other beings. 5. To avoid intoxicating or narcotic drinks. This minimum of true morality also, of course may only be attained by means of the holy eightfold path. Thus, one must travel it at all events as far as is needed in order to gain such sufficient insight into the perniciousness of our inclinations as will induce us to follow it within the limits of these five injunctions. For the monk, these injunctions are extended further. See below!

* Doubt in regard to the four excellent truths is meant. "Ghaṭīkāra the potter, O Mahārāja, does not doubt suffering, does not doubt the arising of suffering, does not doubt the annihilation of suffering, does not doubt the path leading to the annihilation of suffering," it is said in the 31st Discourse of the Majjhima-Nikāya. At this stage therefore, one has already gained such a deep insight into the four excellent truths that the inclination dwelling within us to doubt them, conditioned by ignorance and therefore fundamentally *unreasonable*,—from the highest standpoint it is equally as unreasonable as the inclination towards any kind of passion—is entirely removed and only the complete realization of the four excellent truths by the annihilation of all thirst for Becoming remains to be carried out.

The Five Fetters of the lower earthly life are dealt with in detail in the 64th Discourse of the Majjhima-Nikāya.

** There are four classes of saints: He who "if he wanted to do so, might say of himself: 'I have escaped from hell, escaped from the animal world, escaped from the realm of spectres, escaped from the byway, from the repudiated worlds, I have entered

The Saṅgha is nothing but an institution for the clearing away, in advance, of all those external hindrances that in the world generally make it impossible to keep closely and steadily to the holy eightfold path. In so far as we know how to avoid as much as possible these hindrances, also in the world, and thus to restrain them, successful progress may also here take place. Yea, it may even happen that one who remains in household life, may progress farther then another who has left it. "The Brahmins, O Gotama, speak thus: 'Who lives the household life, may effect true and real welfare. Who goes out from home, cannot do so.' Now what does Lord Gotama think about this?"—"For that matter I distinguish, O Brahmin, not do I pronounce a simple judgment. Whether one lives the household life or whether one goes out from home: if he is living wrongly,

---

the stream, I am safe from torment in the lower worlds and sure of the Full Awakening."[322] Because such an one has thus entered the stream leading to Nibbāna, therefore he is called "one who has entered the stream"—*Sotāpanna.* The Sotāpanna "still seven times among ghosts and men hastening through births, puts an end to suffering." 2. The "Once Returning." *Sakadāgāmī:* "There a man .... after having considerably weakened desire, hatred and delusion, only returns once more; and having returned once more to the world, he puts an end to suffering. This man is called a 'Once Returning One.'"[323] 3. The "Never Returning One," *Anāgāmī:* "There a man, after having annihilated the five fetters of the low earthly life, reappears among the spiriṭ-born beings, and there he is extinguished, never more does he return to that world. This man is called a 'Never Returning One.'" 4. The Perfect Saint, *Arahā,* who still during this life puts a complete end to suffering: "Such a monk nowhere returns."[324]—Thus it is only the reaching of the last stage that is denied to him who lives the household life. How a man has to live in the world, if he wants to reach the stage of an Anāgāmi, is taught by the example of Ghaṭikāra the potter in the 81st Discourse of the Majjhima-Nikāya quoted above. Meanwhile the reaching of perfect sanctity is not absolutely excluded for him who lives the household life; he may reach it at least in his dying hour. "I tell you, Mahānāma, that there is no difference between a lay disciple whose mind has reached this stage of deliverance (to direct his last wish towards the ceasing of Becoming), and a monk whose mind is freed from all influence, as far as the state of deliverance is concerned."[325] That as a lay disciple he can attain the complete annihilation of will only in his dying hour, follows from this, that, if in days of health he should penetrate to the immediate realization of Nibbāna, just because this presupposes the complete renunciation of all earthly things, he would also externally leave the world and thereby in every case reach Nibbāna as a monk.

I do not praise it. For whoso lives the household life, O Brahmin, and whoso goes out from home: if he lives wrongly, on account of his wrong living he cannot effect true and real welfare. Whether one lives the household life, O Brahmin, or whether one goes out from home: if he lives rightly, I praise it. For whoso lives the household life, and whoso goes out from home: if he lives rightly, on account of his right life he may effect true and real welfare."[326]

But of course he who withdraws from household life, other circumstances remaining the same, will make much easier and quicker progress than he who remains in household life. Yea, often his household and business relationships may be of such a kind that only a complete break with them will at all provide him even the possibility of working earnestly for deliverance. But even where they are exceptionally favourable, as remarked above, they can never be of such a kind as to make possible complete deliverance during this present lifetime, and the unshakeable certainty of the same. Therefore to those who make this highest goal their aim, it only remains to enter the Saṅgha. To these elect ones the Buddha appeals first. Hence, it will be clear without further argument that he makes the going into homelessness the starting-point for the realization of the holy eightfold path, and bases this path in all its parts upon this going, by leaving it to all who are not able or willing to fulfil this fundamental antecedent conditions to hold to the several stages of the Path, as far as is possible to them in their individual circumstances. And so he begins his description of the path of Deliverance, as it takes practical shape, with the going into homelessness.

"Here in this world, O monks, there arises an Accomplished One, an Exalted One, a Supremely-Awakened One, Perfect in Knowledge and Conduct, an Auspicious One, a

Knower of the World, an Incomparable Trainer of men who wish to be trained, a Teacher of gods and men, an Awakened One, a Holy One. And this entire universe with its deities, its Māras and its Brahmās, together with the whole race of ascetics and recluses, gods and men alike—this He expounds, having thoroughly understood it by His own superior insight, and he publishes abroad the Doctrine that is excellent in its origin, excellent in its progress and excellent in its goal. He makes known the Holy Life, perfect and pure. And a householder or a son of a householder or a member of some other class comes to hear that Doctrine and to put his confidence in the Accomplished One. And he thinks to himself: 'Cramped and confined is household life, a den of dirt. But the homeless life is as the open air of heaven. It is hard to live the Holy Life in all its perfection and purity while bound to home. Let me go forth to homelessness!' Accordingly, in a little while, he leaves all behind him and vows himself to the homeless life."[327]

2. MORAL DISCIPLINE

In the 125th Discourse of the Majjhima-Nikāya the Buddha compares himself to an elephant's driver. Just as such an one by means of a tamed elephant lures the wild elephant out of the elephant's forest into a clearing—"then the wild elephant has come into the clearing"—to take out of him his "forest-wonted behaviour, his forest-wonted longing, his forest-wonted obstinacy, obduracy, refractoriness," by methodically progressive exercises, and thus "to cause him to become accustomed to the environs of the village, and to adopt the manners in vogue among men," in the selfsame way the Buddha first induces man to wander forth from home into homelessness, there gradually to take out of him all his thirst for the world. With his going into homelessness, "the noble disciple has come into the clearing," starting out from which he has next to traverse that first part of the excellent eightfold path wich we have called "separating from the enemy." It consists in the disciple keeping in check the downward-tending motions of the thirst by which he is possessed, in no longer giving way to them, until in time he becomes entirely *disaccustomed* to them, in doing which, he also has to limit his relations with the world to the strictly necessary. The Buddha calls this first part of the way *"Sīla,"* moral discipline. It is precisely laid down in the following precepts of the Order:

"The monk abstains from all taking of life, shuns taking the life of any living creature. Laying aside cudgel and sword, he is mild and merciful, kind and compassionate towards every living creature.* He refrains from the taking of what has not been given him, shuns taking things ungiven. Taking only what is offered him, waiting for such gifts, he abides heart-free from all thievish intent. Refraining from unchastity, he lives the pure, the chaste life. He shuns the

* The disciple of the Buddha is on no account allowed knowingly to kill a living creature, be it even the most humble insect. If against this any one should refer to the saying of Schopenhauer: "But the insect in being killed does not suffer as much as man from its sting; the Hindus do not see through this," then the reply must be given that Schopenhauer himself has not understood the real point here. It is not a question of whether I or the animal suffers more pain at the moment. The point is, if I defend myself against an insect's sting by killing the insect, then, contemning another creature's welfare, I yield to my own thirst for physical wellbeing, instead of overcoming it, or at least satisfying it only by means which cause no pain to others. From this brutal assertion of my thirst for wellbeing, there will result after my death a new grasping; and this will cause me much more pain than the pain I should have had to stand from the insect's sting.—Then I ought to let myself be eaten up by lice; then we ought to let the animals, especially wild beasts, so increase that at last they exterminate the whole human race? Certainly not. If you are so much interested in maintaining yourself in a world with such co-inhabitants, then, if they endanger your life, or your necessary resources, you may kill them, if there are no other means of keeping them away, without fear of sinking down yourself into the animal kingdom, or even into the hell-world; for in these realms killing is done from malice or wantonly or at least upon the slightest occasion. Hence it is only a man who kills from *such*

sexual act, the vulgar, the common! He refrains from lying, shuns the uttering of untruth. He speaks the truth, holds to the truth; staunch and trustworthy, he is no worldly deceiver. He abstains from tale-bearing, shuns slanderous speech. What he hears in this quarter he does not repeat in that, so as to create trouble for people here; and what he chances to hear in that quarter, he does not repeat in this, so as to cause annoyance to the people there. Those at variance he brings together and those already in union he encourages. Concord pleases him, concord rejoices him, in concord is all his delight. He speaks words that make for concord; he refrains from harsh speech, shuns speaking roughly. Whatsoever words are blameless, pleasant to the ear, loving, heart-moving, courteous, charming and delighting all who hear them—such are the words he speaks. He abstains from idle chatter, shuns unprofitable conversation. Speaking in proper season, in accordance with fact, to the purpose, in accord with the Doctrine, in accord with the Discipline, his words are a precious treasure, full of appropriate comparisons, discriminating and to the point. He abstains from doing any injury to seeds or growing plants. He partakes

motives who generates in himself an affinity with them, and in consequence of this, will come to them. But on the other hand, of course, you must accept it into the bargain, that after death you will again be reborn in a world in which there are vermin and wild beasts with which you again will have to contend. For your thirst is still of such a kind that it desires to maintain itself at all costs also in such a world. But if you manage to let yourself be eaten up by lice or torn to pieces by wild beasts, instead of killing them, then this is only possible because your thirst for existence is already so exalted, and thereby your loosening from an environment such as your present one has gone so far, that on account of is, you would not do harm even to an insect. The consequence will be, that upon death which will follow as result of this, you will only have an affinity with worlds that are too high for such molestations, and therefore you will only be reborn in such worlds. And if all men were to act thus, then, of course, they would all disappear from the earth, but only to be settled in higher worlds more suited to them, and there to find themselves again. They would make their exit from this earth because it had become "too mean" for them, and as would be fitting, would abandon it wholly to the animals who then might be among their number.

of but one meal a day, eats no evening meal; he shuns eating out of proper season. He keeps away from singing, dancing and theatrical representations. He shuns using garlands, scents, unguents, ornaments, decorations, adornments. He abstains from using broad or high beds. He declines to accept gold or silver, uncooked grain or raw meat. He abstains from the possession of women or girls, slaves male or female, goats or sheep, fowls or swine, elephants, cattle, horses, mares, fields or lands. He avoids having aught to do with fetching and carrying messages. He abstains from trafficking and merchandising. He has naught to do with false balances, false weights or false measures. He shuns the crooked ways of bribery, deception and fraud. He keeps aloof from maiming, murder, abduction, highway robbery, wholesale plundering and every deed of violence.

"He is contented with the robes he receives for the covering of his body and with the food he receives for the maintenance of his life, and, whithersoever he goes, he takes with him only such things as are proper and necessary. Even as the winged bird, whithersoever it flies, bears with it only its wings, so the monk is contented with what he gets of clothing and food, and, journeying, takes with him only needful requisites."[328]

The means for a painstaking observation of these Rules of the Order are, as we know, provided by the cultivation of right concentration. The deep contemplation, to which the monk devotes himself till the evening in some secluded place, "under a tree of the forest, in a rocky recess, in a mountain cave, in a place of graves, in the heart of the jungle, or on a heap of straw in the open fields after having returned from his begging-round and partaken of his meal, sitting there with legs crossed under him, body held upright,"[329] furnishes effective motive force first for self-mastery within these limits; while the cultivation of constant recollectedness in general, causes this motive force to be present at every moment and thus to be able to determine our action. This constant recollectedness takes shape more exactly under the form of the Four Right Efforts. "There, ye monks, the monk generates in himself the will not to allow to arise within him evil and unwholesome things that have not arisen. For this he fights, striving courageously, and arms the mind, making it ready for combat. He generates within himself the will to expel evil and unwholesome things that have arisen within him. For this he fights, striving courageously, and arms his mind, makes it ready for combat. He generates within himself the will to make arise within him wholesome things that have not arisen. For this he fights, striving courageously, and arms his mind, makes it ready for combat. He generates within himself the will to maintain wholesome things that have arisen within him, not to let them disappear, but to bring them to increase, to development and full unfolding. For this he fights, striving courageously, and arms his mind, making it ready for combat."[330]

Thus the striving disciple, by systematically suppressing all evil motions and by cultivating the opposite good ones, upon the path of Right Concentration gradually passes round the former. "It is, Cunda, as if there were an uneven road, and another and a level road passed round it; as if there were a rugged landing-place, and another and a level landing-place led past it. In like manner the worker of harm may pass round upon the path of harmlessness, the unchaste person may pass round upon the path of chastity."[331] In other words: Right Concentration in time leads to *perfect morality,* for which very reason this first part of the path is regularly designated as "concentration ripened to morality."*[332]

* How concentrated right thinking in time chokes evil inclinations and causes good ones to arise, thereby leading to morality, may be seen with special clearness in the following passage: "Whatsoever a monk considers in mind and dwells upon at any

As a consequence, already at this stage a feeling of happiness arises, which, because beyond all evil, cannot generate any suffering. "By the faithful observance of this noble body of precepts of right conduct he enjoys cloudless happiness within."[333] But this wellbeing is not yet perfect. "Tell me, Udāyī: 'Is there a perfect wellbeing, is there a plainly indicated path for the reaching of perfect wellbeing'?"—"We have, O Lord, a saying which runs: 'There is a perfect wellbeing, there is a plainly indicated path for the reaching of this perfect wellbeing'."—"And what, Udāyī, is this plainly indicated path for the reaching of perfect wellbeing?"—"There, O Lord, a certain person has rejected killing, has rejected taking things not given him, has rejected debauchery, has rejected lying, or has taken upon himself yet other duties of an ascetic. This, O Lord, is the plainly indicated path for the reaching of perfect wellfare."—"What do you think, Udāyī? At the time, when one has rejected killing, rejected taking things not given to him, rejected debauchery and lying, taken upon himself yet other duties of an ascetic,—does one feel at such a time perfectly well, or well and ill?"—"Well and ill, O Lord."—"What do you think, Udāyī? If one has trodden the path which brings with it weal and woe, can one then attain *perfect* welfare?"—"The Exalted One has cut off the conversation, the Fulfiller of the Path has cut off the conversation."[333]

It was necessary to lay special stress upon this, since, even to-day, virtue is almost without exception taught to be the way to real and perfect happiness. Mere virtue can never lead beyond the world, more especially, not beyond the circle of rebirth. Hence it always provides, also for the period after death, only a relative happiness, that is to say,

---

length, to that his thoughts will incline. If the monk considers and turns over in mind at great length the thought of Craving, he drives away the thought of Renunciation, strengthens that thought of Craving." 333

such a happines as is possible within the world of the transient. It is with reference to this that the Buddha alludes to it as of minor value: "Mean, ye monks, and of subordinate importance; nothing but moral discipline, is what the average man means, when speaking approvingly of the Perfected One."[335]

This, of course, implies no disparagement of morality as such. In passing this judgment, the Buddha rather only wishes to say that the disciple cannot remain content merely with morality, since "there is still more to do."[337] For it is merely the first step leading to the great final goal of holy life; precisely as such, however, it is on the other hand absolutely necessary. For without it there is no real concentration; and thereby also no complete penetrating vision of our personality as *anattā*. But concentrated, that is to say, entirely objective, directly perceptive contemplation of the constituents of this our personality is only possible, when cognition is no longer disturbed by passionate upheavings of any kind, when the storms of willing that darken it have quieted, or when, as the Buddha says, "the coarser corporeal, mental, and vocal motions have been soothed down,"[338] in short, when the mind has become purified of all disturbance. And this same purity is the result of morality: "How then, friend? Is the Holy Life lived under the guidance of the Blessed One for the sake of purity of conduct?"—"Not for that, friend . . . . But, friend, purity of conduct leads to purity of mind; purity of mind to purified understanding; purified understanding to purified knowledge; purified knowledge to purified certitude."[339]

"By correct procedure, Visākhā, is obtained the purification of a spotted mind. But how, Visākhā, by correct procedure is purification of a spotted mind obtained? There, Visākhā, the noble disciple thinks of *the principles of moral discipline*, that are unbroken, comprehensive, always abiding the same, unspotted, liberating, praised by those of understanding, uninfluenced, recommended by the wise, not dictated by personal interests, *directed towards concentration.* In thinking *of morality*, his mind brightens, joy arises, and whatever exists of spots on the mind, disappears, even as a dirty looking-glass is cleansed by correct procedure."[340]

"Just as, monks, a man standing on the shore of a pond that is disturbed, turbid, muddy, notwithstanding that he has eyes, cannot possibly recognize either the oysters and shells at the bottom, the sand and gravel, nor the multitude of fishes swimming about, even because of the disturbed water; just as little, monks, can a disciple whose mind is not purified make his own the holy, the supramundane eye of insight, even because of his unpurified mind."[341]

Perfect morality thus constitutes the indispensable foundation of further progress on the way of deliverance. Its relation to concentration is the same "as if an acrobat, when he wishes to show his tricks, first digs up the earth, removes the stones and hard gravel, smoothens the ground, and so on soft ground performs his tricks:

Just as all life is based upon the earth,
So is the liberating code of morals
The base and soil whence springs all that is good,
The starting-point of every Wake One's doctrine."[342]

3. THE PART OF CONCENTRATION IN THE NARROWER SENSE

Our thirst for the world, that is, the sum of all our inclinations and disinclinations, ever and again from all eternity springs anew out of the activities of the senses. As soon as any object whatever comes within our range in the form of sensation and perception, instantly a motion of willing is aroused, in consequence of which it is either desired or hated. These motions in the passage of time have assumed the form of qualities of our character. As is perception, so is our volition. If at the present moment an object seems to me to be worth striving for, then I want it, I feel thirst for it. But if to-morrow I inspect it more closely, and now perceive that in truth it is something odious, and therefore that I was deceived yesterday in my judgment of it, then my desire is at once transformed into loathing. Now in reality every normal perception includes such a deception, since in truth no actual and possible object of the world proves itself worthy of being desired, since everything is transitory and thereby productive of suffering, and therefore fundamentally unfit for us. It therefore cannot possibly be otherwise but that every course of life is nothing but a continuous chain of disappointments. The tragic thing about it all, however, is this, that in spite of everything we are not cured of our desire. The reason of this is, that ever and again we allow ourselves to be cheated anew by perception into believing ever and again that things are as they represent themselves to be, that is, something really worth while. Hence, the source of all craving, and thereby of all misery, is really to be found in our defective *perception* or knowledge of things. We do not penetrate them to the very bottom, where without exception they conceal for us pain and disgust. In short, we are *in ignorance* of their real nature and of their true relationship to us. "Bhikkhus, I know nothing else on account of which desire, if not yet present, awakens, and if it is already present, increases and becomes powerful, save the perception of the agreeable. In him who takes notice of the perception of the agreeable *without thoroughly investigating it*, desire awakens, if it was not there before, and increases and becomes powerful, if it was already there."[343] As soon as perception in every direction has become correct and exhaustive, and *real* knowledge of things is thereby gained, without further ado complete soberness, *universal* disillusionment sets in, with the result that everything, even our own personality, is abandoned with a smile.

The reason of this defective perception is this, that we simply do not *want* to know what things really are, but only how far they may form suitable objects for our desires. In other words, we place our cognizing apparatus exclusively at the service of our desire, thus degrading the machine of the six senses into a mere machine of thirst. Accordingly, *right* perception is effected by paying no heed whatever to our thirst for objects and by investigating them as to what they are in reality, and independent of their qualities as objects of our desire. Only after having thus cognized their true nature may we proceed to inquire if thirst for such objects will at all pay itself. This may also be expressed in this way. We must use our apparatus of the six senses merely as *an apparatus of pure cognizing;* * we must look at things as cold, disinterested spectators; we must seek to obtain not a merely subjective, but an objective, picture of the world, such as would appear to a being that had no sort of desire whatever for the world, but merely wished to seize the objective facts of the same; a method of investigation which Schopenhauer illustrates by calling attention to the heads of angels with no body attached to them.

In the excellent eightfold path it appears in detail as *the noble restraint of the senses:*

"And having with the eye perceived a form, he does not dwell upon the form, takes no special note of the same. But inasmuch as the eye being unrestrained, occasion is

---

* As always, so also here, we must bear in mind that, as something inscrutable we stand behind our cognizing *apparatus*.

thereby given for the arising of craving and unhappiness and evil and insalutary thoughts, he practises restraint of the eye, keeps a watch upon it, brings it into subjection.

"And having with the ear perceived a sound, with the nose an odour, with the tongue a flavour, with the body an object of contaction, or with the mind an idea, he does not dwell upon the mental image thereof, takes no special note of the same. But inasmuch as these organs of sense being unrestrained, occasion is thereby given for the arising of craving and unhappiness and evil and insalutary thoughts, he practises restraint of these organs of sense, keeps a watch upon them, brings them into subjection."[344]

Thus one maintains incessant watch over the activities of the senses in order that they may never manifest themselves in the form of attachment to the object of sense, that is, manifest themselves in the service of thirst. This we do by never taking any interest in the object as a whole, or in any of its parts, but instead, in face of the thing seen or heard, managing to "call a halt" and soberly ascertain what in itself it may be, independent of the charms which it exerts over our desires. Then, we very soon see something quite different from what we had hitherto perceived. For instance, we no longer see simply a man or a woman, no longer see a delicate hand, a seductive smile that had hitherto kindled our passion, but only filth, put together, organised into this shape which sooner or later, also outwardly, will change back again into its original form, and which, even now has as little to do with that inscrutable out of which an attachment to it has arisen, as will be the case some day when, as a mass of dead matter, it is again thrown away like a worn-out garment. This matter, and this matter alone, albeit in organized form, is what is *really* present. The pleasing body, the graceful movements of which have hitherto enchanted me, the little mouth smiling so charmingly, the dark eye looking so inscrutable, are like a sparkling diamond which consists only of coal, is nothing but a chemical combination of carbon, hydrogen and other matter, built up into this form and kept in motion by a wave of thirst for such activity, a wave rising out of the inscrutable, that is, out of our real and deepest essence, to fall back again with the dissolution of those combinations and to rise again in another place, leading to a new grasping of a new matter. But the inscrutable itself, from which this thirst and this grasping have arisen, is at bottom, as essentially alien to all this as is space to the clouds that arise in it and out of it. As space by the lightnings that flash forth out of the clouds, so the inscrutable is incessantly traversed and set vibrating by the sensations aroused through the organism.

Thus does the world appear, if one looks at it not through spectacles dimmed by desire for it, but emptied of desire and thus in an entirely objective manner. Thus does it look to *purified* vision, even as it appeared of old to the elder Mahatissa. "It is said that once upon a time a certain woman who had married into a family of high rank, having quarrelled with her husband, adorned and embellished herself until she looked like a goddess, and then early in the morning started out from Anurādhapura to return to her family. On the way she met the elder who was just going for alms of food from the Cetiya mountain to Anurādhapura. As she caught sight of him, her vile nature caused her to laugh aloud. The elder looked at her with a searching glance, and noticing her teeth, he penetrated with his vision the disgusting nature of the body and attained Sainthood. Therefore was it said:

'The elder gazed upon her teeth
And thought upon impurity;
And ere he took another step,
The state of Sainthood he attained.'

Then came her husband, following in her footsteps, and seeing the elder, he asked: 'Sir, did you not see a woman passing along this way?' And the elder replied:

> 'I know not what along this way
> Went past, a woman or a man.
> But this I know, a set of bones
> Went moving on along this road.'"* [345]

Such a man no longer also hears simply charming or repellent sounds, but only what is really and alone existent in this direction, namely, vibrations of the air penetrating to his ear and there arousing a contact, an ear-contact, and thereby, the sensation of a sound. What hitherto made this sensation so agreeable or disagreeable to him, he now recognizes to be the mere subjective colouring applied by him to this meagre objective process. For it was pleasing or unpleasing to his will to be affected in this way, and cognition, being until now the obedient servant of this will, of course thought beautiful what pleased this same will, since it is the duty of the slave to admire all the fancies of his master; in short, he recognizes it to be an *illusion*. But who, consciously, would like to live in illusion? Only a child or a fool could do so. The man possessed of reason without further ado will repudiate even the most enchanting illusion, the moment he recognizes it to be such, since he very well knows that with it he is forsaking the world of reality and betaking himself to a world of seeming which, sooner or later,

---

* The teeth are especially well suited for contemplation:

First, they are evidently *anattā*, as the loss of all of them does not concern me in my essence.

Secondly, in their rottenness, often beginning quite early, they manifest with great clearness the all-pervading law of transitoriness.

Thirdly, as they provide us with nourishment, they remind us of everything in ourselves as consisting only of materials of the outer world and having thereby fundamentally nothing to do with ourselves.

inevitably must be shattered against the former, and hence, in the end, must bring him suffering. Therefore it is impossible that a man who has recognized that all music, objectively considered, is nothing but waves of atmospheric vibrations and thereby only a corresponding medley of sounds, can find any further delight in them. Certainly, in addition to this, music is an "agreeable sensation" of the greatest potency. But this sensation is just the "mere subjective colouring" mentioned above, inasmuch as the composer has created the poor objective process *as the language of his feelings and passions,* and the will, in those who subsequently listen to it, understands how to read this language, and thereby obtain that immediate insight into the wildly agitated sea of the feelings and passions of the composer, which moves it so much. But this sea in truth—perhaps the composer himself has died long ago—has long since dried up, in the same way that the present feelings of the hearer again will dissolve into nothing. The whole thing, therefore, in every direction, is nothing but a passing illusion. Whoso has penetrated this, *can* have no more desire for music, as little as a grown-up man can still find delight in the toys of his childhood, to play with which once gave him the keenest feelings of pleasure. Of course he must have *really* recognized it, that is to say, so that this consciousness is always clearly and unmistakeably present with him, especially at times when he actually hears music. *If* this is the case, then he will only smile at his hitherto having been able to become filled with enthusiasm by phenomena so transient in every way, and with the best will in the world he will be unable to see any difference between his former attitude and that of a child who spends his days in jubilantly chasing soap-bubbles. Therefore—one must have the courage to say this also—all great musical composers are nothing but manufacturers of playthings for big children; this, of course, be it well noted, only when viewed from the highest standpoint.*

Exactly the same is of course the case with the materials brought to us by the three other external senses, the senses of smelling, of tasting and of touching.

The sense of taste in particular, transmits to us nothing but the taste of the *corpses* of those plants and animals we use as food. For let this nourishment be prepared with as much refinement as we please, penetrating insight will always discover in it nothing but the odour and taste of corpses.

To be sure, this picture of the world is poor and wretched, so poor and wretched that men absolutely do not *want* to make themselves acquainted with it, for they may well divine that if they did, their appetite for the world might soon leave them. But who can seriously maintain that it is not true? And *if* it is true, if the world of the five senses—and we know of no other, and we can never become aware of another—is in truth poor and wretched, unspeakably poor and wretched, then again it stands sure that it can only be desired in consequence of a powerful illusion, in consequence of a grotesque self-deception, that is in consequence of *ignorance* of its real constitution. And it stands equally sure, that in the same measure in which insight into this its real constitution, thus, *knowledge*, is reached, every kind of thirst for it must die away. We recognize *that we lose nothing, if such objects vanish from us for ever*. Or should we really have missed anything, if we had not experienced all the agreeable sensations of our life up to this moment and were only now about to begin to live?** Surely not.

---

* Whoever feels inclined to revolt at this, thereby only shows that his cognition is not yet quite objective, but is still corrupted by his thirst (for music). Of course what has just been said does not exclude the possibility of noble music, as in general all art, leading upward to purer realms *within* the world.

** We only want to live because of agreeable sensations. From the disagreeable ones we directly flee, and the neutral ones leave us indifferent. But how few in

For every trace has disappeared from our memory of most of these sensations, as well as of all those innumerable sensations of our former existences; by which fact alone it is proven that they deserved nothing else but to be blotted out of our memory. But in the same sense must be answered the question as regards any point of time in our future that we choose to select, especially as regards the moment of our approaching death. So that, let us look at the matter in any way we please, we always come back to the same conclusion: *We really lose nothing if we forever let go that summation of all those sensations which we call life.**

But this not yet the *whole* truth. Were it only thus that we lose nothing by renouncing life, then with equal right it might be answered that in that case it could not be forbidden us to enjoy the harmless pleasures that blossom for us there, once we find ourselves placed in the world, even if these pleasures are only based upon illusion and self-deception. But whoever should speak thus, would not be paying sufficient regard to the statement made above, that every illusion sooner or later must take its revenge. For this revenge, a truly terrible one, consists precisely in this, that as long as we cultivate these illusions, we are unable to get out of the world; and hence, ever and again must accept into the bargain all its sufferings, in the shape of sorrow, sickness and ever repeated death, yea, at last also in the shape of a fall into the *abysses* of existence.

This is the whole truth about the world, as it presents itself when we look into it with *guarded senses,* hence, maintaining an attitude of pure cognition, that is to say, in

number are the former in comparison to the two latter kinds, even in regard to their number, to say nothing of their ingrained, deceptive character!

* In order completely to see into the worthlessness of life, one must as far as possible dissolve it into its several details. One will be astonished at the nothings of which it is made up. But what is worth nothing in its details, is also worth nothing as a whole.

the form of the noble restraint of the senses. Of course, this whole truth is not at once and without further ado realized even by this concentrated activity of mind in the stricter sense,—and it will be noticed that the noble restraint of the senses is nothing but the cultivation of concentration of mind in the stricter sense. For as the restraint of the senses may only be undertaken with prospect of success by a man who in severe moral discipline has already purified his mind of the grossest illusions and thereby of the more brutal expressions of thirst for the world, even so it must itself be gradually perfected, by incessant exercise, in the form of deep contemplation in some lonely place, thus, specially by means of the restrained, that is to say, concentrated, sense of thought, as also in unceasing watchfulness over all the senses in daily life, if the whole truth is to be unveiled to it. Its development, therefore, is also a *gradual* one.

First, the true nature of the objects of the senses can only be perceived as in a mist, in the same way that the unpractised eye can hardly distinguish the hazy contours of a distant mountain-chain on the horizon from a bank of clouds. Corresponding to this degree of cognition, the craving for the objects of sense can only be suppessed by incessant struggle. Attention must therefore chiefly be directed towards not allowing ourselves to be corrupted and caught by them afresh. "Therefore, Sāriputta, a monk has thus to scrutinize himself: 'On the way by which I went to the village for alms, at the place where I stood begging for alms, on the way by which I came back from the village from begging for alms, as respects the forms entering consciousness through the eye, as respects the sounds entering consciousness through the ear, as respects the odours entering consciousness through the nose, as respects the sapids entering consciousness through the tongue, as respects the objects of touch entering consciousness through the body, as respects the ideas entering consciousness through the organ of thought, has perhaps willing or greed or hate or delusion or contention arisen in my mind?' If now, Sāriputta, the monk recognizes during his contemplation: 'On the way by which I went to the village to beg for alms, at the place where I stood begging for alms, on the way by which I came back from the village begging for alms . . . willing or greed or hate or delusion or contention has arisen in my mind,' then such a monk, Sāriputta, has to struggle for liberation from these evil, unwholesome things. But, Sāriputta, if the monk recognizes during his contemplation: 'On the way by which I went to the village to beg for alms, at the place where I stood begging for alms, on the way by which I came back from the village begging for alms . . . willing or greed or hate or delusion or contention did not arise in my mind,' then such a monk, Sāriputta, has to maintain this same blessed and happy exercise day and night."[346] So long as the monk can maintain this exercise, albeit with continual struggle, he treads that stage of the holy path described by the Buddha in the following terms: "There, Udāyī, a certain person is on the way to abandon grasping, to put away grasping; and while he is on the way to abandon grasping, to put away grasping, memories bound up with grasping arise in him. And he gives no place to them, but puts them away, expels them, eradicates them, nips them in the bud."[347]

The more, especially, the insight arises within him that his body represents nothing more than a mechanism built up out of matter into an organized form, the more his efforts are directed above all against that kind of craving which is assumed by thirst in the form of the appropriation of nourishment, that is, in eating. It is precisely this expression of thirst which he will recognize as fundamentally cruel and therefore as especially vulgar and mean, inasmuch as the body generally can only be sustained by the continual destruction of other life. Therefore he confines himself to the strictly necessary in maintaining his body as the indispensable condition of reaching holiness, consoling himself with the thought that along with the one he will also be rid of the other. "There, Mahānāma, the holy disciple thoroughly heedful partakes of food, not for delight and enjoyment, not for pride and vainglory, but only to sustain this body, to maintain it, to avoid damage, to be able to lead a holy life, thinking: 'Thus shall I kill out former feelings and not allow new ones to arise, and I shall have enough for untainted wellbeing.'" * 348

While thus the monk adopts a more and more objective

* What is sinful in the taking of food lies in this, that other life is destroyed, and thereby suffering is caused in the world. Since animal life is more highly organized and much more sensible to pain than plant life, the good man will in no case, either directly or indirectly, be the cause of the killing of animals for his food. In consequence of this, he will not eat the flesh of any animal in any case where he has seen or heard or supposes that it has been killed for his sake. "There are three cases, Jīvaka, where *I* say that meat shall *not* be accepted: Seen, heard, supposed." 349 For the same reason, no one may offer the Perfected One or his disciples the flesh of an animal killed for this purpose. "Whoever, Jīvaka, takes life for the sake of the Perfected One or of a disciple of the Perfected One, incurs fivefold serious guilt. Because he commands: 'Go and fetch that animal,' thereby the first time he incurs serious guilt. Because then the animal, led to him in fear and trembling, experiences pain and torment, he for the second time incurs serious guilt. Because he then says: 'Go and kill this animal,' he for the third time incurs serious guilt. Because the animal then in death experiences pain and torment, he for the fourth time incurs serious guilt. Because he then gives unfitting refreshment to the Perfected One or the Perfected One's disciple, he for the fifth time incurs serious guilt." 349 But if we are in no way guilty of the animal's death, then we may quietly eat its flesh. For what is eaten in this way, is nothing but cast-off dead matter, like any other. Therefore the monk Kassapa replies to a layman who had reproached him for having accepted the prepared flesh of a fowl as alms:

"To hurt, beat, slaughter, prison aught that lives;
Thieving and lying, perfidy and secrecy,
Secretly spying, seducing others' wives,
This is called sinful; not the eating of flesh." 350

Certainly, the holy disciple will partake of this food, as of all nourishment, bearing in mind the death of the creature from which it has been taken, like parents who, on a journey through a desert, in despair kill their own beloved child, so as not all three to perish of hunger; and weeping aud beating their breasts, piece by piece devour it. Whoso thus looks upon food, will never return to this world. 351

attitude towards all the excitations of his senses, little by little his penetration into the real constitution of the corresponding objects, brings him to the point where the impressions of his senses no longer irritate him at all. He becomes "as one blind, dumb and deaf towards agreeable sights, sounds, odours, tastes, feelings, thoughts,"* and therefore becomes more and more free from them. They become of ever less importance to him, although the old serpent of thirst may now and then raise again its head and show its fangs; but already it has become so weak that it can do him no more serious harm. "Again, Udāyī, a certain person is on the way to abandon grasping, to put away grasping, and while he is on the way to abandon grasping, to put away grasping, *occasionally*, now and then, confused thoughts, memories bound up with grasping arise in him. Slowly, Udāyī, the thoughts arise, but quickly he puts them away, expels them, eradicates them, nips them in the bud. As if, Udāyī, a man should let two or three drops of water drip down upon an iron pan glowing the whole day over the fire,—slow, Udāyī, would be the fall of the drops, but very quickly would they be dissipated and disappear. Even so, Udāyī, there is a certain person on the way to abandon grasping,

* Above all, we may no longer occupy ourselves with the world by means of *the organ of thought*. The degree in which we continue to do this, is an infallible indicator of the intensity with which we still cling to the world. In the objects of the sense of thought, in the images of our fancy, in the conceptions and judgments hitherto formed, we preserve the reflection of the entire world hitherto experienced by us, in such a way, that our organ of thought is able to call them up at will, whereas the objects of the five external senses are often accessible to us only with difficulty. Therefore our thirst for the world is chiefly active in our organ of thought. By its means, the poor revel in riches, the rich in plans for the future, the man of science in the vision of the causal concatenations of the world. If therefore we wish to know, how much we still cling to the world, we need only examine how far we still occupy ourselves with it in thought. Therefore the problem of deliverance, in the last resort, consists not merely in becoming poor in outward possessions, but above all else, in becoming poor *in mind*, that is to say, in putting away everything *from the kingdom of our thoughts also*. (Compare chiefly Majjhima Nikāya 121st Discourse.)—This, of course, is also the meaning of that saying of the Christ: "Blessed are the poor in spirit."

to put away grasping, and while he is on the way to abandon grasping, to put away grasping, occasionally, now and then, confused thoughts occur to him, memories bound up with grasping. Slowly, Udāyī, those thoughts arise, but quickly he puts them away, expels them, eradicates them, nips them in the bud."[352]

Along with the intensity of concentration develops also its extension, until at last it extends over the whole behaviour of the monk. "The monk is clearly conscious in drawing near and in retiring; in turning his gaze upon an object and in turning his gaze away from an object; clearly conscious in stooping and in raising himself; clearly conscious in the wearing of his robes and in the carrying of his alms-bowl; clearly conscious in eating and drinking; in chewing and tasting; clearly conscious in voiding the body's waste; clearly conscious in walking, in standing still and in sitting; clearly conscious both in falling asleep and in awaking, both in speaking and in keeping silence."[353]

With this constant complete consciousness, in the light of which everything now takes place, the slavery of consciousness or cognition is now entirely broken through. Now it takes up an entirely objective standpoint in regard to the whole heap of processes constituting personality, and no longer *serves* them, but *rules* them, by now exercising the calling that by right belongs to it. "By cognition is the world guided, to the power of cognition is the world subject," that is, the world we experience in this heap of processes as our personality. Certainly, in regard to the purely corporeal processes it may not at present exercise any immediate and penetrating influence, but all the so-called mental processes, namely, the activities of perception and of mind in its widest sense, are completely subject to its control and thereby under its domination. "One cannot at once make pliant the body, but a mortal can dominate his mind."[354] And because he can do this, he can also free his mind from all inner disturbing emotions, by first of all completely stilling the external five senses and thereby putting a stop to the disturbances coming from without, so that it becomes entirely unified, entirely concentrated, and thus "can think clearly and correctly."[355]

The first condition, the complete quieting of the external senses, is attained, as we already know, by choosing "some solitary spot—the foot of a forest tree, a cleft in the rocks, a mountain cave, a place of burying, a thicket, or a couch of straw in the open fields." "There, however, there are no forms entering consciousness through the eye, that might be seen and seen again and desired; there are no sounds entering consciousness through the ear, that might be heard and heard again and desired; there are no odours entering consciousness through the nose, that might be smelt and smelt again and desired; there are no sapids entering consciousness through the tongue, that might be tasted and tasted again and desired; there are no objects of touch entering consciousness through the body, that might be touched and touched again and desired."[356]

If thus, everything external is silenced, through the power of insight, by way of the Four Right Efforts, the striving disciple can now make disappear, one after the other, all inner motions still alive within him and constituting a hindrance to concentrated and intuitive thought. This he effects by sitting down cross-legged on the ground with body held upright and confronting them in a purely objective manner, and contemplating them so long in all their perniciousness, that eventually they melt away like ice in the sun. What states must thus be overcome to their final residue, the Master tells us by enumerating the Five Hindrances, *nīvaraṇā*, which we have just called the hindrances to pure thinking. We learnt about them above.* They are, love

* See above, p. 345.

for the world or sensual desire; ill-will and pleasure in doing harm, also rendered as grudging and resentment; mental langour and slackness; anxiety and disquietude, and doubt. By entirely removing these hindrances, the disciple has "learned to know the impurities of the mind, the crippling; and free from sensuality, free from evil states of mind," he *meditates and thinks*,[357] no longer disturbed by anything therein, with quieted body, in tranquil serenity and extreme energy, in short, in Right Concentration.* He fixes his attention upon the machinery of his personality. He "sees how sensations arise within him, sees how they are there, sees how they dissolve; he sees how perceptions arise within him, sees how they are there, sees how they dissolve; he sees how thoughts arise within him,** sees how they are there, sees how they dissolve; . . . . he dwells in the contemplation of the arising and passing away of the five groups of grasping: Thus is corporeality, thus is the arising of corporeality; thus is the passing away of corporeality;*** thus is sensation, thus is the arising of sensation, thus is the passing away of sensation; thus is perception, thus is the arising of perception, thus is the passing away of perception; thus are the activities of the mind, thus is the arising of the activities of the mind, thus is the passing away of the activities of the mind; thus is consciousness, thus is the arising of consciousness, thus is the passing away of consciousness."[359]

Thus with iron energy in concentrated contemplation he cultivates the Anattā-view from day to day, from month to month, from year to year, until at last the great moment comes,† when the clouds of ignorance are completely

---

* "He of quieted body is at ease. Whoso is at ease, his mind attains to collectedness and calmness." 358

** The Saṅkhārā in their narrower sense, as forming the fourth group of grasping.

*** To penetrate the passing away of the corporeality, the contemplation of corpses serves.

† When will it come? In the Aṅguttara-Nikāya I, p. 271, it is said: "It does not stand in the power, the capacity of the farmer that to-day his corn may grow,

scattered, and the vaporous veil woven by his desire around his personality and its world, through which, as through some mist, despite all his efforts, he hitherto only has been able to look at reality, is completely torn asunder at a single jerk,* and now "wisely penetrating, while in the body he envisages the highest truth," in seeing before him with pure and direct vision, the nature of this personality in all its naked reality, he recognises its machinery as manifested in the sixfold activity of the senses, as the product of a mechanism built up out of filth which is exhaustively

---

to-morrow bear fruit, and the day after to-morrow ripen, but there will come a time when that corn of the farmer has reached the right moment where it bears fruit and ripens. Even so also it does not stand in the power, the capacity of the monk that to-day or to-morrow or the day after to-morrow his mind becomes totally delivered from the influences; but, ye disciples, there will come a time, when the mind of the monk who trains himself in high morality, high spirituality [concentration] and high science, will be totally delivered from the influences." In the 10th Discourse of the Majjhima-Nikāya, the Master says: "Whosoever, O monks, shall so practise these Four Foundations of Recollectedness for seven years, may expect one of these two results: either he will attain to full deliverance in this present life, or else—a portion of grasping still remaining—to no more returning when this present life is ended. But setting aside all question of seven years: whosoever shall practise these Four Foundations of Recollectedness for six, five, four, three, two, or even for one year,—nay, setting aside all question of one year: whoso shall practise these Four Foundations of Recollectedness for seven months even, may expect one of these two results: either he will attain to full deliverance in this present life, or else—a portion of grasping still remaining—to never more returning when this present life is ended. But setting aside all question of seven months: whoso shall practise these Four Foundations of Recollectedness for six, five, four, three, two months, one month or even for half a month; nay, —setting aside all question of half a month: whoso shall practise these Four Foundations of Recollectedness for seven days even, may expect one of these two results: either he will attain in his present life to full deliverance, or else—a portion of grasping still remaining—to never more returning when this present life is ended." And in the 85th Discourse of the *Majjhima-Nikāya* it is said that a monk who has taken the Perfect One as his guide, if beginning in the evening, in the morning may find the way out; and beginning in the morning, in the evening may find the way out. That is to say, everything depends upon the capacity which a man brings with him to the treading of the Path, as well as upon the energy with which he pursues it, as is specially expounded at more length in the second passage quoted.

* The highest intuitive insight comes like a flash of lightning, "just as, disciples, a man in the gloom and dark of night upon the sudden flashing of lightning might with his eyes recognise objects." 360

summed up in grasping of filth, even if this is ultimately refined and rarified till it takes the form of thoughts,* and which, precisely on account of this its nature, can represent nothing else but a machine of suffering.

Further, he recognizes this mechanism ceaselessly renewing itself from all eternity, as conditioned by his thirst for the world of filth and thereby of death,** and on this very account he also finally recognizes that with the total annihilation of this thirst, at his approaching death he will be completely and for ever freed from the dreadful nightmare of this realm of Anattā, of Not-the-*I*, if he clings to nothing more, so that, after the definitive coming to a stop of all organic processes—*sabbasaṅkhārasamatha*—nothing, nothing at all will disquiet him any more. And he recognizes all this as clearly and directly, sees himself as distinct from all the components of his personality, the elements of suffering, as a man looking into the clear water of a lake spread out at his feet, knows himself distinct from this lake, and at the same time with his vision penetrates the lake in all its component parts.

"Suppose that in a mountain gorge there is a lake, clear, tranquil, still, and that a man stands on the bank of the same and looks down at the shells and pebbles and sand below, and at the droves of fish as they move hither and thither or remain at rest. And suppose that man to say to

* Compare the following: "As, ye monks, even a little bit of filth smells badly, so, not even for a small space of time, should I wish to be reborn, not even for a moment." 361—If any one, in view of this contemptuous characterization of the body endowed with six senses as formed of filth, should refer to the aptness of its construction and the beauty of its form, the Buddhist at the outside would concede this only in so far as it remained noteworthy that anything of this sort could be brought about out of mere filth.

** What dissolves in us, is simply and solely appropriated nourishment. " 'This has become'—see you this, monks?"—"Yea, Lord."—" 'Through that Nutriment originated,'—see you this, monks?"—"Yea, Lord."—" 'With the ceasing of that Nutriment, what has become likewise ceases'—see you this, monks?"—"Yea, Lord." 362

himself: 'How clear and tranquil and still is this lake! There are the shells, there the pebbles, there the sand and there the little fishes moving here and there or remaining quite still!' In the selfsame way the monk cognises: 'There is Suffering, there its Arising, there its Ceasing and there the way that leads to its Ceasing.'"[363]

But though the "four perversities" of his former thinking are thus gone, namely "holding the Not-the-*I* to be the *I*, the perishable to be the imperishable, suffering to be happiness, and the repellent to be the lovely,"[364] still, he has not yet come to the conclusion: "A Supremely Awakened One is the Blessed One, well proclaimed is His Doctrine, well living is His Brotherhood."[365] For at first he only intuitively recognizes the realm of Anattā as to its boundaries, its peculiarities, and its conditionedness. But the condition itself, thirst, is not yet abolished. But now he comes to the conclusion. For "thus perceiving, thus comprehending" this his thirst is no longer able to exist, "it vanishes from him without leaving a remainder," and thus the holy disciple beholds "his mind liberated from the influences of sensual desires, liberated from the influences of (craving for) Becoming, liberated from the influences of ignorance."* Thereby in the delivered one "this insight arises: Delivered am I; Life is lived out, the Holy Goal achieved; done all that was to do; for me this world is no more."[366]

With this, his departure out of the world is fundamentally completed. Though, as a rule, he will wait for the complete withering away of the components of his personality, as the product of his former thirst,** he has become so much a stranger to this personality, that there stirs within him no

* In these three varieties of *Āsavā* are regularly summed up the influences that disturb the cognitive activity.

** The redeemed saint has overcome life. The next thing would seem to be that he should also externally put an end to it by suicide, after having internally separated himself entirely from it. But this, as a rule, he will not do, precisely because life has

self-satisfaction because of its possession, and hence no inclination to bring it into any essential relationship to himself. He has reached that concentration where neither in regard to his body endowed with consciousness, nor in the face of external phenomena, the onslaughts of the pride that thinks "I" and "mine," any longer make their appearance. And in possession of this deliverance of the mind, the deliverance through wisdom, he abides.[368] Hence also, from now on his attitude toward the components of his personality and the whole world is one of the most perfect equanimity, such equanimity being only the positive side of the annihilation of all thirst for the world. Nothing concerns him any more, not even death which only annihilates what he now intuitively recognizes as not belonging to him, and in addition, as full of suffering: "He stands unawed by any in heaven or earth. And perceptions do not lay hold of Him, the Holy One, who lives apart from desires and questionings and distress of mind, and thirsts no longer for existence."[369]

He has swum across the stream that separates this world of death from the realm of deathlessness,* and from "this

---

become indifferent to him, so indifferent that with a smile he would offer his breast to his murderer for the deadly thrust:

> "In dying I do not rejoice;
> In living I do not rejoice.
> In patience I wear out this form,
> Clear, conscious, wisely well aware."[367]

Nevertheless, serious bodily pain may well furnish a reason for his throwing away life by suicide, just because it has become a matter of entire indifference to him. In this way, for example, did Channa act, as narrated in the 144th Discourse of the Majjhima-Nikāya, where the Buddha upon Sāriputta telling him that this seemed blameworthy to the friends and colleagues of Channa, approves of his action in the following words: "I do not say, Sāriputta, that this is blameworthy. Whoever *abandons one body, Sāriputta, and assumes another*, he, I say, is to be blamed. This is not the case with Channa the monk. Channa the monk has taken the weapon without fault."

* The Buddha calls the world the realm of death — *māradheyya* — as opposed to the realm of deathlessness-*amāradheyya*.[370] We call it *Nature*, the realm of eternal birth. This is, of course, just as correct; the world may just as well be called the realm of *nature* as that of *morture* (Schopenhauer). But precisely in this difference of denomination is expressed with especial clearness the difference of standpoint. Who adheres to life, sees only its

shore, full of perils and terrors," he has reached "the other shore, secure and free from perils and terrors."[372] Thereby he has left everything behind him, even the doctrine of the Buddha, which also was only to serve the purpose of "a raft" for this crossing, "meant for escape, not meant for retention."[372] As beyond all wisdom, he is also beyond good and evil: "Understanding the similitude of the raft, O disciples, ye must leave righteousness behind, how much more unrighteousness!"[372]

Thus it was the "mind ripened in wisdom" by concentration[373] which, like a diamond that nothing can resist,[374] annihilated everything, with the result that it is itself thrown away, after its task has been performed.

---

eternal renovation; who is wise, sees the end to which everything is subject. — As a rule, in the Canon, death, in this his quality as supreme ruler of the world, is personified as *Māra, the evil one,* the prince and bestower of all wordly lust, who in fact is nothing else but death in disguise, inasmuch as he who serves it, is subject to death. But this personification, in contrast to the figure of the Lucifer in the Bible, always remains apparent as such, as is made clear in the more specific appellation of Māra, as *Māra pāpimā,* literally meaning not "Māra, the Evil One," but "Māra, the evil." In this obvious personification of wordly lust, reality is reproduced in the most perfect manner. In every man, his passions assume the form of uncanny, independent powers to the *suggestions* of which — notice this peculiar form of speech! — we are given a prey. In one who is becoming a saint, in whom the struggle with them increases to the terrible intensity of an actual fight to the death, of which the average man has no idea, at the culminating point of the struggle in view of the fact that the saint recognizes them as powers alien to his innermost essence and therefore entirely hostile, they condense, before their final collapse, into a last tremendous upheaving in visionary shape, namely, into that of the Fiend, as we find, not only among Buddhists, but also in the case of the Christian saints. — That Māra in every case is really nothing but a personification, is, for the rest, expressly taught. Rādha says to the Buddha: "Māra, Māra, it is said, O Lord; but who, O Lord, is Māra?" — „The body, truly, Rādha, is Māra: sensation is Māra; perception is Māra; mentation is Māra; consciousness is Māra." 371

The foregoing exposition deals with the primary origin of the figure of Māra. Later on, after it had become known to the world through the accounts of those who had experienced it, in consequence of human predilection for such personifications, and in order dramatically to increase the effect of the words of the Master, it was often introduced by the compilers of the Canon into the framework of the narratives wherein those words are transmitted to us.

4. THE ABSORPTIONS
THE HIGHER KNOWLEDGE

We called the body endowed with senses the six senses-machine, and we saw in the foregoing that this machine, if used by way of concentration as merely a machine for cognition, may serve to penetrate to the bottom, the world as well as the machine itself, and thereby to kill every desire for them. But in order that this machine may be placed exclusively at the service of our newly awakened will for perfectly objective cognition that in no wise is influenced by the thirst animating us, all the disturbing influences of the motions of the mind, that in addition arise in a sort of automatic fashion within the machine in consequence of our being accustomed to them, must be excluded. The Buddha vividly pictures to us this gradual concentration of the six senses-machine upon the activity of pure cognition, or the gradual spiritualization of its work, in the following manner:

"There exist, monks, great impurities of gold, like sand mixed with earth and stony gravel. The gold-washer or the gold-washer's assistant therefore pours the gold into a tub, cleans it, purifies it thoroughly, washes it. When now these impurities have disappeared, have been removed, then, ye monks, there still remain mediocre impurities, such as fine gravel and coarse sand. And the goldwasher or the gold-washer's assistant cleans the same gold, purifies it thoroughly, washes it. When now these impurities have disappeared, have been removed, there remain, ye monks, still some small impurities over, such as fine sand and black dust. And the goldwasher or the goldwasher's assistant cleans the same gold, purifies it thoroughly, washes it. When now these impurities have disappeared, have been removed, then only the gold-sand remains. This sand the goldsmith or the goldsmith's assistant pours into a crucible, melts it, melts it together, melts it thoroughly. Now the gold has molten, molten together, molten entirely, but it cannot yet be used, it is not yet free from dirt, it is neither pliable nor malleable nor shining; it is brittle and not yet fit to be worked.

"But, ye monks, there comes a time when the goldsmith or the goldsmith's assistant again melts this gold, melts it together, melts it thoroughly, and when this gold, molten, molten together, molten thoroughly, ready for use, free from dirt, pliable, malleable and shining, is not brittle, but is fit to be worked. In the making of whatever ornaments we wish, be it a diadem, an ear-ring, a necklace or a golden chain—this purpose it fulfils.

"Even so, ye monks, there are in the monk earnestly training himself in high spirituality* great impurities, such as bad behaviour in deeds, words and thoughts. These the thoughtful monk, animated by high aspirations, gives up, puts away, destroys, causes to disappear.

But if these are given up and destroyed, then in the monk earnestly training himself in high spirituality, there still remain the mediocre impurities such as sensual thoughts, hating thoughts and cruel thoughts. These the thoughtful monk, animated by high aspirations, gives up, puts away, destroys, causes to disappear.

"But if these are given up and destroyed, then in the monk earnestly training himself in high spirituality there still remain the small impurities such as thinking about his relatives, thinking about countries, and the thought of not being despised. These the thoughtful monk, animated by high aspirations, gives up, puts away, destroys, causes to disappear.

"But if these are given up and destroyed, then the thoughts about mental states remain. And here concentration is

* That is to say, in pure thinking, or in Right Concentration.

neither quiet nor exalted nor full of peace and unity, but it is a training maintained by painful suppression. But, monks, there comes a time, when cognition becomes inwardly firm, becomes entirely pacified, becomes unified and collected. This concentration, however, is tranquil, exalted, full of peace and unity, is not a training maintained by painful suppression,"[375] the five hindrances of pure thinking are completely thrown down; there reigns "peace and clear-sightedness," that are "valid" for "the analysis of the several elements" and thereby, as we have seen, for the penetration of the constituents of our personality as *anattā*.

This tranquility and clear-sightedness may reach such a depth that not only do we become indifferent to the outer world, but the external senses entirely cease to function, *so that such a man becomes totally insensible to impressions from without.*[376] Thereby he has entered the state of the *Absorptions, the Jhānā*, of which we have already made the acquaintance in regard to their blissful effects.* By becoming completely released from the five external senses, and from every kind of sensual thought resulting from them, we have become pure will for insight. There has set in a complete standstill of all remaining motions of willing, of such sort that only the still living will for pure insight now can act, undisturbed and in perfect freedom. This activity is therefore soon entered upon in the first Absorption which consists in "energetical thinking and contemplating." Of course, here again the five groups of grasping, as comprehending the totality of all suffering, form the object of contemplative thinking.**

---

* Compare above p. 347.

** Compare the passage quoted above, p. 382 *et seq.*: "And what, Venerable One, are the mental images that pertain to Concentration?"—"The Four Foundations of Recollectedness"—having the five groups of grasping for their object—"friend Visākha, are the mental images that pertain to Concentration," wherein we only have to bear in mind that the Absorptions constitute concentration *par excellence*. Because of this, the four first ones are regularly given as examples of Right Concentration. 377

But this contemplation of suffering is here taken as a starting-point in order by its means to effect temporarily a complete overcoming of our personality and thereby a complete "temporary deliverance." The way to this is as follows.

The basis of it is given in the 101st Discourse of the Majjhima-Nikāya. There the Buddha explains to the Jainas who think they can escape the consequences of their former wrong-doing by means of self-mortification, and thereby, as well as by avoiding the doing of new deeds, believe they can attain to the complete drying-up of suffering, that their attempts must be fruitless, since the effect always follows its cause with the iron necessity of a natural law, and therefore it is impossible to escape the consequences of deeds committed in former existences. The means chosen by the Jainas he characterizes as especially foolish, since, to the evils arising in consequence of their former deeds they add the present pains of their entirely useless self-mortifications. Then the Buddha proceeds to show, how in spite of all former wrong living, and its consequences now appearing little by little in the form of suffering of all kinds, "true well-being" may be won. This is effected by not allowing our mind to be overcome by these now-appearing evil consequences, in remaining *undisturbed*. This is reached by "overcoming attachment." For every occurrence only becomes a painful one for us by endangering or destroying an object dear to us, be this object money and property, or a person, or our own body.* If now I am able to tear out my attachment to this object, so that it leaves me in future indifferent, then the occurrence that threatens this object is divested of its pain-producing character. Whoever has become indifferent towards all possessions, to him the loss of these

* Here we may again call attention to our standing, as something inscrutable, behind everything, therefore also behind our own body.

possessions no longer means suffering. Even the physical pains of our own body are not appraised as real suffering, if we have lost all attachment to the body. We then have a man who smiles amid tears. True wellbeing is not denied him even in the midst of pains, since a supramundane happiness transfigures them, as the setting sun overflows with gold the clouds that enwrap it. Thus does the man become who overcomes attachment. But *how* is attachment overcome? By bearing ever in mind that it is just this attachment that is the cause of all suffering, until "what is within me of desire and attachment, is abnegated." In this way, the contemplation of suffering, and of its being causally conditioned, directly becomes the means to true wellbeing in all the circumstances of life. If this true wellbeing has been reached, then the contemplation of suffering has fulfilled its purpose in this particular case. "And later he does not bear suffering in mind any more. And why not? The object, ye monks, for which the monk might bear suffering in mind—this object he has attained."

Thus does the monk act especially in the first Absorption. He contemplates the components of his personality in their quality as factors of suffering acutely and persistently, until all desire and all attachment to them is extinguished, though perhaps only temporarily. As soon as this is attained, there is no more occasion for thinking any further about suffering, and so he thinks and contemplates no more. At the same time it becomes easy for him also to get rid of the *tendency* of will to continue contemplation, by following the admonition of the Master: "Welcome, O monk, with the body keep watch over the body, in order not to hide within yourself a thought pertaining to the body; with the sensations keep watch over the sensations, in order not to hide within yourself a thought pertaining to the sensations; with the mind keep watch over the mind, in order not to hide within yourself a thought pertaining to the mind; with the phenomena keep watch over the phenomena, in order not to hide within yourself a thought pertaining to the phenomena."[378] The monk who has got thus far, will now rather abandon himself entirely to this blessed happiness of being entirely independent of the components of his own personality, into which now deepen the joy and happiness that had already found their way to him with the disappearance of the Five Hindrances,* in consequence of his practice of the contemplation of suffering. He dwells in the state of the Second Absorption: "Stilling thinking and contemplating, in deep inward quietude bringing the mind to One-ness, having ceased from thinking and contemplating, in the joy and bliss that are born of concentration, the monk attains to the Second Absorption."

But the monk does not tarry on in this. He reminds himself that this also is not yet the Goal, for "this also, Udāyī, I call subject to motion. And what is subject to motion? What in this is not eradicated as blissful joy, that passes here as motion... But this I call not enough, and I say, 'Reject it!' and say, 'Overcome it!'"[379] And so the monk proceeds to concentrate his cognizing faculty upon this motion of blissful joy peculiar to the second stage of Absorption, to penetrate it also as a mere expression of thirst, and thereby to cause it to disappear. When this is effected, the result is that complete equanimity enters in face of the upheavals of the elements of personality, not yet pure, but still connected with a new, though still more refined motion of will, namely, happiness over this very equanimity that now has supervened. "Joyous, passion-free, even-minded, the monk abides clearly conscious and recollected, and in the body tastes the bliss of which the Noble Ones say: 'The man of even and collected mind abides in bliss!' So he attains to the Third Absorption."[380]

* Compare above p. 345 *et seq.*

But also of this bliss the words of the Master hold good: "This also, Udāyī, I call subject to motion . . . . I call it not enough, and say: 'Reject it!' I say: 'Overcome it!'"[381] For this very reason the striving disciple does not tarry in it too long, but causes it also to disappear in the fire of his cognition which, like a burning-glass, he sets to work also upon this motion of bliss by means of his will for pure cognition so that at last there only remains perfectly purified, absolute equanimity in face of the totality of the processes of personality, whereby the fourth stage of Absorption is gained. "Leaving pleasure and pain behind, with the fading out of all past joy and sorrow, in the painless, pleasureless purity of an even and concentrated mind, he attains to the Fourth Absorption."[382] "And this, Udāyī, I call subject to no motion."[383]

But now he further recognizes: "This Fourth Absorption also has become, is put together by thought, is changeable, must perish;"[384] hence it is not yet the highest. Accordingly, soon it is no longer enough for him that he dwell in the most perfect equanimity in regard to the world of the senses as this still presents itself to his thought-consciousness; for *immediate* contact with it by means of the five external senses he has long since ceased to maintain. He does not want to know anything at all about it any more, and therefore desires to exterminate from himself this last reflex of it in his thought-consciousness also. This he achieves, as we already know,* by concentrating his cognizing faculty upon the perception of *boundless space*, then, leaving this, upon the perception of the *boundlessness of cognition* itself, to find it at last empty of every kind of contents. This condenses into the perception of absolute voidness which he now sees

---

* See above p. 329. There the monk has reached the realm of boundless space by having first completely quieted his mind by concentrating it upon the representation of "earth." To this point we shall return later on.

before him, *the realm of Nothingness*. But these states also he recognizes to be the result of an operation of the sixth sense, the sense of thinking,* therefore as something "thought together," and therefore something that has *become*, and so still belongs to the realm of transitoriness. The consequence is, that out of this insight there now grows up the will not to think any more, therefore also to will nothing more, since at this stage all willing exhausts itself in the activity of the organ of thought. And so he next abandons activity of thought also up to that last residue in which he only just perceives how now also all perception comes to an end—*the boundary of possible perception*—until finally also this last and most refined motion of willing is entirely extinguished, and with it also the last remainder of cognition still maintained by it. With this, complete freedom from sensation and thereby perfect peace are realized.**

As we see, this "temporary deliverance," that is, the transient complete abrogation of all willing, exactly like eternal deliverance, becomes possible first through all willing corresponding to thirst, that is, to our inclinations, being overcome by the newly awakened will for pure insight, and then next, by this pure will for insight itself being also stage by stage stifled by means of insight attained. *All willing is killed by an ever new willing that is directed towards the recognition of our former willing as something unsuited to us*, whereby the omnipotence of cognition is once more made manifest.

But this omnipotence of cognition reveals itself in yet another way. For as soon as we have it completely in our

* "When the activities of the five senses are suspended, with the purified, mental consciousness the Sphere of Boundless Space is to be known, the Sphere of Boundless consciousness—the Sphere of Nothingness is to be known." [385]

** The first Four Absorptions are called *rūpa-jhānā*, because they are perfected within, and in face, of the corporeal world. The four others, that is, the realm of boundless space, of the boundlessness of cognition, of Nothingness and of the boundary of possible perception, are called *arūpa-jhānā*, as lying beyond the corporeal world.

power, as soon therefore as we are able to concentrate it upon any object we choose in all its keenness and clarity, no longer dimmed by anything, and at the same time, continuously, without a break; so soon, therefore, as it becomes, not only "purified, pure, spotless and undimmed," but also "yielding and pliable," and on the other hand again, "firm and unshakeable," which comes about in the Fourth Absorption, whereby it becomes independent of all the influences of the world of the senses, it penetrates the whole realm of Anattā and thereby the whole world in every direction, spatially as well as temporally, as also in its causal concatenations. For it is just as boundless as its object, the world itself,—a quality about which the striving disciple becomes immediately clear, when he immerses himself in the "realm of the boundlessness of cognition." If, however, cognition in itself is boundless—apart from the *actual* hindrances, the which precisely the saint has overcome—as well in respect of its intensity as of its extension, then there is nothing astonishing in its being able, in its entirely free and pure activity, to convey to us corresponding knowledge. To doubt this in advance as an impossibility is therefore just about as reasonable as it would be if a South sea islander were to laugh at the assertion of an astronomer that he could so strengthen his power of sight by means of ground and polished glasses as to be able to see in the depths of the vault of heaven stars that no mere eye could ever behold, and could plot out the course of the heavenly bodies for hundreds of years, in the past and in the future. Why should things cognizable generally in themselves, not be actually attainable to cognition brought to the climax of its development? Or, to use the words of the Buddha, why should not, to the man who has brought his cognition to this highest point of development, "to whatever thing attainable by cognition he directs his mind in order to attain it by insight, precisely there and there attainment be granted, according to the mode of its effecting?"[386]

These things to which the saint directs his purified cognition, are as follows:

"If the monk should wish: 'With the Heavenly Hearing, the purified, the superhuman, may I be able to hear both kinds of sounds, the heavenly as well as the earthly, the distant as well as the near'—then there he always attains the faculty of realization.*

"If the monk should wish: 'Penetrating with my mind, and beholding the inmost hearts of other beings, of other men, may I perceive in their actual condition the minds that are given to Craving or to Hatred or to Delusion, as well as those that are free from Craving, free from Hatred, free from Delusion,'—then there he always attains the faculty of realization.

"If the monk should wish: 'May I recover the memory of my many varied existences'—'With the heavenly eye, the purified, the superhuman, may I behold how beings

* The saint is also able to come into touch with the beings of other worlds, and to hold conversation with them. These worlds of the gods are distinguished from one another by the degree to which their inhabitants have become loosened from the dominion of the six senses, as this loosening is realized step by step by the saint in his gradual ascent to Nibbāna; because of which precisely, he experiences already here below all the heavens, one after the other. In accordance with this, the lower heavens consist in a refined sensuality, whereas the highest ones are identical with the *arūpa-jhāna*, (see above p. 451**; compare Majj. Nik. 120th Discourse). For this reason we get those descriptions of the bliss and supernatural peace experienced by the traveller upon the path of deliverance —(cf. above, p 345 *et seq*) — in the course of his gradual loosening from the world, as also those descriptions of *heavenly* pleasures and *heavenly* peace. — As soon as the disciple, in cultivating concentration, reaches the state corresponding to a certain heaven, he *to this extent* is able to realize the powers slumbering in us all, of acting at a distance, such powers, for example, as clairvoyance, but especially, second sight, the foretelling of death. In order to understand this somewhat, we must specially remember what is said in the text above, that the element of cognition, by means of which we are connected with the world, is "infinite," so that we are able to reach the whole world in all its heights and depths, if only the will, bearing and directing it, is powerful enough.

disappear and reappear, according to their deeds'—then there he always attains the faculty of realization."*[387]

Because thus with his cognition he penetrates everything, and because, as we already know, the world is governed by cognition, is subject to its power, therefore the man possessed of cognition deals with the world, his own body included, as we can always deal with a foreign thing that we have brought entirely into our power. He "delights in the various magical powers, one after the other; as being single, to appear manifold of form; and having been manifold, again to become single of form; to appear and disappear; to float unhindered through walls, barriers and rocks, as if through air; to sink into and rise out of the earth as if it were water; to travel on water without sinking, as if upon dry land; to move through the air like the winged bird; in the greatness of magical power and might, to hold and handle the very sun and moon, wielding his body at will even up to the world of Brahma." **[388]

To be sure, *how* this comes about, cannot be penetrated in detail by normal cognition, just because it is excluded from this domain; therefore it is quite useless to launch out into hypotheses and theories regarding it.*** The Buddha himself warns us against this, by expressly declaring, "the sphere of the Absorptions—*jhāna-visaya*—is another of the four incomprehensible things about which one ought not to

---

* As to the two last mentioned kinds of knowledge, see above p. 302 *et seq*.

** The five powers treated above, together with the complete arising of the vision of Anattā, and thereby of complete deliverance, constitute the six higher kinds of knowledge *(chaḷabhiññā)*.

*** Only this must be said, to avoid misunderstandings, that these faculties, especially the magical powers mentioned last, — of becoming manifold, while being one, and so on,—manifest themselves in their totality in the state of deepest Absorption. "Panthaka has bodily multiplied himself a thousand times by magic, *sitting thus quietly in the serene grove.*" (Thera-Gāthā, v. 563) They therefore are experiences obtained by the saint only in *this* state, and *only by him alone*. To the external world, they thus are imperceptible. Therefore they have nothing in common with the biblical miracles.

ponder, for if a man ponders about them, he will fall a prey to madness and mental disturbance."[389] As always, so also here, the Buddha merely invites us to put the matter to practical proof, leaving it to any one who does not wish to do so, to think about it whatever seems to him good. Here, by way of exception, many an one must remain content with mere belief in the words of the Master, who otherwise might also possess the will for the practice and ultimate achievement of this "culminating point of concentration" or this "wisdom ripened into concentration." For not only is it the case that all the Absorptions, and particularly the higher ones, are not attainable to every one, but it may happen that a person, in spite of all his exertions, does not even attain to the first one, since the disappearance of the Five Hindrances does not necessarily lead to the complete ceasing of the activities of the five external senses, but often is followed only by such a *quieting* of them, that they no longer constitute a hindrance to clear and intuitive thinking, in particular, no longer in the form of the sensual thoughts that emanate from these. But also in the latter case—as dealt with in the previous chapter—thinking is entirely purified, so that it is able to lead also in this state to the perfect vision of Anattā, and thereby to definitive deliverance. One who in this way has attained to full deliverance, that is, one who has not even reached the First Absorption, is called a *Sukkhavipassaka*, meaning "he who is filled with dry insight;" whereas one who has gained one or several or all the Absorptions, is designated as a *Samatha-yānika*, that is, one who has taken as his vehicle the complete pacification, *samatha*, of the activities of the six senses. If we ask the reason why every one is not able to gain the Absorptions, the answer of the Buddha is: "This depends on difference of capacity."* Though there is here an exception,

* Majjh. Nik. 64th Discourse. There it is described, how the monk reaches the

and indeed the only one, to the fundamental principle dominating the entire doctrine of the Buddha, that every individual for himself may test its truth, nevertheless no one who for the rest has become convinced of the solidity of this doctrine, will have the least doubt as to the reality of the domain of the Absorptions, as "he beholds the Exalted

---

several Absorptions, one after the other, and overcomes them, whereupon Ānanda asks the Master: "How is it, that some monks are *delivered in mind* and some are *delivered by wisdom*?" He receives this answer from the Master: "This, Ānanda, I say, results from the difference in their capacity." — According to this, he especially is *delivered in mind* who is able to bring about the complete ceasing of all sense activities during his lifetime, whereas he is called *delivered by wisdom* who merely by means of deep insight has struggled through to the complete vision of Anattā, and thereby brought about the destruction of all thirst. But the latter, of course, along with the deliverance through holy wisdom, also realizes the deliverance of the mind in such a way that at least in death it supervenes to its full extent. Therefore it is always said of such an one, that he has reached "The deliverance of the mind, the deliverance that is through wisdom." (*Cf.* the ascetic who resembles "the red Lotus" in the Aṅgutt. Nik. II, p. 86 and p. 380* above.)

From these explanations, as well as from our whole book, the complete one-sidedness of that conception will probably become clear which seeks the essence of the path, even *exclusively*, in the Absorptions, and accordingly declares the Path to be nothing but *Yoga*. To be sure, a *Buddha* always reaches these Absorptions with their sphere of power and insight, and only from this highest standpoint is he able to point out and teach the four holy truths in their complete all-embracing meaning; but they are not necessary for other men in order to reach holiness. On the contrary, a man who has realized them up to the boundary of possible perception,—(see above, p. 331**)— may nevertheless be a bad man.[390] To realize them, nothing more is necessary than intensive training in extreme concentration of will, be it only by means of the *Kasiṇā* exercises which we shall deal with below. Because the Absorptions are only the consequences of such concentration of will, therefore a worldling cannot realize *nirodha-samāpatti*. (See above p. 332*) To this belongs more than mere *Concentration* of will; to it belongs at least temporarily, complete *abrogation* of will. But this the worldling cannot possibly attain to, because he has not yet struggled through to the sober insight that willing also does not belong to his essence, and therefore is not able, even only temporarily, to free himself from it *entirely*. This *sober insight* is therefore the basis of all holiness, that is, of the killing of the will. Of course, as a *consequence* of this insight and of the thereby conditioned exterminations of our inclinations which disturb mental activity, the pure will to insight may become concentrated in such a way that it opens out into the Absorptions. The reason why in the Discourses, when the path leading to deliverance is described, these Absorptions are always referred to, and even as its crowning close, must be sought in this, that the Buddha always gives the ultimate view which includes in itself every other, as may, for example, be gathered in another direction from the 129th Discourse of the Majjhima Nikāya.

One guaranteeing it."[391] Rather precisely from the description of these supramundane faculties which accrue the nearer we come to Nibbāna, and thereby to "Nothingness," will he, not without right, derive a fresh hint that behind this seeming Nothing, the true and real is hidden.*†

C. THE MEANS OF CONCENTRATION

In the foregoing we saw that the concentration of the mind, or the concentrated intuitive activity of cognition, is the heart of the Buddha's path of deliverance. It alone leads to intuitive *knowledge*, and thereby to the annihilation of our thirst for the world, hence to deliverance. Precisely to it, therefore, the whole path leads. But because so very much depends on it, even everything, for this reason the Buddha repeatedly sets forth in more or less *formal* fashion the mode of procedure for the development and cultivation of the faculty of concentrated contemplation. To understand these means, we must remind ourselves again of the following facts.

Our cognition by its nature is entirely at the service of thirst. Consequently it is at once entirely occupied by every motion of the latter, so that, like a searchlight sweeping a section of country, at almost every moment it is turned upon another object, whether this object is immediately made

* As to this expression, see Majj. Nik. I, p. 245: "That is true which is real, Nibbānam."

† From the foregoing expositions it will be seen that the essence of the Absorptions, from the first of them up to the higher knowledge, consists in sober heedfulness carried to its ultimate in intuitive insight. Compare, besides other passages, Aṅgutt. Nik. I, p. 40: "But he overcomes them and understands: '*I know, I see.*'" Accordingly, there is nothing more perverse than to translate *jhānā* by "ecstasies" or "raptures." Such conceptions mean, on the contrary, states wherein man abandons himself without restraint to the feelings that well up in him, so that clarity of understanding is obscured and the freedom of the will circumscribed.

accessible through the outer senses, or consists in one of the motions of thought incessantly rising within us. It can also be said that our cognition in its usual activity resembles the light in a lantern that in the darkness of night is by its owner directed at every moment towards some other object, in order to find his way and *for no other purpose*, thus, not at all that he may inspect things more closely. As little as this traveller obtains a *real* insight into the things upon which his light falls, just as little can cognition in its normal mode of action gain a real insight into what enters, or is brought within, its range. If this insight is to be attained, cognition must rather rest upon the object concerned with the utmost possible persistency and keenness; in fact, it must be *concentrated* upon it.*

Now this power of concentration, like everything else in the world, is gained by exercise. Thereby it is clear that this exercise can not only be cultivated by the usual activity

* Be it noted that in this lies the reason for the oft occuring repetitions in the Dialogues which he only will blame to whom the spirit of the latter has not become clear.

If we wish to do away with a false appearance deluding our eyes, for instance, when at night a curiously shaped tree-stump mimics a muffled form, this is only possible by fixing our gaze long enough and acutely enough upon the object which gives rise to the false appearance, until the reality appears. Thus must we also, for long, and ever and again, regard everything in reference to its three characteristics, "transitory, causing suffering, and not-the-*I*," until the opposite *transcendental appearance*, in consequence of which "we mistake ourselves for the cognizable," that is, for the five groups of our personality, disappears. But this is what the Discourses of the Buddha are meant to effect; therefore they always again and again, from the most varied points of view, direct, and *must* direct our gaze towards this transcendental appearance. Whoever finds this monotonous, has not yet even the barest idea of the problem of this transcendental appearance, and of the importance of annihilating this appearance along with which all other problems are disposed of. Because a false appearance, even a false *transcendental* appearance has to be got rid of, it is therefore not enough to go through the present work once or twice, and then to put it away for always, for the right thoughts given us by it all too soon again would be extinguished by that tendency to "wrong thinking," which dwells within us (comp. above, p. 441). But by daily directing our thinking for years towards insight into the three characteristics, we must *force* it to take this way, whereupon in like measure this transcendental appearance will disappear.

of the senses, but also specially *trained* by concentrating the attention upon a definite object with no other purpose than this, to become accustomed to collected thought. Because we thus make the struggle against the main hindrance to all concentrated mental activity, namely absent-mindedness, our only and self-determined aim, this method of procedure will soonest lead to the goal through our giving our will for insight, in time, complete supremacy and thereby full mastery over the other motions of will that still arise within us and seek to bring it into their service. Thus this training finally leads us to being able at will to maintain an attitude of pure cognition with regard to any object whatsoever. Therefore it is not to be wondered at—rather is it the contrary that would appear curious—that the Buddha has incorporated this special training for the strengthening of the will for insight, and thereby for insight itself, into the Path of salvation devised by him. And this he has done in a threefold mode.

First, we have to exercise ourselves in looking with the mind so long and so intently at a given object, for instance a tree, that at last it completely fills our direct ocular cognition; and in this contemplation of the object we come to perfect rest, all our remaining motions of will thereby becoming allayed. If we succeed in doing this, then we proceed to exercise our cognising activity also in this direction, so that together with its intensity, its extension also increases through the "mono-idea-izing" of our cognition by means of intuitive representations of ever more extensive objects. Because in this way the pure cognizing activity becomes more and more independent of all impulsive willing and more fixed in itself, thus, its freedom from all hindrances ever greater, therefore the result of this training is called "a grand deliverance of the mind." Indeed we must have attained a considerable degree of freedom of willing, especially of will to cognise, if we have our will so far in our power that we are able to remain for hours or even for days in deepest contemplation of a represented object, moreover one of large extension.

"But what, householder, is grand deliverance of the mind? There, householder, a monk has conceived a single tree as 'grand,' and becomes stilled thereby . . . . Then, householder, a monk has conceived two or three trees as 'grand' and becomes stilled thereby . . . . There, householder, a monk has conceived a single meadow as 'grand' and becomes stilled thereby . . . . There again, householder, a monk has conceived two or three meadows as 'grand' and becomes stilled thereby . . . . There, householder, a monk has conceived a single kingdom as 'grand' and becomes stilled thereby . . . . There again, householder, a monk has conceived two or three kingdoms as 'grand' and becomes stilled thereby . . . . There again, householder, a monk has conceived the earth girdled by the ocean as 'grand' and becomes stilled thereby. This, householder, is called 'grand deliverance of the mind.'" [392]

It is clear that with a cognitive power, developed in this manner, it can no longer be so very difficult to penetrate the machinery of personality to the bottom and thus to realize the vision of Anattā. But further, it also becomes clear that this training leads in the easiest manner to the Absorptions right up to their highest point, to the higher knowledge, and thereby to unrestricted, arbitrary domination of all the processes of our personality. Of course, if *this* is attained to, then the training must be pursued still further, as it is more closely described especially in the 128th Discourse of the Majjhima-Nikāya. There the Buddha describes, how he himself on this path reached the culminating point of concentration. After he had reached a certain measure of inner collectedness, there arose before his spiritual eye a splendour, and forms. But concentration was not yet sufficiently intensive to retain those appearances. "Then, Anuruddha, I thought: 'What may be the cause, what the reason, why the splendour disappears from me, and the view of the forms?' Then, Anuruddha, I said to myself: 'I have become uncertain; uncertainty has been the cause why my concentration was destroyed. And because my concentration was destroyed, therefore the splendour vanished, and the view of the forms. Therefore I will now direct my efforts towards no longer falling into uncertainty. And now, Anuruddha, while I dwelt earnest-minded, eager and unwearied, again I perceived a splendour and a view of forms." But they again vanish. The Bodhisatta* again seeks the cause of this, and finds it in his having become inattentive. He labours towards no longer falling into uncertainty and inattention. In this he succeeds. The splendour and the forms again appear, but only to disappear again soon. As the new cause of this he discovers that he had become dull and languid, and now labours towards no longer becoming uncertain nor inattentive, nor dull and languid. Nevertheless, it is again the old game: the splendour and the forms appear again and again, but he is not able to hold them fast. But the Bodhisatta remains unshakeable in his energy, ascertains each time the cause of the breaking up of his concentration, and finds out, one after the other, that he had become horrified, enchanted, clumsy, too much strained, that he had become too slack, too careless, then, that he had fallen into absent-mindedness, lastly, that he had looked too sharply at the forms. One disturbance after the other he gets rid of, until he perceives "a certain splendour", and obtains a "view of certain forms, and an immeasurable view, and a view of immeasurable forms, through a whole night, through a whole day." But he is not yet satisfied with this. He also wants

---

* A being endowed with wisdom, a name given to the Buddha before his complete awakening.

to know how it comes that at one time he perceives a certain splendour, and the aspect of certain forms, and then again an immeasurable splendour, and the aspect of immeasurable forms. "Then, Anuruddha, I said to myself: 'At a time when my collectedness* is a definite one, there my eye is a definite one, and with a definite eye, I behold a definite splendour, and the aspect of definite forms. And again at a time when my collectedness is immeasurable, then my eye is immeasurable, and with an immeasurable eye, I perceive immeasurable splendour, and the aspect of immeasurable forms, through a whole night, through a whole day, through a whole night and a whole day."

With this all disturbances of mind were discovered and done away with, for which very cause also the pure will for insight had become sovereign lord of all and every further form of willing. Especially everything pertaining to inclination was definitively annihilated, and for the Buddha there remained only such kinds of willing as, in the light of all-prevailing, all-determining insight, he himself deliberately allowed to rise within himself. He had become absolute sovereign over the heap of processes that represented his personality. From here it was but a last small step to the culminating point of concentration, from which then upon him "dawned the knowledge and the sight:

> 'Forever am I released,
> This is the final life,
> And never is there new Becoming.'" [393]

It has seemed necessary to follow this kind of training in concentration of mind up to its conclusion, in order, on one hand, to make known the immense amount of stubborn endurance required in working towards deliverance, such as here is particularly in evidence, but also, on the

---

* That is, concentration.

other hand, in order to make known its results, which may seem impossible to the average man.

Still greater stress does the Buddha lay upon another training of concentration, namely, that which has the act of breathing as its object. If we could call concentration the heart of his path of deliverance, then the special concentration of cognitive activity upon inhalation and exhalation, constitutes, as it were, the heart within the heart. Ever and again in the Discourses, attention is called to the importance of this variety of the practice of concentration. "Inhalation and exhalation, ye monks, thoughtfully exercised and cultivated, causes the attainment of great merit, high promotion."[394] The Buddha himself even after his complete Awakening regularly spent the four months of the rainy season "immersed in watchfulness over inhalation and exhalation."[395] If we ask for the reason of the pre-eminent importance of this training, the Buddha himself tells us: "Inhalation and exhalation, ye monks, thoughtfully exercised and cultivated, produces the Four Foundations of Recollectedness; the Four Foundations of Recollectedness, thoughtfully exercised and cultivated, produce the Seven Constituent Elements of Awakening; the Seven Constituent Elements of Awakening, thoughtfully exercised and cultivated bring about deliverance through wisdom."[396] The Buddha also explains to us, how this is meant:[397]

At first, one merely practises concentration of the cognizing activity upon exhalation and inhalation in itself. "The monk, O monks, betakes himself to the depths of the forest, or to the foot of a tree, or to any solitary spot, and sits himself down with legs crossed under him; and, body held erect, earnestly practises Recollectedness. With conscious intent he breathes in, with conscious intent he breathes out. When he takes a long inward breath, he is aware, 'I take a long inward breath'. When he makes a long outward breath, he is aware, 'I make a long outward breath'. When he takes a short inward breath, he is aware, 'I take a short inward breath.' When he makes a short outward breath, he is aware, 'I make a short outward breath.' 'Perceiving the whole breath,* I will breathe in'—thus he trains himself. 'Perceiving the entire breath, I will breathe out'—thus he trains himself. 'Quieting this activity of the body, I will breathe in'—thus he trains himself. 'Quieting this activity of the body, I will breathe out'—thus he trains himself."

The monk thus practises concentrated thinking in that activity of his body in which the totality of the purely corporeal processes again concentrates itself, in such a way that from the very outset he seeks to gain an immediate influence over them: "As regards the bodies, I call it changing the body, that is, inhalation and exhalation. Thus, as respects the body, does the monk keep watch upon the body."

But now the process of respiration is closely connected with all the other activities of the six senses-machine, as being their basis. Therefore it offers the best way of closely observing the rest of the mechanism of this machine of the six senses and at the same time of learning how to influence it, if we make this process the fulcrum of concentrated thinking, to which it may always return in order to avoid distractions by other motions of the mind.

"'Serenely feeling—that is inhalation and exhalation—I will breathe in,' 'serenely feeling I will breathe out'—thus he trains himself. 'Blissfully feeling I will breathe in,' 'blissfully feeling I will breathe out'—thus he trains himself. Thus, as respects sensations, does the monk keep watch upon the sensations. As respects the sensations, I call it changing sensation, that is, carefully *giving heed to it*, when inhaling and exhaling.

---

* Though the original text says "*Sabbakāya*, the whole body," nevertheless only the breath is understood by this, as not only appears from the whole context, but especially from the immediately following passage: "As regards the bodies, I call it changing the body, that is, inhalation and exhalation."

"'Perceiving the thoughts, I will breathe in,' 'perceiving the thoughts I will breathe out'—thus he trains himself. 'Enlivening the thoughts, I will breathe in,' 'enlivening the thoughts, I will breathe out'—thus he trains himself. 'Loosening the thoughts, I will breathe in,' 'loosening the thoughts I will breathe out'—thus he trains himself. Thus, as respects mind, does the monk keep watch upon the mind.

"'Perceiving transitoriness, I will breathe in,' 'perceiving transitoriness, I will breathe out'—thus he trains himself. 'Perceiving unattractiveness, I will breathe in,' 'perceiving unattractiveness, I will breathe out'—thus he trains himself. 'Perceiving estrangement, I will breathe in,' 'perceiving estrangement, I will breathe out'—thus he trains himself. Thus, as respects the phenomena, does the monk keep watch upon the phenomena, untiring, clear-minded, thoughtful, after having overcome worldly wants and cares. And how wants and cares are overcome, he has wisely observed, and well has he equalized it."

As we see, this kind of concentration-training is a combination of purely formal training and Right Recollectedness. Pure cognition precisely here is exercised by its being directed from the very beginning upon the vision of Anattā. For this very reason the latter in this manner is realized in the easiest and quickest way. For by thus exercising concentration of mind in Right Recollectedness, during this exercise itself, we come ever nearer to the *ascertaining of reality*. But precisely from this does the will for pure insight, on its side, derive ever new *strength* to assert itself more and more in face of the other motions of willing. The more we succeed in doing this, the more, thus, that the latter motions vanish, the greater *the joy* that arises, until at last wirh the progressive domination of the pure cognizing activity, this joy also again ebbs away, and at last complete *peace* of mind ensues. In the whole six senses-machine, only the will for pure cognition, and the knowledge born of it, are now active. For which very reason the latter has become wholly unified, wholly pure, like a flame that, nourished by the best wood, burns without smoke or fumes, quite clear and steady. *Concentration* has become complete.* But along with it there supervenes *equanimity* in regard to everything. For where pure cognition has come to reign, there is no more inclination or disinclination in regard to anything. For these would be expressions of thirst which now, though only for the time being, has been silenced. Pure cognition is cold and passionless. It can be touched neither in an agreeable nor in a disagreeable manner. It is like water that is not horrified, nor becomes indignant nor revolts, whether "there are washed in it things pure or impure, things smeared with fæces or urine, slime or pus."[398]

But this pure insight in time will unfailingly lead to the pure vision of Anattā, whereby every kind of thirst will be annihilated for ever, and thus deliverance through wisdom achieved. The Seven Constituent Members of Awakening *(Sambojjhangā)*—which we have just seen develop from Right Recollectedness up to Equanimity—have led to the *end*.

Besides the chief kinds of concentration-training thus far dealt with, there is still a third, but purely external method for the quieting of all the motions of the mind that hinder pure thinking, and thereby for bringing about concentration. They are the *Kasiṇā* exercises. "The disciple exercises Kasiṇa—entireness**—by means of earth, of water, of fire, of the wind, of blue, yellow, red, white, space, consciousness, light."[399] This method is as follows.

The undivided attention is concentrated upon a visible object, preferably upon a coloured round disc made specially

* But it is not necessarily concentration in the sense of being accompanied by Absorption, *jhāna*.

** This means, that cognition is entirely absorbed in the respective representation.

for this purpose, ('blue, yellow, red, white Kasiṇa'), or upon a spot of earth clearly visible, ('earth Kasiṇa'), or upon a pond lying at a distance, ('water Kasiṇa'), and so on, until at last a moon-like reflex is distinctly behold with eyes opened as well as with eyes closed. This reflex is called "*uggaha-nimitta,* conceived reflex." Proceeding now to fix concentration upon this reflex—which must remain, even if meanwhile one moves to another place—there arises the inner reflex, *paṭibhāga-nimitta,* without colour or form, resembling a sparkling star or the moon becoming visible between the clouds. At the same time, the Hindrances, *nivāraṇā,* disappear, and *upacāra-samādhi,* concentration lasting to the first *Jhāna,* the first absorption, and "bordering upon it," is reached. All the motions of thirst have gone to sleep, the light of knowledge, no more dimmed by any of them, beams forth in all its clearness. Hence, also on this basis, if it is directed upon the personality by the will for the complete penetration of this personality, now coming into action, it may, in time, penetrate it through and through.*

Of course, it depends on personal qualities as to which of these trainings** is best suited to the individual concerned. But hardly will any one be able to neglect them entirely, if he wants to make definite progress within any reasonable time in the struggle for the killing out, or only for the weakening, of his inclinations by means of pure cognition. For in the course of the endless round of our rebirths, our cognition has become so much accustomed to place itself at the service of every rising motion of will, and thus,

* As to the other *Kasiṇā* not yet dealt with at length, in the space Kasiṇa, the portion of space seen through a round opening, for instance in the roof of a hut, forms the object. Consciousness-Kasiṇa has the boundlessness of cognition itself for its object, and is able to generate the realm of boundless consciousness. In the light Kasiṇa, daylight falling through a window, a keyhole *etc.*, serves as object. — The coloured round discs, mentioned above, usually measure from eight to twelve inches in diameter.

** There are still two other kinds of training, the eight Overcomings, *Abhibhāyatanā,* and the eight Liberations, *Vimokhā.* They are extensions of the *Kasiṇa* exercises.

like diffused light, to illumine everything meagrely, but nothing entirely, instead of turning itself upon one object so as completely to penetrate the same, that it must by hard work be directly trained for this latter achievement, which at bottom is its only appropriate activity.

D. THE FOUR HOLY STATES

If we look over the Way, as up to this point we have learnt to know it, we find it saturated by the most unbounded charity. The disciple of the Buddha is "mild and merciful, kind and compassionate towards every living creature."* This his all-embracing love even extends to the vegetable kingdom, since he also avoids destroying seeds and plant-life.* He even goes so far in his consideration for this part of the living world, that he empties out the remains of his scanty meal "upon ground free from grass, or into flowing water."[400]

For the rest the sacred texts are inexhaustible in their praise of sympathy.

> "May all beings be full of happiness and secure!
> May they all be happy!
>
> Whatever there are of living beings,
> Whether they move, or are bound in their places,
> Whether they are weak or strong,
> Whether long or short, whether big or small,
> Whether medium of size, or slim, or stout,
> Whether visible or invisible,
> Whether near or far,

---

* Compare above, p. 417 *et seq.*

Whether now in life or longing to come into life,
May they all be happy!

As a mother protects her only child with her own life,
Cultivate such boundless love towards all beings!"

Thus it is said in the Mettasutta of the Suttanipāta. And in the Aṅguttara-Nikāya the Master says: "Whoso of my disciples cultivates mind-delivering love only for a moment, that disciple meditates not in vain, and follows the doctrine and the discipline of the Master; how much more those who constantly cultivate the thought of love." Further in the Itivuttaka, in a passage that might directly be called the Song of Songs of Buddhism, it is said:

"All means in this life for the earning of merit are not worth one sixteenth* part of love, the deliverance of mind. Love, the deliverance of mind, takes them up into itself, shining and glowing and beaming.

"And as all the shining of the stars is not worth one sixteenth part of the brightness of the moon, but moonlight takes it up into itself, shining and glowing and beaming, so all means in this life for the earning of merit are not worth one sixteenth part of love, the deliverance of mind. Love, the deliverance of mind, takes them up into itself, shining and glowing and beaming.

"And as in the last month of the rainy season, in autumn, the sun in the clear and cloudless sky climbing the firmament clears away all darkness in the space of air, shining and glowing and beaming; and as in the night, early in the morning, the morning star shines and glows and beams, even so all means in this life for the earning of merit are not worth one sixteenth part of love, the deliverance of mind. Love, the deliverance of mind, takes them up into itself, shining and glowing and beaming."

* We should say: one thousandth.

Moreover, this love is not limited by dislike on the part of others. Rather does it flood through the disciple of the Buddha in such an immeasureable stream, that no hostility is able to set up bounds to it, that it cannot be exhausted by any hate, even as the earth cannot be made earthless. On the contrary, every hostile attack only brings it to fuller unfolding.

"Suppose, O monks, that a man armed with spade and basket should come, saying: 'I will make the world to be void of earth,' and should dig everywhere all around, scattering the earth abroad, delve holes and fling away the soil, crying: 'Be thou void of earth! Be thou void of earth!' What think ye, monks? Could this man so cause the world to be devoid of earth?"

"Nay verily, Lord."

"And why not?"

"The world, O Lord, is deep beyond all measure, not easily to be made void of earth, however much toil and trouble that man might give himself."

"Wherefore, monks, however men may speak concerning you; whether in season or out of season, whether appropriately or inappropriately, whether courteously our rudely, whether wisely or foolishly, whether kindly or maliciously, thus, my monks, must you train yourselves: 'Unsullied shall our minds remain, neither shall evil word escape our lips. Kind and compassionate ever, we will abide loving of heart nor harbour secret hate. And that person will we permeate with stream of loving thought unfailing; and forth from him proceeding, enfold and permeate the whole wide world with constant thoughts of lovingkindness, as the world wide, ample, expanding, measureless, free from enmity, free from ill-will!' Thus, my monks, must you train yourselves." [401]

The Buddha even goes so far as to say: "Yea, monks, even if highway-robbers with a two-handed saw should take and dismember you limb by limb; whoso grew darkened in mind thereby, would not be fulfilling my injunctions."[401] Even then, we have rather "to abide kind and compassionate," and forth from them proceeding, we have "to enfold and permeate the whole wide world with constant thoughts of love, ample, expanding, measureless, free from enmity, free from ill-will."[401]

But this love is a love of a quite peculiar kind. When *we* speak of love, even of the purest love, we connect with it inseparably the conception of something due to feelings and affections. In other words, we always think of *inclination* towards some or all men, or towards beings in general. But the kind of love the Buddha teaches is far removed from this. Everything that is inclination or feeling is nothing more than a stirring of thirst, perhaps of thirst in its most noble form, but nevertheless of thirst, which therefore must be overcome at all costs, as the source of every sort of misfortune. Hence, the Buddha's love is something that is free from every kind of inclination. But what remains, if everything of the nature of inclination is separated from love? *Kindness* remains, pure kindness. Kindness is love purified by insight from the dross of passion, as which, in principle, all mere inclination, of whatsoever kind, must be regarded. Passionate love is a thing of every day; passionate kindness is a contradiction in itself. The conception of kindness therefore in itself excludes everything pertaining to inclination. It is the love that comes from pure insight, as contrasted with the love of a man still dominated by his passions. For this reason it is also the love of the Buddha, and therefore we shall henceforth call it by this its name of honour. The Buddha teaches unlimited *kindness* towards all that lives and breathes.

But because kindness is the fruit of pure insight, therefore it can only ripen, where this pure insight in all its fullness illuminates the darkness of life, that is, in a pure and concentrated mind, the only source of all such insight. "He of quieted body is at ease. Whoso is at ease, his mind attains to collectedness and calmness .... His mind overflowing with Kindness, he abides raying forth Kindness towards one quarter of space, then towards the second, then towards the third, then towards the fourth, and above and below; thus, all around. Every-where, in all places the wide world over, his mind overflowing with Kindness, streams forth ample, expanded, limitless, free from enmity, free from ill-will."[402]

We see: on whatever path we encounter anything really great and exalted in the world, it always shows itself to be the fruit of concentration of mind.

But if kindness is thus the fruit of pure insight, then it must also be closely connected with the great final goal of all such insight, with complete equanimity such as results from the killing of all thirst. Indeed, this relation is so intimate, that the Buddha has directly made it a vehicle for the attainment of this final goal. This he does in the *Brahmavihārabhāvanā*, the four Holy States,* the first of which consists in the monk's radiating through the whole world with a mind of Kindness. The other three he cultivates, in immediate connection with the first, as follows:

"His mind overflowing with Compassion, he abides, raying forth Compassion towards one quarter of space, then towards the second, then towards the third, then towards the fourth, and above and below; thus all around. Everywhere, into all places the wide world over, his mind overflowing with Compassion, streams forth ample, expanded, limitless, free from enmity, free from ill-will.

"His mind overflowing with Sympathetic Gladness, he abides, raying forth Sympathetic Gladness towards one quarter of

* Literally "the Cultivation of the Holy States."

space, then towards the second, then towards the third, then towards the fourth, and above and below; thus all around. Everywhere, into all places the wide world over, his mind overflowing with Sympathetic Gladness streams forth, ample, expanded, limitless, free from enmity, free from ill-will."

"His mind overflowing with Even-Mindedness, he abides, raying forth Even-mindedness towards one quarter of space, then towards the second, then towards the third, then towards the fourth, and above and below; thus, all around. Everywhere, into all places the wide world over, his mind overflowing with Even-mindedness, streams forth ample, expanded, limitless, free from enmity, free from ill-will."[402]

But with this perfect equanimity, in so far as it has become lasting, the monk has again reached complete deliverance. "'Thus is it," he understands; "there is a lower and there is a higher; and there is a refuge beyond this sensuous sphere." And thus knowing, thus perceiving, his mind is delivered from being influenced through Desire, delivered from being influenced through Becoming, delivered from being influenced through Ignorance."* [402]

But now the question arises as to the last and deepest reason for this boundless sympathy with all living beings, such as, in the form of the four holy states, is an essential requirement in all holiness. None can become a saint who has not realized it within himself. According to Schopenhauer, this sympathy is based upon the penetration of the principle of individuation, on our identification with other beings, thus in the doing away of the dividing wall between "You" and "*I*," whereby we recognizes ourselves in everything, exactly according to the saying of the Vedānta: *"Tat tvam asi."* But it is clear that this explanation cannot hold good

---

* If on pp. 242, 243 above, the four holy states only lead to being reborn in a Brahma-world, the reason of this is that the monk still clings to these four states themselves.

for the Buddha, since it strays into the domain of the transcendent which is once and for ever closed to cognition, into that "untrodden land," in regard to which there is only one correct attitude: absolute silence. But the Buddha is in no need whatever of such explanations as are based upon trying to explain the inexplicable. For from his highest standpoint this problem also unveils itself in the simplest possible manner; indeed its solution, as in general the whole doctrine of the Buddha, is even self-evident, if only it is once understood. For the true reason for that boundless sympathy which the saint feels towards all beings, is summed up in the saying: "*We are beings that desire weal and shrink from woe.*"[403] Of course this saying must not be taken as it represents itself to the superficial glance, but it must be regarded with the eye of the Buddha. To this latter it presents itself as follows: If I desire weal and shrink from woe, then this *I* is of course not my body nor my sensation; neither is it my perception nor the activity of my mind nor even my cognition; in short, it is not the totality of my personality; for all this is *not* the *I*, *anattā*. As we know, I myself am something totally different from all this, which does not allow of being determined in any way; I am the inscrutable itself. Only so much I know in the light of my cognition, that I am nothing belonging to the world, that is to say, I am able to state in purely negative fashion that nothing in the world has fundamentally anything to do with me. On the contrary, my personality and thereby the world, only represents a *limitation* of me. As a saint, I free myself from this limitation by realizing holy *freedom*. This freedom becomes complete, if in my last death I definitively cast away the mechanism hitherto connecting me with the world, the body endowed with senses. Then I am absolutely free, and thereby unrestricted and unlimited, which conceptions only declare that every partition, every boundary-line restricting my freedom has fallen. "Liberated from what is called corporeality, Vaccha, the Perfected One is indefinable, inscrutable, immeasurable, like the great ocean."[404] But if I am fundamentally unlimited and boundless, and on the other hand a creature desiring weal and shrinking from woe, then of course also this desire for wellbeing and this shrinking from woe is boundlesss. Indeed, everyone experiences this at every moment in the insatiability of his desire for wellbeing, and his boundless aversion from all suffering.* But he does not experience the boundlessness of his essence itself. For *he himself* has limited himself to his personality and to a certain circle of interests. Because of this, his boundless desire for wellbeing and aversion from suffering concentrate themselves upon this limited circle, and work within this circle. But in one who is becoming a saint, in the same measure that he recognizes everything, his personality also, as *anattā*, the boundlessness of his essence itself also becomes manifest. Thereby, however, his craving for wellbeing and his shrinking from suffering are liberated from their confinement to the circle that up till now has been arbitrarily drawn. The former is widened in the form of a boundless benevolence — merely another expression for kindness — his shrinking from suffering, however, in the form of boundless compassion for everything. He suffers wherever suffering is felt, were it away off in starry space.** But, of course, just as boundless also is the joy that rises in him through the satisfaction of his desire for wellbeing in the same measure that he directly recognizes himself as different from his personality, and thereby knows himself to be, in his real essence, above this primary source of all suffering. And finally, just as boundless

---

* Thereby the riddle of the insatiability of thirst in itself is solved.

** We may also say: he becomes a being which only feels quite well when he does not even need to *perceive* suffering any more, who therefore himself suffers wherever he encounters suffering.

also is the holy equanimity, wherein his boundless desire for wellbeing, at the end of all, when he has also recognized this holy joy as a transitory emotion, is satisfied just as boundlessly, and thereby comes to rest forever.*

Because the higher a man rises morally, ever the more increases, and at the same time, ever the more universal becomes, his kindness, therefore, conversely, the amount of kindness shown by a man is an infallible gauge for measuring his moral value. Following what has been said, in appraising him it will be specially important to know what is the radius of action of this his kindness, whether it extends not merely to mankind, but also to the animal world, yea, even to vegetable kingdom. The saint takes them all without restriction to his breast.[405] In him this kindness, in harmony with the perfect purity of cognition from which it originates, also shows itself in the purest manner, by his raying forth holy equanimity to all beings as the highest feeling possible; and in his pity —this is the form which compassion has taken in him who himself is no longer open to feel mental pain—he exerts himself exlusively in giving to men the highest, that is, *truth,* —"The gift of truth is the highest gift,"[406]—while leaving all the other innumerable possibilities of doing good to those still striving, according to the degree of insight they have already attained. Also with respect to these lower degrees of the manifestation of kindness, we must bear in mind that they are the fruit of cognition. Therefore kindness, also in these lower stages, contrary to mere love that only too

---

* Here therefore the concepts, *egoism* and *altruism*, find their solution in a higher unity. We are only happy when we are wishing well to all other beings. The latter is only possible in so far as, and to the degree that, we separate ourselves from our personality. But in so far as this happens, we also lose our Ego, by which term, as we know,—comp. above, p. 187—in general is only meant the imaginary essential relationship beetween ourselves and the components of our personality. But if we are no Ego, no *I*, as a positive quantity of this world, then, of course, the distinction, "another," has also lost its distinctive relation, so that every limitation to the realization of good-will is removed.

often causes us to act in a blind and therefore stupid manner, will always endeavour to give that which in each case is best and most wholesome, be it alms or personal help or—for in comparison to eternal welfare, temporal well-being is of small importance—as far as possible, by wholesome advice and instruction.

But besides this, the striving disciple will always himself cultivate kindness in the form of The Four Holy States, as far as ever he is able to do so. Not only is this indispensably necessary for his own welfare, inasmuch as precisely thereby he more and more frees himself from being restricted to a certain circle, and thus in truth again finds his way back to himself—"whoso, clear-minded, awakens limitless kindness, thin are the fetters for him who beholds the perishing of mortal nature,"[407]—but by the cultivation of The Four Holy States, he does a much greater service to other beings than he could ever do by external works of compassion. For he *penetrates* them all, as far as they are receptive of the same, with the radiations of his kindness, his compassion, his joy, and, to conclude with the highest of all, with his unshakeable equanimity, thus pouring immediately into them, quietness, serenity and peace. Of course, our grossly materialistic conception of nature which only wishes to acknowledge the purely mechanical effects of impact and pressure, will not permit us to admit this. But is not this conception of nature long since refuted by our natural science itself? Can we not send out the Hertzian waves for thousands of miles into space without wires, with the result that they can be caught up by any equally attuned recipient? Why then should not man be able to send forth into space waves of kindness, of compassion, of joy and of equanimity, with the effect that they are received by every heart susceptible to them, since we know that the so-called spiritual is only something of more refined materiality, therefore something similar to the

Hertzian waves? Besides this, the phenomenon of the radiation of waves of kindness coincides with that of the radiation of Hertzian waves also in this, that the further the waves are to reach, the stronger must be the source of energy by which they are generated. The more concentrated will is, the farther its circle of action extends.* What a thought! A holy monk from his lonely cell sends forth waves of compassion or of joy into space, and hundreds of miles away they impinge upon a mind tormented by sorrow and grief, which now, in consequence of the same, in a manner inconceivable to itself, suddenly feels within itself an upwelling of peace and serenity. Is not the judgement of the average man who characterizes every monk without discrimination as an idler of no use to the world, here again transformed into its direct opposite? Are not those monks who flee from the world, when they so act, in truth at that moment the greatest benefactors of their fellow-countrymen? Truly: "You ought to know that these people practise the most useful practices: they create more of eternal use in a moment than all the outward works that are ever done outwardly," says also the great German, Master Eckhart.** Instances of the power of this radiation are furnished by the Buddha himself. Devadatta, the Judas Iscariot amongst his disciples, turns a wild elephant loose against him in a narrow lane. "But the Exalted One directed towards the elephant Nālāgiri his power of kindness. Then the elephant Nālāgiri, smitten by the Exalted One with his power of kindness, lowered

* On a small scale, this phenomenon may be observed every day. The presence of the mother has a soothing effect upon the child, also if the infant does not notice her. An eminently kind man by his mere presence calms perturbed minds. Retrospectively the field of action of the will may even extend to those departed in death. "If a monk should wish: 'May my kinsfolk and relations departed, who passed away established in Faith, thinking upon me, thereby inherit rich and abundant reward!' then let him aim at perfection in virtue; let him labour for inward peace of mind, withstand not the approach of absorption, strive after penetration, betake himself to solitude!"[408]

** Hence, in this direction lies also the real solution of the so-called social question.

his trunk, went to the place where the Exalted One was, and stood before him."[409] On another occasion, Ānanda asks the Exalted One to convert Roja, a nobleman of the Malla clan, who was a stranger to the doctrine of the Buddha. "This is not difficult for the Perfected One to effect, O Ānanda, that Roja the Malla may be won for this Doctrine and for this Order. And Roja the Malla, smitten by the Exalted One with his power of kindness, went like a cow seeking her young calf, from one house to another, from one cell to another, asking the monks: 'Where, ye reverend ones, is now the Exalted One staying, the holy, highest Buddha? I crave to see him, the Exalted One, the holy, highest Buddha.'"[410]

It is this kindness radiated forth by the saint, which, if he lives in the wilderness among wild beasts, gives him greater security than could any external measures for his protection. "Dwelling on the mountain's slope, I drew to me lions and tigers, by the power of kindness. Surrounded by lions and tigers, by panthers and buffaloes, by antelopes, stags, and boars, I dwelt in the forest. No creature is terrified of me, and neither am I afraid of any creature. The power of kindness is my support; thus I dwell upon the mountain side."[411]

If, living according to these principles a monk works, not only for his own welfare and salvation, but also for that of many others, "for the benefit, welfare, and salvation of gods and men,"[412] we can understand that the making possible of such a holy life by the provision on the part of the lay adherent of the indispensable necessaries of existence, is praised by the Buddha as the best and most meritorious form of almsgiving, — a giving of alms that increases in value the higher stands the monk who is its object, and therefore, the more effectual is his activity. For in this way the lay adherent also may have his part in the building of the great edifice erected by the wholesome activity of the *true* monk, — and, of course, it is only of such that we here are speaking.*

But from the foregoing it will also be understood that only one who, to begin with, effects his own salvation, can be a real helper to his fellow men. "But, Cunda, that a man who himself is sunk in a morass can drag out another who has sunk therein, — such a thing is not to be found. But, Cunda, that a man who himself is not sunk in a morass, can drag out another who has sunk therein, — such a thing is to be found."[414] Hence, it is not in the least surprising when we find it said: "His own welfare for another's, how great soever, let none neglect."[415] For these words only mean: Never neglect your own salvation out of regard for the salvation of others, for in this case you will only ruin yourself without really being of use to others. This admonition is every whit as necessary to-day as when it was uttered long ago, since to-day also the general motto is: "Unhappy in one's own skin, the general weal is chosen!"[416] The proper procedure is to work for one's own welfare *as well as* for the welfare of others. Such a man "is the greatest, the best, the worthiest, the most exalted."[417] He closely follows the footsteps of the Buddha who also was not content to secure his own salvation only, but throughout a long life sought to save what could be saved, and further, saw to it that also as regards all the generations that should follow, in his doctrine there should stand open to them a clearly visible way to salvation. For even when on the point of death, he admonishes his disciples: "But for this reason ye have to take good care of, and preserve, the things that I have shown you for your penetration .... in order that this holy life may run its course and exist a

* Of the others holds good: "For a bad, unrestrained man it were better that he swallowed a red-hot iron ball, than live on the charity of the land."[413]

long time, that it may make for the wellbeing and salvation of many, out of compassion for the world, for the profit, welfare and salvation of gods and men." [418] Thus, the doctrine handed down was intended to take the place of his personal instruction. As said in the Dīgha Nikāya: "It may well be, Ānanda, that you may perhaps think: 'Gone is the instruction of the Master; we have a Master no more.' But, Ānanda, the matter is not to be looked at in this way. Whatever, Ānanda, I showed you and gave you as Doctrine and Discipline, that, when I am gone, will be your master."

We also have now acquired an exhaustive knowledge of this Doctrine. If we cast our eyes over it once more as a whole, it may be summed up thus in a few words.

We are sick, we suffer from the disease of willing.* The symptom of this disease is the wound of the six senses,** that is, our body endowed with the senses. The disease is chronic: we have suffered from it all through beginningless time. According as it assumes a milder or a more serious form, we adhere, on one hand, either in the heavens or in the human kingdom, or on the other hand, either in, hells or in the animal kingdom; and thus the wound of the six senses exhibits itself to us in the form of "the five heavenly capacities of craving," or of a human or an animal organism, or else of a rejected creature,—all this in endless sequence. The physician who can cure us of this disease is the Buddha. The medicine by means of which he effects this cure, is intuitive insight. In contrast to its merely symptomatical treatment by the ordinary person —who only temporarily soothes the incipient stirrings of

---

* "Sabbaṃ dukkhaṃ chandamūlakaṃ chandanidānaṃ: chando hi mūlaṃ dukkhassa: All Suffering is rooted in willing, springs out of willing; willing is the root of suffering." [419]

** "The wound, this is a name for the six senses." [420] "And how does a monk bind up wounds? If a monk has perceived a form with the eye, heard a sound with the ear . . . . then he neither adheres to the whole nor to the particulars. *Thus does a monk bind up wounds.*" [421]

desire by yielding to them, with the result that the disease only grows worse*—the latter by the Buddha is removed at its root by way of intuitive insight. We become entirely will-less. But along with the disease also disappears its symptom, the wound of the six senses. At first it remains as a scar, for the saint also, up to the time of his death, is bound to his body. With this death, however, the body is cast away entirely and for ever: the wound closes up completely. We are cured for ever. We are free, absolutely free,—free, namely, from all willing, free from our long sickness.**

This single change only will deliverance from the world bring about in us. We ourselves will remain entirely untouched. Only this eternal and unwholesome willing, this ever-tormenting sickness will be taken away, and thereby at last peace arise within us, so that we shall be able to say with the Master: "Once there was Craving, and that was of evil; now that exists no more, and so it is well. Once there was Hatred, and that was of evil; now that exists no more, and so it is well. Once there was Delusion, and that was of evil; now that exists no more, and so it is well."[422]

Whether we ever shall be able to say this, will depend above all upon whether the Doctrine of the Buddha, as we now have learned to know it, has aroused in us the *will* to be able to say it. Everything else is then *self-evident*.

---

* In the same way that the wounds of a leper only become worse through the rubbing by which he seeks to relieve the annoyance of the itching. *Cf.* the great 75th Discourse in the Majj. Nik.

** *Cf.* Shakespeare, Timon of Athens: "My long sickness now begins to mend; and nothing brings me all things."

APPENDIX

I. THE DOCTRINE OF THE BUDDHA AS THE FLOWER OF INDIAN THOUGHT

> "I, O Disciples, am the Brahmin in holy poverty, whose hands are always pure, the bearer of his last body, an incomparable Saviour and physician."
>
> Itivuttaka 100.

The Buddha calls his doctrine "timeless." This means: It is an absolute truth, which was valid for his time as well as it also is for ours, and as it was valid for eternities past, and will be valid for eternities to come. And because this is so, it can also be understood, even if it is entirely severed from the conditions and relations under which it came into the world. But it will be easier to understand it, if we know at the same time the whole environment out of which it sprang, and which alone made it possible for the Buddha and his doctrine to appear. Therefore we wish here briefly to expound the kernel of striving for religious insight current in Ancient India before the appearance of the Buddha, as to its contents, its form, and its relations to the doctrine of the Buddha. Our data may be partly based upon the expositions given by Deussen in his General History of Philosophy, since Deussen was a pioneer precisely in this direction.

The striving of Ancient India for insight had, in gradually progressive development, concentrated itself upon finding out the fundamental principle which underlies everything existing. This fundamental principle is accessible only within ourselves.

For it is only within himself that each may plumb the deepest depths; of everything outside himself he only cognizes the external garb in which it presents itself to his five external senses. Thus, men in Ancient India, in searching for the fundamental principle within themselves, at the culminating point of development, got so far as to proclaim as this fundamental principle, themselves, their own *I*, the Ātman. For this *I*, this Ātman, every one has to search who desires to find the ultimate. But that this Ātman must be *sought* for, involves this, that everything that offers itself to us *without being searched for*, thus, our body with all its organs of sense, cannot be the Ātman, our true essence: and that it is a delusion, if we think it to be this latter. Accordingly, the conception of Ātman from the outset was generally connected with the interpretation of *the Self* "*as opposed to what is not the Self*." This fundamental meaning pervades all the more usual applications of the word Ātman, in so far as by the same is indicated:

1. our own person, as distinguished from the outer world;
2. the trunk of the body, as distinguished from the external members;
3. the soul, as distinguished from the body;
4. the essence, as distinguished from the inessential.

Here, to begin with, we only want to lay it down, that Ātman essentially and originally is a *relative* conception, inasmuch as, in regard to it, we always think of something that is *not* the Ātman; and it is a *negative* conception, inasmuch as its positive content does not consist in itself, but in what is thereby excluded. Such *relatively negative*, or, as we might also say, *limiting* conceptions have often been used by philosophers with great advantage, to designate the incognizable principle of things by excluding from it the whole content of the cognized world. Of such a kind is the "essentially existing" of Plato, as opposed to the arising and passing away; the "substance" of Spinoza, as opposed to the modes of existing, of which the whole world consists, the corporeal as well as the mental; and lastly, the "thing in itself" of Kant, as opposed to the whole world of phenomena. All these conceptions, the essentially existing, the substance, the thing in itself, are negative, that is, about the principle they only tell us what it is not, and just therein lies their value for metaphysics which has to deal with something for ever incognizable. Of such a kind is also the conception of Ātman, which exhorts us to look at the self of our own person, at the self of every other thing, and to put away everything that does not in a strict sense belong to this self. It is the most abstract and therefore the best name ever devised by philosophy for its one and eternal theme; all other names, as, the essentially existing, substance, the thing in itself, still smell of the world of phenomena, from which they are ultimately derived; Ātman alone goes to the point where the inner, dark, never appearing essence opens out to us. It is therefore no mere accident that it is precisely the Indians who have arrived at this most abstract and therefore best designation for the eternal theme of all metaphysical science; for in the Indian genius there resides a restless instinct for penetrating into the depths, a desire to get beyond everything which still appears as something external and inessential, as is beautifully borne out in the second part of the Taittirīya-Upanishad, to give only one example. There man is presented to us, first in his external bodily appearance. As such he consists of the juice of nourishment. But this body is only a wrapping that covers from us the inner essence. If we take it away, we come to the life-breathing Self. But this also again becomes a wrapping, which we have to remove, in order to arrive at our mind-like Self, and from this, in the same way, penetrating deeper and deeper, at the cognition-like Self.

Here we have arrived at the centre; and it is highly characteristic, that the philosopher here at the end, adds a warning not to desire to penetrate still farther, and not to try to make this ultimate interior of nature also an object of cognition. "For it is the bliss-creating. For when one in this invisible, incorporeal, inexpressible, inscrutable finds the peace, the standing-place, then has he entered peace. But if therein he still assumes a distinction, a break, then has he disquietude, the disquietude of him who thinks himself wise."

"In view of this ability of the Indian mind, to penetrate into the depths and to grasp the innermost kernel beneath everything of the nature of a husk, we may understand how Indian philosophy, to express what it had to say, made use of the word Ātman, taken from every-day life and even reduced to a reflexive pronoun, at first, shyly and tentatively, then still more frequently and confidently. We can understand how for Indian thinkers all other denominations of the highest being, mythological, anthropomorphical, and ritual, became a shell, through which, as their innermost kernel, here more, there less clearly, the Ātman radiates, until thinking has become so far strengthened as to find in the Ātman the purest expression for the principle of things."

In former times, the "invisible and inscrutable," in short, the *immaterial* which was found because it was searched for in the right direction, that is, in our own depths, and in the right manner, that is, the indirect one, by stripping off everything inessential to us, was called the "boneless," that is, formless, by which everything bone-like, that is, formed, was borne. Thus is it in Ṛigveda I, 164. But according to the Ucchishṭa-hymn, Atharvaveda II, 7, "All names and forms of the world are based upon the Ucchishṭa, *that which remains*, if we take away all forms of the apparent world. The conception of *Ucchishṭa* is therefore in a similar manner at once as negative and relative as that of Ātman, and closely related to it. The hymn contains an exhortation to direct our attention to *that which remains* if we think everything cognizable away, as which, then, "that within myself," *(tán máyi)* "the splendour within me," is designated. Lastly, in Atharvaveda 10, 7. 8 it is asked concerning the Skambha, *the supporter* who carries everything without himself being carried: "Proclaim this Skambha, who may he be?" until at last, after many inserted contemplations, which nevertheless are not far from the point, at the close of the second hymn the word *Ātman* appears, with which the standpoint of the Upanishads is reached.

This standpoint of the Upanishads itself is very beautifully illustrated in the narrative in the Chāndogya-Upanishâd 8, 7—12: "The Self, *Ātman*, the sinless, free from age, free from death, free from suffering, without hunger, without thirst, whose desiring is true, whose counsel in true,—that one ought to investigate, that one ought to seek to know." Impelled by this demand, among the gods, Indra, and among the demons, Virocana, rise and go to Prajāpati as disciples, remaining with him for thirty-two years. Then Prajāpati said to them: "Look at your Self in a pot full of water, and what you do *not* perceive of your Self, tell me that." Then they looked at themselves in the pot of water. And Prajāpati said to them: "What now do you see?" And they said: "Reverend sir, we see *this our entire Self* in reflection, unto the tiniest hair, unto the nails." And Prajāpati said to them: "Now adorn yourselves, put on your finest garments, embellish yourselves, and then look again in the pot of water." Then they adorned themselves, put on their finest garments, embellished themselves, and looked again in the pot of water. And Prajāpati said to them: "What do you see?" And they said: "Just as we, reverend sir, stand here, adorned, dressed in our finest garments, and embellished, just so, reverend sir, those there are adorned, dressed in finest garments, and embellished."

And Prajāpati said to them: "This is the Self, this is the immortal, this is the fearless, this is the Brahman." This answer satisfies both disciples, and they go home: But Prajāpati, looking after them, says: "There they go, without having perceived and found the Self." Virocana and the demons are content with this answer, and so are all demoniac men who see the Self in the body, therefore pamper their body here below, make much of their body here below, and therefore ornament this body even after it has become a corpse with all kinds of trumpery, as if for it there was another life, a world to come. But Indra, reflecting that this Self is smitten by all the sufferings and illnesses of the body, and perishes by death, "feels—*what everybody may feel*—that all the changes that happen *to* us, for that precise reason cannot change us ourselves, and returns to Prajāpati, who invites him to stay for another thirty-two years as disciple. Indra remains for another thirty-two years as disciple, and then Prajāpati gives to him the second answer: "That [spirit] which in dreams gaily wanders about, he is the Self, he is the immortal, the fearless, he is the Brahman." But also with this answer Indra does not feel satisfied. "Most, certainly this [Self], even if the body is blind, is not blind; if the body is lame, is not lame; certainly it is not struck by the diseases of the body; it is not killed, if the body is killed; it is not lame if the body is lamed; yet it is as if it were killed, it is as if it were oppressed, as if it experienced the unpleasant, and it is as if it wept; in this I can find no comfort." And again he came with the fuel—[that is, as a disciple]—to Prajāpati, and told him of his doubts. And Prajāpati said: "Certainly, this is the case, O Maghavan, but I will explain to you the Self still further. Stay for another thirty-two years as disciple!" And Indra stayed for another thirty-two years as disciple. Then Prajāpati said to him: "If one has thus gone to sleep, so perfectly come to rest that he sees no more dream-pictures, this is the Self, this is the immortal, the fearless, this is the Brahman." Thereupon Indra went away satisfied. But before he had come to the gods, another doubt arose in him. And again he returned to Prajāpati, carrying the fuel in his hands, and said to him: "Oh, reverend sir, in this state one does not know himself, and does not know that one is this one, neither does one know other beings. *One has come to annihilation*. Herein can I find nothing comforting." "Certainly, this is the case, O Maghavan," Prajāpati replied. "But I will explain it to you still further. But it is not to be found anywhere else but in this. Remain five more years as my disciple!" And for five more years Indra remained as his disciple. Then Prajāpati said to him: "O Maghavan, truly mortal is this body, possessed by death; it is the abode of that immortal, *incorporeal* Self. Possessed is the corporealised by pleasure and pain, for because he is corporealised, no defence against pleasure and pain is possible; *the incorporeal*, however, pleasure and pain cannot touch." And so we must become *incorporeal* by entering into the highest light, by retiring to pure and entirely quieted spirituality, such as reigns in deep sleep.

The meaning of this narrative is clear. To the question "What is the *I*, the Self?" Prajāpati gives three answers. The materialistic or demoniacal answer is this: The Self is the body together with its sensitive and vegetative functions and perishes therefore together with this body. The second answer means: I can be an *active* spirit, released from the body. This state of active spirituality is illustrated by the dream-state, as that normal state in which even here below we may observe the spirit freed from corporeality. In the third answer, finally, spirituality entirely without any object, or spirituality in its complete quietude, is declared to be the state really suited to the Self, and thereby the real Ātman.

About this third and highest state of Ātman, thus, the state in which the Ātman dwells even here in deep sleep, the Bṛhadāraṇyaka-Upanishad 4, 3, 19 says: "But just as there in airy space a falcon or an eagle, after having flown about, wearied, folds up his wings and nestles down, even so also does the mind hasten to that state where, gone to sleep [that is, become entirely quieted] it feels no more desire, and sees no more pictures in dream. This is its essential form, wherein it is exalted above desire, is free from ill will, and void of fear. For just as a man, in the embrace of a beloved woman, has no more consciousness of what is external or internal, so also the mind, embraced by the cognition-like Self, has no more consciousness of what is internal or external. This is its essential form, wherein it is of satisfied desire, is itself its desire, is without desire, and severed from grief. Then is the father no father, and the mother no mother, the worlds are no worlds, the gods no gods. Then is the thief no thief, the murderer no murderer, the ascetic no ascetic. Then there is no being touched by good, no being touched by evil. Then has he overcome all torments of his heart. If then he is without sight, yet is he seeing, although he does not see, for to the [essentially] seeing one there is no interruption of seeing, but there is nothing second beside him, nothing other divided from him, that he might see."

The three states of the *I* or Ātman dealt with so far, are the only ones that come under consideration in the older Upanishads. Only later, with the rise of Yoga practices, did men learn in Yoga of a state of the *I* that is still higher than even the perfect quieting of the mind, such as supervenes in deep sleep. In deep sleep, the extinction of the world's expanse takes place *unconsciously,* and in such wise that cognition also is no longer its own object. But by means of methodically exercised concentration—these same Yoga practices—the liberating of cognition from the material organism, and further, the extinction of the whole world's expanse, can be attained with *full consciousness*. One practises concentration at some lonely spot, by calling the five external senses "home," so that one "no longer cognizes externally," by bringing even the bodily functions, inhalation and exhalation included, to a complete standstill, and fixing the mind exclusively on the representation of boundless space, and then, by entirely abandoning this representation, bringing it to the intuitive representation of how cognition itself is boundless. Thus, so to say, we float in our own *pure* cognition by making this cognition itself the sole object of cognition, and thus we cognize ourselves as "through and through consisting of cognition." Then we proceed to the intuitive representation of there being nothing any longer to cognize—the realm of nothingness—and at last, by dismissing also this representation of nothingness from our mind, we rise to the highest representation, that there is no more representation at all for us, so that we only know ourselves to be entirely without representations. This is the realm of neither perceiving nor non-perceiving. This *conscious* state of purest *objectless* mentality is then "the fourth" *(caturtha)*, the very highest state of the *I*, of the Ātman or *the Turīyam:* "Not cognizing internally, and not cognizing externally, not cognizing in both directions, also not consisting through and through of cognition, neither perceiving nor non-perceiving, invisible, intangible, incomprehensible, incharacterizable, unthinkable, indescribable, only *founded upon the certainty of the own Self,* extinguishing the whole expanse of the world, quieted, blissful, without a second,—this is the fourth quarter *[caturtha]* this is the Ātman, that man should cognize."[423]

All this was thus *immediate experience*, direct cognition, and therefore stood, and stands, firm beyond all doubt *in actuality:* the *I,* the Ātman, is able to remain in these four states. On this *intuition,* by means of *reflection,* the *system* of the Vedānta was built up. It was said: If even during our lifetime it is possible to get free from the body—in Turīya the body is a mass without sensation, by which we are no more touched—and to retire completely to pure and objectless mentality, then the death of a delivered one is nothing more than the *permanent* throwing away of the body, by *permanently* retiring to pure mentality. The eternal, and at the same time, blissful state of the *I* seemed thereby to be discovered. But later on it was concluded: If the true essence of man, his real *I* is discovered, then thereby also the real essence of the world must be revealed. For this essential nature of the world must, precisely as such, be contained in everything existing in the world, in the sun in the firmament, as well as in airy space; above all, also in ourselves, since we certainly belong to the world. If I cognize *myself,* I thereby also cognize the ultimate, primary cause of the world; in other words: The principle of the world must be identical with the principle of the *I.* "As a piece of salt that has dissolved in water can no more be found, but must still be existent in the water, as the salty taste indicates, even so you do not perceive the existent here in the body, but nevertheless it is there. What this subtle is, of that this world consists. This is the real, this is the *I,* this thou art *(tat tvam asi),* Çvetaketu."[424] From this, without any break followed the equilibration of Atman and Brahman, the principle of the world. And from this it also ensued, that this latter also is to be defined as pure mentality, as the great, endless, shoreless essence consisting only of cognition.

Thus did men philosophize in India, on the heights of the Vedānta. They dived into the depths of their own *I,* in order to grasp this their real *I,* and to sever themselves from whatever showed itself in truth not to be this *I,* not to be this our real, deepest, and ultimate essence. Proceeding from this our real *I,* they then tried to comprehend the rest of the world, thus exactly reversing the method in vogue among ourselves, our scientists completely losing themselves in the external world under the childish delusion that thereby they will also be able to comprehend their own nature. Thus did men philosophize in India ever since, down to the present day. Especially did they philosophize thus in the period—from about B. C. 500—that followed the Vedānta of the Upanishads, thus, during the epic era of the Mahābhārata. In this later period also, all philosophical and religious striving for insight was directed towards penetrating to the real kernel of man—because this is obviously the right way—by peeling off everything which, showed itself not to be kernel-like or essential, thus, which seemed like a shell. And at that time also they tried to penetrate to this kernel by means of *Yoga,* hence, by practically laying hold of this kernel or real *I,* in this way that they turned away from the outer world and tried to lose themselves ever more deeply in their own innermost, and by *Saṃkhya,* by reflection. Therewith they succeeded in correcting the fundamental error of the Vedānta system, namely, the error of considering the Ātman and the world to be the same. They began to understand, that for pure objective cognition the totality of the objective apparent world, now called *Prakṛiti,* is as an independent factor opposed to the cognizing subject, thus to the *I,* and therefore is not merely *Māyā,* to which it had been reduced by the idealistic Vedānta of the Upanishads: "One thing am I, and another is she *(Prakṛiti).*" [425]

Thus, in the genuine Indian spirit, the Buddha also philosophized, standing at the beginning of the epic period. He also wanted to find our *kernel,* our real and innermost essence, that which simply cannot be separated from us, thus the *I,* the Ātman—Attā in its Pāli form—by which word is precisely designated the essential within us, or *what is held to be this*, by the removal of which we therefore should be absolutely annihilated.* "What do you think, ye youths, which may be better? if you search for the woman, or *if you search for your I?*" Thus also in the Discourses of the Buddha everything circles round the Ātman, the *I*. This *Attā* is the unchangeable centre, to which all the Discourses of the Buddha point, or from which they proceed. It is the great problem in the doctrine of the Buddha also. And as we can hardly read a page in the doctrine of the Upanishads, without coming upon the Ātman, in the same way there is hardly a Discourse of the Buddha, which does not deal with the Attā in some form or other. When the Upanishads are therefore simply characterized as the doctrine of the Ātman, this qualification is not less true of the doctrine of the Buddha. This, *in the sense here dealt with,* is Attā doctrine, as much as the Upanishads are always only Ātman doctrine.

But with the Upanishads, and thereby with the general mode of Indian thinking, the Buddha is also in harmony inasmuch as he sought to find the Attā by taking away from it everything inessential to us, to our *I,* to our Attā, and thereby separable from it. He even has brought this method to its highest, classical perfection, by substituting for the fundamental question: "What is the Ātman? What is my *I*?" the other one: "What is the Attā in any case *not?* What in any case is *not* my *I*? What is *An*attā?" And he also tried to solve this question by means of Sāṃkhya and Yoga, and solved it definitively. By means of Sāṃkhya, of sober consideration, of reflection, he decided it in the following way:—As criterion of what is in no case essential to us, what therefore can be separated from us without ourselves being touched thereby at our core, he laid down the formula: What

* *Cf.* above p. 161.*

I behold in myself to perish, and, with the setting in of this perishableness, to bring suffering to me, cannot possibly be my *I*, my Attā, but must certainly be *not*-the-*I*, *An*attā,—a criterion that is obviously infallibly right.* By this criterion he then investigated all the components of his personality, the body, sensation, perception, the activities of the mind, the cognizing faculty, and found them all to be transitory and thereby bringing suffering to us, and therefore that they could not possibly be our real essence, our actual *I*, our true Attā. And yoga practice confirmed this result of his reflection since he actually succeeded in separating himself from his body, his sensations, his perceptions, the activities of his mind, all his cognition, by annihilating all perception and sensation *(saññāvedayitanirodha)*, and then returning to the body to experience new sensations, new perceptions, new activities of the mind, new cognition. Thereby was given practical proof that our *I*, our true Attā, is essentially different from all the elements of personality.

But thereby *everything* recognizable in us was recognized to be inessential, *nirātman*, *an attā*. Only think: You lose your whole body, and together with it all capability of sensation, and all cognizing of every kind, what then shall remain? But how, then, about my *I*, my Attā, that certainly is not in any way touched by the establishment of what is *not* the *I*, *not* the Attā? How is the result of the Buddha's investigation to be interpreted, that *everything* is *An*attā, *not* the *I*? To this we must reply with Einstein, the modern physicist: "*Interpret not, but acknowledge!*" Acknowledge what is right beyond all doubt; regardless whether we are able to

---

* How very close this criterion lies to the human mind, though in its world-annihilating importance it could only be penetrated by a Buddha, may be gathered from this, that even *Deussen*, like so many others, understood it by his own divination: "But Indra, reflecting that this Self is smitten by all the sufferings and illnesses of the body, and perishes by death, feels—*what everbody may feel*—that all the changes that happen *to* us, for that precise reason cannot change us ourselves." Compare above!

digest this truth or not. If we cannot digest it, that is, cannot bring it into harmony with our world-view, then this would only prove that we are not able to digest *truth*, that our present world-view is so false that an indubitable fact of reality, yea, a *fundamental fact* of this reality, finds no room in it. "Interpret not, but acknowledge!" But to acknowledge means, ruthlessly to draw all the consequences that follow from the discovered fact of reality. But these consequences are: If everything I can cognize within myself is inessential to me, then I am also able to separate myself from everything that is in any way cognizable, accordingly, from everything transitory, and thereby from everything that causes suffering to me; I can lose all this, without being touched by it at my core. But what will happen, if I have indeed liberated myself from everything cognizable, if I, accordingly, at my last death, have abandoned my body, thereby all capacity of sensation conditioned by it, and thereby for ever all becoming conscious? "Interpret not, but acknowledge!" here also again holds good. That is to say, even if this question cannot be answered, there would follow from this as consequence, merely a further incognizable alongside the incognizability of our real essence, and in addition to the countless other incomprehensibilities with which in this world we find ourselves confronted. There would follow, in fact, the incognizability of the *condition* into which we should be transferred at our last death.

This incognizability also would then have to be taken into account as the necessary consequence of a fact of reality. But this condition called by the Buddha *Nirvāna*, is not at all incognizable, since the Buddha himself speaks of the "seer of Nirvāna." It is cognizable that there all factors which might produce suffering in any way are absent, and that I shall there be entirely and absolutely desireless and thereby absolutely happy. For what higher bliss can there be than not to be any more disquieted by any, not even by the slightest, unsatisfied wish?

Another consequence of the incognizability of our real *I*, our true Ātman, is this, that I, separated from everything that in truth is *not* my *I*, am boundless and unlimited, inasmuch as everything bounding and limiting me belongs to the realm of *not*-the-*I*, of the cognizable. "Liberated from corporeality, a Perfected One is deep, immeasurable, unfathomable as the ocean."

But the most important *practical* consequence is this: If my real *I*, my true Attā is entirely and absolutely incognizable, then even the question: "What am I?" "What is the Attā?" is in principle wrong, since this question already presumes the Attā to lie within the realm of the cognizable and thereby to be able to be found out. Indeed the Vedānta, as we saw, sought for the Ātman in the realm of the cognizable and *also found it there*. "It is of the nature of cognition, and what is of the nature of cognition, follows it."[426] "Only of being, bliss, and thought does the Ātman consist."[427] But the Buddha was forced to the conclusion that the Attā, our kernel, cannot be grasped at all by means of cognition, that especially it cannot consist in thought, be of the nature of cognition, since he found all cognition, especially all thinking, to be conditioned by *the organs* of cognition that are quite evidently alien to us.

According to this, however, every one who wants to probe to the bottom his real *I*, must inevitably lose himself in a *cul de sac*, if he insists upon doing so in a positive manner; that is, if he formulates the problem thus: "What am I? What is my Ātman?" he must land in "a cave, a gorge of views." The right way to get at least on the track of our essence, our *I*, our Ātman, is only to ask: "What in any case am I *not*? What at all events is *not* my *I*, *not* my Ātman?" In short: we must regard as the fundamental problem we have to solve, not: "What is the Attā?" but "What is *An*attā?"

This is all the more necessary, since only if the case is thus formulated, is it possible really to overcome the realm of Anattā, of not-the-*I*: As soon as anything cognizable inside or outside of me arouses even the slightest thought of myself, this is a proof that I have brought it into some relation to myself and thereby to my will, be it in form of inclination or of disinclination, whereby this will receives new nourishment, and liberation from it is thereby again postponed. But if I am able to regard everything without exception, also my own body, my sensations, my entire cognizing, exclusively from this point of view: "This I need *not*, this I am *not*, this is *not* my self," then in time, infallibly, every kind of volition, every wish for the realm of what is thus cognized as being Anattā, *inessential* and *unsuited* to me, and thereby also every kind of willing whatsoever, must become extinguished, and so deliverance ensue.

For *these* two reasons the doctrine of the Buddha is also called the doctrine of not-*I*, *anattā-vāda*, as contrasted with the *I*-doctrine, the *attā-vāda* of the Vedānta. But it is not called thus because the Buddha *denies* the Attā, in contrast to the Vedānta.* What would it mean to deny the Attā, to deny thereby myself, me, the primary fact which alone I cannot doubt? For am I not *the* most real thing of all for myself, so real that the whole world may perish, if only I, this all and one for every single individual, remains unaffected by the general ruin? We may identify our *I*, our Ātman with the components of our personality, or with

* The Buddha rejects the Atta-vāda as well as the Loka-vāda.428 Who concludes therefore from the rejection of the Atta-vāda that the Buddha *denies* the Attā, the *I*, must also conclude from the rejection of the Loka-vāda, that he denies the world *(loka)*! Really, he only rejects the *Vāda* about the Attā, every *doctrine* about the *I*, as well as he rejects only the *Vāda* about the Loka, every *doctrine* about the world as such.

some of them, or with only one of them, and therefore say: "The body is my *I*, the sensations, the perceptions, the activities of the mind are my *I*, *thinking is my I*." But to *deny* the *I* and thereby ourselves, therefore to say: "I am neither something perishable nor something imperishable, I am absolutely nothing at all," this surely is a dictum "before which thinking turns back." For absolute nothingness neither denies nor affirms anything. But if thus the absolute non-existence of the *I*, the Ātman, cannot be "brained," then neither will the Buddha probably have "tongued" it.

Rather has the Buddha brought the Vedānta to its utmost perfection. He also has sought for the Ātman, as all great minds have sought it. "Know thyself!" ran the inscription on the temple of the Pythia. And Herakleitos, in the search for his *I*, had come so far that he was able to assert that the boundaries of the soul could not be found, even if all roads were run through. Further, like all India, the Buddha also had sought for the Attā in the *indirect* way, by taking away from the Attā everything that is not the Attā. But he followed this way so radically and with so much success, that everything cognizable, especially also the mental, especially also *thinking*, revealed itself to him as *An*attā and thereby as something that had to be overcome by us. And *therefore* he says: You teach the Attā, but I teach what the Attā is *not*. You know the Attā, but I only know what the Attā is *not*. Therefore you are always talking about the Attā, but I only speak of *An*attā. In short, you have the Attā-method, the *attā-vāda*, whereas I have the Anattā-method, the *anattā-vāda*. And this I have because only thus is the Attā, that is, myself, able to become free from suffering and happy. "But, monks, cleave ye to any *I*-doctrine *(attā-vāda)*, whereby no sorrow more can come to him who cleaves, neither lamentation nor suffering, neither grief nor despair? Know ye of any such *I*-doctrine?"—"Indeed, we do not,

Lord."—"Well said, monks. Neither do I know of any such *I*-doctrine." *[429]

Thus the Buddha has not become untrue to Indian thinking; rather is his doctrine *the flower* of Indian thought. He is "the *true* Brahmin," who has *completely* realized the ideal of the Upanishads. And precisely because this is so, India will again greet him as her greatest son, as soon as she again shall have recognized this.

Yea and more, hail to the age that philosophizes in the direction of the Anattā-vāda! Hail in every case to the man who follows the Buddha on this way, first by turning his thoughts in the direction shown by the Buddha, and then, in time, also by practically moulding his life more and more in accordance therewith. He is no longer in need of religion and philosophy, no longer in need of theosophy or "mystics;" he is also no longer in need of *natural science.* He is in need of nothing more at all. For very sōon dawn will break within him. Just because he has the right *method,* very soon and very easily he will raise the veil that enfolds the primary problem of the human heart, the primary secret of all religion:—the great riddle of deathless and tranquil eternity will be solved for him. For very soon he himself "will mark,

---

* From this explanation it will probably become clear without further ado that our modern form of saying "the *I* is *transcendent*" is not the mode of expression used by the *Attā-vāda,* for whom the *I* is not absolutely transcendent, in as much as it is ultimately found in pure cognition; but it is really the language of the *Anattā-vāda,* since the statement "the *I* is transcendent" means: "the *I* is beyond all cognition, it absolutely cannot be found out." How stupid, how incredibly stupid it is to accuse him who teaches the transcendence of the *I,* of adhering to the *Attā-vāda,* will certainly become clear to the greatest simpleton, when he learns that the Buddha even verbally teaches about the *I,* what is involved in the conception of transcendency: "I am not anywhere whatsoever, to any one whatsoever, in anything whatsoever."[430] "But since the *I* and anything belonging to the *I* is not to be found *(anupalabbhamāne)* . . ."[431] "Even in this present life is the Accomplished One not to be found out *(ananvejjo).*"[432] Because no kind of cognition penetrates to the *I,* nothing whatsoever, absolutely nothing, can be told about it; the rest is—silence! And it is only this *silence* about the *I,* no more, that the Buddha teaches.

he himself will see: This is the sick, the painful, the diseased; there the sick, the painful, the diseased is done away without any remainder over."

2. THE METAPHYSICS OF THE BUDDHA

"The supreme blasphemy is the denial of the indestructible essence within us."
Schopenhauer.

The primary and fundamental question of all philosophy and religion is this: "What am I?" not: "What is the world?" What the world is, ultimately interests man only in so far as it is related to himself and must therefore be taken into account in any attempted solution of the first, fundamental question. But the question, "What am I?" has always been answered by the immense majority of men thus: "I am body and soul"—under the latter concept being understood the willing and cognizing principle within us, which, in contrast to the body, is supposed to be immortal. This view of the average man has been left behind by the great leaders in religion and philosophy, inasmuch as they have held the essence of man to consist exclusively in the faculties of willing and cognizing, holding, therefore, the soul to consist of these functions, and declaring the body to be only an inessential addition to this same soul. A higher definition of our essence will nowhere in the world be found outside the realm of the Buddha. Even in the Upanishads, which in their grandeur come nearest to the doctrine of the Buddha, our essence is defined as "being, bliss, and thought."

Such definitions were reached through the idea that the essence of man ought to consist at all events in one of his cognizable qualities, more especially in his most noble and exalted qualities. Of course this presupposition has especially been made their starting-point by all the smaller minds, particularly by those in whom is lost even that primary consciousness proclaimed also by Spinoza, the Jew, when he says: "We feel and experience that we are eternal." But to these small minds the uniform definition of what constitutes the essence of a human being, formed a mighty weapon against those greater ones who, being such, without exception teach that our essence, in one form or another, is indestructible. This weapon enabled them, in spite of their smallness, to take up fight against those great ones, that is, against their doctrine that our essence is indestructible, and thus to establish *the opposition between science and religion* in the human domain This opposition, in particular, is also a typical peculiarity of our time. For small but talented minds are very well able to track out the defects and weak points of great systems, but they cannot as easily put reality in the place of the discovered defects and the blanks caused thereby. Again it is only the true genius who is capable of this. And so the small minds very soon succeeded in proving that all the mental functions of man, especially thinking, were essentially bound up with his corporeal organism, thus, were organic functions. As such they form part of the corporeal organism, and must therefore perish along with the organism when this breaks up in death. Accordingly, in consequence of the common assumption that the essence of man consisted in these mental functions, annihilation of the *essence* of man at the moment of death seemed a settled fact. The gulf was opened between religion culminating in all its forms in the doctrine of the immortality of our essence, and science, demonstrating beyond denial that what religion, together with science itself, declared to be the essence of man, fell prey to annihilation at the moment of death.

Are there any who can bridge this gulf? Certainly, there are very many who labour incessantly to bridge it. The zeal developed by the representatives of modern religions in this direction, is admirable. Many a time, the proud work really seemed to have been accomplished, until another bomb of scientific acumen burst in, and again brought about the crashing collapse of the proud arch bridging the gulf. So religion and science, now as before, stand opposed to each other as irreconcilable enemies. In particular, the fact remains, that neither of the two adversaries is able to vanquish the other. Religion is unable seriously to contest the scientific standpoint that even the highest mental functions are of a material kind, and therewith the doctrine that the essence of man, supposed to consist in these functions, is, along with the bodily organism, annihilated in death. On the other hand, no science can weaken the overwhelming supporting grounds in favour of that fundamental dogma of every religion, the doctrine of the indestructibility of our essence. This makes it quite clear, that on both sides error and truth must be closely interwoven, the strength, nay, the invincibility of each party, consisting in the truth it maintains, its weakness, however, in the error it has associated with the truth.

But if thus there is error also on both sides, why do not the contending parties succeed in discovering the error of *the opponent*, a thing possible, after what has just been said, even to merely talented minds? They do not succeed in this, because it is the *same* error which dominates both parties, so that in discovering it, they would disavow themselves. This error consists precisely in the *basis* common to both contending parties, that the essence of man must be sought for in his mental qualities. Because this common basis is intangible for both sides, and *because it is false*, therefore there is no hope of filling up the gulf between science and religion *as long as this common basis is not proved, and generally acknowledged, to be false.*

But thereby also an immense difficulty arises. For if it

is declared to be an error to seek for the essence of man in his mental or even in his corporeal qualities, in what, then, is man to consist? What remains of him, if he is stripped of all his mental and corporeal qualities, above all, of his will, and of his consciousness? Surely, nothing more is left. Consequently, for all that, since he is still there, he must be understood to consist in his qualities, or in some, or at least, in one of them. Indeed, upon this consideration is founded the seemingly unshakeable security of the common basis of religious and materialistic thinkers; but, at the same time also, the incompatibility of both their standpoints. Only if we could succeed in proving this common basis to be false, only then would there be a prospect of bringing to an end the conflict between science and religion. But how might this be possible? Who would venture merely to make the statement that man consists neither in his corporeal nor in his mental qualities, and therefore is nothing at all? Would not such a man declare himself to be a madman, in declaring something not to exist which quite evidently does exist, namely, himself? Would he not be turning upside down all words and conceptions, and converting them to their contrary? What reasonable man would dare do such a thing?

Nevertheless, there is one who has ventured to do this, who has really inverted all words and conceptions and converted them to their contrary. For example, he declares to be unwholesome what has always been thought to be wholesome and salutary; he designates as ugly what has always been looked upon as beautiful; he defines as woe what from all time has been called happiness. He even calls that the *non-existing* which, ever since man existed has been called the *existing*; and that which all men have always called *nothing* he decides to be the highest reality, not merely in appearance, and by sophistical casuistry, but in perfect earnest, in the literal sense of the words and "in accordance with *actuality*." It is clear, that such a man, if he is wrong, stands out as the greatest fool the world has ever seen. But if, against all apparent possibility, he should turn out to be right, then he ought to be hailed as the greatest genius ever born on earth. For then he would verily appear as the only reasonable man of the whole human race. And indeed he regards himself as such, for he has further the unparalleled audacity to declare all men, himself and his followers only excepted, to be mentally ill, to be insane.[433] This unique man was the Indian mendicant monk, Siddhārtha Gautama who in consequence of this his standpoint just set forth, called himself the *Buddha*, the Awakened One, he who has awakened from the dream of life to reality *as it is*.

He says: You want to know what you really are, what in you constitutes your essence, that means, you wish to know the substratum lying at the basis of what you call your *I*, by which word you mean precisely that wherein you at bottom consist. You think it self-evident that this your *I* must consist of something which you *cognize* within yourself. In this way you come to designate the qualities with which you see yourself endowed, as the substratum of the *I*-concept, foremost of all, your sensation, perception, and thinking. But how now, if your self-evident presupposition, that you must consist of something cognizable, were false, if there were also something *incognizable* in you, which was your real essence; if, further, this your incognizable, but real essence were removed from the jurisdiction of the laws of arising and passing away, and if I could prove all this to you with compelling logic, nay, with palpable, visible evidence? Of course, you shake your head and think this entirely incognizable to be contradictory in itself, as it is surely a contradiction to desire to ascertain something *incognizable* by means of *cognition*. But this is not at all what is meant. For the reality of this finally incognizable thing stands fixed from the very beginning, as primary, pre-eminent fact. It is simply *your own* reality, the reality of that which you call your *peculiar essence*, your *I*, thus, the most immediate fact of consciousness there can ever be. What is in question is rather only this: Whether with your cognitive faculty you are able to grasp this your *peculiar essence* as such, *apart* from its reality. That is to say, whether this your faculty of cognition is able to penetrate beneath into the depths of your own real essence; or, in other words, how far the light of your cognition reaches in a certain direction, to wit, precisely in the direction of that in which you are objectively absorbed. And *this*, surely, is no transcendental realm for your cognitive faculty; on the contrary, it is again a primary function of cognition to recognize its own limits. Why, then, do you oppose my proposal, first of all, to fix these limits of cognition? Did not your own Kant too undertake this task, to whom you could not declare yourselves sufficiently thankful for thereby freeing you from all false metaphysics? Certainly, I very well know the reason why you are opposed to me and my doctrine. The *consequences* resulting from my fixing the limits of cognition, together with my judgment of what is cognizable, are displeasing to your *will*, and therefore, on this ground, my doctrine is not allowed to be true. But is not such a standpoint the very opposite of all true science? Is it not, in fact, childish to want something not to be true, when quite obviously it *is* true?

Of course, I am bound to offer you the proof of the *evident* correctness of my fixing of the boundaries of cognition, the more so, as I may thus be able to cure you of the extravagant views of your Kant. Hearken! Your Kant wanted to derive the boundaries of cognition from the nature of the process of cognition itself. But this undertaking is quite impossible. Whoever should undertake such a thing, to begin with, ought to have developed his own faculty of cognition to the highest point possible, or he will infallibly declare the boundaries set to his own individual cognition in consequence of his own *limited development* to be the immanent boundaries of cognition itself, as is proven precisely in the case of your Kant.* But have you got any other great thinker who claims for himself to have climbed to the *summit* of all possible development of cognition? Apart from this, however, it must be just as impossible to determine accurately the boundaries of cognition from its own structure, as it is impossible to determine the strength of the eyes from a mere physiological examination of the eyes themselves, or the distance covered by a telescope by a mere physical and chemical examination of its lenses. Everybody knows, that this is practically, and therefore really, impossible, but that an incontestable and certain determination of the strength of our eyes or of the distance covered by a telescope can *only* be arrived at by fixing the eyes or the telescope upon a distant, external object, and then examining, if, and to what degree, this object is seized by the eyes or by the telescope. *Only* thus, by means of a *practical* test, do the boundaries of our cognition permit of being determined with absolute certainty. Well then! It is in this way that I, the Indian mendicant monk, am going to ascertain, if, by means of our faculty of cognition, we are able to penetrate to our real self.

Of course, this method of determining the boundaries of our cognition opens up an immense difficulty: When it is a question of making out a quite definite object and of

* Kant reached his *a priori* judgments only by failing to recognize the circle of rebirths, whereby he had to make life commence only with the birth of the single individual. In this case, there certainly is no other possibility than to declare the notions with which we come into the world, (space, time, causality), and which are really acquired by us during earlier existences, to be *a priori* forms of our cognizing faculty itself.

identifying it as such, then at least one infallible characteristic marc of it must be known. For otherwise, the possibility is never excluded, that a wrong object may be taken as the one sought for. If I am looking for gold, I must know at least one specific characteristic mark of gold, if I do not want to run the risk of taking any copper or brass I may hit upon for the gold I am in search of. Thus also as regards my *I*, as regards that in which, in the end, I am completely subsumed, at least one infallible characteristic marc must be known, if I am to be able successfully to examine the objects of my cognition as to their identity with my *I*, if I do not want to run the risk of taking something for my *I* which in reality is *not* my *I*, be it that it has really nothing at all to do with my *I*, be it that it is only an inessential addition to my *I*.

Fortunately, the relation between our *I* and our faculty of cognition is such, that in every case this indispensable criterion may be obtained. Indeed, this criterion, quite as much as the *reality* of our *I*, is again an *immediate* fact of consciousness, which, precisely as such, requires no proof, nay, is not at all capable of such a thing; it can only be immediately *experienced*. If I see a passing train, I know that this train has certainly nothing to do with my essence. Why not? Because I was here before the train came near me, and because I am still here after it has thundered past me. What only reaches me after I have long been here, and then again vanishes from me, so that *I* remain, cannot have anything to do with my essence. If the iron money-chest I had bought to keep my money in, is stolen from me, this theft unquestionably has taken away nothing belonging to my essence. For the loss of the money-chest causes *suffering* to *me* for a long time after it has been committed. In these simple facts is contained the long sought-for and infallible criterion for our *I*. My *I* cannot possibly consist in what *I* behold perish, and afterwards recognize to have vanished, yea, from the total loss of which *I* still suffer. Myself in my *real* essence I have therefore by means of my cognition failed to find in any case, so long as to this my cognition those objects alone present themselves, the vanishing of which I *observe,* and by the loss of which I *suffer.* On the contrary, only an object appearing before my cognition might be regarded as my real *I,* which showed itself to this cognition as remaining always the same for as long as this cognition might last and as often as it might repeat itself, as surely as at the same time I know myself—again an *immediate* fact of consciousness—to be the cognizing subject, which, itself unmoved by everything, beholds life together with all its vicissitudes passing before itself: *I* was born, *I* was a boy, *I* was a youth, *I* am a man, *I* shall be an old man, *I* shall leave my body in death, being always the same indivisible *I.*

In this manner the Buddha first fixed the special *object* which he wished to grasp, to comprehend, to embrace with his cognition.

And now it was a question of really grasping this object with the cognition. To effect this, he directed his power of cognition towards everything cognizable within him and around him, turning it principally upon his power of cognition itself, all the more so, that it is precisely in cognition, as we already know, that the essence of man has always from of old been found. And he arrived at the following result:—

Cognizing is no simple process, but to a closer inspection resolves itself into several elements, namely, into sensation, perception, and thinking. In this, the inner relationship between these elements is such, that *sensation* originates first, followed by *perception* of the object sensed, which cannot be temporally separated from sensation, whereupon *thinking* about the object which thus has entered the domain of cognition, begins. Where nothing at all is sensed, there nothing is perceived; and where nothing is perceived, nothing is thought, for want of any object upon which thinking might act: "What one senses, that one perceives. What one perceives, that he thinks." According to this, the process of cognizing dissolves upon still closer scrutiny, into a countless number of sensations, perceptions and thoughts, incessantly following one another. This very summary analysis of the process of cognizing* shows, if we adhere to the criterion we found for the establishing of our *I*, that at all events, the various sensations, perceptions, and acts of thinking are not essential to us. For I have had millions of such sensations, perceptions and thought-acts, and though they are all scattered and gone to nothing, I still exist. At this present moment, I have new sensations, new perceptions, new thoughts, and also in future I shall have new sensations, perceptions, and thoughts, and they also will pass away without taking *me* away with them.

But now arises the principal question: I know not only that I have sensations, perceptions and thoughts; I also know immediately that they are dependent on me, proceed from me, and are based upon me; in short, I know myself to possess the *capacity* of producing sensations, perceptions and thoughts. And it is just this which at bottom we mean when we say that feeling, perceiving and thinking are *essential* to man. We wish to express thereby that ultimately we are not summed up in the various concrete sensations, perceptions and thoughts, but in the *capacity* of having such things, so that in every case, with the annihilation of this *capacity*, we ourselves ought to be annihilated.

To become clear about this, we must examine how this capacity is realized in an individual case. How, to begin

* See for this, the chapter on personality!

with, do we come to have a sensation? If I direct my eye towards a form, a sensation of sight flames up; if a sound reaches my ear, a sensation of hearing; if my nose is affected by an odour, a sensation of smell; if my tongue comes into contact with some kind of food, a sensation of taste; if my body touches a tangible object, a sensation of contact; and when an object of thinking is presented to my organ of thought, be it a concrete representation or an abstract idea, a sensation of thought is effected. With the arising of this sensation, I further *perceive,* and with the same corresponding organ of sense, the object sensed, and then, by means of the organ of thought, I begin to *think* about it. If I have lost my eyes, then all sensations of seeing, as well as all sight-perceptions, are gone. If I become deaf, or lose the organ of smell, then for me all sensations and perceptions of hearing or smell have ceased. The same is the case with the other senses. In particular, if my organ of thought, that is, my brain, is seriously damaged, I am no longer able to think. From these observations of reality, in face of which all phantasies of any other kind have to keep silence, it results with infallible certainty, that every activity of the senses as well as of the mind is bound up with the corresponding organ, and conditioned by it. A function of cognition without an organ of cognition is all as impossible as digestion without a stomach. But of course it does not follow from these statements that I myself consist in these activities of sense and mind. To this theorem the dependence of the mental functions upon the organs of my organism stands in no relation whatever. Rather is this relationship only created by our bringing the knowledge of the conditionedness of our mental functions by their corresponding organs, into relation with the criterion we found for determining our real *I.* When we do this, the following consequences ensue:—

Every organ of sense, the organ of thought included, is material, be it of a coarse or of a refined material. Like the whole corporeal organism, it represents a high-potential chemical combination of the four chief elements.* As soon as this organ, so composed, is stimulated by an external object corresponding to it, it begins to *vibrate*, thereby arousing *sensation*, and later, *perception* of the object sensed, just as, when a match is rubbed on any friction-surface, heat is produced and light appears. Now I recognize without further ado, that the four chief elements, building up the whole apparatus of cognition as well as, in particular, its several *organs* of cognition, can on no account have anything to do with my essence. For I *seize* them in the form of nourishment; hence, I must have existed *before*. Further I myself, in my real essence take no part whatever in the incessant *vibrations* of these organs of cognition, producing the sensations and perceptions *for* me; rather do I behold also the incessant origination and annihilation of these vibrations. Finally, I myself, untouched by all this, perceive the gradual wearing out of these organs of cognition and their ultimate decay, with the result that I experience sorrow, grief and suffering over it. Consequently, these organs of cognition also, and with them, also the entire apparatus of cognition, are entirely alien to me, and have nothing to do with my real *I*.

Thereby it is established for cognition that is entirely objective, thoroughly unprejudiced, that also the entire *capacity* to feel, perceive and think, is not an immediate and organ-less effectuation of our essence itself, but that we possess this capacity also only so long as we possess *the organs* of cognition, that are *obviously* alien to our essence. In other words: I also may possess, or I may not possess, the capacity to have qualities, especially mental qualities, without being thereby affected myself-in my essence. This

* See the chapter on personality!

capacity also, therefore, is not essential to me, but is only an inessential "appendix" to me.

But if thus even the mere capacity to feel, perceive and think is inessential to me, then this of course is much more the case with every *object* that I feel, perceive, and think by means of this capacity. Not even my *will* belongs essentially to me, that is, in such a manner, that I should be annihilated through its annihilation. For it is only a will for *objects* felt, perceived, and thought, in respect of such objects ever and again springing up anew in its manifold variations, as desire, repulsion, passion, hatred, and so on,—where nothing at all is felt and perceived, there nothing is wanted,—and dying out in the measure that I recognize an object I first longed for, as bringing me suffering, and therefore not worth longing for. Yea, by this dying out of a certain definite willing, I am so little affected, that I may possibly feel relief and even pleasure at its extinction. Hence, in willing also an arising and passing away is to be observed.

With this, however, we have caused everything cognizable to pass before our cognizing power, without recognizing anything of it as our *I*. This true *I* is therefore not to be discovered as an *object* of cognition; it does not enter our consciousness in any way; it is *transcendent*.

But how, then, can we know anything about it? How are we possibly able—this being, after what we have just seen, an immediate fact of consciousness—to ascertain the *reality* of our *I*? And how, further, can we establish the criterion we set up for the identification of our *I* by means of consciousness, if the *I* in no wise appears in this consciousness, presents itself in no wise to it? Is not this, in spite of, or rather because of, the foregoing exposition, a contradiction in itself, whereby also our exposition itself must appear to be contradictory? It would be a contradiction, if what is here taught about our *I*, was taught on the basis of a pretended *immediate* perception of the *I*. But this is not the case. What up till now we have heard about our *I*, has been exclusively gained from contemplation of the realm of *not-I*, as we contemplated the objects of this realm that alone are accessible to our cognition, *in a certain direction,* namely, in so far as their relations to ourselves are concerned. It is the same as if an automobilist whose car is provided with an electric reflector drives at night along the highway. Everything entering the field of the streaming light of the reflector he beholds as clearly as in daylight, and of course *recognizes it also in its relations to himself*; but he himself does *not* enter the light of the reflector since he sits behind it; hence, he cannot see *himself*. In exactly similar fashion we are only able to recognize the objects of the realm of *not-I* that enter the light of cognition, but not ourselves. For we are the *subject* of cognition, literally translated, *what underlies* all cognition, and *for* which alone the light of cognition shines. But on the other hand, we are of course also able to recognize every object of cognition *in its relations to ourselves*, since this also only represents a cognition of the *object* in a certain direction. Reduced to a brief formula, our exposition means: "Things I know immediately, but myself mediately."[434] To put it yet otherwise: There is really no self-consciousness, but only a not-self-consciousness, only a consciousness of what is really *not* our self, *not* our *I*; an insight also proclaimed in the words of the Bhagavad-gītā (II, 71): "Whoso lets go all enjoyments of the senses, and wanders on without desire, *without self-consciousness*, and without selfishness, will gain peace." And to teach us to think in this same manner about everything entering the realm of our cognition, is the sole purpose of the Buddha's doctrine. Thus this doctrine teaches us to think *in harmony with the highest reality*, in contrast to the ordinary thinking of all others who mistake something that really is not their *I* for their *I*, thereby reaching the empirical *I*- or self-consciousness.

Because all possible qualities and processes are thus only qualities and processes within the realm of *not-I*, therefore of course all possible conceptions and words are only valid for this realm of *not-I*, since they have only been devised for the designation of these qualities and processes.

Thus, in reality, to the cognizable stands opposed the incognizable, to the physical the metaphysical, since "cognizable" and "physical" in the last analysis, are identical conceptions. The incognizable am *I*, the cognizable is the world, to which of course also belongs what is cognizable in myself, that is, my feeling, perceiving, and thinking.

But thereby the realm of the incognizable, and thereby of the *meta*physical, is not yet exhausted. If I am not summed up entirely in the physical, thus, myself am no part of the world, then it must be possible for me to free myself from the whole world. But what, then, for me, will take the place of this world? Of course, *nothing*. For if we could say, that *something* would take the place of the world, then this something again would be bound to be something *cognizable*, and thereby something *of the world* itself, seeing that the notion "something" also is wholly and entirely abstracted from the realm of the world, of the cognizable, and therefore can only have reference to something within the world. But this whole world of the cognizable is annihilated there "where there is nothing whatsoever."[435] But though there, there is no "anything," nevertheless there, there is the *reality*, as certainly as that I, after having overcome the world, will be just as real as I really am now, and as that there, there can be no more arising and passing away, inasmuch as these conceptions also are entirely and exclusively devised for the designation of processes within the world of the cognizable. That "nothing" with which I find myself confronted after having overcome the world, is therefore a nothing *cognizable.* And because there is nothing more there that can be cognized, therefore, at my last death, upon my entry into *this* domain of *reality,* I cast off for ever the whole apparatus of cognition. *This* reality is what the Buddha referred to in these solemn words: "There is a not-born, a not-become, a not-created, a not-formed. If there were not this not-born, this not-become, this not-created, this not-formed, then here an escape from the born, the become, the created, the formed, could not be known."[436] "There is yonder realm where neither earth is nor water, neither fire nor air, neither the boundless realm of space nor the boundless realm of consciousness, neither this world nor another, neither moon nor sun. This I call neither coming nor going nor standing, neither origination nor annihilation. Without support, without beginning, without foundation is this. This same is the end of suffering."[437] *This* realm of reality is also called our "home," "the Void," "the quiet place"; "that is not connected with becoming in the world of the senses, that does not change, that does not lead elsewhere."[438] Further, it is characterized as "the unshakeable, the immovable," "eternal stillness," "the true"; "the other shore," "the subtle," "the invisible," "the free from illness," "the eternal," "the incognizable," "the peaceful," "the deathless," "the sublime," "the joyful," "the secure," "the wonderful," "the free from affliction," "reality *(dhamma)* free from oppression," "the free from suffering," "the free from incitement," "the pure," "the free from wishes," "the island," "the refuge," "the shelter."[439] This reality of *Nirvāna,* wherein everything is extinguished—that is, everything *cognizable*—for only for the realm of the cognizable, of course, is the conception "everything" also valid—is "highest bliss,"[440] on which account the Buddha ever and again proclaims "the glory of Nirvāna."[441] In *this* realm of the reality as "in the Deathless," the delivered "are submerged,"[442] for which reason nothing more can be said about them: "Just as of the fire that flames up under the strokes of the smith's hammer it cannot be said as to whither it has gone, after it is extinguished, so just as little can be discovered the abode of the truly delivered ones who have crossed over the stream of the bounds of the senses, have reached the unshakeable bliss."*

Such are the metaphysics of the Buddha, such are the *real* metaphysics. This *science* of metaphysics is as exact, and therefore just as certain in its results, as the science of physics,—taking this word in its most comprehensive meaning, as the science of everything natural. For *these* metaphysics have exactly the same things for the objects of their investigation, namely, the things of this cognizable world; and they contemplate these things after exactly the same method that physics does, that is, according to the methods

---

* *Cf.* above p. 360.* In *this* domain of Actuality, or in the *Absolute*—"*Paramatthasāro nibbānaṁ*: Nirvāna is the highest reality"—there naturally also is no more *multiplicity*, no more of all the individual Holy Ones who have returned to the highest Actuality. Just as little is there a *Unity* there, such as is taught by Pantheism and absolute Monism. These latter picture to themselves the absolute actuality as an ocean out of which the individual beings emerge, somewhat as steam rises out of the ocean; later these beings return to this ocean like drops of water, in which, like the latter, they again dissolve.

The actual fact is rather somewhat as follows. Those beings who as perfected Holy Ones have rid themselves of all "attributes" (Upadhi) through which alone they are sundered from the Absolute Actuality, sink back again into the latter, not, however, as a drop of rain, but as a *stone* sinks into the ocean. The stone thus thrown in disappears in the ocean and precisely thereby withdraws itself from all further speculation as to its future fate: whether it becomes one with the ocean, or retains its individuality, or some other unknown possibility comes into play. Only a reflection which is strictly confined to *this* foundation remains wholly within the sphere of *intuition*. This intuition accompanied by the highest thoughtfulness the Buddha has exercised here also, in saying of the Delivered One that he is "submerged in the Deathless." (See above.) Neither this Deathless, Nirvāna, is thus my *I*; it is rather my *home* in which I am submerged. Compare with this, Suttanipāta, v. 1076: "*Atthaṁgatassa na pamānam atthi.*" Those acquainted with the older Sanskrit literature will see at once that in the Pāli word, "*atthaṁgatassa,*" is hidden the ancient well-known compound word, already found in the Vedas: "*astaṁgata,*" the root meaning of which is "gone home." Verse 1076 thus means: "For him who has gone home there is no standard of measure. (*Cf.* Ṛigveda 10, 14, 8, and Chāndogya Upanishad 6, 14.)

of logic and direct experience. Their only difference is the same as that which exists between the several special branches of physical science; that is, *the point of view*, from which they look at things. Physical science regards things in their relations *to one another*; true methaphysics regards the cognizable in *its relation to my own self*.

Accordingly, the metaphysical is just as certain as the physical that lies stretched out before my eyes; nay, it is even much more certain than this; for it is just as certain, just as indubitable, just as impossible of being argued away, as my own essence is certain, indubitable, and impossible of being argued away. For this same metaphysical I myself am, and it is the highest situation possible to me.

Because *this* kind of metaphysics is only reached by means of a certain scientific contemplation of *things cognizable*, therefore *these* metaphysics also do not transgress the boundaries set up to cognition, do not dabble with imaginary worlds and their just as imaginary inhabitants, as pseudo-metaphysics are wont to do.

Because the metaphysics of the Buddha discover the completing portion of that part of reality that alone is known to us, therefore in the Buddha's doctrine of reality as in the highest Unity, the great contradictions also between religion and science are dissolved without further ado. To renounce the world becomes just as intelligible as to enjoy it; nay, to renounce it is recognized as wholesome and sublime. Alongside of the physical order of the world, the moral one appears, which stands as high above the physical order, as the metaphysical goal it aims at, stands above physical aims. First of all, the gulf closes, that exists between the fundamental dogma of every religion, the axiom of the indestructibility of our essence, and the no longer doubtful doctrine of modern science, that, like everything in the world, so also our entire personality, therefore everything that is cognizable within us, is subject to incessant change and ultimately to complete dissolution. Assuredly our essence cannot die, since everything that is mortal in us is precisely not our essence. And so, sheltered by the wings of the doctrine of the Buddha, the contending sisters shake hands. Religion becomes science, and science, without contradicting itself, again may lead on to religion and religious feeling. What noble, what feeling man will not rejoice at the possibility of such a prospect? But you who do not rejoice about this, you fanatics of pseudo-metaphysics, to whom your *creed* stands higher than *religion* itself, and you sworn enemies of every kind of metaphysics, in whom the consciousness of the supra-mundaneness of your essence has so utterly and completely disappeared, that every hint at this supra-mundaneness only arouses the blind instinct to oppose it at all hazards, approach and ram your heads against the metaphysics of the Buddha. Even thus you will be serving them, for "every attack that fails to down its man, only makes him more strong."[443]

3. RIGHT COGNITION

> "In so far only is there any process of verbal expression, in so far only is there any process of explanation, in so far only is there any process of manifestation, in so far only is there any sphere of knowledge, —*in as far as this is, to wit, the corporeal organism together with consciousness.*" 444

I.

True cognising is *direct* cognising, consisting in the *immediate* perception of an object by means of our sense-organs. This direct cognising, taken by itself, as yet knows nothing of concepts and words, of consideration and reflection, of proofs and conclusions. Rather do these things represent expressions of another independent faculty called *reason*, which *may* be associated with direct cognition, but is not bound to be so associated.

Direct cognition by itself, unaccompanied by any activity of reason, provided that it is perfect, is called by Schopenhauer, *æsthetic contemplation*. Suppose, for instance, that I attempt to lose myself in æsthetic contemplation of the starry sky at night. I am alone on a wide plain. Solemn stillness reigns all around. Above is spread out the mighty dome of heaven. Innumerable stars sparkle and glitter in the depths of the celestial vault. Now and then a meteor majestically and tranquilly describes a flaming bow through the dark void. Slowly, with equal pace, travels along the whole carpet of the stars. One star after another sinks below the western horizon. New stars rise in the eastern sky, to complete their path in the same lofty and silent manner. That *I* behold all this, that I am the see-er,—this thought does not arise; no thoughts, no reflections at all, arise. In this direction my cognitive faculty remains inactive; for such an activity of *reason* there is no room, since everything is *perceived* so overwhelmingly, so clearly, that all reflecting activity may remain quiescent. Only when, from this immersion in æsthetic contemplation, I return to the unæsthetic and uncontemplative activity of reason,—only then does thinking again begin; and I perhaps say to myself: "*I* have had a wonderful experience. I temporarily rose to the heights of pure æsthetic contemplation free from any admixture of reasoning activity."

As we see from this example, the pure, direct action of cognition is at the same time the highest kind of cognition. Why, then, do we not confine ourselves to this form of cognition? Why do we bring into play the activity of *reason* at all? The answer is: This activity of reason is necessary, first of all, if we are unable fully to *apprehend* any given object; thus, for the completion of a *defective* apprehension. We try to fill up the gaps in our apprehension with rational conclusions. Further: the activity of reason becomes necessary when I am no longer a mere spectator of the world-drama, but become a player along with others. Then mere perception is no longer enough. Then I must come to an understanding with my fellow-actors, must look out for my living, must think of my security in the future, were it only the future of the following minute. But in order to determine the nature of this future and then to be able to realise it, I must from perceived reality, draw *conclusions* with regard to that which is not directly to be cognised, and is as yet unreal, but is becoming real,—such a conclusion as this, for instance: "If this exists, then that will come into existence. If this does not exist, then that will not come into existence." But in order to be able to draw conclusions, we have to translate our perceptions into concepts and words. For it is only by means of concepts as well as of memory (which now also comes into play) and of imagination, that a comparison of the innumerable separate phenomena as they present themselves to perception, becomes possible. But the forming of concepts in itself presupposes a sorting out of the innumerable perceived objects into classes, since every concept represents the subsumption of a particular class of single perceptions from a certain definite point of view.* In consequence of this sorting out or classification, the Eternal Now which alone is known to the primary variety of cognition, that is to perception, is differentiated into past, present and future. At the same time, in the same way that the individual phenomena are subsumed under concepts, the mutual *relations* of the various individual phenomena are subsumed under forms of thought for the linking up of the concepts. These

* Compare above p. 140.

forms of thought, taking shape by gradual adaptation to perceived reality, produce in their totality the web of logic as the reflected image of the causal sequence of the perceived world, concepts and forms of thought, on their side, having as their deposit, language.

From these considerations it also clearly follows that the exercise of reason, as such, yields nothing new, but only by means of reflection, analyses what is perceived, and registers it in concepts and words; and later, using logical conclusions, under general rules. Even the most self-evident judgments are based upon some logical conclusion, albeit we are not always conscious of this. Thus the statement: "The earth exists," is arrived at by the following syllogism: "What I perceive exists; I perceive the earth: therefore the earth exists." Accordingly a statement only needs to be put into the form of a syllogism if we wish to ascertain whether it is true or not. Everything arrived at by reason, in some form or other must beforehand be perceived. In any other case, the activity of the reasoning faculty can only be compared to a mill running empty, and therefore, notwithstanding all its clatter, producing nothing.

Hence a false cognition may be caused, either by there being no perception at all at the base of the reason's activity, or else by the perception of the object to be cognised being an incorrect one, or, at least, not penetrating it sufficiently; in which latter case, of course, the abstract reproduction by the reason of the phenomena perceived will be bound to be wrong; or, lastly, by the laws of reason being violated during the process of translating the, in themselves, correctly perceived phenomena into abstract form.

To this translation of what is perceived into the higher conceptional form of cognition, corresponds the plastic reproduction by an artist of something he has seen. This latter reproduction, also, will be the more perfect, the more truly and profoundly the artist saw the thing in question, and the greater his mastery of the technique of his art.

II.

Our own essence, that which at bottom we always mean when we speak of our *I*, never under any circumstances can become an object of perception, for the simple reason that it is *the subject* of cognition, that which lies at *the basis* of the process of cognizing; these last words constituting an entirely adequate translation of the word "subject," *for* which alone this process takes place. That is to say: It can never present itself to any of our senses which are always directed wholly outwards. On the contrary, we can only perceive those objects which we see *opposite* us, the totality of which we call "the world," to which world, of course, belongs also our cognizing *apparatus* and the element of consciousness itself which this yields. This is expressed by the very word "object," which is derived from the Latin *objicere*, meaning, *to throw against*. The concept, object, is thus a *relative* concept which essentially presupposes at least *two* factors, one which throws itself against, and another against which it is thrown, the latter being called the subject. It is here the same as, for instance, with the word "poison," where a thing thus defined is so defined with reference to some living creature for which it is poison. Just as there is no such thing as poison in itself apart from a creature *for* which it acts as poison, so there can be no object if there is no subject independent of it, standing over against it, *for* which it is an object, and which, precisely on this account, can never itself become an object. Accordingly, the subject of cognition, or the *I* in itself, must be unperceivable by the very nature of the whole process of cognition.

Let us imagine a being the antecedent conditions of whose *reasoning* activity have ceased, a being therefore which dwells in the profoundest bodily and mental isolation, but is able to apprehend in the most perfect manner everything that is presented to its senses. Such a supposed being could never arrive at the reflective action of reason, and so never arrive at thoughts or concepts, and thereby just as little at words, which always presuppose concepts. Rather would it remain confined entirely to immediate perception, and with this find itself completely satisfied, since for it such perception would constitute perfect apprehension, and it would therefore stand in no need whatever of the added activity of mind as made possible by reason. From this it is certain that within the consciousness of such a being its own essential feature, that is, its *I*, could not present itself as such, neither in consequence of immediate perception—for, as we have already seen, our *I* cannot in any wise become perceptible to our sense-organs—nor as a mere abstract thought or concept as an *I*-thought or *I*-concept. For the thought or concept of *I* can only appear in our consciousness, purely as the result of the activity of *reason*; but the being we have imagined exercises no such activity in any shape or form. First of all, such a being would not think. "*I* perceive;" that is, it would not possess the idea of *I* even in the form of the logical subject. Because it *does not think at all*—taking thinking in its general sense as the reflecting and abstracting activity of reason—therefore, of course, neither does it think in the form of "I perceive all this."

None the less, this being also becomes conscious of its *I* after a certain fashion, namely, in so far as everything it perceives is perceived precisely as *object*, as something opposed to it, that "throws itself against it," that passes before it. Therewith, in the thing perceived it also lays hold of its own actuality which, so to put it, is *reflected* by this thing which precisely thereby becomes an *object*. It is much the same as if our supposed being should gaze upon the light of the full moon shining in the sky at night. Just because it apprehends everything perfectly, without more ado it would *perceive* this light as mere *reflected* light, and would therefore, in this light also perceive the reality of *the source* of the light, that is, *indirectly*, the reality of the sun, though it would be quite unable to discover the sun itself in the night sky no matter in what direction it might turn its gaze. In exactly the same way, in the perception of a thing as an object the reality of *the subject* is also *indirectly* perceived, if the object is really seen *as an object*. For which reason precisely, Schopenhauer has said: "Of things we have direct knowledge, of ourselves only indirect knowledge."

If our imagined being should now pass from mere perceptive activity to *reasoning* activity, thereby translating his perception into the abstract form of cognition, then the beholding of the radiant full moon would unfailingly also give rise to the thought of the sun as being the source of the light, though the being, in reflecting, would have to say to himself: "I am nowhere able to find the source of the light." And in the same manner, the perception of every object inevitably is bound to give rise also to the *thought* of the subject, imperceivable in itself,* on account of which alone perception precisely takes place, since otherwise the quality of being *an object*, apprehended also in the perception of a thing, would never get itself translated into the abstract form of cognition.

But not only this. If the translation of what is perceived into the higher form of cognition of reason is perfect, then in this higher form of cognition this also must become evident, namely, that the subject presents itself only *indirectly* to perception. This *indirect perceptive* apprehending can be

* So the passage quoted above on p. 186* without further words will be perfectly clear, nay, self-evident: "But since, ye monks, the *I*, and anything belonging to the *I*, is not to be *found* really and truly . . . ."

expressed in entirely adequate rational form *only* by the thought: "This is *not* my *I*." For by the word "I" one designates just oneself as the subject corresponding to the object, only then giving to the latter the character of object. And by qualifying the thing perceived as *not* one's *I*, we show that the I does not immediately present itself to our perception; but that it is only the thing perceived, which in its quality as object, reminds us of the subject opposed to this.

Accordingly, since a being endowed with perfect perception apprehends everything that can be perceived, and before all else, its own entire personality, as mere *object,* in passing from the perceptive to the reflective activity of reason, our imagined being can first arrive at the ego-idea only in its *negative* form: it can only grasp the idea of not-I, thus: "Everything is *not* my I, not my true essence, is Anattā."

This perfect method of cognition *(ñāyā*, also called *ñāṇadassanaṁ),* that is, cognition perfectly accordant with "reality as it is," is what the Buddha teaches, here again proving himself the greatest of gods and men. Because our *I* is not perceivable, and therefore is "not to be found" in any way, therefore has the Buddha never occupied himself with it; therefore does he even qualify all statements relating to this *I* as empty fancies. He concerns himself solely with that which alone is cognisable, namely, with the things of the world which he summarises in the elements of our personality *(sakkāya).* But those things which alone are cognisable he has seen *correctly*, perfectly apprehending them as being mere *objects* for us, and precisely therefore, not our true *I (anattā).**

* To the *I*-idea in its positive form: "This am *I,* this is *mine,*" one comes when, contrary to actual fact, one "confounds" oneself with the knowable, that is, with one's personality. (*Cf.* above on p. 185 *et seq.*)

III.

As the Anattā-idea is true of every being, it has for outcome the following general view of the course of the world and the real task of our life.

Whatever we may look at in the world, whether ourselves or anything else, whether great or small, complex or simple, as soon as we make the attempt to lay hold of the essential in it, its kernel, its innermost substrate, which once laid hold of, all its other qualities without further ado, would become clear, we find to our astonishment that it cannot be laid hold of, nor even found: the realm of essences is hidden from us by an impenetrable veil. This discovery leads to the establishment of the first fundamental truth,—this, namely, that our faculty of cognition is *not* adapted to cognise realities *in themselves,* that is, the essential that lies at the foundation of every single thing; and above all else, our own essence.

The reason of this is that what is innermost and primary in every reality is not cognition, but that this cognition comes forth from it as something secondary, accidental, and external, after it has provided itself with "attributes," *(upādhi), i. e.,* a corporeal organism, and thereby has come into contact with the attributes of other realities. The faculty of cognition is designed purely for the cognising of the mutual relations of these attributes. Thus cognition is, as it were, a light which only illumines a quite definite region amidst the boundless unlighted realm of origins within which it is lost. This obscurity which reigns throughout the entire domain of origins, becomes the more noticeable the stronger the light of cognition shines, since at all the more points it touches the borders of the unilluminated realm of origins.

Within the domain of the cognisable, again, there is one fundamental axiom which is absolutely irrefutable, to which pertains unshakeable certitude. Though everything in the world should totter, though all cognition should prove rotten, though heaven and earth should crash together, *this* axiom does not shake, and never can be shaken. On it, as upon a granite rock, rests the entire edifice of the Buddha's doctrine. It is the *Anattā-idea* which fixes, determines the fundamental relations between ourselves and everything cognisable. This fundamental idea the Buddha has also been able to set forth so clearly in the form of a syllogism that it is impossible in any way to put it more clearly. This Great Syllogism runs like this: "What I perceive to pass away within me, and in consequence of this passing away, cause suffering to me cannot be my real essence. Now I perceive *everything* that is cognisable within me to pass away, and with the advent of this transiency, bring me suffering; therefore nothing cognisable is my real essence."

The Anattā-idea creates the possibility of deliverance. Everything cognisable is *not* my *I*, therefore I can free myself from everything cognisable. To liberate myself from everything not my *I*, I must become *selfless:* I must seek nothing cognisable, that is, nothing at all for myself. I may not relate anything at all to myself. But this I am able to do only if, first of all, I learn how to *think* in accordance with highest reality. With a gaze thus alienated I must learn so to look upon the mechanism of my personality that in the course of this my activity of thought, "the inclinations of pride which thinks the thoughts, 'I' and 'Me'—*(ahaṁkāra-mamaṁkāra-mānānusayā)*—may arise within me no more," but everything meet me simply and solely as *an object:* a method of thinking which finds its classical expression in the Paṭiccasamuppāda.

Thus, it is, of course, *I* who think in this entirely impersonal form. And this kind of thinking is the greatest art I have to learn. I must dismiss not only the thought "village," the thought "man," the thought "forest," the thought "earth;" I must not only dismiss the thought of boundless space and that of my own boundless consciousness,* but also and above all else, the thought of myself, and the thought that there can exist anything belonging to me. This one thought only may I think: "Empty is this [whatever I may be able to cognize] of myself and of everything belonging to me"[445]—"This does *not* belong to me; this am I *not;* this is *not* my Self." And this kind of thinking I must practise for the purpose of realising also that other saying: "What exists, what has become, shall not be, shall not be there present *for me;* shall not become, shall not become *for me;* I let it go."[445] For just because I am thus able, as the culminating point of selflessness in thinking, to think everything stripped of any positive relation to myself, I become fully and entirely clear that at bottom *I* have absolutely nothing to do with it.

How could this ever be misunderstood? How could men ever be so mad as to assert that the Buddha taught that when *I* think, then, not *I* am thinking, but—?!

When I have understood this also, then the whole Canon, if only I take its words as they are given, will become an ocean of light for me. Then deliverance also will become easy for me. For then I know that for the Buddha also remains true what has always been true, what I even cannot seriously represent to myself in any other way, namely, that *I* am he who acts and works, that *I* am he who sins and struggles, that *I* am he who suffers and delivers himself, that *I* am he who may win timeless, eternal bliss, that, especially, *I* am he who thinks the non-ego thought, the Anattā-thought, and who thinks it precisely in following the injunction of the Buddha: "Bhikkhus, *when* you think, thus shall you think: 'This is suffering;' thus think: 'This is the arising of suffering;' thus think: 'This is the annihilation of

* *Cf.* the 121st Discourse of the Majjhima-Nikāya.

suffering;' thus think: 'This is the Way that leads to the Annihilation of Suffering.'"

To be sure, also after this exposition thereof, the doctrine of the Buddha will remain for the majority of men an entirely inaccessible realm; and even for those who may divine its immense depth, this depth will remain only "a comfortless, fathomless depth" comparable to that melancholy lake in Norway in whose surface, encircled by its dark wall of steep rocks, never the sun, but only the starry sky of mid-day is reflected, and over which no bird, no wave ever passes, so that they also make their own those other words: "Happily, I can only praise this doctrine, not subscribe to it," and so withdraw to other systems more within their scope.

But on the other hand, there are also minds which only need instruction in order to recognise the doctrine of the Buddha as "a lotus pond, with a clear, mild, cool, glittering surface, easily accessible, refreshing; and with deep forest-groves near the water," and who thereupon, "scorched by the fiery summer sun, devoured by the fiery summer sun, exhausted, trembling, athirst," bathe and drink in this lotus pond, "and after having assuaged all the pains and torments of exhaustion, sit or lie down in the forest grove, filled only with delight." These too, at one time may have taken their refuge in other systems. None the less, now they say: "Certainly there were many columns standing there, and the selfsame sun shone upon them all, *but it was only Memnon's column that sang!*"

For such as these, the foregoing expositions have been written.

KEY TO THE QUOTATIONS

In the translation into English of the after-mentioned texts from the Pāli Canon, use has been made also of the following already extant volumes of translations of the same.

1. The Majjhima Nikāya. The First Fifty Discourses from the Collection of the Medium-Length Discourses of Gotama the Buddha. By the Bhikkhu Sīlācāra. London, Probsthain & Co.—*This work is marked with an asterisk* (*).

2. Dialogues of the Buddha. Translated from the Pāli By T. W. Rhys Davids. London, Henry Frowde.—*Marked with two asterisks* (**).

3. Buddhism in Translations By Henry Clarke Warren. Cambridge, Mass.—*Marked with a dagger* (†).

4. Die Reden Gotamo Buddho's aus der Mittleren Sammlung Majjhima-Nikāyo des Pāli-Kanons von Karl Eugen Neumann. München 1922.

5. Buddhistische Anthologie. Texte aus dem Pāli-Kanon. Übersetzt von Dr. Karl Eugen Neumann. Leiden 1892.

6. Dīghanikāya. In Auswahl übersetzt von Dr. R. Otto Franke. Göttingen 1913.

7. Die Reden des Buddha aus dem Aṅguttara Nikāya. Übersetzt von Nyāṇatiloka. München-Neubiberg 1922.

8. Puggala Paññatti. Übersetzt von Nyāṇatiloka. München-Neubiberg 1910.

Abbreviations. A.=Aṅguttara Nikāya.—C.=Cariyā-piṭaka.—CV.=Cullavagga.—D.=Dīgha Nikāya.—Dhp.=Dhammapada.—It.=Itivuttaka.—M.=Majjhima Nikāya.—MV.=Mahāvagga.—Mil.=Milindapañha.—PP.=Puggalapaññatti.—S.=Saṃyutta Nikāya.—SN.=Suttanipāta.—Th.=Theragāthā.—Ud.=Udāna. (Issues of the Pāli Text Society.)

---

1. M. I p. 246
2. M. I p. 172
3. M. I p. 173
4. M. I p. 140
5. CV. IX, 1, 4
6. M. I p. 184
7. S. V p. 437
8. M. I p. 8
9. A. II p. 71
10. Ud. VI, 4
11. M. I p. 429†
12. S. III p. 138
13. M. II p. 145
14. M. I p. 488
15. M. I p. 486
16. M. I p. 265
17. A. II p. 191
18. M. I p. 520
19. M. II p. 170
20. M. I p. 520
21. M. I p. 319
22. M. I p. 479
23. M. I p. 480
24. M. III p. 6
25. M. II p. 134
26. M. II p. 44
27. M. III p. 130
28. M. I p. 268
29. M. I p. 201
30. S. IV p. 312—314
31. M. III p. 17
32. M. III p. 6
33. M. I p. 32

34. M. III p. 18
35. D. XIX
36. S. V p. 443—445
37. M. I p. 133
38. M I p. 490
39. M. III p. 6
40. MV. I p. 9
41. S. II p. 17
42. S. IV p. 1
43. S. IV p. 216
44. M. I p. 299
45. A. II p. 165
46. D. II
47. M. I p. 190
48. M. I p. 185*
49. M. I p. 295*
50. M. I p. 190
51. M. I p. 259*
52. M. I p. 256*
53. M I p. 111*
54. M. I p. 111*
55. M. I p. 190
56. D. XV
57. S. IV p. 15
58. M. I p. 295
59. S. II p. 3 *et seq.*
60. D. XV**
61. D. XV**
62. D. XV**
63. M. I p. 295*
64. D. II**
65. M. III p. 107
66. S. II p. 114†
67. D. XV†
68. D. XV†
69. D. XI
70. SN. v. 1114, 1037, 734—735
71. D. XV**
72. M. I p. 190
73. A. II p. 47
74. M. I p. 185*
75. S. III p. 23
76. A. II p. 261
77. M. I p. 138
78. S. V p. 158
79. Th. v. 277—278
80. M. N. I p. 73*
81. S. I p. 133
82. A. I p. 36
83. Th. v. 785
84. S. II p. 178 *et seq.*
85. S. II p. 178 *et seq.*
86. S. II p. 187 *et seq.*
87. M. I p. 515; D.N. II**
88. M. I p. 516
89. M. I p. 410; II p. 170
90. S. I p. 133
91. M. I p. 233*
92. MV. I, 14
93. M III p. 282
94. M. I p. 57 *et seq.**
95. M. I p. 59*
96. S. I p. 135
97. M. I p. 232
98. S. II p. 94
99. Mil.
100. M. I p. 138
101. M. III p. 17
102. M. I p. 141*
103. S. IV p. 15
104. Mil.†
105. SN. v. 1114
106. Dhp. v. 279
107. M. III p. 18
108. M. III p. 31
109. S. IV p. 400
110. M. I p. 137*
111. M. I p. 140*
112. MV. VI, 31
113. M. I p. 150
114. S. III p. 109 *et seq.*†
115. A. I p. 46
116. Ud. VIII, 1—3
117. M. I p. 38
118. D. XV
119. The Light of Asia, p. 177
120. SN. v. 1074, 1076
121. A. II p. 161
122. S. IV p. 374 *et seq.*
123. A. II p. 45
124. S. IV p. 54.
125. M. I p. 433
126. D. IX
127. D. I
128. D. XXIII
129. D. XV
130. SN. III, 12
131. S. III p. 30
132. A. II p. 38
133. M. I p. 247*
134. M. I p. 167
135. A. II p. 34
136. MV. VI, 31
137. A. II p. 18
138. Th. v. 258, 259
139. S. II p. 13
140. S. II p. 2
141. D. XV
142. S. II p. 3
143. Th. v. 1002
144. S. IV p. 20
145. M. I p. 167
146. S. II p. 3
147. D. XV
148. D. XVIII
149. (Schopenhauer)
150. S. III p. 101
151. D. XV
152. M. I p. 265
153. M. III p. 99
154. (Schopenhauer)
155. S. I p. 91 *et seq.*
156. A. II, II, 6
157. Dhp. v. 127
158. A II p. 172
159. Dhp. v. 219, 220
160. S. II p. 64
161. S. IV p. 132
162. A. III p. 72
163. A. I p. 265
164. D. XVI
165. A. II p. 80
166. A. II p. 38
167. A. II p. 230
168. D. XV
169. Dhp. v. 153, 154
170. S. V p. 421
171. S. III p. 87
172. S. II p. 192 *et seq.*
173. D. XVII
174. A. VII, 62

175. S. I p.135
176. M. I, 301*
177. A. I p.176
178. M. I p.293
179. M. III p.17
180. S. IV p.216
181. It. 43,2
182. SN. III, 12
183. SN. v. 732
184. M. II p. 237
185. M. I p 53
186. M. I p. 54
187. SN. v. 730
188. It. 114
189. Ud. I, 3
190. S. II, 73
191. M. I p.265*
192. M. I p.265*
193. D. XI
194. M. I p.292
195. M. II p.202
196. M. II p.261
197. S. II p.99
198. M. II p.230
199. S. II p.100
200. S. I p.135
201. M. III p.16
202. M. III p.251
203. SN. v. 864 *et seq.*
204. M. I p.450
205. M. III p.205
206. M. III p.130
207. M. I p.51
208. D. I
209. S. II p.86
210. M. I p.251
211. S. IV p.13
212. M. III p.286
213. S. I p.120
214. Ud. I, 3
215. M. I p.92
216. M II p.101
217. M. III p.286
218. M. III p.244
219. M. III p.301
220. M. III p.136
221. C. III, 15
222. D. XVI
223. M. I p.122
224. M. III p.104
225. M. II p 263 *et seq.*
226. M. I p.333*
227. M. III p.27 *et seq.*
228. M. I p.456
229. MV. I, 23
230. S. IV p.201 *et seq.*
231. M. I p.430
232. S. V, 230
233. M. I p.38
234. M. I p.304
235. S. IV p.251
236. M. I p. 303
A. III p 55
237. M. I p 185
238. M. I p. 436
239. Dhp. v. 383
240. M. I p.302
241. M. II p.159
242. S. III p.29 *et seq.*
243. M. III p. 267
244. M. I p.364
245. M. I p.91
246. D. IX
247. D. IX
248. D. II
249. D. II
250. M. III p.233
251. M. III p.233
252. M. II p.203
253. M. II p.37
254. M. I p.41
255. MV. I, 7—10
256. M. I p.301
257. M. III p.110
258. A. I p.132
259. M. I p 455
260. M. I p.352
261. M. III p. 246
262. M. III p. 246
263. A. V p. 414
264. Dhp. v. 203
265. Dhp. v. 368
266. A. V p.414
267. M. I p.89
268. (Goethe)
269. S. V p.272 *et seq.*
270. M. I p.511
271. M. I p.82
272. M. I p.167
273. M. I p.435
274. Dhp. v. 218
275. M. II p.245
276. M. III p.8
277. M. I p.114
278. Th. v. 1150
279. M. I p.30
280. M. III p.72
281. M. I p. 294*
282. M. I p. 116
283. M. I p.301*
284. A. II p.177
285. M. III p.107
286. M. III p.225
287. M. II p.262
288. A. II p.202
289. M. I p.251
290. D. XI
291. M. III p.223
292. M. I p.301*
293. M. I p.219*
294. M. III p.1
295. Ud. V, 5
296. M. II p.265
297. M. I p.445
298. A. I p.5
299. M. I p.241
300. M. I p.464
301. M. III p.72
302. M. III p.72
303. M. III p.251
304. M. I p.420
305. M. I p.281
306. M. III p.230
M. I p.309
307. M. II p.56
308. M. II p.205
SN. v. 621
309. M. I p.483
310. P. P. I, 17, 18
311. S. V p.343
312. M. I p.353
313. MV. I, 23.
M. II p.56
314. Ud. I, 8

315. M. II p.64
316. D. XI
317. A. III p.295 *et seq.*
318. M. I p.451
319. M. I p.450
320. M. I p.168
321. M. I p.478
322. D. XVI
323. P.P. I, 40
324. M. III p.103
325. S. V p.410
326. M. II p.197
327. M. I p. 267*
328. M. I p. 179 *et seq.**
329. M. I p.181*
330. M. II p. 26
331. M. I p. 43*
332. D. XVI
333. M. I p. 64
M. II p.35
335. D. I
337. M. I p.272
338. D. XVIII
339. M. I p.149
340. A. I p.208
341. A. I p.14
342. Mil.
343. A. I p.3
344. M. I p.180
345. *cfr.*† p.297
346. M. III p.294
347. M. I p.453
348. M. I p.355
349. M. I p.369
350. SN. v. 242
351. S. II p.98
352. M. I p.453
353. M. I p.181*
354. A. X No 208
355. M. I p.324
356. M. III p.293
357. A. II p.211
358. M. I p.37*
359. A. II p.45
360. A. I p.124
361. A. I: XVIII, 13
362. M. I p.260
363. M. I p.280 *et seq.**
364. A. II p.52
365. M. I p.183
366. M. I p.184
367. SN. v. 1002
368. A. I, III, 32
369. M. I p.108
370. M. I p.226
371. S. III p.195
372. M. I p.135
373. D. XVI
374. A. I p.124
375. A. I p.249
376. (*cfr.* above p. 329)
377. M. III p.251
378. M. III p.136
379. M. I p.454
380—383. M. I p.454 *et seq.*
384 M. I p.350
385. M. I p.293
386. M. III p. 96
387—388. A. I p.255
M.N. I p. 34*
389. A. II p. 80
390. M. III p.42 *et seq.*
391. M. I p. 369
392. M. III p. 146
393. M. III p. 160
394. M. III p.82
395. S. V p.326
396. M. III p. 82
397. M. III p. 82 *et seq.*
398. M. I p. 423
399. A. I p. 41
400. M. I p.207
401. M. I p. 127 *et seq.**
402. M. I p.38*
403. M. II p.159
404. M. I p.487
405. SN. v. 149
406. Dhp. v. 354
407. It. 27
408. M. I p.33*
409. CV. VIII, 3, 12
410. MV. VI, 3, 6, 4
411. C. III, 13
412. M. I p.211
413. Dhp. v. 308
414. M. I p.45
415. Dhp. v. 66
416. Th. v. 936
417. A II p.35
418. D. XVI
419. S. IV p.328
420. M. II p.260
421. M. I p.223
422. A. I p. 197
423. Māṇḍ. Up. 7
424. Chānd. Up. 6, 13, 2
425. Mahābhāratam 11437
426. Bṛh. Up. 4, 42
427. Nṛs. Up. 9
428. M. I p.40
429. M. I p.137
430. (*cfr.* above p. 331*)
431. (*cfr.* above p. 186*)
432. (*cfr.* above p.164)
433. A. IV, 157
434. (Schopenhauer
435. SN. v. 1094
436. Ud. VIII, 3
437. Ud. VIII, 1
438. SN. v. 1076
Dhp. v. 93
MV. I, 22
439. S. I p.133
M. III p. 110
S. IV p.369 *et seq.*
440. Dhp. v. 203
441. D. XIV, 3, 13
442. SN. v. 228
443. (Schopenhauer)
444. (*cfr.* above p. 77)**
445. M. II p.203